Not Native American Art

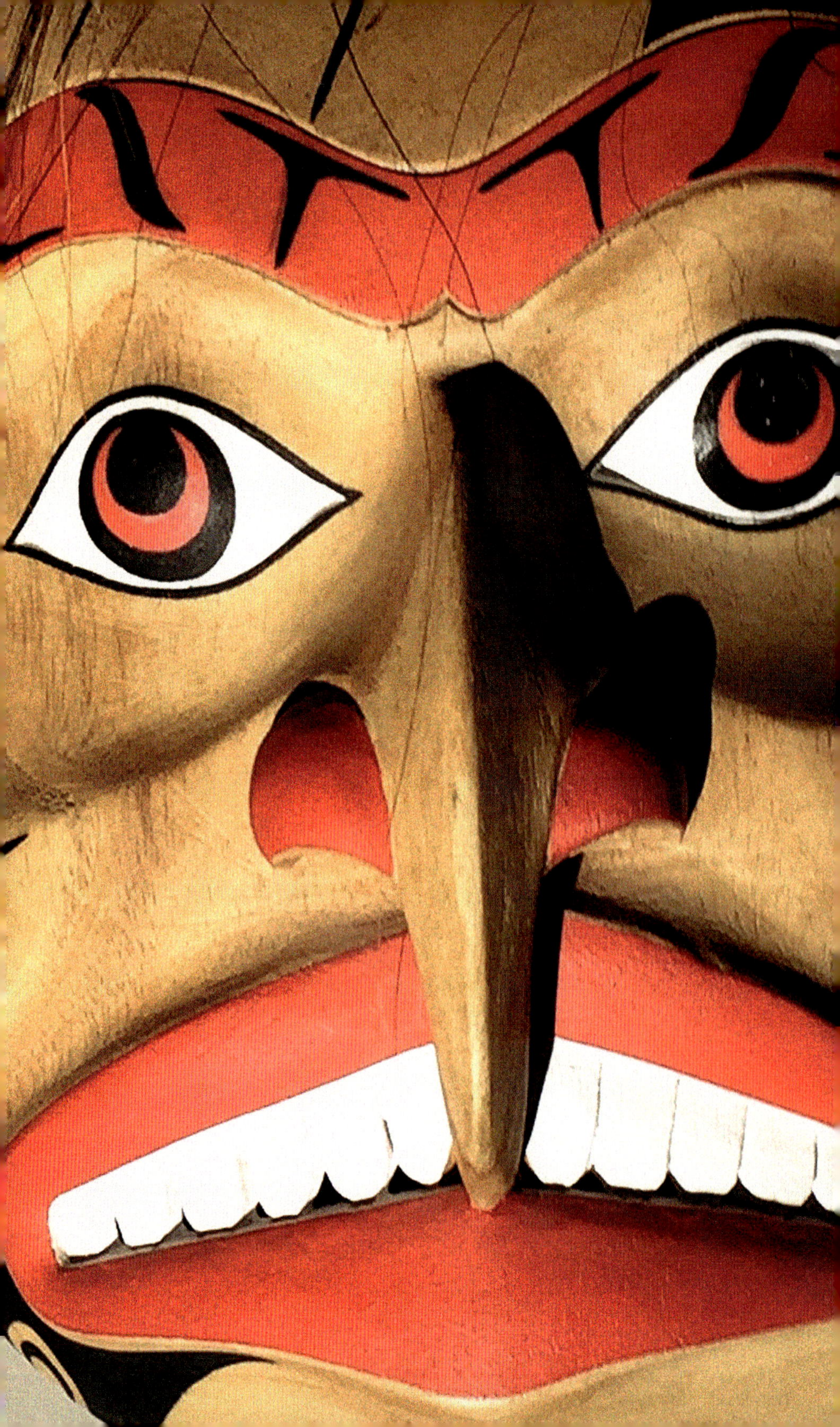

JANET CATHERINE BERLO *Foreword by Joe D. Horse Capture*

Not Native American Art

FAKES, REPLICAS, AND INVENTED TRADITIONS

University of Washington Press | Seattle

Not Native American Art was made possible in part by a generous gift from Jill and Joseph McKinstry.

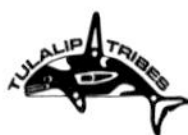

This book was supported by the Tulalip Tribes Charitable Fund, which provides the opportunity for a sustainable and healthy community for all.

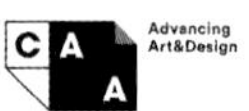

Publication of this book has been aided by a grant from the Wyeth Foundation for American Art Publication Fund of CAA.

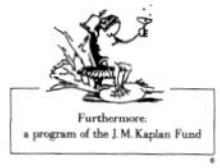

This book was made possible in part by a grant from Furthermore, a program of the J. M. Kaplan Fund.

Design by Mindy Basinger Hill
Composed in Garamond Premier Pro

27 26 25 24 23 5 4 3 2 1

Printed and bound in the United States of America

UNIVERSITY OF WASHINGTON PRESS | uwapress.uw.edu

LIBRARY OF CONGRESS CATALOGING-IN-PUBLICATION DATA
NAMES: Berlo, Janet Catherine, author. | Horse Capture, Joseph D., writer of foreword.
TITLE: Not Native American art : fakes, replicas, and invented traditions / Janet Catherine Berlo ; foreword by Joe D. Horse Capture.
DESCRIPTION: Seattle : University of Washington Press, [2023] | Includes bibliographical references and index.
IDENTIFIERS: LCCN 2023007534 (print) | LCCN 2023007535 (ebook) | ISBN 9780295751368 (hardcover) | ISBN 9780295751375 (ebook)
SUBJECTS: LCSH: Indian art—North America. | Cultural property—United States. | Authenticity (Philosophy) | Tradition (Philosophy) | Art and society—United States.
CLASSIFICATION: LCC E98.A7 B485 2023 (print) | LCC E98.A7 (ebook) | DDC 704.03/97—dc23/eng/20230331
LC record available at https://lccn.loc.gov/2023007534
LC ebook record available at https://lccn.loc.gov/2023007535

♾ This paper meets the requirements of ANSI/NISO Z39.48–1992 (Permanence of Paper).

Contents

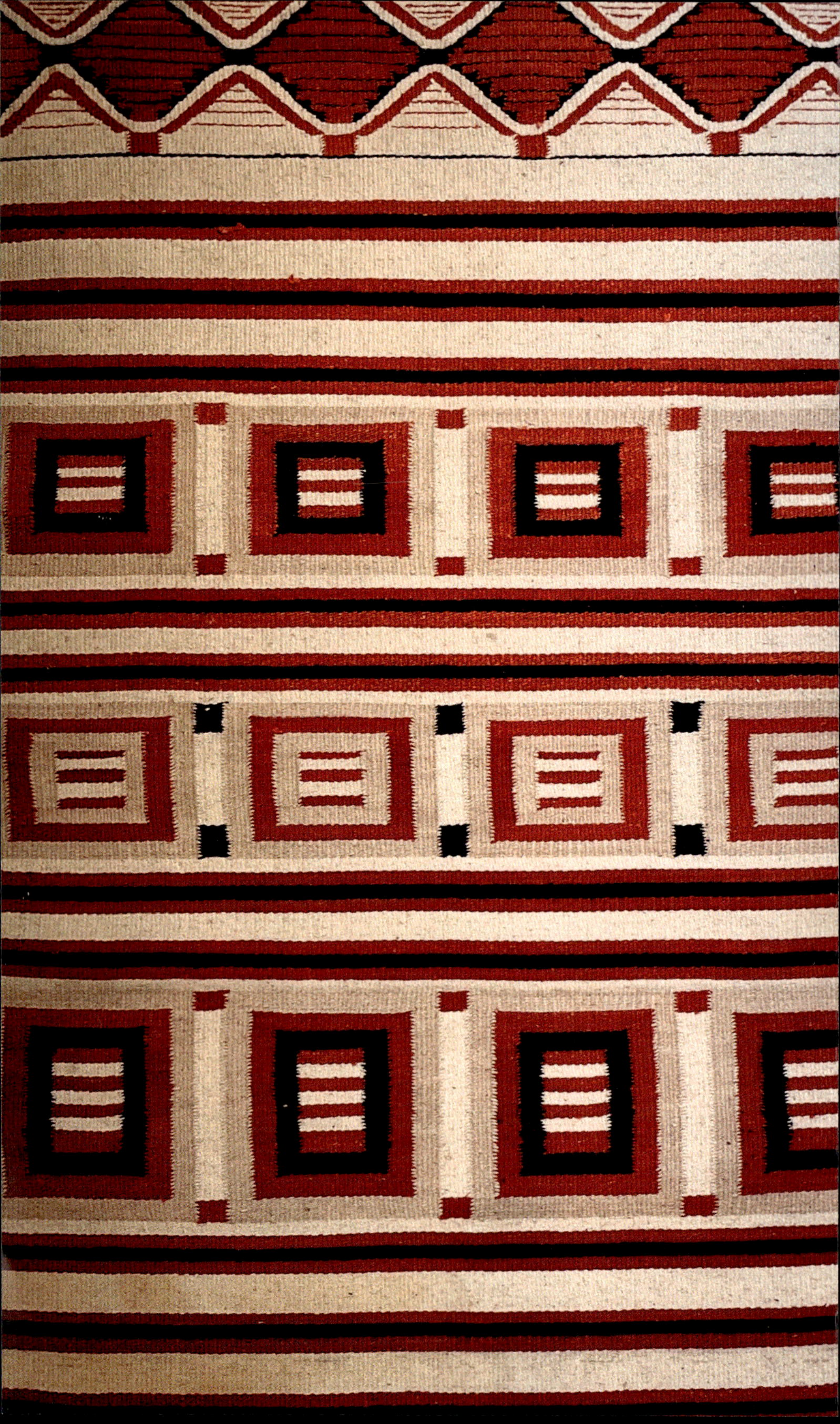

Foreword

JOE D. HORSE CAPTURE (A'ANININ)

I first met Janet Berlo in 1997 at the inaugural meeting of the Otsego Institute for Native American Art History, an effort organized by the Fenimore Art Museum to further the study and understanding of Native American art. Funded by the fabulous Eugene Thaw, a retired dealer of old master prints and drawings, the Otsego Institute was founded to pass knowledge about Native art on to the next generation of potential scholars, curators, and professors. All of the sessions featured a Who's Who in Native art history at the time, and although the presentations were informative and enlightening, one of the best aspects of this several days' gathering was the time one got to spend with the students and the other presenters.

I got my first real museum job in 1997, after receiving my BA from Montana State University in Bozeman and serving two years as a curatorial intern at the Minneapolis Institute of Art on the exhibition *Visions of the People: A Pictorial History of Plains Indian Life*. I found myself back in Minneapolis working as the assistant curator of Native American art under director Evan Maurer. I am fortunate that my father, George P. Horse Capture Sr., was well established in the museum field as one of the first Native curators in the country. Unknown to me at the time, some of that knowledge was passed on to me.

Honestly, during my early museum career, I was a bit intimidated; it was a combination of What am I doing here? and Why are these non-Native folks specializing in the culture of Native people? And that was the attitude that I had at my first Otsego gathering. I remember it clearly: I showed up wearing a T-shirt and camouflage pants, with a long black braid, and channeling my father's Alcatraz experience, I had an attitude. Although I was generally polite, there was honestly something odd about the experience—there were not many

Native people there. It was challenging for me to understand why non-Native folks were teaching about Native American art history. Today I see a similar perspective among some young Native curators and scholars. To that specific audience, let me tell you now: the attitude that I had decades ago was a mistake.

As we try to build what has been lost, or what needs repair in our culture, we need to think about how and where we get our resources. These can come in many shapes and forms, all valuable in some way. They have included Native knowledge embedded within the community, mostly through elders; historical records; early anthropological writings; Native collections; and those non-Native scholars who have done so much work over the decades. Each of these sources has its advantages and pitfalls. For example, not all elders are knowledgeable about their own culture. Some elders, or their parents, have gone through the boarding schools, a traumatic experience whose fundamental nature is to take the "Native" out of Native youth. Furthermore, some of these elders, or their parents, have turned to Christianity, which historically discourages (polite word) the celebration and knowledge of our traditional ways.

Historical records also present challenges. Questions to ask include: Who is actually recording this? and Do they have an agenda? The same is true for early anthropologists. It is important for us to carefully take pieces of knowledge from everywhere, while also being aware that it is challenging to find one source that is truly complete. As for non-Native scholars, I tend to lean toward those who have spent time with actual Native people. There are several non-Native scholars/curators who have dedicated their careers to the study of Native art history and contribute to Native communities. I will not create a listing here, but I have the deepest respect for those who have created friendships with Native people and use their resources to assist in rebuilding our culture.

Continuing with the puzzle metaphor, Janet Berlo is certainly a corner piece of this puzzle of knowledge. She has consistently been generous with her knowledge and time with everyone and has made countless close friends in Indian Country. In my experience with her, she has been nothing but kind and generous. She has invited me into her home, and we have had many discussions that have enlightened my personal knowledge. During her decades of teaching, she has empowered generations of students who continue her legacy—and many of her students contribute to the field and to Native people. For many years, it was challenging for me to think about Berlo without thinking of her comrades in Native art history, Ruth B. Phillips and Aldona Jonaitis. These three scholars have literally changed the study of this field. I, tongue in cheek, called them the Charlie's Angels of Native American art history, although that is a bit inaccurate, because there is no Charlie. Believe me, no one could or can tell them what to do.

As they say, Janet Berlo is a good one.

There has always been a bit of a gray area in the study of Native American art history. How do we look at and interpret works that were created by non-Natives who either have close ties to Native people or learned from them? And what if these same non-Native people have been adopted into Native families? The traditional methods of kinship within many Native communities do not fit with Western laws of kinship—which is often centered around blood quantum and enrollment. Today, there are so many Native hobbyists that for museum professionals it can be challenging to discern the historic work from the new. This situation can be very problematic when it comes to auctions and galleries that specialize in Native objects. In fact, some museums collecting historic Native art fear that it may not have been produced by the Ancestors. I am sure that questionable works have slipped into many museum collections. Berlo's brilliant book opens the door to some of those stories.

Of particular interest to me are Reginald and Gladys Laubin. I met Gladys Laubin in 1991 when I was working as an intern at the Minneapolis Institute of Art. Quite elderly at the time, she was charming and very much enjoyed *Visions of the People*. The Laubins wrote the definitive book about the Plains Indian tipi. I am embarrassed to admit that I consulted that book when I was learning to erect a tipi; my father did too. Berlo's section on the Laubins is fascinating. It not only delves into the perspective of the Laubins at the time, but it also puts their story within a contemporary context.

One of the aspects of Berlo's book that I very much enjoy is her emphasis on telling these important stories while simultaneously helping us understand how they play out in today's Native world. Often books that address important stories neglect to assist the audience in the broader implications of their story; not this one. A refreshing insight into the challenging, and often troubling, aspect of the creation of Native art by non-Native artisans, *Not Native American Art* is a must-have for those interested in the complexity of the creation of Native art by both Native and non-Native artists.

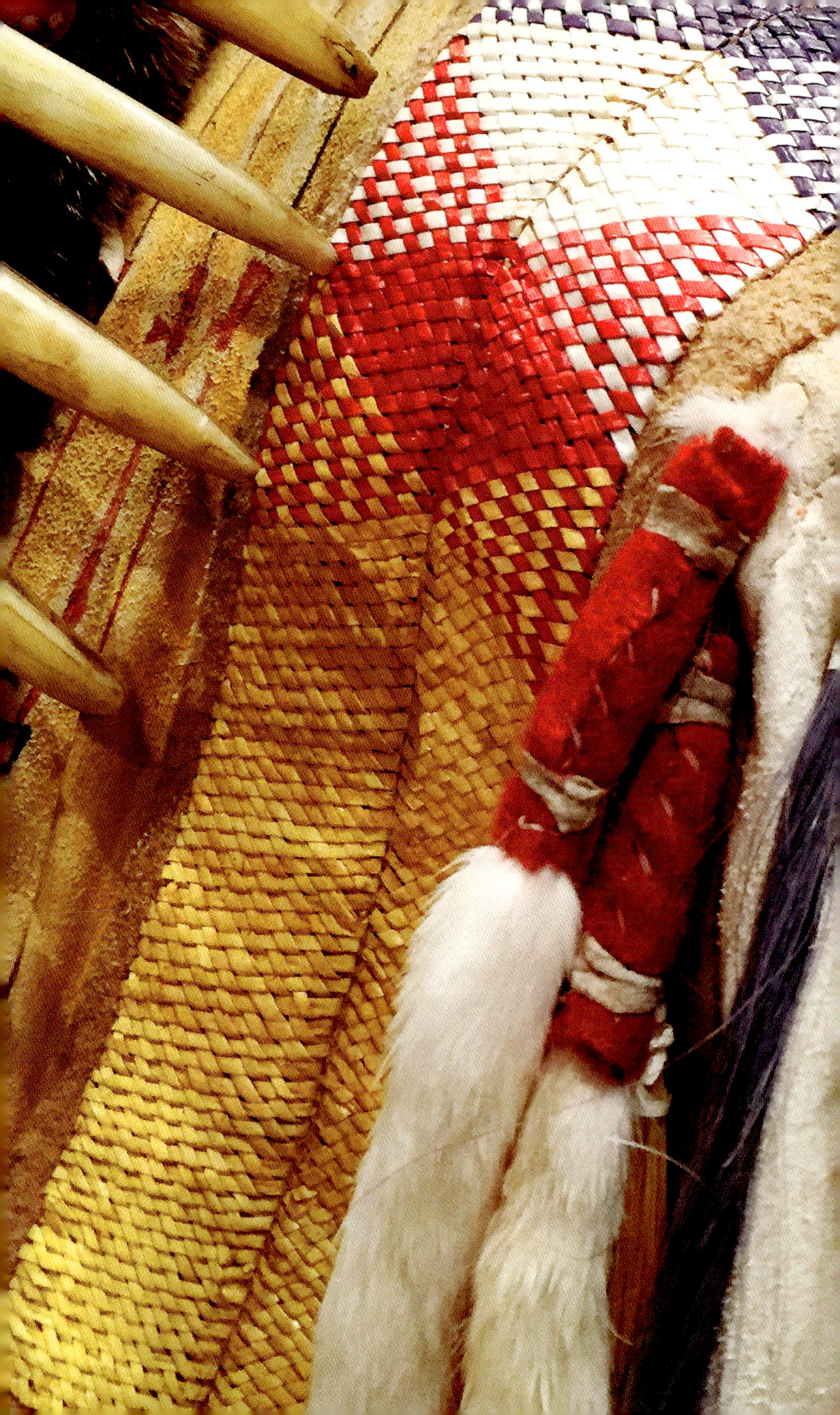

Acknowledgments

This book gestated for more than ten years, with many midwives, critics, helpers, and consultants. It may take a village to raise a child, but it takes a transcontinental metropolis of scholars connected in cyberspace to write a book. The metropolis of Native American art history (and its adjacent fields) is a particularly generous one, and I am pleased to offer my thanks here.

The University of Rochester has been my happy intellectual home since 1997. This project has benefited from research funds allotted by the College of Arts and Sciences, as well as time away from teaching duties facilitated by department chairs A. Joan Saab and Rachel Haidu. Stephanie Frontz, head of the Art and Music Library, bought every book I ever asked for on the topics covered herein. The staff of the Interlibrary Loan Department at Rush Rhees Library got everything I requested, no matter how arcane, into my hands in a matter of days, or even hours. In the university's Graduate Program in Visual and Cultural Studies, I have had the pleasure of working with some remarkable young intellectuals as they earned their PhDs. They have taught me a great deal about new ways of thinking about objects and theory, and about ethical scholarship. Moreover, they continue to give me helpful feedback about my own work. I am particularly grateful to former students Jessica Horton, Norman Vorano, Elizabeth Kalbfleisch, Alexander Brier Marr, Alicia Guzman, Vicky Pass, and Abigail Glogower. At the final hour, graduate student Daly Arnett helped with bibliography, formatting, and other technical issues.

My work on Gladys and Reginald Laubin commenced while I was the Mellon Distinguished Scholar in Residence in the Department of Art History at the University of Illinois Urbana-Champaign in the spring of 2007. Tandy Lacy and the other staff of the university's Spurlock Museum, which houses the

Laubin Collection, facilitated my research there. I am grateful to Gwendolyn DuBois Shaw, who invited me to be part of the symposium "Racial Masquerade in American Art and Culture" at the National Portrait Gallery in 2016; my work on the Laubins benefited from what I learned from the scholars of "blackface" and African American masquerade who spoke there. I am grateful to Jonathan Batkin, Cheri Falkenstien-Doyle, and Leatrice Armstrong, all formerly at the Wheelwright Museum in Santa Fe, who fostered my research in their archives on Hosteen Klah and sandpainting replicas. Carole Ann Fabian and Lillian Vargas at Columbia University's Avery Art Library allowed me to study the sandpainting replicas in the Bush Collection.

A fellowship from the Center for Craft and Creativity (2011–12) allowed for travel to New Mexico and Arizona to interview contemporary potters—both Native and non-Native—who draw inspiration from ancient Mimbres pottery. A National Endowment for the Humanities Faculty Fellowship (2012–13) supported the first drafts of several chapters. In the spring of 2017, I held a senior research fellowship at the Georgia O'Keeffe Research Center, where final drafts of several chapters were written. I thank Eumie Imm Stroukoff and Carolyn Kastner of the O'Keeffe for their gracious hospitality and Kristine Ronan, my fellow fellow, for her comradeship and discerning feedback. While I was a visiting research scholar at the Rochester Museum and Science Center in July 2019, curator Kathryn Murano Santos, registrar Elizabeth Pietrzykowski, and archivist Stephanie Ball extended every courtesy to me as I researched women's participation in the Seneca Arts Project for chapter 5.

During the first months of 2020, I held a senior research fellowship at the Sainsbury Research Unit at the University of East Anglia in Norwich, United Kingdom. While this was regrettably cut short by the COVID-19 pandemic, the two months I spent there were crucial in writing the final version of chapter 1. My colleagues at the university, particularly Steven Hooper, George Lau, and Chris Wingfield, as well as Jacqueline Fear-Segal of the history department, graciously welcomed me, engaged with my work, and recommended important publications. My office mate, the archaeologist Emmanuelle Honoré (the only office mate of my entire professional life!), was a marvelous intellectual companion as well as a coconspirator in chocolate and laughter.

I have found that art dealers and collectors often look more closely at the physical aspects of works of art than do modern art historians. I am grateful for deep conversations with Jonathan Holstein, Donald Ellis, and Toby Herbst over several decades, in which each demonstrated his profound knowledge of

Native American objects and of the thorny issues of attribution, forgery, and pastiche. I thank the many artists, restorers, conservators, and replica makers whom I interviewed for this project. Some are named within the chapters, and some have chosen to remain anonymous. All have taught me a great deal. My valued colleagues heather ahtone, Arthur Amiotte, and Joe D. Horse Capture have, over the years, offered deep insights into Native epistemologies and Native ethics. I am grateful for your intellectual generosity, and for your friendship. Thank you, Joe, for graciously consenting to write the foreword.

Perceptive comments on drafts of various chapters were offered by Kathryn Bunn-Marcuse, Paul Duro, Robert Foster, Mary M. Fox, Jessica Horton, Aldona Jonaitis, Carolyn Kastner, Alexander Brier Marr, Christopher Patrello, Ruth B. Phillips, Kristine Ronan, A. Joan Saab, and Norman Vorano—thank you. Paul D. Weiss performed the herculean task of reading every word of the manuscript twice and commented on grammar, word choice, logic, and understandability to the nonspecialist, for which I feel enormous gratitude.

Clyde Ellis, thank you for being my long-distance writing buddy for more than four years, as we each waded through endless chapter drafts. Your good humor helped to see me through. Jill Ahlberg Yohe, Jonathan Batkin, Karen Kramer, John Lukavic, Evan Maurer, and David Penney—you are all curators and scholars extraordinaire, and I thank you for every conversation, as well as your rapid response to every query. Bruce Bernstein, I admire tremendously your encyclopedic knowledge of all things Southwestern, and I thank you for your generosity in sharing your knowledge during my many sojourns in Santa Fe. Phil Deloria, I am grateful for several crucial conversations and for your enthusiasm for this project; it rests on the shoulders of your distinguished books about representation and misrepresentation. Jim Enote, thank you for a memorable day at Zuni in the summer of 2017 and for your writings on Native topics. Chip Colwell, your marvelous book *Plundered Skulls and Stolen Spirits* was most inspiring to me, as was our wide-ranging conversation in Rochester, New York, in March 2019. Michael F. Brown's *Who Owns Native Culture?* was an early inspiration, as were our deep conversations in Santa Fe in 2017, 2018, and 2019.

I am also grateful to D. Y. Begay, Tony Berlant, Barbara Brotherton, Robert N. Brown, Arni Brownstone, Christina Burke, Diana Fane, Ivan Gaskell, Aaron Glass, Adriana Greci Green, Candace Greene, Chelsea Herr, the late Bill Holm, Jennifer McLerran, Juan Antonio Murro, Judith Ostrowitz, the late Zena Pearlstone, Matthew Robb, Khristaan Villela, and Jason Weems. Surely,

I have unwittingly omitted others who offered assistance over the decade in which I worked on this subject. I offer my blanket thanks and apologies to them.

At the University of Washington Press, I am grateful for the guidance and enthusiasm of editorial director Larin McLaughlin and editorial assistant Caroline Hall. Senior project editor Joeth Zucco, copy editor Jane M. Lichty, and indexer Sally Brown helped to make the book more readable and searchable.

Portions of chapter 1 were originally published as "From 'Artifakes' to 'Surrogates': The Replication of Northwest Coast Carving by Non-Natives," written with Aldona Jonaitis, in *Unsettling Native Art Histories on the Northwest Coast*, edited by Kathryn Bunn-Marcuse and Aldona Jonaitis, 76–91 (Seattle: University of Washington Press, 2020). Portions of chapter 2 are condensed from "Men of the Middle Ground: The Visual Culture of Native-White Diplomacy in Eighteenth-Century North America," in *American Adversaries: West and Copley in a Transatlantic World*, edited by Emily Ballew Neff, 104–15 (Houston: Museum of Fine Arts, 2013). Portions of chapter 5 are a greatly abbreviated version of "Navajo Sandpainting in the Age of Cross-Cultural Replication," *Art History* 37, no. 4 (2014): 688–707.

I save the best for last. Aldona Jonaitis and Ruth B. Phillips: for nearly forty years you have been my sounding boards, my best friends, my teachers, my sometimes coauthors, and my consistent coconspirators in the world of Native American art history. My work is always better for your insight and counsel. You have been my closest companions on this long journey and every chapter is better for your discerning judgment.

Aldona and Ruth—I dedicate this book to you.

Introduction
Of "Santa Fakes" and Other Illusions

I began this introduction and wrote much of chapter 1 of this book while a senior research fellow at the Georgia O'Keeffe Research Center in Santa Fe in the spring of 2017. Santa Fe is an excellent place to think deeply about the misrepresentation and replication of Native American art. In shops around the city's plaza (which is itself a picturesque simulacrum of an ideal that never existed), real century-old Zuni ollas (pottery jars) selling for $16,000 sit cheek by jowl in shop windows with ersatz Native jewelry.[1] Potholders labeled "Made in India" sport ancient Mimbres designs, and more nineteenth-century Navajo rugs than could possibly have been made by a veritable army of industrious Navajo women are offered for sale. In one shop, exquisite historic Navajo blankets and contemporary Navajo-made homages to mid-nineteenth-century third phase chief's blankets are sold next to Mexican reproductions of Navajo rugs. In even tonier galleries, yet another too perfectly preserved nineteenth-century Plains war shirt or Great Lakes beaded bag is offered up for the delectation of those willing to pay the five- or six-figure price tag.

Two weeks before I arrived in Santa Fe in February 2017, a federal grand jury in Albuquerque returned indictments in what US Fish and Wildlife Service special agent in charge Nicholas E. Chavez called "the largest investigation ever into fraudulent Native American jewelry sales under the IACA [Indian Arts and Crafts Act]."[2] This legislation, enacted in 1990, prohibits advertising or selling art objects as Native American–made if they are not, in fact, made by an enrolled member of one of the United States' federally recognized tribes.[3] The jewelry in question was allegedly made in a factory in Cebu City, Philippines; based on real Navajo and Pueblo prototypes; and sold in shops owned by members of the Palestinian American Aysheh family in Gallup, Santa Fe,

Albuquerque, and elsewhere. Surely, the cosmopolitan global circuit is complete when Middle Eastern entrepreneurs have jewelry made in Southeast Asia to sell to American tourists in New Mexico as authentic American Indian art. In 2019, a motion by the Aysheh family to dismiss the indictments was denied by the US District Court for New Mexico.[4] When this book went to press in summer 2022, the case remained in pretrial hearings.

Those of us who study the indigenous arts of the Americas, Africa, and the Pacific have long been aware of fraud and reproduction.[5] The day the first European set foot in Samarai, New Guinea, or Zuni Pueblo in the American Southwest, the stage was set for making objects to sell to outsiders, none of whom understood local aesthetics or cultural practices. In addition to buying (or looting) some of the finest works of art created in those cultures, they also bought objects that were outright spurious, they commissioned replicas, and they influenced what would be made in the future.

How does one make sense of the welter of material loosely described as "Native" that is on offer in Santa Fe, a city that is probably the economic epicenter for ancient, historic, and contemporary Native American art? While this book does not specifically focus on Santa Fe, writing there in the spring of 2017, and during shorter sojourns in April of 2018 and 2019, certainly focused my mind, for every day I confronted the subject of my research—in shop windows, in museums, in the galleries on Canyon Road, and in the objects worn and carried by the tourists who flock here. This book is a first attempt to look broadly at the overlapping, troubling, confusing categories that are loosely (and often erroneously) called Native North American art, even though they are sometimes made by non-Native people, or Natives and non-Natives working collaboratively, or indigenous people in Nepal or Mexico. Sometimes they are replicas, homages, or outright fakes. I examine these and other slippery categorizations in chapter 1.

Like many other scholars, I have long been interested in what the anthropologist Arjun Appadurai has called "the social life of things."[6] In studying works of art, it is essential to understand as much as we can about their original makers and users, and the meanings those individuals invested in their belongings. That is the traditional role of the historian of art, and that is how I have spent much of my professional career. Yet increasingly, many of us scholars of visual culture are finding that it is also imperative to consider the complex trajectories of objects as they have been removed from their original contexts, rediscovered, and placed in new social realms, or in some cases the ways in which they have been rediscovered, reclaimed, remade, and reinterpreted by the descendants of their makers. For this reason, the reuse, translation, and duplication of objects (whether as inspiration for new makers or as pawns in an international marketplace that values the pristine, the flawless, and the antique above all else) are prime concerns in this book.

My earlier books and essays dealt with the real stuff, from ancient Mesoamerican pottery to nineteenth-century Plains drawings and contemporary Indigenous art.[7] But I am also keenly interested in how the "real" gets translated, filtered, transformed, and copied in numerous ways. While this book is in some ways about the art market and its slippery practices, it is more than that. I am also curious about the ideas that animate people. Why would an Anglo couple spend decades at the turn of the twenty-first century perfecting the art of making Mimbres pottery the same way it was made one thousand years ago? What did it mean for another Anglo couple in the early to mid-twentieth century to relentlessly market themselves as "more Indian than the Indians," as they toured the globe demonstrating Indian dance? How did discerning twentieth-century art collectors such as Nelson Rockefeller and Robert Woods Bliss, who had so much money and expertise at their fingertips, get taken in by fakes? How do ideas about replication and duplication operate in various Native cultures, so that in some instances works that to my eyes might seem to be lifeless copies by outsiders are imbued with the same power as the originals?

As Native American art historical studies have come of age within the academy, and Native objects are of increasing value in the marketplace, there is also an urgent need to grapple with issues of forgery and misattribution, as well as issues I group under the rubric of "vexed identities," by which I mean complex situations that cannot easily be defined. In contrast to the larger field of art history, there is almost no literature on these topics in Native American art history. Discussed privately among dealers and scholars, they are seldom addressed publicly, though I have organized sessions at professional meetings, where my colleagues evinced great interest in these issues. This book is not limited to issues of forgery and erroneous identifications, but also focuses on more complex social issues sometimes having to do with questions of identity, sovereignty, and rights.

In my opinion, in the twenty-first century the world of Native art is increasingly shadowed by notions of essentialism that sometimes threaten to straitjacket what cultural identity is. These involve questions of who has the "right" to engage in acts of cultural translation and who is a "real" Indian making "real"

Indian art, despite the fact that in the rest of the academic community, such one-dimensional notions were, thirty years ago, increasingly being replaced with notions of hybrid or unfixed global identities, *Créolité* (Creoleness), and other cosmopolitan constructs.[8] This is an issue far too complex to take on fully within these pages, but it shadows many of the examples I write about.

Through a series of case studies, I pose questions about issues of representation, authenticity, and reproduction as they have played out in specific communities and with particular object categories since the mid-nineteenth century. For example, I examine non-Native makers of Plains-style quillwork and beadwork as well as of ancient Mimbres-style pottery, in each case executed to impeccable standards. I discuss Reginald and Gladys Laubin, non-Natives who introduced the international modern dance world to Plains-style dance in the first half of the twentieth century. I examine collaborations between Navajo sandpainters and non-Native artists who recorded the ephemeral images of sandpaintings in paint on paper and published them in the first half of the twentieth century. Objections have arisen as to the legitimacy of all of these actors and actions, and I discuss such objections as well. I also focus on a few Native makers of replicas and copies, both historically and today. Each chapter can be read alone, or out of order, but I have placed them in a sequence meant to elucidate ways of thinking about the multiple and slippery categories of authenticity.

Right at the outset, I seek to clarify for the reader what this book is not. *It is not a handbook for collectors or curators hoping to discover whether an individual work of art is real or fake.* I was trained as an art historian at a time when connoisseurship was out of fashion; in the 1970s, we were animated by the social history of art, by feminist reinterpretations of art worlds, and by transdisciplinary practices.[9] After decades of working with an older generation of museum professionals and art dealers, and more recent experiences with Native and non-Native makers of objects, I have come to appreciate how very useful it is to understand pigments, hides, clay surfaces, and the like. A deep knowledge of the materiality of works of art allows a small number of individuals to "read" the manufacture and the history of an object in ways that most of us cannot. Few people trained in art history PhD programs in the past few decades have had much exposure to the close scrutiny of materials. But as the generation of scholars and curators who had such skills dies off, it is remarkable that a new generation of (mostly) Native practitioners has arisen who can provide indigenous expertise in such topics. Navajo weaver D. Y. Begay, for example, is widely consulted for her knowledge of historic Navajo textiles and indigenous dye use, while Canadian Métis curator Morgan Baillargeon has written a definitive ethnography of hide tanning.[10] They, and others like them in areas ranging from quill- and beadwork to pottery making, have revived interest in Indigenous ways of knowing and making, and they lead in the deep understanding of such processes.

It is not an exhaustive survey of forgeries or misrepresentations in the field of Native American art history. In 2009 and 2010, two archaeologists wrote useful companion books tracing the issues of the forgery of pre-Columbian works of Mesoamerican and Andean art.[11] While a similar volume on indigenous North America would be useful, this book is not it. Instead, I make selective inquiries into issues of interest to all who study or collect Native North American art, be it ancient, historical, or contemporary. I explore these issues by means of case studies that will allow the reader to gain insight into the histories (and in some cases the personal or cultural motivations) of individuals who have replicated nineteenth-century Plains quillwork or thousand-year-old Mimbres pottery, to name just a couple of object types.

This is not a book focused on legal issues. Issues of legality (such as the Indian Arts and Crafts Act and the Native American Graves Protection and Repatriation Act, both enacted in 1990, as well as earlier legislation), however, do arise in particular chapters. My work here treads a more slippery slope having to do with issues of representation, epistemology, and material objects themselves. My aim is to analyze the complexities of these issues in examples drawn from different times and places, in part to show that essentialist claims not only may be increasingly hard to justify but perhaps always have been. Probably I will have succeeded in my aims if, in certain instances, I have made some issues seem even more confusing than they had been or have infuriated certain readers who prefer their notions of authenticity to remain uncomplicated.

It is not an examination of the fraudulent appropriation of Native identity. Egregious cases continue to be uncovered in which non-Native individuals have assumed Native identity, usually for professional gain. This book focuses on objects, and the actions of people who have made and used them in performance, but does not address the larger issue of ethnic identity.

It is not a denunciation or a polemic against the work of non-Native makers of Native-style art. I am a historian who seeks to understand the social contexts within which people make objects, be they replicas, reconstructions, fakes, pastiches, or homages (tricky words, some of which are examined in chapter 1 as well as throughout the book). I attempt to offer many sides to complex issues. In my opinion, simple denunciation of such practices precludes understanding. My work is neither a celebration of nor an apology for such work; I seek to understand it. There are good reasons why some Native makers of objects may vociferously object to non-Native people earning income by making objects that they may have no legal or socially sanctioned right to make; I will explore these issues without necessarily offering rousing denunciations of them.

This book builds on the work of many colleagues in the fields of Native American art history and anthropology, as well as theoretical works in cultural studies and critical race studies. Some of what I have written here will not be "news" to many who work in these fields, but I hope that juxtaposing topics and issues from various regions helps to frame them in a way that makes room for new methods of analysis and discussion. We all tend to be circumscribed within our own regional or temporal specializations; sometimes it is only by looking comparatively that we see either how similar certain practices are or, conversely, how distinctly different they are, making a simplistic "one size fits all" response unsuitable.

Like many others working today, both Native and non-Native, I believe it is important to specify my own place in these complex transcultural queries. I have been a scholar of the indigenous arts of the Americas since beginning a PhD program in the history of art at Yale in 1974. My publications have been multi-sited and transdisciplinary, ranging from close examination of archaeological and historical materials to examinations of contemporary materials within their communities of origin, historiographic inquiries, collaborative projects with both Native and non-Native colleagues, and critical writing on contemporary arts and artists. Much of my work has considered issues of cultural boundaries: ancient central Mexican art made in a Maya context in the sixth century CE, for example, or nineteenth-century ledger drawings made by Plains artists for white patrons. My first publication that considered "authenticity" was a short article written in 1985, after my fieldwork among contemporary Maya weavers in Guatemala revealed that a few contemporary women were producing textiles of a quality that most people believed was no longer possible and that these were being marketed as rare historical textiles.[12]

While this is a book of art historical and visual studies scholarship, it also chronicles a personal journey, and to keep this in the forefront, I open most chapters with an anecdote that helps to illuminate the issues at hand. My reasons for this are many. I believe that twenty-first-century scholarship requires that we make our own personal interests and intellectual investments transparent. While some might find such insertion of the author into her text self-indulgent, the older I get, the more I seek to leave behind the dry, impersonal stance of much academic writing. For more than three decades, changing trends in the discourses of anthropology and cultural studies have exhorted us to remember that we are all implicated in the worlds that we study. This approach also reminds the reader that this is an idiosyncratic exploration of a vast topic. Every reader who is conversant with Native art will think of a host of other byways I could have traversed. This is the first book to broadly consider issues of forgery and misrepresentation in this field, and I hope that it will open the door to many more publications on different facets of this topic.[13]

Readers should not be alarmed or offended to find some "real" Native art in a book titled *Not Native American Art*. I do not mean to impugn the artistic integrity of these works by having them rub shoulders with items of far more "vexed identity." They serve as place markers, standards, and ways to locate and position other works that appropriate, copy, respond to, or draw on Native art.

I interviewed curators, conservators, restorers, replicators, reenactors, Native artists, and Native cultural specialists over the course of a decade. My protocol was that, after a formal interview, I gave each interviewee the opportunity to see what I had written and to amend or cut. In only two instances did this result in individuals not wanting their names used (see chapters 4 and 5). In one case, I created a composite identity, and in the other, I simply omitted the name.

Finally, as many authors now do, I find it necessary to explain my use of terminology. When talking about the field as a whole, and indigenous people of North America in general, I interchangeably use Native American, American Indian, Aboriginal, and Indigenous. Each of these terms has its partisans and its detractors, but all are in current usage. When discussing Canadians, I follow the customary use of "First Nation," which has not gained currency in discussing the indigenous inhabitants of the United States. When discussing specific ethnic groups, I specify Zuni, Lakota, and so forth, usually using the terms that are most widely recognized or the terms that individuals used in speaking about themselves.

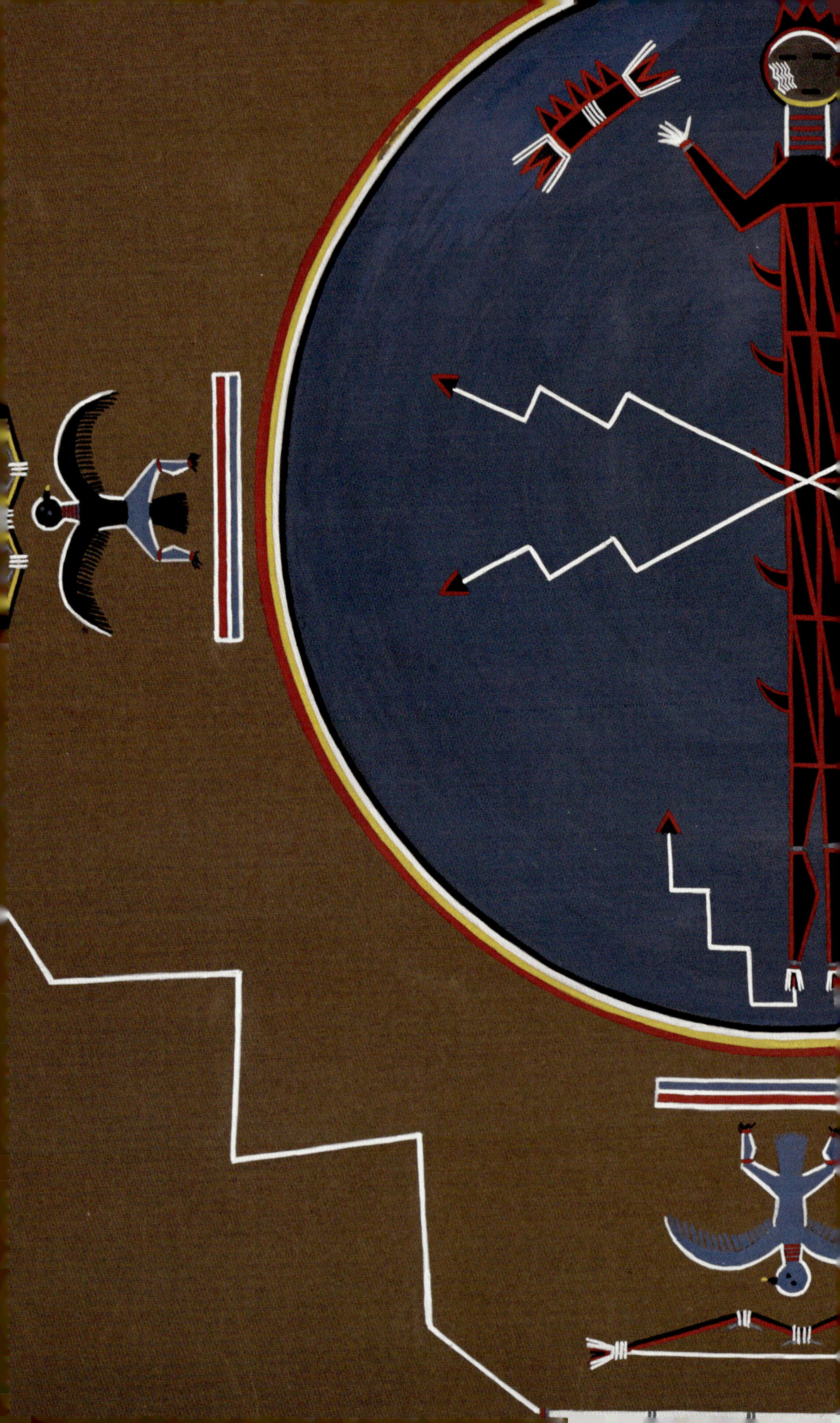

Not Native American Art

1

Authenticity and Its Discontents *What Is "Real" Native American Art?*

Strands of mystery, nostalgia, connoisseurship, obfuscation, and sleight of hand wrap around historical objects assumed to be Native-made. Is it real? Was it used in ceremony? Is it a reconstruction? Or, even more shockingly, "Does it have the soul of the Indian?," as one twentieth-century collector claimed that he asked about every item he considered for purchase.[1]

Two men well known in the study of Native art history, one from the twentieth century and one from the nineteenth, are Milford Chandler and George Catlin. Both collected Native objects and contributed a great deal to our knowledge of Native artistry. Both also tried their hands at making Native-style objects, with varied motivations and degrees of success. These examples are meant to complicate the reader's understanding of what "real" Native art is and why some objects we assume are real may not be. They also set the stage for unpacking some of the messy terminology that is often used indiscriminately and imprecisely when discussing objects that may or may not be Native-made: What is a replica? What is a pastiche? Is a fake different from an invented tradition? I examine nine different terms, generally providing one example for each, in the hopes that by the end of the chapter the reader will be ready to think critically about the longer case studies in subsequent chapters that employ these terms.

As is customary when Native people get together to discuss issues of importance, let's begin with a pipe.

Milford Chandler's Pipe

In the collection of the Spurlock Museum at the University of Illinois Urbana-Champaign is a red stone pipe bowl carved with the image of a small buffalo

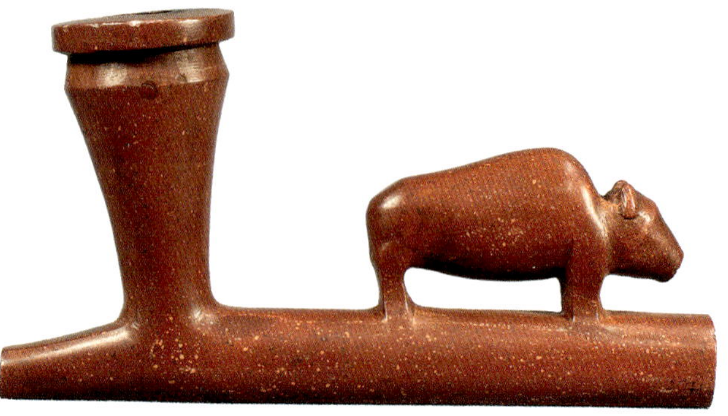

FIG. 1.1 Milford Chandler, pipe bowl, 1955. Catlinite, 6¼ × 3 in. Reginald and Gladys Laubin Collection, Spurlock Museum, University of Illinois Urbana-Champaign, no. 1996.24.0041a.

(figure 1.1). Milford Chandler's pipe is a beautiful object. About six inches long, it nestles comfortably in the palm of the hand, as a pipe bowl should. It is both a ceremonial instrument and a miniature sculpture, meant to be handled and admired during the act of passing and smoking the pipe.

Chandler (1889–1981) was a collector of Native artifacts as well as a "hobbyist" who learned about such artifacts by making replicas of them. While he owned many Native-made objects, this pipe is not one of them. Chandler made this himself in 1955 and gave it to his friend Reginald Laubin, who shared his interest in all things Indian. When Reginald and Gladys Laubin gave their collection to the Spurlock Museum, this pipe was part of the gift. (On the Laubins, see chapters 2 and 3.) So, a pipe made *by* a white man *for* a white man surely falls under the rubric "not Native art." But Chandler had an unusual relationship to historic Native American art. He was close to some Native people, especially in the Osage and Potawatomi communities, and as a central figure in the rise of the American Indian hobbyist movement, he learned about Native art through looking and making, not by reading books.

Long before there were lavish full-color art books and detailed treatises on everything from Acoma pottery to Plains parfleches, a small group of enthusiasts and collectors were learning about Native objects by making their own replicas. They came to be called hobbyists, for the study of Indian material culture and the reproduction and wearing of such items was their hobby.

A full discussion of the rise of this movement is beyond the scope of this book, but it is impossible to understand the culture of making copies and replicas without understanding hobbyism in the United States, particularly between about 1930 and 1980, when a generation of people—mostly white men—learned about Native American art by replicating it.[2] One social anthropologist describes dedicated Indian hobbyists as "amateur researchers who learn through imitation." "They combine theoretical study, practical training, and experimentation to re-experience the sounds, smells, tastes, visuals, and 'feeling' of eighteenth- and nineteenth-century Native American life. Instead of contenting themselves with disembodied contemplation, Indianists seek to bodily engage with the materiality and sensoriality of former life-worlds, that is, with material culture as it used to be embedded in social contexts."[3] When working on the exhibition *The Spirit Sings* in the early 1980s, Canadian art historian Ruth B. Phillips was surprised to discover that nearly every ethnologist in Europe who specialized in Indigenous North America had been a hobbyist.[4] In North America, too, twentieth-century hobbyism bled into ethnology, with scholars such as Ted Brasser, William K. Powers, Bill Holm, and Bill Mercer all having been active hobbyists. Hobbyists were part of what the historian Clyde Ellis and others call the Indian lore movement, which grew out of the Boy Scouts in the early twentieth century, as well as the general love of "playing Indian."[5]

Chandler was an important figure in this movement; he wrote many articles in hobbyist magazines and taught a younger generation of non-Native people about the material and cultural aspects of Native life.[6] As with many of the non-Native people discussed in this book who worked during the middle of the twentieth century, he was respected by Native people of an older generation because of his sincere interest in the old ways—in subjects that many of the elders believed would fade from memory, as a younger generation became educated outside of their communities and entered the mainstream workforce.

But back to Chandler's pipe: the stone is catlinite, which is most often red.[7] Pipes such as this are well known across the Plains and have been used by Native peoples for countless generations. Offered in ceremony as well as in intercultural negotiation, the smoking of a pipe with one's peers, one's enemies, or those with whom one has entered into an agreement is akin to both a legal and a spiritual contract. In some cases, pipe smoking turned outsiders into kin. Most catlinite comes from a quarry in southwestern Minnesota that has been mined by Native peoples for centuries. Thousands of such pipes are in museum and private collections; surely thousands more have been passed down within Native families.

The history of catlinite pipes has long been a story of the intertwining of Native and white interests. For Native people, the quarry was said to be sacred and a place where people from various Native nations came, unmolested, to quarry the soft, easily worked stone. It became Pipestone National Monument in 1937, and only members of federally recognized tribes are allowed to mine the stone. American artist George Catlin visited the quarry in 1836 and painted Native men working the stone.[8] Catlin claimed that he was told, "No white man has ever been to the Pipe Stone quarry, and our chiefs have often decided in council that no white man shall ever go to it."[9] Yet the fur trader Philander Prescott had been there five years earlier with some Native men and wrote that all had worked the quarry for one long day and gotten material for about twenty good pipes.[10] Various nineteenth-century treaties assured that Indian people would have unfettered access to the quarry, and, indeed, they have continually used this resource. Yet by 1865, when the trader John Boyd Hubbell had bought the American Fur Company's interests on the upper Missouri River from the Chouteau family, he wrote:

> I venture to say the residents of Pipestone City and that beautiful section are not aware of the fact that a large quantity of the pipestone was hauled to Lake Shetek and manufactured into Indian pipes and other things by machinery. . . . Gen. Sully had expected to be ordered to make a treaty with the Sioux, and as the red stone pipes were prized highly with them, he engaged with me for 5,000 pipes at $5 apiece. I employed men to make them under the supervision of A. B. Smith, one of the earliest settlers of Dakota. Gen. Sully did not make the treaty as expected, but the pipes were no loss, as we traded them to good advantage with the Indians all along the Missouri, receiving a well-dressed buffalo robe or its equivalent in other skins for a pipe. Robes at that time were worth over $10.00 on an average.[11]

So nearly a century before Chandler made his pipe, there was a veritable industry in white men making pipes for Indian trade and diplomacy. It is not surprising, then, that in 1907 one scholarly source claimed that the Indians who mined pipestone at the end of the nineteenth century sold "much of the stone to whites, who ha[d] taken up the manufacture of pipes and various trinkets, using lathes to aid in the work." A local authority in Pipestone in

1892 stated that "not 1 percent of the pipes then made and disposed of were of Indian manufacture."[12] Therefore, Chandler's pipe stands within a long history of white men carving Native-style pipe bowls.

If indeed so few of the pipes known in the late nineteenth century were Native-made, what does this mean for all of the pipe bowls held in museum collections across the world? If the maker is unknown, should we no longer assume that these are Native American objects? Or is it more important to know if these were objects owned and used within a Native community?

I begin chapter 1 with this example because it illustrates how facts may differ from received wisdom about objects. Just because a catlinite pipe has "Indian" iconography on it does not mean it was necessarily Native-made. Object makers in all cultures tailor their imagery to their clientele. But this story also brings up an important flaw in the way that we think about Native art. Most people see it as a category with strict boundaries around it: either something is "Native American art" or it is not. But neither cultures nor artists have walls around them, as will be evident in many further examples, including another made by Chandler. Moreover, I will repeatedly quote authors writing more than a century ago who marveled at how many fakes and copies existed in the world of Native North American material culture at the end of the nineteenth century.

The Limits of "Authenticity" in the Historical Era: George Catlin

In the twenty-first century, it is easy to think that objects dating from the mid-nineteenth century must be authentic; after all, there were so many Native objects in circulation then, and most were not considered valuable in the way they came to be some one hundred years later. Yet the man who was so celebrated for his depictions of Native people before 1840 also took part in the falsification of both objects and depictions.

It is impossible to talk about the work of the self-taught American painter George Catlin (1796–1872) without introducing two of his European contemporaries, for their travels and interests paralleled each other. The German explorer Prince Maximilian of Wied-Neuwied (1782–1867) and his Swiss artist companion Karl Bodmer (1809–1893) sailed to North America in 1832 and traveled up the Missouri River, providing the most detailed accounts and the finest and most accurate images of peoples of the Northern Plains. Before major North American publications and exhibits of the 1980s, their work was not nearly as well known to English speakers (except for scholars) as Catlin's.[13] But Bodmer's work haunted Catlin and was part of the impetus for his many proclamations of the veracity of his images.

Catlin was celebrated for his hundreds of paintings of Native life and his enormous collection of regalia and other objects. From his *Letters and Notes on the Manners, Customs, and Condition of the North American Indians* to his Indian Gallery displayed in many countries in the 1830s and 1840s and his paintings, drawings, and prints that were replicated and circulated in multiple ways, Catlin introduced Native worlds—principally of the Plains and Great Lakes—to many Americans and Europeans. Today, his paintings hang in the Smithsonian American Art Museum and the National Portrait Gallery, as well as in many other American museums. Some of his objects are in the National Museum of Natural History, and he remains a crucial source on early nineteenth-century life and art. Two aspects of Catlin's work are of interest here: first, his concern with "truth" as revealed in his need both to publish documents written by men of renown attesting to the veracity of his artwork, which he called "certificates of authenticity," and to publish excerpts from reviews of his book, lauding him for the same thing, and, second, in stark contrast, his falsification of some objects presented in his Indian Gallery and in his publications.

Catlin's life is well known and thoroughly chronicled. In 1828, intrigued by the Indian delegates he saw in Philadelphia, he began painting their portraits. He moved to St. Louis in 1830—the gateway to the "Indian Country" he sought to explore. He first traveled up the Missouri River on a steamboat in the spring of 1832, arriving at the villages of the Mandan and Hidatsa a year before Prince Maximilian and Bodmer. Smithsonian anthropologist John Ewers estimated that Catlin's trip lasted eighty-six days.[14] Except for traders, few outsiders knew anything about this region, and Catlin's prodigious visual and textual output solidified his claims to the authenticity of his representations.

From 1833 to 1836, Catlin made subsequent trips to various forts to paint Native people. In later writings, he repeatedly referenced this, with great hyperbole, as "eight years in the west."[15] His encounters with Mandan, Hidatsa, and many other peoples were recorded both in paintings and in the newspaper reports that became *Letters and Notes on the Manners, Customs, and Condition of the North American Indians*, published in 1841.[16] Catlin toured with his paintings and objects to New York, Boston, and other eastern cities in 1837, and he set sail to London via Liverpool in the autumn of 1839, with some six hundred paintings and "several thousands of Indian articles," taking a long-term lease on a large exhibition space in the Egyptian Hall, in Piccadilly.[17] In *Notes of Eight Years' Travels and Residence in Europe, with His North American Indian Collection*, Catlin bitterly complains about the "constant efforts by artists and amateurs to make copies" of the work on display there. He writes, "After having risked my life and spent my little fortune in the wilderness to procure such exciting and such original studies, and bring them to England, I did not consider it fair that these gentlemen should step into my rooms just when they had an hour of leisure, and industry enough to use it, and copy whatever they could most easily convert into cash."[18] Indeed, despite the posting of a sign reading "No copying allowed in the rooms," there were times when the gallery guard confiscated sketchbooks and presented them to Catlin.[19]

CERTIFICATES OF AUTHENTICITY

Issues of authenticity preoccupied Catlin. As the art historian Kristine Ronan has chronicled, he "developed a variety of tactics to work against the potential uncertainty in viewers' responses to the accuracy of his works."[20] For example, he printed certificates signed by various notable men who attested to the authenticity of his portraiture (figure 1.2). Ronan suggests that being self-taught, and lacking Bodmer's prodigious talents, Catlin was insecure about how his artwork would be received, and that explains his preoccupation with veracity; he was gratified by the reception of his work in London and made sure to note that those who wrote about him always mentioned such certificates in their writings.[21] The topmost of three printed/handwritten certificates is signed by "K McKenzie," who attests that the "Ojibbeway" (i.e., Ojibwe) portrait of Ka-bes-kunk, no. 189, "was painted from the life, at Fort Union, Mouth of Yellow Stone, in the year 1832, by Geo. Catlin, and that the Indian sat in the costume in which it is painted." Kenneth McKenzie (?–1861) was a Scots Canadian who worked in the fur trade on the upper Missouri throughout the 1820s, joined John Jacob Astor's American Fur Company, and helped to build Fort Union. In *Letters and Notes*, Catlin refers to "M'Kenzie" dozens of times, and he makes an appearance in a cluster of eighteen testimonials, some with multiple signatures, at the start of the book. Catlin refers to these as certificates "voluntarily furnished to me by men whose lives, it will be seen, have been spent, in great part, in the Indian Country, and in familiarity with the men and manners set forth in the work."[22] Among them are Joel R. Poinsett, secretary of war, Washington; William Clark, superintendent of Indian affairs, St. Louis (well known from the Lewis and Clark Expedition of 1804–6); and Henry Schoolcraft, Indian agent for Wisconsin Territory, whose own opus on Native cultures would not be published for another decade.[23]

In this group of testimonials, McKenzie assures the reader,

> I have seen Mr. Catlin's Collection of Indian Portraits, many of which were familiar to me, and painted in my presence at their own villages. I have spent the greater part of my life amongst the tribes and individuals he has represented, and I do not hesitate to pronounce them correct likenesses, and easily recognized; also his sketches of their *manners* and *customs*, I think, are excellent; and the *landscape views* on the Missouri and Mississippi, are correct representations.
>
> K. M'KENZIE, *of the Am. Fur Co. Mouth of Yellow Stone.*[24]

Similarly, when *Letters and Notes* was published in 1841, while Catlin was in London, he made sure to include encomiums (which he called "critical notices") excerpted from many British publications. The *London Morning Chronicle* called his descriptions "not merely animated or life-like, but *life* itself." *Dublin University Magazine* lauded his "faithful and accurate observations," and the *London Atlas* was reassured that his descriptions were "verified by the concurrent testimonials of many individuals intimately acquainted with the scenes and races delineated." *Chambers's Edinburgh Journal* made the definitive pronouncement: "No one, it seems to us, can be compared in point of accuracy and extent of research with that of Mr. Catlin."[25]

Indeed, much of what Catlin presented to the world was both groundbreaking and accurate. But in recent decades, scholars have been attending to what is *not* accurate in his work. A shirt he claimed to have gotten from a high-ranking Mandan named Mató-tópe is one egregious example, along with his drawings of several bizarre painted hides, none of which—mysteriously—has survived for our examination.

MATÓ-TÓPE'S SHIRT—OR CATLIN'S?

Mató-tópe (ca. 1784–1837), whom Catlin called Mah-to-toh-pa, or Four Bears, was the distinguished second chief of the Mandan. He became a talismanic

Smithsonian Report, 1885, Part II.—Donaldson, Catlin Indian Gallery. PLATE 4.

No. 189 Ojibbeway.
Ka-bes-kunk.
he who travels the whole country
I hereby certify that this Portrait was painted from the life, at Fort Union mouth of Yellow-Stone. in the year 1832, by Geo. Catlin, and that the Indian sat in the costume in which it is painted.
K. McKenzie

Chippeway
Gaw-zaw-que-dung.
He who halloos.
I hereby certify that this portrait was painted from life by Geo. Catlin, in my presence at the Sault De St. Marys, in the year 1836. and that the Indian sat in the Costume in which it is painted
James L. Schoolcraft
S. B. Porter Ast. Surgn. U.S.A.

No 234 Menomonie.
Chēh-ko-tong.
he who sings the War Song.
I hereby certify that this portrait was painted by Geo Catlin in 1835 at Prairie Du Chien & that the Indian sat in the costume in which he is painted.
E. A. Hitchcock
Capt U.S. Army

FACSIMILES OF CERTIFICATES TO AUTHENTICITY OF CATLIN'S INDIAN PORTRAITS.

FIG. 1.2 "Facsimiles of Certificates to Authenticity of Catlin's Indian Portraits," after plate 4 of Thomas Donaldson, "The George Catlin Indian Gallery in the United States National Museum," in *Annual Report of the Board of Regents of the Smithsonian Institution, July, 1885* (Washington, DC: Government Printing Office, 1886), pt. 2, appendix.

personage for Catlin as well as for Prince Maximilian and Bodmer. Both artists painted him many times; he gave them items he had made and painted himself. Mató-tópe figures prominently in Catlin's *Letters and Notes* and in his claims of authenticity. Catlin pronounced him "the most popular man in the nation" and chronicled their smoking and eating together in Mató-tópe's lodge, after which the chief offered Catlin the painted robe on which he had been seated.[26] Catlin painted the illustrious warrior several times and described in detail his ornate regalia and the battles represented on his pictographic robe.[27] Indeed, Mató-tópe seems to have become, for Catlin, emblematic of his whole endeavor; the frontispiece to *Letters and Notes* depicts the chief posing for Catlin's portrait of him. The intrepid artist-explorer and the noble Mandan stand together as dozens of Natives observe the artistic encounter. The fact

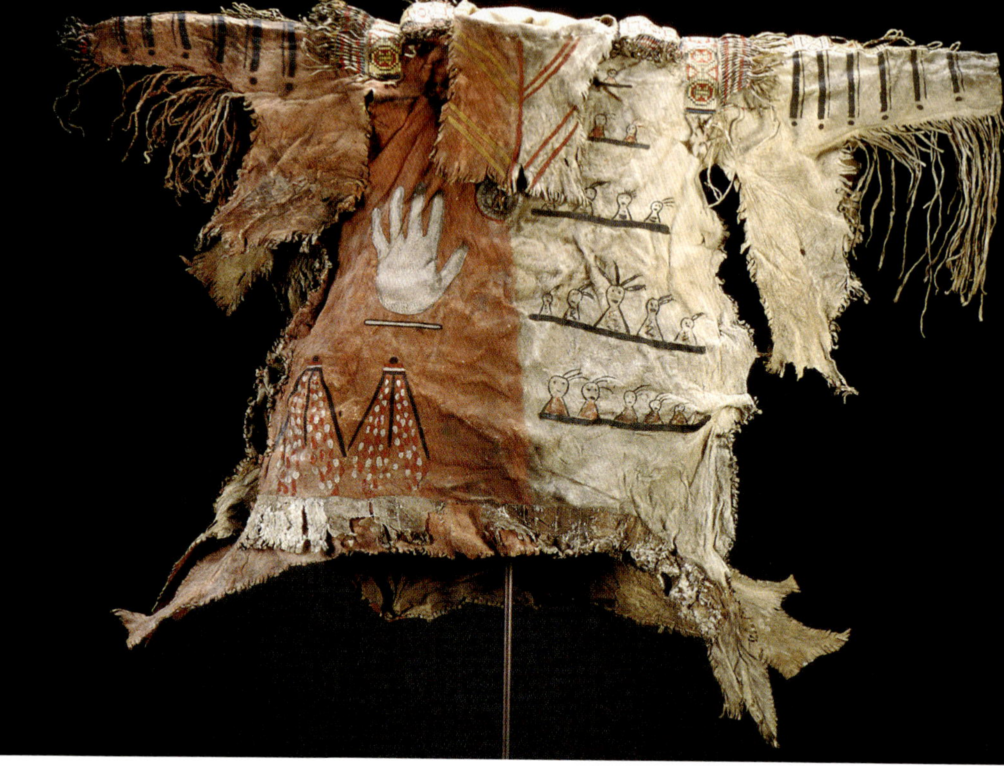

FIG. 1.3 "Mato-tope's Shirt," likely made by Catlin himself. Height 34 in. Department of Anthropology, National Museum of Natural History, Smithsonian Institution, no. E386505.

that they pose in front of a Plains tipi instead of a Mandan earth lodge suggests that this vignette stands for Catlin's larger enterprise, rather than simply being the recording of one encounter.

In the Smithsonian is a shirt Catlin claims was painted by Mató-tópe (figure 1.3). Superficially it resembles the one Mató-tópe wears in the full-length portrait in *Letters and Notes*.[28] Bill Holm, who was both a distinguished scholar of Native art and an acclaimed maker of objects, carefully studied the shirt that Catlin claimed to have gotten from its maker and discovered many differences between this example and authentic Northern Plains shirts of the early nineteenth century: it is far too short; its shoulder bands are Cree-style loomed quillwork rather than Northern Plains style, and they are poorly attached to the shirt by coarse cotton thread; its forked neck flaps are sewn on rather than being integral to the hide itself; and its pictographs are rendered not only in oil paint but in a cartoonish style. Holm concluded his analysis by saying that even "the least talented" Plains artist "would have been appalled by the crude images and inexpert workmanship."[29]

Proposing that Catlin himself made the shirt, Holm writes, "I wonder whether Catlin actually ever possessed Four Bears' shirt, or was he, for display in his gallery, forced to supplement his collection, many pieces of which are (or were) fine examples of early nineteenth-century Indian art, with objects of his own manufacture?"[30] Clearly this shirt and many other pieces in the Catlin collection are what Holm used to call "artifakes," most of them combining pieces of fine, original Indian objects with newly, and crudely, made parts.[31] It is possible that Catlin did own a shirt belonging to Mató-tópe, but we will never know. A substantial number of paintings and artifacts were stolen from his cabin on the steamboat *Warrior* when it docked in St. Louis in the summer of 1835.[32] If the splendid shirt from the acclaimed warrior was among those items, his impulse to re-create it would perhaps be understandable.

Our familiarity today with superb early to mid-nineteenth-century Plains hide shirts through museum exhibitions and high-quality color photographs makes it easier for us to recognize the problematics of the shirt in figure 1.3.[33] In Catlin's time, of course, there was almost nothing to compare it with, and no one was analyzing the subtleties of Plains pictorial representation as we do today. Catlin was known for his sometimes hasty renditions; as John Ewers pointed out long ago, a man who painted some 135 works in eighty-six days on the upper Missouri had to work quickly.[34] Plains artists, in contrast, seldom appeared to draw hastily on their shirts: they gave their war exploits the careful rendering that they deserved.

One of the *tableaux vivants* that played daily in the Egyptian Hall was "Mr. Catlin at his Easel, in the Mandan Village, painting the portrait of Mah-to-toh-pa," in which, the program guarantees, "the costumes of the chief and the painter [are] the same that were worn on the occasion."[35] Catlin was reenacting a historical moment as well as his own painting of that moment. The artist played himself, but the Mandan chief in the *tableau vivant* was one of the white Londoners Catlin paid to "play Indian," reenacting a pivotal moment in Catlin's career night after night for the edification of the public.

"LEGERDEMAIN AND HUMBUG": A PRIAPIC HIDE PAINTING

Catlin's time in Europe in the 1840s and 1850s was a public success but a financial failure. He was never able to make a profit on his Indian Gallery tours and performances. In 1852, he was forced to sign over his entire Indian Gallery to wealthy American Joseph Harrison, in order to pay off his creditors.[36] As finances grew ever more precarious, he was consumed with making more drawings, prints, and paintings, as well as special portfolios to sell to the wealthy.[37] A couple of these portfolios contain drawings of pictorial buffalo robes allegedly in Catlin's collection.[38] Some are variants of robes he illustrated in *Letters and Notes*, while others, as Plains scholar Arni Brownstone has noted, comprise "a varied and extensive array of bogus pictographic works."[39]

In a bound portfolio of twenty-three oil paintings on cardboard in the British Museum, Catlin's description of the final painting (figure 1.4) calls it "*Facsimile* of a painted Buffalo Robe (N° 33) in Catlin's Indian Collection" (italics in the original). He claims that he obtained it from an Assiniboin medicine man in 1832.[40] The scene is painted in a bizarre mixture of pictographic abstraction and European naturalism. Simple inverted triangles represent the torsos of the many male figures, while use of a ground line, foreshortening, one-point perspective, rendering of spatial depth, and figures shown in three-quarter view make it clearly a European sketch. The iconography is even more outlandish.

In the foreground, five Native men in fringed leggings sit around a cauldron into which their long pipes are inserted. Three of the men have giant erect penises, as do the two men at right who walk away from the seated figures. Catlin describes the robe with this unlikely scene as the property of a great "Medecine Man," whom he characterizes as an "adept in legerdemain and humbug." This painting is, Catlin alleges, the man's walking advertisement for the botanical substance he discovered that, when smoked, "produced the most inveterate and infallible priapism in both old and young."[41] Because this condition did not last until the men got home to their women, the women destroyed the medicine man's tent and accoutrements, and the fur trader gave the robe to Catlin.

When Ewers published the British Museum portfolio in 1979, he commented circumspectly: "No other white observers of the Assiniboin during the 1830s appear to have mentioned this humorous happening in their writings. Nor is the robe known to be preserved in any collection of Plains Indian artifacts. We must rely upon Catlin alone for a record and interpretation of it."[42] Brownstone, writing about other hide paintings, observes that while such frank images were taboo in European society, they could be "smuggled in" under the guise of a factual ethnographic depiction, thus satisfying European

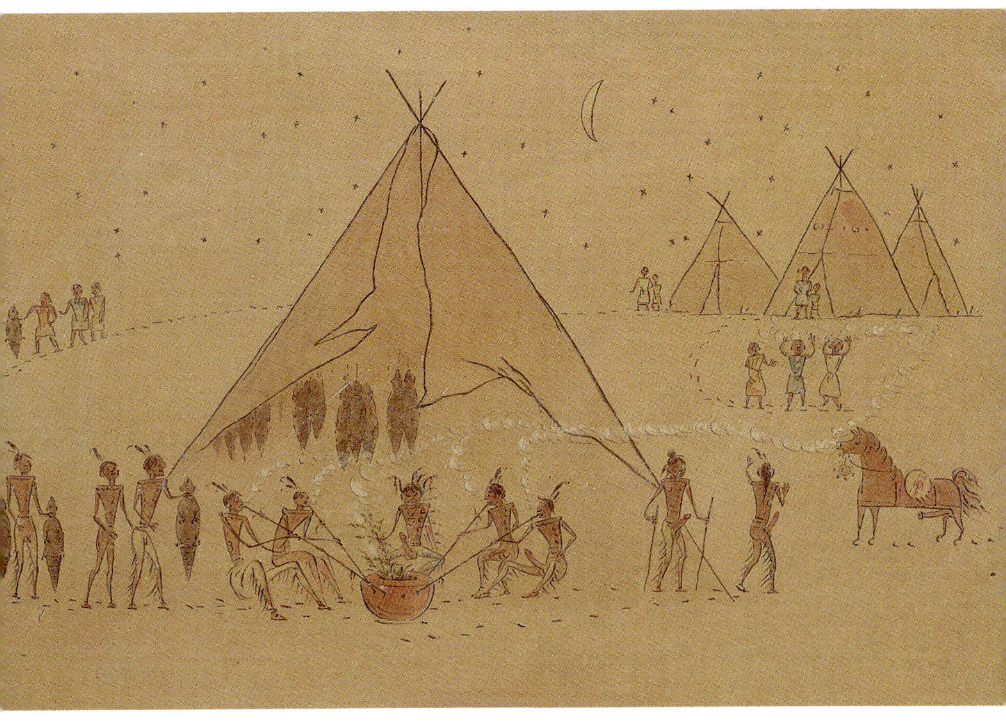

FIG. 1.4 So-called "*Facsimile* of a painted Buffalo Robe (N° 33) in Catlin's Indian Collection" (Detail). Plate 23 in *Portfolio of Pipes*, oil on cardboard, 44.3 × 57.8 cm. No. Am2006,P tg.42. Photo © Trustees of the British Museum.

erotic appetites with imagery that did not actually occur in Plains Indian art.[43] It is not that Plains people were prudish—far from it, as many examples from ethnography and literature demonstrate.[44] Yet this particular painting is thoroughly Euro-American in sensibility and style.

Perhaps such examples signal the desperation of an aging and financially ruined man whose commercial efforts turned increasingly from the original to the pastiche and outright invention, or "legerdemain and humbug," in the description he penned of the alleged Assiniboin medicine man. Perhaps he hoped that the good name of his earlier decades would carry him through.

In summary, by the mid-nineteenth century, many of the themes that will be amplified in the rest of this book are already in play: complicated genealogies of making and use, non-Natives "playing Indian," and the copying or falsification of Native works by non-Natives.

A Welter of Words: The Language of Replication

A powerful tipi painting or shield design could come to a Kiowa warrior in a dream. A Lakota woman might devise a truly extraordinary beadwork design during menstrual seclusion, when she was empowered to spend her time making art and dreaming of Double Woman (the spiritual muse of the female artist). A Tlingit chief owned—and still owns today—the rights to totemic images associated with his particular family or clan.[45] It stands to reason that within Native North American artistic systems, there is no single definition of an original, a copy, or a replica. Each clan or nation might have its own way of thinking about such issues. In some cases, an individual might sell the object itself, or transfer to another artist the rights to remake such an object, for it is the ownership of the *image*, *emblem*, or *idea* that is fundamental. As will be evident both here and in later chapters, subsequent versions of an object were sometimes thought to have the same status as the original, though in the case of objects with spiritual efficacy such powers might begin to fade by the third or fourth version, as Crow men told the anthropologist Robert Lowie early in the twentieth century.[46] But in each case, the ownership of intellectual or spiritual property was to be scrupulously acknowledged and promiscuous copying avoided.

Within the history of European art, in contrast, there long was collective agreement about the meaning and the worth of copies and replicas. Artists learned by copying the masters. Sometimes famous artists would make what is called an "autograph replica"—an exact, signed copy—of one of their own paintings, when commissioned to do so by a patron. In the nineteenth century, most major American museums displayed copies of famous Greek and Roman sculptures, for in this way knowledge of the masters was made accessible to all, not just those who had the means to do the grand tour of Europe.[47]

Modern European thought about copies is preoccupied with value judgments: the original is the best, and any replication is usually conceived as a lesser representation. The anthropologist Gwyneira Isaac has examined the inadequacy of European definitions of copies and replicas for the study of the material replication of knowledge in non-European societies, using the Zuni as an example. At Zuni, she argues, *copy* and *original* are spurious terms, for repetition is "an affirmation of the continuity of knowledge."[48] In many cases, as we shall see, Tlingit and Haida peoples of the Northwest Coast are in agreement with this.

Definitions founded in European philosophy or aesthetics may be flawed when we apply them to Native contexts. Nevertheless, it is useful to examine the vocabulary for divergent sorts of replication. In this section, I offer various terms with which to understand replication and how it plays out in particular circumstances. Some definitions and standards are drawn from the fields of European, Asian, and African art history in order to test their applicability to Native North American situations. These categories are, of course, fluid; some of these objects could fit more than one category. This is simply a first effort at finding a language with which to discuss the complex issue of replication and its many variants. I fully understand that for some Native makers and users of these objects, the terms and definitions that derive from five hundred years of European art may be of little interest or seem irrelevant or even repugnant. Yet because Native-made objects have circulated in an international marketplace for nearly that long, I believe that such terminology can provide helpful ways of thinking about objects and of understanding their many conflicting placements within the politics of representation and the politics of replication.

THE REPLICA: TWO VERSIONS

Most dictionaries define a replica as an exact copy of some original, be it a painting, an antique firearm, or a totem pole. (Sometimes people think of a replica as being smaller, as in a replica of the Empire State Building or the Eiffel Tower, but that is not central to the definition.) Of course, the definition of a replica is culturally specific and rose out of philosophical discussions during the European Enlightenment. Replication was conceived of differently in earlier eras and in other cultures.[49]

Since the 1960s, both Native and non-Native carvers have deliberately made replicas of Northwest Coast carvings. I offer two examples that illustrate different uses to which replicas can be put. I have chosen replicas made principally by non-Native carvers, both well known and well respected within the world of Native Northwest Coast art.

Bill Holm (1925–2020), legendary as a scholar and an artist, was also known for his generosity in sharing knowledge with Native people.[50] Wanting to understand how artists had created the earlier works of art he had studied in museums, Holm in the 1950s began deciphering the formal rules of historical arts, making objects that conformed to those rules, and published his findings in *Northwest Coast Indian Art: An Analysis of Form*.[51] This book provided the vocabulary for articulating the aesthetic rules for understanding (and re-creating) historic northern formline style. Both Native and non-Native artists studied this book and worked with Holm to learn how to make art that adhered more closely to these prototypes. An explosion of artistic creativity followed.

Holm's work in this area was educational rather than commercial; a firm believer that making something provides the best way of understanding it, he made Northwest Coast–style objects to comprehend them more fully. Holm often spoke of his carvings as "artifakes," for he never wanted them confused with objects made by Indigenous carvers with inherited rights.[52] This term casually denigrates the importance of his own work in order to distinguish it from the towering artistic achievements of the past. Belying this self-deprecating term is the fact that Holm's carvings are masterful, well-researched copies that have proved useful for understanding the history of Northwest Coast art. In 1970, he made a replica of a Dzunuk'wa figure that had originally stood in the village of Gwa'yasdams on Gilford Island, north of Vancouver Island (figure 1.5). Dzunuk'wa (sometimes translated as "Wild Woman of the Woods") is understood in Kwakwa̱ka̱'wakw belief to be a wild and antisocial being, but one who gives gifts during winter ceremonials.[53] Over the years, the original had seriously deteriorated; only its head, in the collection of the Burke Museum of Natural History and Culture in Seattle, survived.

The Holm example is essentially a replica of a lost artwork, one known only from its worn head and historic photos; this replica serves to enhance the understanding of Kwakwa̱ka̱'wakw art in a museum context. In general, Holm carved not only to understand the original better, as mentioned above, but also to provide students and museum visitors with the experience of seeing (or sometimes handling and using) works to better understand their formal and material characteristics.[54] In contrast to Holm's replica carved on his own initiative for a university museum audience, the next example involves a non-Native carver commissioned by a local cultural heritage committee to head up a project that involved both restoration and replication.

Four magnificent house posts stood for well over a century in Chief Shakes's house on Wrangell Island in southern Alaska.[55] The artist and scholar Steve Brown has called them "among the greatest and best known masterworks of classical Tlingit art." Because of Brown's research, we now know they were created by a late eighteenth-century master artist named Kadjisdu.áxtc.[56] This artist is known for his many magnificent sculptural works; these complex figural posts were likely commissioned by Chief Shakes IV of the Stikine Tlingit.[57]

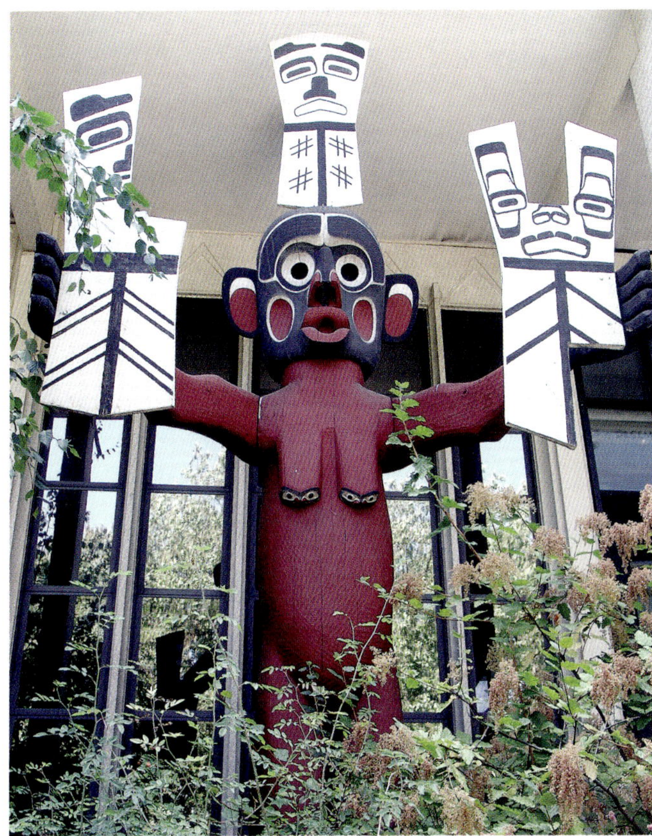

FIG. 1.5 Bill Holm, Dzunuk'wa figure holding coppers (replica), 1970. Red cedar, height 23 ft. Burke Museum of Natural History and Culture, University of Washington, no. R-200.

While much northern Northwest Coast figural carving of the past two centuries is far more stylized and abstract than this, Kadjisdu.áxtc carved lifelike forms with volumetric presence; they seem to emerge from the wood with, as Brown has eloquently described it, "a quality of life and emotional power that few others have attained."[58] All four posts were considered important enough in the 1830s to have been brought from Khasitláan (Old Wrangell), seventeen miles away, when Chief Shakes IV established a new community for his clan on Wrangell Island. A century later, his clan house was renewed, and many poles and other objects were recarved during President Franklin Roosevelt's New Deal initiatives of the 1930s, though the house posts stayed in the clan house until 1980, when worry about their poor condition of preservation led to their removal for conservation and for replication.[59]

Notions of replication are complicated among many cultures of the Northwest Coast. Replication does not necessarily mean making an object that looks exactly like the one being replicated, for the most crucial element is the clan information that must be displayed; as long as the proper wolf or raven clan emblem appears, for example, the artist making the replica may do so in an innovative way. The art historian Emily L. Moore distinguishes between what she calls "regenerative replication" (with its interest in making a new visual from for the "intangibles" that were part of the life of a crest) and "preservative replication," which, as she defines it, "privileged the preservation of appearance over anything else."[60] While many eighteenth- and nineteenth-century Northwest Coast objects have been reimagined by contemporary makers and presented in artistically innovative ways, it was the desire of the Wrangell Native community that the house posts' replication follow closely the design of the originals. In 1984, the Wrangell Cultural Heritage Committee charged Brown, a non-Native carver and restorer, with the job; he was aided by three Tlingit carvers, Wayne Price, Will Burkhart Jr., and Nathan Jackson.[61]

As a restorer, Brown was deeply familiar with the visual grammar of Tlingit art. He followed what a classically trained art historian would call the "Morellian details" in the works of art he researched: the shape and proportion of the eyes, lips, ears, and fingers of figural sculpture, for example, which are the places where an artist demonstrates his particular style.[62] Brown, Price, Burkhart, and Jackson sought to adhere closely to Kadjisdu.áxtc's style. They made both cardboard and wooden templates to measure against the original posts in order to closely follow the sculptural curves, and they used traditional hand adzes in order to achieve the fine surface texture of the originals.[63] In the one replicated post illustrated here, a large frontal human with a frog emerging from his mouth holds a smaller figure with the head of a bear, who, in turn, holds another frog (figure 1.6).

As in many replication projects, missing elements had to be resolved using knowledge attained over many years of doing restoration work. Some of the posts were missing noses and teeth; the one depicted here had facial features that were weathered and worn down. The replica depicts the human face in a fresh new state.[64] For his work in leading this ambitious carving project, and giving new life to the work of an eighteenth-century master carver, the Kiksadi

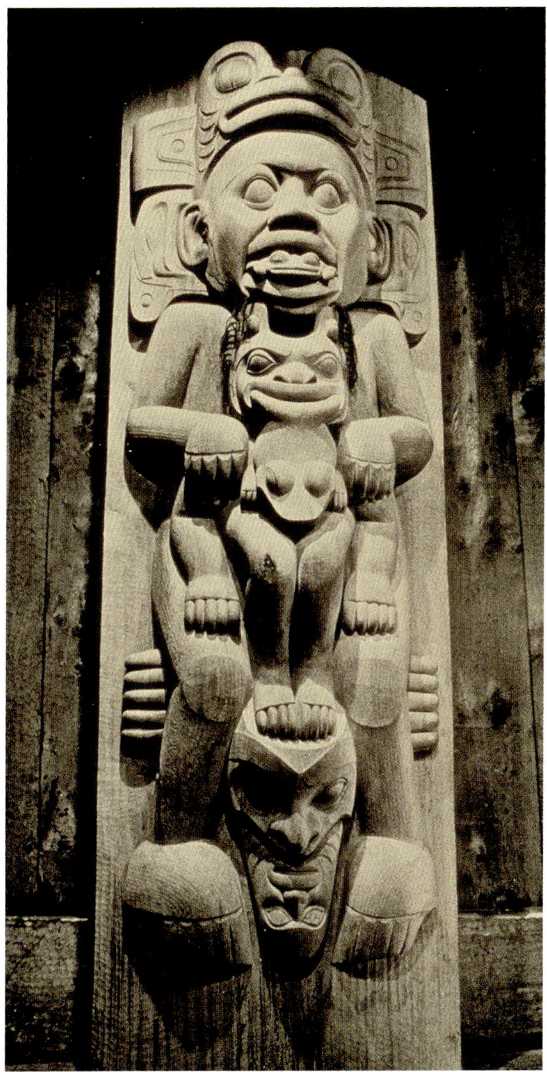

FIG. 1.6 Steve Brown, Wayne Price, Will Burkhart Jr., and Nathan Jackson, replica of early nineteenth-century Tlingit house post from Chief Shakes's house, 1984–85. Installed in Chief Shakes House, Wrangell, Alaska.

Tlingit bestowed Kadjisdu.áxtc's name on Brown, indicating that not only does this master artist's work live on but so does his talent.

The replicas just discussed were carved in the 1970s and 1980s. Today, however, most Kwakwa̱ka̱'wakw, Tlingit, Haida, and other people of Northwest Coast heritage feel strongly that only those who are of the proper cultural heritage and who have inherited the rights to specific clan images should be making culturally specific objects. They resent outsiders benefiting economically from an artistic practice that is not theirs to own. (Indeed, one Tlingit artist, Nicholas Galanin, has made art about this subject, as discussed in the book's conclusion.) But I have deliberately chosen these two examples because they were NOT made for economic gain (though, of course, Brown and his Native colleagues were paid for their work on the Tlingit house posts) and they were made by non-Native carvers. It is crucial to evaluate the relationship that non-Native makers of art have with source communities before dismissing their work. It is also important to recognize that situations change, and what was considered appropriate or helpful in the 1970s or 1980s is not necessarily considered so in 2023.

Holm spent a great deal of time in Kwakwa̱ka̱'wakw territory and was highly regarded by numerous Native people there. His relationship with Kwakwa̱ka̱'wakw carver Mungo Martin (1879–1962) began in 1953, and in 1957 Martin bestowed on Holm the first of his many Kwakwa̱ka̱'wakw names and a position in the sacred Hamatsa society.[65] As an invited participant, Holm always wore the regalia he made. While it has become common for a younger, more politicized generation to decry the participation of outsiders in ceremony and in the making of regalia, it is important to know that this is not the only view. When asked about Holm's place, seated among the chiefs at potlatches for decades, Chief Calvin Hunt of Fort Rupert, British Columbia, replied: "During my childhood, even before my teens, I knew of Bill and admired his work. It was only later I found out he was adopted by Peter Smith, who is my Grandmother Abaya's brother. There were very few non-Native artists around at the time. Our Elders embraced his commitment to our culture, and he still has the passion to learn. He is always willing to share his knowledge, which is the same teachings of our Elders and Ancestors."[66] Holm honored Native culture by researching and analyzing their arts deeply and with respect, and he was honored in return numerous times by the Kwakwa̱ka̱'wakw and other Native peoples for studying and participating in their cultural practices in a respectful way and for unstintingly sharing his research with community members.[67]

Steve Brown was born in Seattle in 1950 and attended the University of Washington, where he worked with Holm. In the 1970s, he was hired by the Makah tribe to lead the work of five young Makah carvers to create the four traditional cedar canoes now in the Makah Cultural and Research Center in Neah Bay, Washington. Like Holm, Brown became a serious scholar and curator of Northwest Coast art.[68] He lived for many years in Wrangell, Alaska, and it is there that Brown was hired to lead the replication of the house posts. He has collaborated with many Indigenous artists, has taught dozens of workshops in southeast Alaska, and was invited to make art for the Sealaska Heritage Institute's Walter Soboleff Building in Juneau.[69]

The German cultural theorist Walter Benjamin (1892–1940) is famous for his observation that even the most perfect reproduction of a work of art lacks the "aura" of the original.[70] Those Tlingit who gave Kadjisdu.áxtc's name to Brown apparently disagreed.

CROSS-CULTURAL REPRODUCTION: A ZAPOTEC "NAVAJO" RUG

A common cliché has it that "imitation is the sincerest form of flattery." Navajo weavers do not agree. For decades, male weavers of Zapotec and Mestizo (mixed) heritage in Oaxaca, Mexico, have been copying Navajo textiles, producing less expensive knockoffs on their treadle looms. The books on their shelves attest to the global circulation of images: when lecturing in the village of Teotitlán del Valle on a Smithsonian tour in the early 1990s, I saw copies of exhibition catalogues of Navajo textiles, as well as books on South African rock art, Picasso paintings, and ancient Mexican mural painting, all of which provided inspiration for the rugs they weave for tourists.[71] I bought one of the inexpensive "Navajo-style" rugs to use in teaching about the globalized tourist art industry; two decades later I gave it to Ohio University's Kennedy Museum of Art, which has a substantial collection of Navajo textiles, for its use as an example of the global appropriation of Native culture (figure 1.7). Roughly three by five feet, and woven with beige, red, and black yarn, this rug alternates long stripes with a series of rectangular boxes with thinner stripes within. The easiest way to tell a cross-cultural reproduction like this one from a real Navajo rug is that almost all Navajo weavings have a continuous warp,

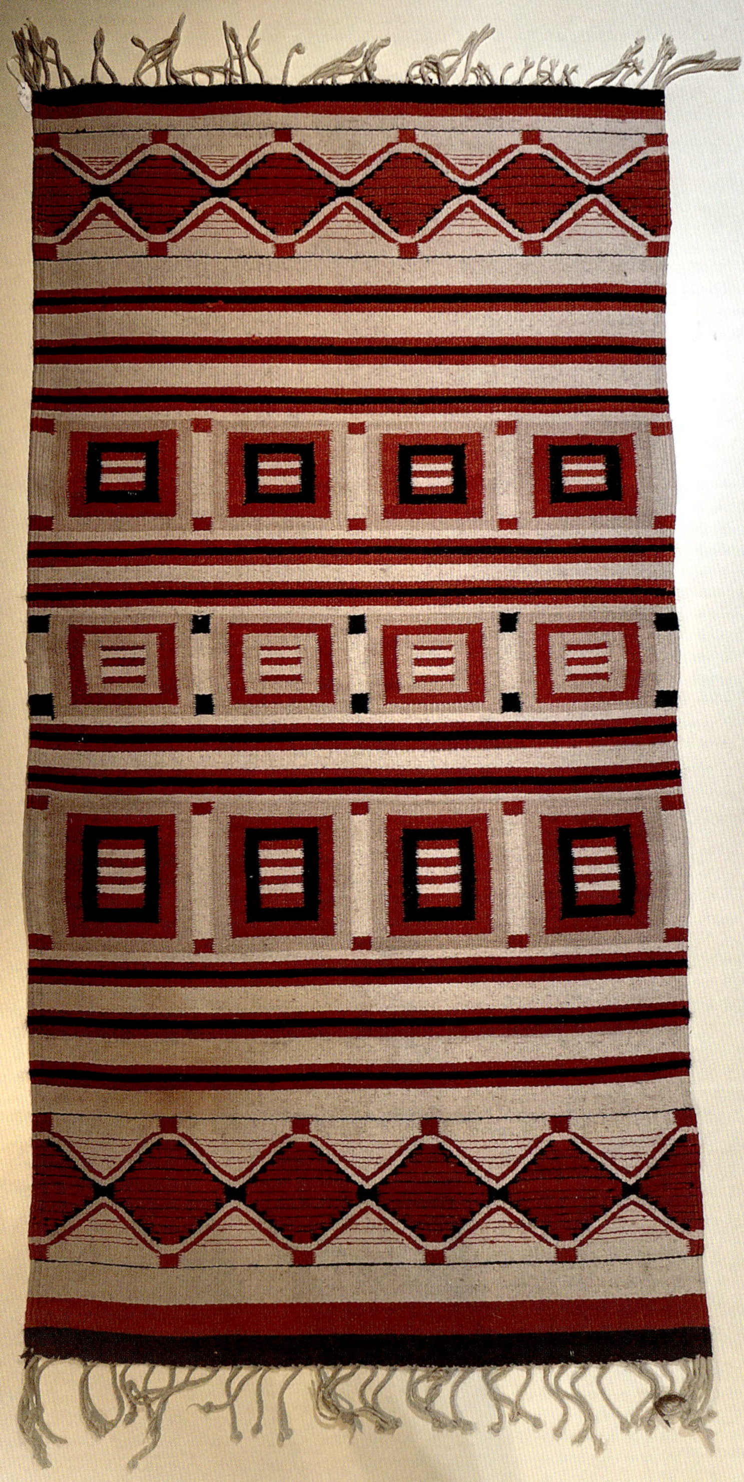

FIG. 1.7 Navajo-style Zapotec rug, ca. 1990. Kennedy Museum of Art, Ohio University, Athens, Ohio, no. 2007.41.01. Gift of Janet Catherine Berlo.

which produces four completely twined selvedges, whereas Zapotec rugs have fringe at the top and bottom, as this one does.[72]

Teotitlán del Valle is the center of the Zapotec weaving industry. A village of some five thousand people in the state of Oaxaca in southern Mexico, its reputation as a center of weaving dates back to pre-Hispanic times. Aztec pictorial documents show that the inhabitants of many towns in this region paid taxes to their Aztec overlords in textiles.[73] The building of a better road system in the mid-twentieth century made it easier to expand the market throughout Mexico and abroad; yet many tourists travel to buy the weavings at the source. There they can observe demonstrations of natural dyeing, especially with the red cochineal dye made from insects harvested from *Opuntia* cacti, a practice that also dates to the pre-Hispanic era and that has gained in popularity in the past few decades.[74]

The anthropologist W. Warner Wood, in *Made in Mexico: Zapotec Weavers and the Global Ethnic Art Market*, brilliantly demonstrates that to really comprehend Zapotec weavings (or any other example of the modern ethnic art market, for that matter), one must understand them as part of a global aesthetic and economic discourse.[75] Framing them only in terms of the local and the traditional prevents a deeper understanding of their complex meanings. So it is instructive to examine the way Zapotec textiles are presented to the consumer on commercial web pages: images are often decades out-of-date, precisely because most consumers seek to purchase a piece of authenticity. They would rather hear about traditions, symbols, and ancestors than about marketing, globalization, and the internet.

A short video on Vimeo about a Zapotec weaver named Porfirio Gutiérrez exemplifies consumers' desires for romantic stories. In his nearly unaccented English, the weaver invokes the ancestors seven times, and "Mother Earth" four times, within the six-minute video. He says, "My father told me that my ancestors started this art form more than two thousand years ago," and "the loom helps me bring these pieces alive . . . and keeps teaching me what I can do, what will be my next process, because it is not me that dictates what I need to do, it is Mother Earth, it is my ancestors."[76] While this may not be inaccurate, it is disingenuous, for it is only part of the story, the sliver that feeds the limitless hunger that modern Euro-Americans have for romantic and noble narratives about Indigenous peoples. While some few weavers may still fit this narrowly circumscribed profile, it omits, for example, the Zapotec entrepreneur who runs his business from Santa Ana, California. In *Made in Mexico*, Wood terms this attention to romance rather than reality "descriptive denial," an excellent characterization of the way such mythmaking carefully conceals global circuits behind a romantic narrative of Indigenous production, thus denying the makers their modernity and agency.[77]

Since the beginning of the twenty-first century, natural dyes of all sorts, including cochineal, have come to the forefront in Zapotec weaving. This anchors the process more firmly in the traditions of the distant past. On his web page, the weaver Demetrio Bautista Lazo recounts that he "grew up at his parents' knees using the popular aniline dyes of the 1960s and 70s. But times have changed and so has the marketplace." He focuses on local natural dyes.[78] In this way, Zapotec weavings have found a niche in North America that positions them as something other than "Navajo knockoffs."

Wood carefully charts the ways that Zapotec weavings have been positioned throughout the Southwest in general, and in Santa Fe specifically. He notes the particular importance of one initiative in the rise in popularity of this genre. In 1988, after seeing the important exhibition *Art from the Navajo Loom: The William Randolph Hearst Collection* at the Los Angeles County Museum of History, a gallery owner in Beverly Hills got the idea to market a new line of rugs based on this significant collection that had been formed in the early twentieth century.[79] He worked with Teotitlán dyers and weavers to ensure that the colors and patterns closely matched the plates in the exhibition catalogue. Many of the large rugs in the "Hearst Series," as the gallery owner called it, were direct copies of textiles in this famous collection and were sold at high prices to Hollywood notables.[80] The one I bought in Teotitlán del Valle was much smaller and only loosely followed the pattern of one of the Hearst rugs without being an exact reproduction.[81]

In a world in which images circulate globally not only through publications but now instantaneously through the internet, the copying of everything is ubiquitous. Zapotec replicas of Navajo rugs have provided a way for the less affluent to have a version of what they admire. Perhaps Navajo weavers would not find this such an egregious affront if these cross-cultural reproductions, as I call them, were not sold in the same spaces in Santa Fe, Albuquerque, and Taos, New Mexico, and Scottsdale, Arizona, where Navajo textiles are featured.

To the uninformed consumer, one looks just like the other, but the Navajo version—woven more slowly on a fixed vertical loom—may cost 200–500 percent more than the Mexican version.

If we take the long view, it is remarkable to consider all the cultural strands that have been woven into Navajo textiles over the past two centuries: influences from Pueblo wearing blankets and Saltillo serapes from Mexico, Germantown yarns from Pennsylvania, and even the design patterns of Middle Eastern carpets that began to influence some Navajo weavers at the beginning of the twentieth century. In the 1980s, textile impresario Gloria F. Ross paired Navajo weavers with American abstract painters, commissioning a line of tapestry weavings that took excellent advantage of the abstraction and geometric precision of both genres.[82] So the Navajo weaving tradition has never been a closed system either. Navajo weavers have not, historically, "stayed in their lane," so to speak, but have been vigorous participants in global visual culture. Of course, in the twenty-first century, Zapotec weavers, too, can voice their outrage—for in some cases their rugs have been co-opted by less expensive Navajo-style rugs now woven in northern India or Turkey or by Tibetan refugees in Nepal.[83] At the beginning of the twentieth century, the trader J. B. Moore, at the Crystal Trading Post in western New Mexico, sought to make Navajo rugs more appealing to householders in American cities who were used to having cut-pile carpets from Turkey and Iran on their floors. He introduced the idea of bordered rugs with central designs from these regions to Navajo weavers—a fascinating episode in cross-cultural replication. Some one hundred years later, the circulation of weaving designs has come full circle.

PASTICHE: THE "NOTORIOUS" BEAR CLAW NECKLACE

In seventeenth-century France, the painter and art critic Roger de Piles (1635–1709) proposed a definition for the term *pastiche* that still holds up today: "Paintings that are neither Originals, nor Copies, are called Pastiches, from the Italian *pastici,* which means pastries, because as the different things that flavor a dish are mixed together in order to produce a single taste, so, too, all of the imitations that compose a pastiche aim to make one truth appear."[84] In Baroque Italy, the pastiche was sometimes admired as the ambitious artist's way of selecting from among the best features of the work of different painters to make an even better painting; later the pastiche would be derided as unoriginal. In postmodern architecture, the word *pastiche* often is used for the whimsy that results, for example, from Philip Johnson placing the profile of an eighteenth- century Chippendale chest atop his 1984 AT&T skyscraper in New York City. Today, the prevalent meaning of the term *pastiche* has to do with the often parodic sampling and quotation that is a staple in film and music.[85] For art historical purposes, we will stick with the words of de Piles. The term in modern art history is generally derogatory—and I follow that trend in the way I use it here.

In the distinguished Native American art collection at the Detroit Institute of Arts is an object of complex cross-cultural parentage: a supposedly Meskwaki bear claw necklace (figure 1.8) that is well known in the field of Native American art history. Published many times, and exhibited both at the institute and in an important exhibit that traveled to the National Gallery of Art in Washington, DC, and the Seattle Art Museum, the necklace has forty bear claws, each separated by a blue European trade bead, and is attached to an otter fur ruff.[86] (Not apparent in the photo is the fifty-inch otter fur tail with beaded emblems that would cascade down the back of the wearer.) It came from the collection of Milford Chandler (discussed earlier in this chapter) and graced the cover of *The Art of the Great Lakes Indians*, a 1973 catalogue that helped define the stylistic features of this geographic region.[87] Yet David Penney, former curator of Native American art at the Detroit Institute of Arts, terms this piece "notorious" and describes it as having been "assembled by Milford Chandler from several other necklaces, fragments of beadwork, and fresh otter pelts."[88] Indeed, as de Piles reminds us, such is the quintessential pastiche—fragments put together "to make one truth appear."

Chandler, by all accounts, was obsessed with the bear claw necklace as an object type. In 1961, he and fellow hobbyist-turned-curator Norman Feder wrote an essay about it for a hobbyist magazine.[89] Chandler made three of them, and one was offered for sale at Skinner's auction house in Boston in 2013. The writer and collector Benson Lanford wrote in the auction catalogue that Chandler "managed to assemble three superlative grizzly claw necklaces of differing tribal styles—each composed of the long, very much preferred, honey-colored bear claws. One necklace was of the Chippeway (Ojibwe) type, one Meshquaki (or 'Fox' Tribe), and the magnificent Pawnee-style necklace offered here."[90] I find it curious that in a sale of "American Indian and ethnographic arts," such a pastiche would be offered. Yet the catalogue was completely transparent about its history, calling it only "Pawnee-style" and saying that it was "assembled by Milford Chandler." Like the necklace in the Detroit Institute

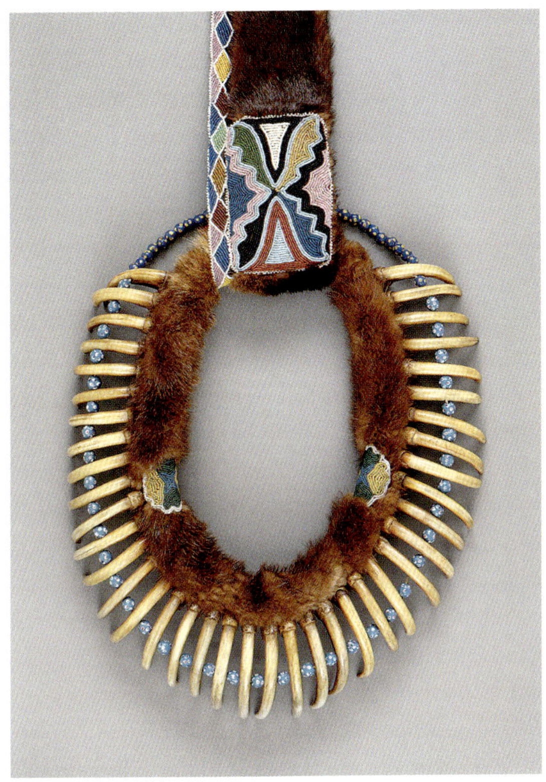

FIG. 1.8 "Meskwaki" bear claw necklace. Nineteenth-century object with mid-twentieth-century modifications. Bear claws, fur, glass beads, ribbon, horsehair, and cloth. 17½ × 14 × 4 in. Detroit Institute of Arts, no. 81.644. Founders Society Purchase with funds from Flint Ink Corporation.

of Arts, it is indisputably a beautiful object, composed of forty claws, rare nineteenth-century Italian lampwork beads, a beaded strip on red trade cloth, and an otter tail "drop" at the back of the neck. In the associated essay, Lanford recounts that Chandler added to it over time: "In the late 1960s, shortly after returning from a cross-country trip, Mr. Chandler showed the author the antique pair of pony-beaded bear paws that he had purchased from a Pawnee acquaintance. Subsequently he sewed the paws to the underside of the otter tail."[91] So this example was a work in progress, always able to be improved on while in the collector/hobbyist's hands. According to the auction catalogue, it was displayed at the Buffalo Bill Historical Center in Cody, Wyoming, from the 1970s until 2002, presumably as a real object of American Indian art. In the world of American Indian artifact collecting, Chandler's name has its own pedigree, and surely the combined mythos of the disappearance of the grizzly bear from the Plains and the well-known collector Chandler is what caused this pastiche to achieve at auction a price of $57,000—nearly three times its estimate.

Are Chandler's bear claw necklaces "artifakes"? They are more than replicas, for portions presumably had legitimate pedigree—the beaded bear paws from a Pawnee acquaintance and perhaps the claws themselves. Certainly many paintings that would later be dismissed as mere pastiches have been owned and exhibited in art museums of the world, so it is not surprising that this work of art has been widely exhibited. Yet if one applies the standards of the American Institute for Conservation's Code of Ethics (see chapter 4), which states that the aim of restoration is to "preserve and reveal" the aesthetic value of the original work of art, this object does not hold up to current museological standards, for it is presented as a coherent whole. Often in art history the hunger for the object in a perfect state of preservation supersedes common sense. That is why an object such as Chandler's bear claw necklace, put together beautifully by an expert (but non-Native) hobbyist/collector, can hold pride of place on the cover of an exhibition catalogue and become a canonical object. Unfortunately, those not in the private circuit of information of an older group of curators and scholars will take it for the real thing.

This impulse to finish or perfect a bear claw necklace—even by proxy—is apparently an old one. In 1833–34, when Maximilian and Bodmer overwintered at Fort Clark on the upper Missouri, the men developed a close friendship with the high-ranking Mandan statesman Mató-tópe (discussed earlier in relation to Catlin; see also figure 3.8). On November 24, 1833, Maximilian wrote in his daybook: "I gave Mató-tópe a necklace of bear claws to take along, which he will finish for me. I bought an otter skin and blue glass pearls in the store for added decoration."[92] So even one of the earliest chroniclers and collectors of Northern Plains materials could not keep from being helpful and "improving" a Mandan object that he intended to collect, thus turning it into a pastiche of sorts.

SURROGATE: A 3-D MODEL OF A TLINGIT CLAN HAT

A surrogate is a proxy or a replacement: someone or something that stands in for another. The twenty-first century has produced a new category of replica in Native American art: the 3-D digital surrogate made by machine. In 2005, a Tlingit Killer Whale clan hat was repatriated to the Dakl'aweidi clan of Angoon, Alaska, from the Smithsonian's National Museum of Natural History; it was carried back to the Smithsonian in 2010 so that a 3-D model could be made in order to more vividly show to museumgoers the meaning of repatriation of culturally significant objects (figure 1.9).

The National Museum of Natural History replicated the clan hat because it was determined that it had been illegally sold to Smithsonian anthropologist John Swanton by the son of its owner in 1904. Its repatriation was timely: it was flown to Alaska and placed on the head of Mark Jacobs Sr., its legitimate caretaker, in a hospital room in Sitka just days before he died.[93] After Jacobs's death, a new clan leader, Edwell John Jr., became the caretaker of this prestigious item, and it was once again danced in ceremony after a hiatus of one hundred years. John is a computer specialist who believed that if the clan hat were replicated, there would be great potential for education about the repatriation process; he liked the idea of a surrogate being placed in the museum to tell the story of the Killer Whale clan hat's journey home. He and other Tlingit leaders worked out a protocol with Smithsonian staff that the surrogate would be accessioned into the Department of Anthropology, used only for educational purposes relating to the repatriation issue, and always accompanied by labels describing it as a replica of an important clan-owned crest object. Not only did John authorize the project, but he also worked closely with Smithsonian staff and participated in the publication describing this historic collaboration.

The replication process is described in detail in the publication. In brief, 3-D laser scanning was used in conjunction with photogrammetry to accurately measure both the exterior and the interior of the object. A computer numerical control milling machine shaped the surrogate, using alder, the same wood as the original. John provided the abalone to be cut and inlaid in the hat. Human hair was donated to the project, and commercial paint was painstakingly matched to the colors of historic Tlingit objects in the museum. The Smithsonian's surrogate does not precisely copy the state of the original at the time of replication. John did not want the copy to be indistinguishable from the original. The copy reveals aspects of the ceremonial splendor of the original that were no longer extant: the original has small holes at the back for the attachment of ermine skins, but no skins were attached when it came to the Smithsonian in 1904. Ten ermine skins were sent from Hoonah, Alaska, and affixed to the surrogate.

While John was adamant that the surrogate was not *at.óow* (i.e., a precious object that had been instilled with power and status), it *was* danced along with real clan hats at a Tlingit clan conference in Sitka in 2012 and at the

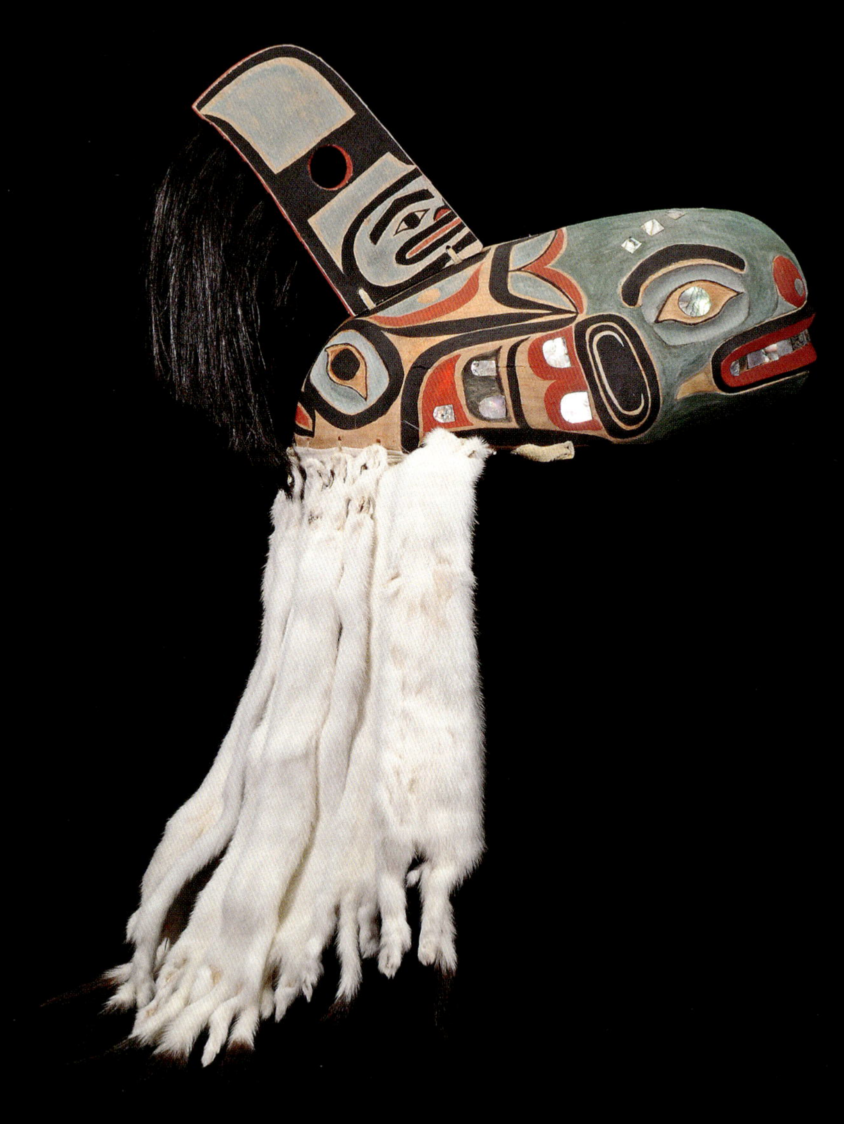

FIG. 1.9 Digital replica of Kéet S'aaxw (Tlingit Killer Whale clan crest hat), 2011. Alder, abalone shell, commercial pigments, ermine skins. Department of Anthropology, National Museum of Natural History, Smithsonian Institution, no. E433020. Photograph by James Di Loreto.

National Museum of Natural History in 2013.[94] In Tlingit protocol, every time an object is danced and witnessed by others, it accumulates prestige. But the journey toward gaining prestige begins when a clan leader pays an artist for his commission. Clan leader Herman Davis was concerned about the surrogate, asking, "How do I pay a machine?"[95] By this he meant, how can technology be integrated into traditional protocols?[96] Both the dancing of the surrogate and Davis's query suggest that this new technology adds complexity to standard notions of originals and replicas, provoking some tension as this idea is incorporated into both Tlingit culture and museum culture.

Gwyneira Isaac of the Smithsonian has pointed out that complex alliances (such as those between the Tlingit and their Smithsonian colleagues) will need to be forged in this new world of digital replicas. She asks, "When we replicate an object of cultural significance, to what extent do we replicate the social relationships and obligations embodied by the original? Do we reproduce or transform these? The presumed and deceptively simple nature of copies and replicas belies their potentially hidden powers of social transformation."[97] Some Tlingit leaders believe that participating in digital scanning and replication processes may have value for their communities. As the authors of "Tlingit-Smithsonian Collaborations with 3D Digitization of Cultural Objects" wrote:

> Clans that have their objects digitally scanned and archived can call upon the digital files for whatever purposes they deem appropriate. . . . Some may be interested in displaying their 3D digital images of their crest objects on a web site to teach clan members about the history of their crests and crest objects. Others may wish to have replicas made for educational purposes. At the very least the digital files serve as a back-up should anything happen to the originals.
>
> Some clans have expressed interest in using the technology to make replacements for their original but aging and badly worn crest hats. Tlingit have a long tradition of reproducing crest hats such as those cremated with clan leaders or lost in disasters such as the burning of the village of Hoonah.[98]

In an era when talented Native carvers are plentiful, it seems odd to consider using precise machine-made surrogates to replace old or destroyed carved regalia. Because of the current cost and complexity of the technology, this seems unlikely to transpire in the near future.

OBFUSCATION: PSEUDO-KATSINAS

For decades, scholars have written about the ways in which artists in communities in Africa, Oceania, and the Americas have altered their customary work for the tourist market.[99] In some cases, aesthetic standards are lowered, for artists have observed that outsiders do not necessarily appreciate the fineness of a complicated weaving technique, or painstaking inlay work in jewelry, or the exact iconographic details of a carved sculpture, for example. In other cases, artists who are cognizant of the proper strictures and standards within their communities can successfully navigate the outside market through what I call obfuscation—intentionally blurring the lines of what is correct and what is not.

The late art historian Zena Pearlstone has written about the trade in Hopi figural sculptures called katsinam (singular: katsina; in the older literature, kachina)—dolls made by Hopi, Navajo, and non-Native carvers.[100] Because of his stature in his community, Hopi carver Wilson Tawaquaptewa (1873–1960) provides an excellent example of how particular individuals can negotiate and blur strictures and prohibitions about sharing proprietary information. From 1904 to 1960, Tawaquaptewa was the chief of Old Orayvi on Third Mesa, in northern Arizona. By the early twentieth century, Hopi "kachina dolls" had been sold to outsiders for several decades. But as Pearlstone has written, "As the chief in charge of all katsina ceremonies, Tawaquaptewa would have been committing a great breach of authority by selling dolls that could be used in ceremonies. Yet Tawaquaptewa is one of the first named carvers who, probably beginning in the 1920s, made substantial numbers of dolls for sale. However, the 'katsina' dolls that Tawaquaptewa sold to the public are unique and idiosyncratic. They are distinguished from all other 1920–1960 Hopi-made carvings in that his dolls bear little, if any, resemblance to the katsinam who dance in the villages during the ceremonial cycle." Pearlstone goes on to assert: "Although other Hopis were carving for sale at the same time, the impact of Tawaquaptewa's dolls, because of his lofty position, could only send a message that selling pseudokatsina carvings was permissible, at least under certain circumstances. . . . From this time it became easier for Hopis and others to make and market dolls that were inaccurate according to Hopi standards."[101] Tawaquaptewa's small painted figure illustrated here (figure 1.10) has an eclectic array of features: the ear-like knobs of a Mudhead, a bill, and a protrusion with a cloud symbol atop its head. Tawaquaptewa's adopted son, Stanley Bahnimptewa, said that his father did not think that the dolls he made for sale "should be made like the ones given to the girls by the Katsinas at the dances."[102]

In the "anything goes" world of the auction market, Tawaquaptewa's "inaccuracy" has become a selling point. In a Sotheby's sale in 2010, one of Tawaquaptewa's dolls depicting a snake priest sold for $31,000. The catalogue description states, "What distinguishes his dolls from all others of the same era is that his carvings, ostensibly representing specific Kachinas, bear little resemblance to the actual Kachina figures that dance in the villages. . . . Thus one cannot make a positive identification as to what Kachinas Tawaquaptewa's dolls are intended to represent. Tawaquaptewa's Kachina dolls are now valued by collectors and museums for their quirky creativity, their distorted realism, and their artistic presence."[103] In later chapters, I provide other examples of such "inaccuracies" in objects made for the market. Such irregularities may indicate that objects are fakes made by outsiders or objects made by community members who lack the specialized ritual knowledge to make something accurately. In the instance of Tawaquaptewa's dolls, it is a pattern of deliberate obfuscation on the part of a maker who sought to walk a careful path between the demands of the art market and the demands for discretion in the community where he served as a high-ranking official for many decades.

The art historian Sascha Scott, writing about what she calls "the politics of knowledge" in the work of early twentieth-century Pueblo painters, has suggested that artists aiming to negotiate the demands of the market and the rules of their communities came up with "evasive visual strategies, including silences, misdirection, coding, and masking."[104] *Silences* might include a careful selection of subject matter, focusing on images of daily life rather than ceremony. *Misdirection* involves altering details in order to safeguard private knowledge, as in the case of Tawaquaptewa. In *coding*, some layers of meaning in visual symbols will be clear to insiders, but remain elusive to outsiders. And *masking* can involve a simplification of imagery in order to limit what is available to the uninitiated.

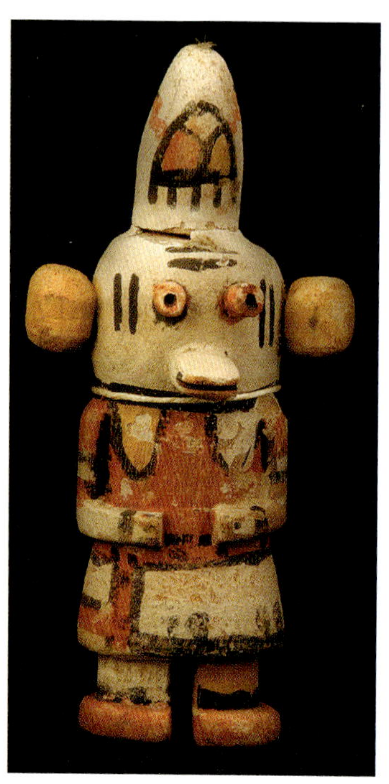

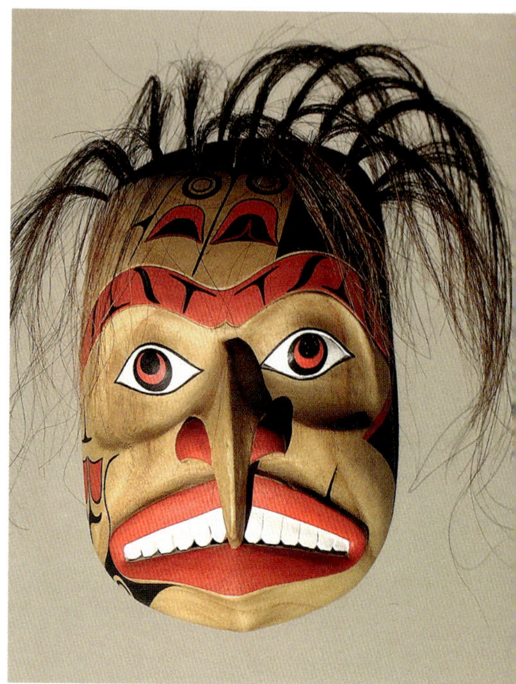

FIG. 1.10 / LEFT Wilson Tawaquaptewa, pseudo-katsina. Private collection.

FIG. 1.11 / RIGHT Fake Northwest Coast mask from Indonesia, 1994–2000. Albizia wood. Height 9.5 in. Collection of Richard and Joan Chodosh, Santa Fe, New Mexico.

FAKE: A "HAIDA" MASK MADE IN INDONESIA

The first known fakes date from the Upper Paleolithic era, more than thirty thousand years ago. In a cave in Spy, Belgium, far inland from the sea, archaeologists found imitations of seashells and deer canine teeth carved from ivory.[105] In this case, the makers wanted something that was not easy for them to obtain because of distance (seashells), so the faking is in the substitution of local materials for rare ones. Any contemporary maker of an elk-tooth dress on the Great Plains would sympathize: in the nineteenth century, the bodice of a Plains woman's dress ornamented with dozens of sets of the eyeteeth of the elk (two per elk) represented a considerable investment and showed the esteem in which her male relatives held her. By the early twentieth century, purchased cowrie shells were sometimes substituted for the rare eyeteeth.

Today, a dressmaker can purchase one hundred plastic elk teeth, predrilled, for twenty dollars.[106] The resulting dress is still a thing of beauty, but the wearer knows the difference.

Since 1980, perhaps the greatest number of faked works of art have been made in workshops in Dafen Oil Painting Village, on the outskirts of Shenzhen, in southern China. Few of these are sold as forgeries; the scholar Winnie Won Yin Wong, who has written an ethnographic account of this phenomenon, says that in these works "the high art of the world has been democratized for global consumers."[107] Indeed, customers in Kansas City, Lyon, or Bern can order a fake Leonardo, Van Gogh, or Warhol, in a range of sizes.

Around 2001, Richard and Joan Chodosh, a Santa Fe couple with an important collection of Northwest Coast contemporary art, were browsing the wares at the popular Tesuque Flea Market, adjacent to the Santa Fe Opera House. At first, it was one of those moments that every collector who haunts flea markets and thrift stores hopes for: they spotted a contemporary Northwest Coast mask in excellent condition, on sale for very little money (figure 1.11). But on closer inspection, they realized something was not right about it. Richard Chodosh said, "As soon as I held it in my hands, I knew it was too lightweight to be cedar or alder. I asked the dealer, 'Where is this from?' And he readily admitted it was made in Indonesia. He wasn't trying to pass it off as an authentic Northwest Coast mask." I asked why they had bought it. "It cost less than fifty dollars, and I thought it was a good example of what's happening now in the world, with knockoffs being made everywhere," Chodosh replied.[108]

The mask combines human and birdlike features, with medium-length strands of hair inserted into a number of holes at the top. The skin area of the mask is unpainted, revealing the grain of the wood. The lips, nostrils, and eyebrows are red, and Northwest-style designs are painted in red and black on the cheeks, eyebrows, and forehead. These designs, called formlines, are the hallmark of northern Northwest Coast painting and carving as done by Tlingit, Haida, and other northern artists for more than two hundred years. The anthropologist Marjorie Halpin has eloquently described formlines as the "continuous, flowing, curvilinear lines that turn, swell, and diminish in a prescribed manner."[109] At first glance, the mask looks good, but after some inspection, it is clear that the artist was not adept at the elegant tapering of formline designs that a skilled Northwest Coast painter will do nearly automatically. The black designs in the eyebrows, for example, do not have the calligraphic grace of real formline designs.

Since the 1980s, Northwest Coast–style masks have been made in workshops in Indonesia and imported to the United States and elsewhere. Some are sold as outright forgeries of the work of well-known artists. Before the widespread use of Google images, and the advent of online sales at eBay (established in 1995), these were not easy to track. But Stephen Lazarus, who has sold authentic First Nations art in Montreal since 1990, has been documenting the flood of these fakes since the early 1990s.[110] When I sought him out to discuss this issue, he recognized the source of this mask immediately: "That's a knockoff of a Don Yeomans mask published in 1994 in [Gary] Wyatt's book *Spirit Faces*. It's clear the Wyatt book went to Indonesia, and the carvers passed it around."[111]

Don Yeomans (Haida, b. 1958) is a well-known contemporary carver whose work has been featured in many exhibits of Northwest Coast art. His totem pole commissions grace the Stanford University campus; the McMichael Canadian Art Collection in Kleinburg, Ontario; and the Vancouver International Airport, British Columbia. When pictures of the original and the fake are compared side by side, the deficiencies of the Indonesian mask are all too apparent. The painted designs on Yeomans's Thunderbird Spirit mask (1993) are masterful. Moreover, his mask has inset operculum shell teeth, which would not have been clear to a carver copying from a book; the teeth on the Indonesian mask are delineated by shallow cuts in the wood. The hair on the fake is much shorter and sparser than the long, lustrous horsehair in Yeomans's mask. The fake also lacks the four feathers that rise from the top of the mask. Presumably, the middlemen who commission these masks are well aware that the inclusion of feathers would bring up questions when the carvings entered the United States, because the Migratory Bird Act of 1918 prohibits the importation of items containing feathers from a long list of restricted species. It is likely that the carver was instructed to omit them.

While most authentic Haida, Tlingit, and Kwakwa̱ka̱'wakw masks are made of red cedar or alder, Indonesian forgeries are usually made of *Albizia falcataria*, a fast-growing tropical wood. Lazarus explains that cedar and alder are tight-grained, while tropical woods are not: albizia, a softer wood, is open-grained, and this shows up on the wood as straight broken lines.[112] These broken lines are evident all over the mask in figure 1.11, for the main part of the mask is unpainted. Moreover, Lazarus points out that since the Indonesian carvers are working from photos rather than three-dimensional objects, the backs of their masks are smooth and flat. Most Northwest

Coast contemporary carvers leave the adze marks showing on the back of the mask.

When I queried Yeomans about this theft of his work, expressing my outrage on his behalf, he pointed out that his Thunderbird Spirit mask sold for around $7,500 in 1993 and would be worth more than twice that today. He went on to say: "The truth is most people interested in our art cannot afford to buy the real thing. Sweatshop products from wherever do not threaten the value of the real object. In every art form, not just Northwest Coast art, there is a very small core of original artists; everything else is derivative. If your business is being original, dwelling on what anyone else is doing tends to stop the creative process."[113] This reply surprised me, but I admire the artist's ability to rise above the tawdriness of the international circuit of appropriation and forgery. Lazarus, too, was surprised that Yeomans was unconcerned, pointing out that, as an art dealer, he found it discouraging when neophyte collectors could not discern the difference and would question him about the reasons for the great disparity in price between a one-hundred-dollar mask in a tourist shop and a mask offered for several thousand dollars by a named Haida artist in a real art gallery, where a dealer invests time and money in nurturing artists and their work and educating collectors. I believe that not all Northwest Coast artists would be as sanguine as Yeomans about this problem. In the book's conclusion, I consider briefly the work of contemporary Tlingit artist Nicholas Galanin, who has dealt with issues of forgery and appropriation in a very direct manner in his own work (see figures C.2, C.3).

Lazarus notes that Indonesian carvers seem to keep up with at least some of the books, for the mask types that were prevalent in the 1990s have been "retired" in favor of newer masks. Lazarus has been collecting images of fake Northwest Coast masks from the internet for years, amassing over one thousand. He has seen a dozen variants of the Yeomans mask and emailed me low-resolution images taken from eBay and auction house websites that depict nine different versions of it, each seemingly by a different hand.[114]

Trevor Isaac (Kwakwa̱ka̱'wakw), who works at the U'mista Cultural Centre in Alert Bay, British Columbia, had firsthand experience of these Indonesian workshops. In April 2015, he took a vacation in Bali. His family had hired a taxi driver / tour guide to show them the region around Ubud, an arts-rich town where they were based. "We were driving in the hilly area around Ubud, and we went by a small house that had totem poles outside. We commented on it and kept driving, but then I said, 'Wait! We have to turn around and investigate.'" They went into the compound, where Isaac took photographs.[115] With the tour guide translating, they discovered that this was a modest family workshop, with father and son carvers, who had been approached by a white man from Alaska and commissioned to make these. He was going to take them back to Alaska to sell at tourist destinations as "hand-carved totem poles." Moreover, in the larger town of Kuta, near the airport, where there are lots of tourists, Isaac saw souvenir shops selling painted totem poles.

Isaac and I discussed the fact that from the time of the earliest Russian and American incursions into the Northwest Coast in the eighteenth century, Native peoples had welcomed material from new worlds and incorporated them into their art. Yet there is a difference between new expressions and outright theft of images that are essentially "copyrighted" within a Native system, like Yeomans's mask.

The anthropologist Jennifer Esperanza studied the makers of such objects for the global tourist market in the town of Tegallalang, in central Bali. She describes that village as "a one-stop shopping resource for ethnic/tribal art of distinctly different and varied world cultures."[116] She writes that North American and European buyers found that, beginning in the 1980s, Balinese wood-carvers—long known for their own distinctive styles—were equally talented at producing art made to order, based on sketches, photos, books, and catalogues.

It is noteworthy that in these cases in Indonesia, the makers are likely not the ones intent on deceiving; they are showcasing the versatility of their talents. The middlemen are trying to offer what the North American art consumers want—"real" Native art—at a far lower price. The consumers are complicit in this too, of course; if they are not well enough informed to realize that notable Native artists command prices commensurate with their talents, then perhaps they deserve what they get?

FORGERY: ZUNI "PSEUDO-CEREMONIAL" VESSELS

All forgeries are fakes, but not all fakes are forgeries. Forgery implies deliberate deception, whereas a fake is simply something that is not "the real thing" whether or not there is an intent to deceive. In the long history of forgeries of European paintings since the Renaissance, the issues have been principally economic: forgery provides the market with substitutes for something that is rare or out of reach financially, and it provides the skillful forger with a means of making a living in which "getting away with it" seems to be part of the pleasure. The scholar Thierry Lenain observes that an object is only a forgery if its intent is to "imitate the appearance of an artwork with a different origin in order to usurp its place in the system" and if the deception is "susceptible to harming someone's interests."[117]

In Native art, copies are made for many reasons—as homage, as renewal, as a privilege given to one artist by another. But, as the art historian Alexander Nagel has said, forgery is the copy's "evil twin."[118] A class of deceptive pottery made at Zuni Pueblo in the early twentieth century is a clear-cut case of Zuni artists and middlemen providing for the market precisely what the market wanted. Unlike the Zapotec copies of historic Navajo weavings, both in the case of the Northwest Coast–style contemporary masks made in Indonesia and in this Zuni example, the intent is unmistakably to deceive, but I label the Northwest Coast example as simply a fake rather than a forgery because the deception was almost certainly on the part of the middlemen, not the carvers.

The authors Bruce Bernstein and Karen Lucic have documented a remarkable situation in New Mexico in the 1920s, when some Zuni people and Anglo traders at Zuni conspired to sell a wide range of fake vessels, principally to the Laboratory of Anthropology in Santa Fe. These were said to be rare ceremonial objects, never before seen by outsiders, but Bernstein and Lucic term them "pseudo-ceremonial vessels."[119]

It is important to note that Zuni Pueblo had been the site of intensive anthropological and archaeological research from the time of Frank Hamilton Cushing (there from 1879 to 1884); James and Matilda Coxe Stevenson (from 1879 to 1888, and Matilda Coxe Stevenson for fifteen years beyond that); Frederick Webb Hodge excavating at nearby Hawikuh (1917–23), which was a particularly rich source for historical pottery; Ruth Bunzel in the 1920s, and others.[120] This set the stage for a situation in which a few Native people, having learned all too well how outsiders were intensely interested in secret and ceremonial affairs—and how much money they were willing to pay for access to information and objects—turned such a situation to their entrepreneurial advantage. This occurred in concert with some of the Anglo traders at Zuni, principally C. G. Wallace.[121]

In 1904, Matilda Coxe Stevenson observed, "At present the less orthodox men will manufacture almost anything a collector may desire. Spurious ancient fetishes are made by the sackful and passed off as genuine. . . . Any number of fraudulent objects may be obtained at the prices set by the clever Indians."[122]

Nonetheless, in 1928, at the newly established Laboratory of Anthropology (under the financial patronage of John D. Rockefeller), the director Jesse Nusbaum and curator Kenneth Chapman had no compunctions about beginning to purchase some "specimens of antique pottery of special form and decoration, which they [i.e., Zuni] still use in their secret rites," as Chapman wrote to Rockefeller.[123] Rockefeller provided the funds for these vessels, for which the traders asked prices far higher than anything previously seen.

Many of these vessels have iconographic elements from sixteenth- and seventeenth-century pots that had recently been unearthed at Hawikuh, where Zuni men had been on the crew that excavated hundreds of pots. As Lucic and Bernstein describe it, the vessels mix archaeological designs and those of nineteenth-century style and iconography in an "eclectic and freewheeling" manner (figure 1.12).[124] The one illustrated here, for example, combines an abstract face adapted from the interior of an ancient Zuni bowl with much later rosette patterns.[125] After painting, the vessels were sanded and then overpainted with soluble brown paint so that they would appear aged from smoke and use. Suspiciously, for vessels said to have been in ceremonial use in kivas, they exhibit no chipping on the rims.[126] Religious leaders at Zuni whom Bernstein consulted agreed that these were not Zuni ceremonial vessels.[127]

The collection was kept in a vault until the 1990s, ostensibly because the traders had told the director of the Laboratory of Anthropology that they feared reprisals from the Zuni community if it were known that such sacred vessels had left the village.[128] Eventually numbering more than 250 objects, this collection provides a cautionary tale of how museum experts can see what they want to see when offered objects unlike any known before. Instead of finding it suspicious that no similar objects existed among some five thousand Zuni pots purchased for the Smithsonian by the Stevensons, Nusbaum reasoned that the fact that Matilda Coxe Stevenson worked among the Zuni for more than two decades and yet never illustrated a single such ceremonial jar was proof of their rarity and of her inability to pierce the veil of secrecy surrounding them.[129]

I would characterize these as forgeries—made and sold from within the community with the intention to deceive. Yet Lucic and Bernstein present an interesting take on this: they coined the term *pseudo-ceremonial* for them and pronounce the collection "genuinely Zuni—a Zuni response to new conditions of patronage." As they explain, "It gives evidence of the Zuni people's understanding of the Anglo longing for entrance into private arenas of their ceremonial life. Beyond the obvious profit motive, the Zuni makers perhaps

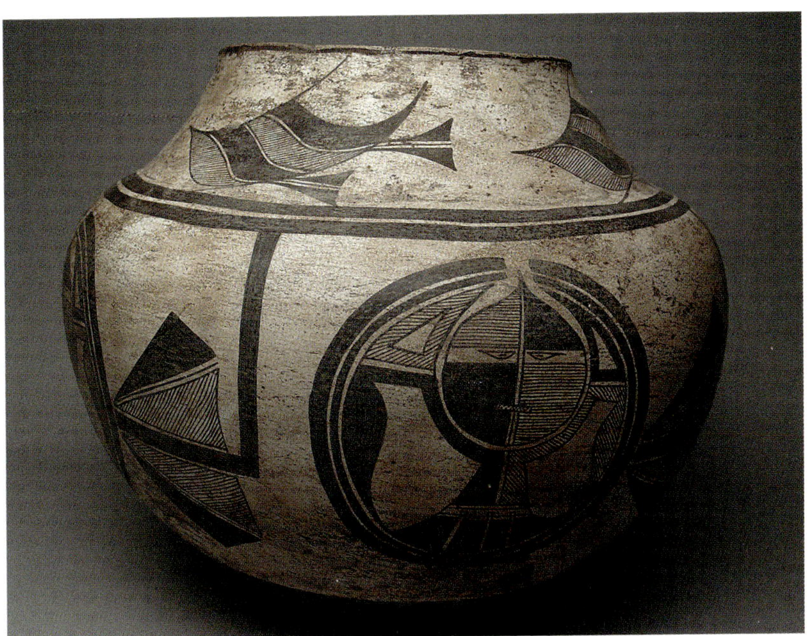

FIG. 1.12 Zuni "pseudo-ceremonial" jar with medallion design derived from vessel excavated at Hawikuh. Ca. 1920. 16 × 20.5 in. No. 7564/12. Courtesy of the Museum of Indian Arts and Culture (MIAC/LOA), Santa Fe, New Mexico.

adapted to requests for such material as a way to satisfy this longing at a distance."[130] Nagel, who called forgery the copy's "evil twin," also observed that "forgery aims to subvert the cult of the authored artifact."[131] Perhaps those Zuni who participated in the making of pseudo-ceremonial wares intended not only to deceive and make money but also, as Lucic and Bernstein suggest, to satisfy the Anglo lust for ceremonial objects "at a distance." This conveniently deflected attention from real ceremonial objects—a more extreme case of what Sascha Scott calls "evasive visual strategies" designed to protect secret knowledge.[132]

INVENTED TRADITION: ZUNI TURQUOISE-ENCRUSTED FETISH POTS

Historians have long talked about the way that ethnic groups and nations invent traditions in order to cement social cohesion or incite patriotism. An invented social tradition is a set of practices said to be ancient or customary

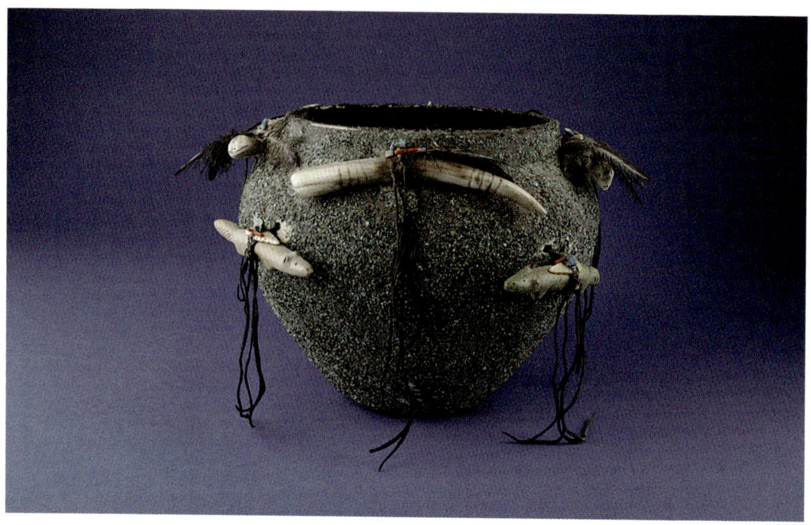

FIG. 1.13 Edna Leki (or Leekya), fetish jar, ca. 1980. Height 8.5 in. Turquoise-encrusted pottery vessel with stone and antler fetishes. Denver Art Museum, no. 1997.94.

but, in reality, is a recent innovation that has met with wide acceptance.[133] An invented tradition is not the same thing as the adaptation of tradition to new circumstances, for all visual and social traditions change. For our purposes, an invented artistic tradition is one that is usually an innovative response to a new market, yet one that seeks to ally itself with tradition in order to make it more appealing to the non-Native consumer for whom anything "sacred" or "traditional" has more social currency and perhaps a higher monetary value. One example is the so-called Zuni fetish jar (figure 1.13).

Throughout the indigenous Southwest, turquoise is a sacred healing substance, not only for wearing but also for use in ceremonial contexts and even as food, crushed and mixed with cornmeal.[134] And small stone and shell carvings of animals, known by the Western anthropological term *fetish*, have long been a part of Zuni ceremonial life. Frank Hamilton Cushing, who was initiated as a Zuni bow priest in 1881, wrote about Zuni fetishes and their role in hunting.[135] In the twentieth century, "fetish carver" became a job geared toward the tourist trade, for the fetish was, indeed, the ultimate tourist object: miniature, durable, and imbued with historical resonance.

Since the mid-twentieth century, some collectors have sought fetishes made by particular carvers.[136] But before this became a trend, a new hybrid form had developed: the turquoise-encrusted bowl embellished with stone, shell, and antler fetishes tied on with leather cord. It is tempting to assume that this arose to make use of all the debitage (the detritus left over from carving turquoise) that a carving workshop accumulates and to develop an art form in which the maker would be selling multiple carved fetishes at once. In fact, the story of its origin is tied directly to the episode of forged vessels in the previous example. Among the group of fake Zuni pots offered to the Laboratory of Anthropology by the trader C. G. Wallace in 1931 was one covered in clay and deer blood into which turquoise and jet chips had been embedded. The following year, Charles Kelsey, of the Ilfeld Indian Trading Company at Zuni, offered the laboratory two large storage jars encrusted and embellished with fetishes, for what Lucic and Bernstein call "the unprecedented sum" of $1,000, to which Nusbaum counter-offered with the (already extraordinary) price of $100 each.[137]

By now, such jars have been sold all over the Southwest for decades and remain popular on eBay and other internet sites. They are of varying sizes, as befits a tourist commodity. Typically, a pot from the relatively nearby village of Acoma would be covered with pine pitch, rolled in crushed turquoise, and then embellished.[138] The one illustrated here has two antlers and six stone animals, each laden with tiny arrow points, turquoise and coral beads, and feather attachments. These are affixed to the drilled sides of the vessel with leather cords. It is often repeated that Zuni turquoise carver Teddy Weahkee (ca. 1890–1965) and his daughter Edna Leki (ca. 1924–2003) produced the first fetish bowls for sale; Leki made the one illustrated here.[139] Wallace promoted fetish carving as a commercial endeavor and worked particularly closely with a small number of Zuni men, including Weahkee.[140] Moreover, a series of published articles incited desire on the part of the art-buying public for this invented tradition. Perhaps the first to sell the idea of the mysterious sacrality of such jars was published in 1938 in the *Masterkey*, with an illustration of one in the Southwest Museum in Los Angeles.[141] As is useful in an invented tradition, the story is cloaked in mystery: "The old men of Zuñi say that no one living has any idea of the origin of the turquoise-incrusted jars. They are as old as Hlíakwa, the Turquoise Boy, who came from his mountains in the northeast (the Cerillos Mountains in New Mexico) to show the ancients how to mix human blood with turquoise and chips of the stones sacred to them."[142] Notably, this was written by Aileen Nusbaum, wife of the archaeologist Jesse Nusbaum, who, as discussed above, was director of the Laboratory of Anthropology when the Zuni "pseudo-ceremonial ware" was acquired; she is clearly building on the stories told to laboratory staff by Wallace and Kelsey. The romance of the fetish jar was further advanced by Ruth F. Kirk, in a series of articles for *El Palacio*, the magazine of the Museum of New Mexico in Santa Fe.[143] The wife of a Gallup trader, Kirk presumably grew interested in these bowls because her husband's trading post had some of them. Echoing the mysterious tone set by Aileen Nusbaum, Kirk writes that "fetishes find their way into the hands of the white man with the darkest secrecy surrounding such operations" and that her own work on this topic was also done "with the greatest possible secrecy."[144]

When asked about such vessels, Jim Enote, director of Zuni Pueblo's A:shiwi A:wan Museum and Heritage Center, told me, "No, they are not ceremonial; they were always made to sell. Of course, you *could* use it in a ceremony and then you *could* call it a ceremonial vessel." We chuckled together. "But it is just a pot. This is true of those prayer meal bowls with the stepped slides that everyone calls ceremonial bowls. They are just bowls."[145] Enote thought that "invented tradition" was a good phrase for them. Many noteworthy museum collections contain such vessels.[146]

VEXED IDENTITY: DON SMITH OR "CHIEF LELOOSKA"?

The domain of Native American art contains many examples (both historical and contemporary) of vexed identity, some of which will be addressed in later chapters. *Vexed*, of course, has many meanings: *controversial*, *annoying*, *in dispute*, *contentious*, and *nettling* are among its many synonyms. An object may have a vexed history—unclear provenance, disputed claims of ownership, uncertain tribal style, or questions about the identity of its maker. The bear claw necklaces "assembled" by Milford Chandler (see figure 1.8) certainly qualify as objects with vexed identities. But here I am using the term *identity* literally and specifically to refer to the maker of the objects. In discussing objects of Northwest Coast style made by an artist who was not born into a Kwakwaka̱'wakw family, we examine the complexities of what it means to have a Native identity or rights to use Native imagery—a complex issue with ramifications that extend far beyond the pages of this book.

In the collection of the Montclair Art Museum in New Jersey is a late twentieth-century Kwakwaka̱'wakw-style transformation mask (figure 1.14).

FIG. 1.14 Don Smith, Kwakwaka̱'wakw-style transformation mask, 1984. Cedar, pigment, and muslin. 40 × 40 × 13.5 in. Montclair Art Museum, Montclair, New Jersey, no. 2006.19.2.

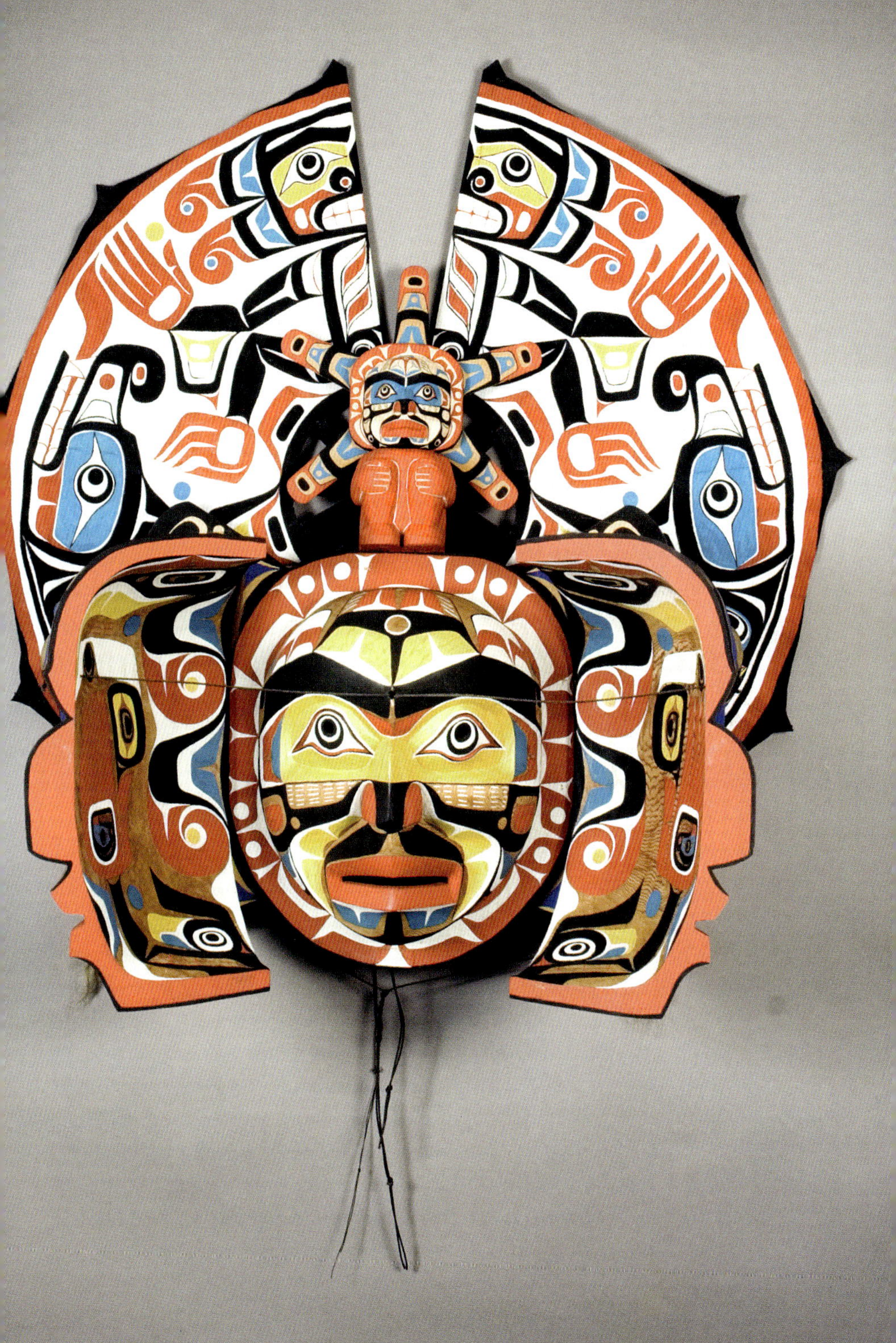

Such masks have long been a hallmark of Kwakwa̱ka̱'wakw stagecraft, in which the wearer controls hidden cords that open one carved face to reveal another within.[147] During a key moment in a potlatch, the mask will fly open, seemingly of its own volition. In this mask, cords also control a pleated muslin cloth behind the head. The cloth (bearing painted images of a frontal human at the top and the flanking profiles of the *sisiutl*, or supernatural double-headed serpent) opens into a full circle, forming a corona behind the head. The carved face is that of K'umugwe, chief of the Undersea Kingdom, a male whose home is guarded by sea monsters. It is a well-made example of late twentieth-century Northwest Coast–style art.

The model for this impressive mask was one carved by Kwakwa̱ka̱'wakw master carver Bob Harris (also named Xániyus; ca. 1870–ca. 1935) a century earlier.[148] Harris's mask has had a troubled history, and a detour into its story illustrates why replicas of nineteenth-century masks needed to be carved for late twentieth-century ceremonial use. Harris's mask was danced in Chief Dan Cranmer's 1921 Village Island potlatch from which masks and regalia were infamously confiscated by Indian agent William Halliday (1866–1957) and for which some participants were jailed. Halliday put the confiscated masks on display in the Alert Bay church hall, and this mask, along with thirty-four other objects, was purchased by New York collector George Heye for $291.[149] As we shall see, the removal of cultural property essential for the legitimizing rights of high-ranking families left something of an artistic void in the Kwakwa̱ka̱'wakw communities of Vancouver Island for some decades in the mid-twentieth century, a void that would be filled not only by a small number of local Native carvers but by some outsiders as well.

The modern mask was a gift from private collectors to the Montclair Art Museum in 2007, some eighteen years after the Indian Arts and Crafts Act of 1990 (Public Law 101-644) was enacted. This legislation was designed to ensure the livelihood of Native artists, by requiring that objects made for sale as Indian art are, in fact, made by a member of a federally or state-recognized tribe. Although this law does not cover the exhibition of art in museums, surely the viewing public would like to know that the art they see in museums is held to the same standards.

In 2017, the label on this work read "Don Smith (Lelooska) (1933–1996), Cherokee/Kwakwa̱ka̱'wakw."[150] The museumgoer might surmise that the artist has a parent, or perhaps a grandparent, of each of those ethnicities (though, of course, ethnic heritage can be far more complex than that). If a museum label identifies Smith simply as a Cherokee artist, as some do, one might ponder the legitimacy of a Cherokee carving a Kwakwa̱ka̱'wakw-style transformation mask. Kwakwa̱ka̱'wakw custom dictates that, in order to wear such regalia, one must have inherited the rights to particular totemic images—killer whale, *sisiutl*, raven, and so forth. A carver who does not personally own such rights might be commissioned to carve a mask by a person who does. That person, rather than the carver, would then own the object. These rights, and the objects that make them manifest, are a source of power and prestige.

In all Northwest Coast cultures, for carvers who do not own those rights, it is an extreme breach of protocol to appropriate highly specific individual, family, and clan crests for their own personal or commercial use. But there are other ways, in addition to descent, that individuals gain rights to such privileges, such as having rights bestowed as a gift in a formal, public ceremony by the one who owns them. And that is precisely what happened in the case of Smith, which makes this an excellent example of what I call "vexed identity."

Many American art museums have (or once had) in their Native North American art collections objects made by Smith.[151] He was born in California to parents of undocumented ancestry. His mother was the daughter of a woman who had been adopted by a wealthy white southern family and was said to be Cherokee. Smith recalled that throughout his childhood, his mother had made Indian baskets and curios to sell. His father, born in Montana, was not Native.[152] As a child, Smith took it for granted that he would learn how to make Indian art. His parents had an Indian curio shop (which he also characterized as "a roadside museum") near Salem, Oregon, and Smith remembered learning from every Native person he met who had a song, a story, or carving tools.[153] He dropped out of school in the ninth grade, and from that point on making "Indian" art was his full-time job. He sold Plains- and Plateau-style objects at his parents' shop, the Oregon State Fair, and the Pendleton Round-Up. As an adolescent who wore Plains- and Plateau-style chiefly regalia, participated in dances, and made objects, he was given the Flathead name "Lelooska" by the Native men with whom he worked at the Pendleton Round-Up.[154]

Smith began to experiment with Northwest Coast–style carving in the 1950s, when the hobbyist Norman Feder commissioned some Northwest Coast replicas from Smith for his demonstrations.[155] In the early 1960s, the Indian Arts and Crafts Board sent Smith to Neah Bay to "teach" Northwest Coast–style carving to the Makah people, and the board bought everything he had made in the demonstrations.[156] From 1959 to 1969, Smith was learning the fundamentals of Northwest Coast design. He carved a totem pole for the 1959 Oregon Centennial Exposition that was erected, and still stands, at the zoo in Portland. He carved four poles for his then home city of Kalama, Washington. Smith carved Haida-style figures of Christian iconography for both the St. Augustine's Indian Center in Chicago and the chapel at Oregon's Lewis and Clark College in Portland.[157] Though later he felt that these were not his best works, Smith got enough attention for this output that he was included in the pivotal 1967 exhibition and catalogue of Northwest Coast art titled *Arts of the Raven*.[158]

For Smith, the most important event of the 1960s, however, was being asked by Kwakwa̱ka̱'wakw chief Jimmie Sewid (1913–1988) to carve a transformation mask for the potlatch that Sewid was to hold in 1967.[159] In 1965, Smith had accompanied the anthropologist Edward Malin and artist Bill Holm to a series of potlatches held in Alert Bay. The next year, Malin sent an article he had published on "Lelooska" to Sewid, and, in summer 1967, Sewid traveled to Portland to speak to Smith in person about commissioning a mask for his upcoming potlatch.[160] In the December 1967 potlatch, Smith's younger brother, who was also an invited guest, danced in the ceremony wearing the Xwixwi (Undersea Eagle) mask that Smith had carved for Sewid.[161] This first Kwakwa̱ka̱'wakw commission was a simpler version of the imagery Smith used in the Montclair Art Museum mask illustrated here: the Undersea Eagle mask opens to reveal a Sun Hawk. In Sewid's mask, the folding, painted cloth is hidden inside the large curved beak of the Eagle and opens to surround the Sun Hawk within. In the 1984 mask, Smith follows more closely the complexities of Harris's late nineteenth-century mask.

Clearly, some museums believe that Smith is a Native maker of Northwest Coast objects. But Smith's case actually puts into conflict the individual and family rights that are the cornerstone of most Northwest Coast cultural protocols and the collective rights of an indigenous nation that seeks to control its heritage in the modern world. In other words, as the anthropologist Aaron Glass has observed, in the period between 1950 and 1980, decisions made by individual chiefs who granted privileges to outsiders "were made at particular historical conjunctures and for specific personal reasons having to do with preserving Kwakwa̱ka̱'wakw art and culture as well as negotiating productive social and intercultural relations" at a time when they were revitalizing the potlatch and negotiating emerging relations with the larger art world.[162] Nonetheless, some contemporary Kwakwa̱ka̱'wakw decry the work done by

Smith, especially the Kwakwa̱ka̱'wakw dance performances still being put on by family members at what is today called the Lelooska Foundation and Cultural Center in Ariel, Washington.[163]

Is there—or should there be—a distinction between a Don Smith mask commissioned by a Kwakwa̱ka̱'wakw chief (who obviously has the right to ask anyone he chooses to carve for him) for use in ceremony and a Don Smith mask in Kwakwa̱ka̱'wakw style made for sale? Is the latter completely illegitimate, or does Chief Sewid's commissioning of ceremonial masks from this carver confer some quasi legitimacy on his other work? According to the Indian Arts and Crafts Act of 1990, one can be certified as a "non-member artisan" if one is "of Indian lineage" and this is documented by the governing body of an Indian tribe.[164] This was included in the law as an accommodation for non-enrolled artists, because, of course, the complexities of individual family histories do not track precisely with federal regulations; legal definitions (whether federal or tribal) do not cover every permutation of lived experience.

In the final years of his life, Smith was, in fact, so certified, through the Cow Creek Band of the Umpqua Tribe, a federally recognized entity. So while Smith might be covered by the letter of the law, many Native artists might believe that he had no standing to make art for sale in the style of a nation of which he is not a member and a nation other than that group in which he has been certified. Ariel, where the Smith family home (and now the museum and cultural center) is located, is more than two hundred miles north of the Cow Creek Band's home in Roseburg, Oregon, a fact that I found perplexing. What was the connection between the two?

In order to understand a situation that seemed problematic, I interviewed Stephen Dow Beckham, a historian at Lewis and Clark College, for in Chris Friday's biography on Lelooska Beckham was said to have helped the artist and his family gain their certification.[165] As in many other case studies in this book, what I discovered only complicated my understanding of the intercultural politics present in all such situations and made it harder to fully dismiss Smith's legitimacy. I have long been skeptical of Smith's claims to Native standing, but Beckham described having seen numerous Kwakwa̱ka̱'wakw performing alongside the Smith family, when he repeatedly took his college students in the 1980s and 1990s to see the masked performances at the Lelooska Cultural Center.[166]

Beckham said that since the late 1970s, some ten thousand to twelve thousand schoolchildren from the Portland metropolitan area have visited the

Lelooska Foundation annually to learn about Native dance, art, and oral traditions:

> The passage of the Indian Arts and Crafts Act of 1990 would have put such opportunities in jeopardy. The Cow Creek Band was sympathetic to the Smith family's plight, for they themselves had been legislated out of existence in 1956. From 1977 to 1989, many confederated groups in Oregon re-earned federal recognition, but it was a long process. They endorsed the educational work that was being done by the Smith family, for at that time nothing else was available. They firmly believed that it made their lives easier if their non-Native neighbors had some exposure to Indian history and traditions.[167]

Beckham went on to explain that today, primarily with casino money, many Native peoples in Oregon do have their own educational programs. Foremost among them are the Confederated Tribes of Grand Ronde, with their Chachalu Museum and Cultural Center, but in 1990 there was not much in the way of education about Native culture.[168]

Conclusion: Native Art and the "Fantasy" of Identity?

This chapter's title, "Authenticity and Its Discontents," signals how fraught the concept of authenticity is. And, of course, authenticity in Native art cannot be considered without at least a preliminary unpacking of the vexed concept of an authentic Native identity. While a discussion of the myriad complexities of racial identity is far beyond the scope of this book and the expertise of this author, it is worth remembering that definitions of Native identity are themselves problematic and contested. So-called scientific concepts of race developed in the nineteenth century were imposed on Native people and plague us still; from such concepts developed legal definitions of blood quantum—how much "Indian blood" an individual has.[169] By such means, the dominant culture to this day polices Native identity, and sometimes Native people police each other. In the United States, being a "card-carrying Indian," as it is often called, means having a CDIB card—the Certificate of Degree of Indian Blood issued by the Bureau of Indian Affairs.

In *Fantasies of Identification: Disability, Gender, Race*, the literary scholar Ellen Samuels considers fixed notions of identity as part of the regulatory structures that police something far too complex for such simplistic regulation. Such structures, she notes, not only "cover over the incoherence of the past but must be continuously circulated to reassemble a coherent present, without which the nation ceases to function" (as apposite an observation of the Zuni Nation or the Navajo Nation as it is of a nation-state such as the United States of America). Notably, Samuels finds that the present mirrors the mid-nineteenth century in its "acceleration of anxieties about identity."[170]

Much of what I examine in this book toggles between the two nouns of Samuels's book title: *fantasy* and *identification*. There is the fantasy that has driven so much collecting of Native art since the mid-nineteenth century, an imposed ideal about what constitutes the "real" Indian and "real" Indian art. This is clearly articulated in a quotation from John Painter, a white collector of Native art. While written in 1991, it unfortunately exemplifies attitudes still held by some collectors and fostered by many galleries that sell Native art:

> "Does it have the soul of the Indian?" During the past ten years, Kurt Schindler and I have asked this question of each other several hundred times, as we have pondered whether one of us should buy an Indian artifact. What are we searching for? In our imagination, we see the Indian riding his small pony, hunting the vast buffalo herds with a short bow and arrow. We see him performing special rituals, such as carefully unwrapping a sacred medicine pipe so that he can perform, dignify, and ratify a special meeting with proper ceremony. We see his pride in wearing or using an object, whether it is a war shirt, moccasins, knife sheath, quirt, strike-a-light, saddle blanket, doll cradle, or drum—the pride which comes from knowing that the item was made with great skill, loving care, and tradition in the style of his particular tribe. Passed down through many generations by telling, showing, instructing, and explaining, objects with this soul were not made to sell to tourists, who could not possibly fully appreciate or understand the heritage and the special sense of values displayed by Native Americans.[171]

Seldom does one see the longings of a non-Native collector so nakedly revealed: To collect fine Native art, then, is to touch "the soul of the Indian"? The anthropologist Steven Hooper, in his compelling theorization of the role of relics across many cultures, provides insight. He asserts that the hunger for "relics" (be they religious or secular) is the animating force behind much collecting. He classifies relics into three types: body relics, contact relics, and image relics. A sliver of bone alleged to be from a Christian saint is a body relic. In the realm of celebrity culture, Michael Jackson's glove would be a contact relic, and an image relic is a statue of Christ or the Buddha.[172]

Similar primitivist tropes underpinned much collecting in the modernist era and have been elucidated by many scholars. While we might hope that such overbearing romanticism is a thing of the past, it still informs the choices made by some, be they buyers, non-Native makers, or performers, as examples from subsequent chapters illustrate.

How can ethical people form any sense of clarity about art making and ethnic identity in a globalized world? In this chapter, I distinguished Zapotec "Navajo-style" rugs and Indonesian "Haida-style" masks from those made by Native North American artists themselves. It is an inescapable fact in the twenty-first-century global village that nearly every commodity appearing on social media is immediately knocked off, replicated, or faked. Discrete visual languages soon break down into gibberish. To many scholars of a globalized anthropology who take this as a given, what is of salient interest is how this phenomenon plays out, and the roles of different stakeholders, as W. Warner Wood's work on Zapotec weaving exemplified.[173]

Most educated people understand that "Buy American-Made" is a feel-good initiative meant to engender patriotism. For some, it also involves a wish to somehow transport us back to the "good old days" when American workers belonged to unions and made a good wage (without acknowledging the racism and sexism of those unions, and the equally American tradition of union busting). Yet it can seem to be a self-congratulatory gesture at best, for our economy is inexorably part of an international web, or a "global supply chain," to use the business term. The jeans we wear, the aspirin we take, the cars we buy (even from "American" companies) link us to makers and manufacturers around the world.[174] And so do many of the so-called Native art objects in the marketplace, as the Zapotec and Indonesian examples in this chapter demonstrate.

We have long had "Buy Native American–Made" initiatives. The Indian Arts and Crafts Board Act of 1935 was intended to protect Indian-made objects (particularly in the Southwest) and their makers from various sorts of imitation;[175] the Indian Arts and Crafts Act of 1990 was built on the foundation laid in 1935. In Canada, the Igloo Tag trademark was established in 1958 to distinguish art in the marketplace made by Inuit from copies and replicas.[176] Yet even with legal mandates in place, the heterogeneous array available in the marketplace or the gallery is unlikely ever to diminish. How could Native artistry be the sole exception in a world gone mad with copies and replicas? Of course, educating affluent consumers to channel their money to Native artists is admirable and important. But there will always be buyers for every price point;

for some, it is simply a notional connection to Native art that holds sway. If a buyer cannot afford an argillite stone sculpture hand-carved by a Haida artist, a replica cast from crushed quartz and resin will do, for as the anthropologist Solen Roth has argued, such a manufactured object "acquires a veneer of nobility through its association with the much-valued stone it imitates."[177]

As Jennifer Esperanza has written about handicrafts made in Indonesia, the entrepreneurial carvers in villages such as Ubud and Tegallalang are proud of the range of objects they offer—from "African" sculptures to "Mexican" Day of the Dead figurines and "Haida" masks. She says they see these as "their tickets to a more cosmopolitan identity" despite the fact that such objects are also "stereotypical, romanticized images made at the expense of other subaltern communities."[178] Esperanza terms this phenomenon "outsourcing otherness," and it will reappear here in chapter 4, in the examination of Mimbres-style pottery made in Nicaragua. As we have seen, lovers of Navajo textiles with limited budgets have turned, in the past few decades, to Zapotec rugs with Navajo patterns. As these have become marketed in more canny ways, with evocations of Zapotec identity and natural dyes, their prices have risen. So middlemen have sought newer, cheaper sources in Turkey and Nepal. This process replicates, on a small scale, trends that have been at work in the global textile market for centuries.[179]

For decades, Native artists and writers have taken up this issue, too, sometimes with humor or lacerating wit, among them James Luna (Payómkawichum [Luiseño] / Mexican American, 1950–2018) and Tanis S'eiltin (Tlingit, b. 1951).[180] Contemporary novelist Tommy Orange (Cheyenne and Arapaho, b. 1982) says it more succinctly than any scholar could: "Enough Blood times Not Enough Blood equals eligibility or ineligibility for tribal enrollment and therefore citizenship in a sovereign nation. But I am half Native—Cheyenne—from my dad. This half of me is a cutting fraction, which cuts if I rub up against it too firmly, if I slide my finger along its edge. Halving is the beginning of erasure."[181]

"Blood Quantum Physics" (figure 1.15), a design for T-shirts, mugs, stickers, and COVID-19 masks made and marketed by Robert Martinez (Northern Arapaho / Euro-American, b. 1977), is a humorous take on the impossibility of understanding the complexities of blood quantum—a conundrum as deep as quantum physics. Within a "blood red" border is a blackboard on which are scribbled complex equations that combine Native words and foods, mathematical equations into which are factored the CDIB card, and both incoming

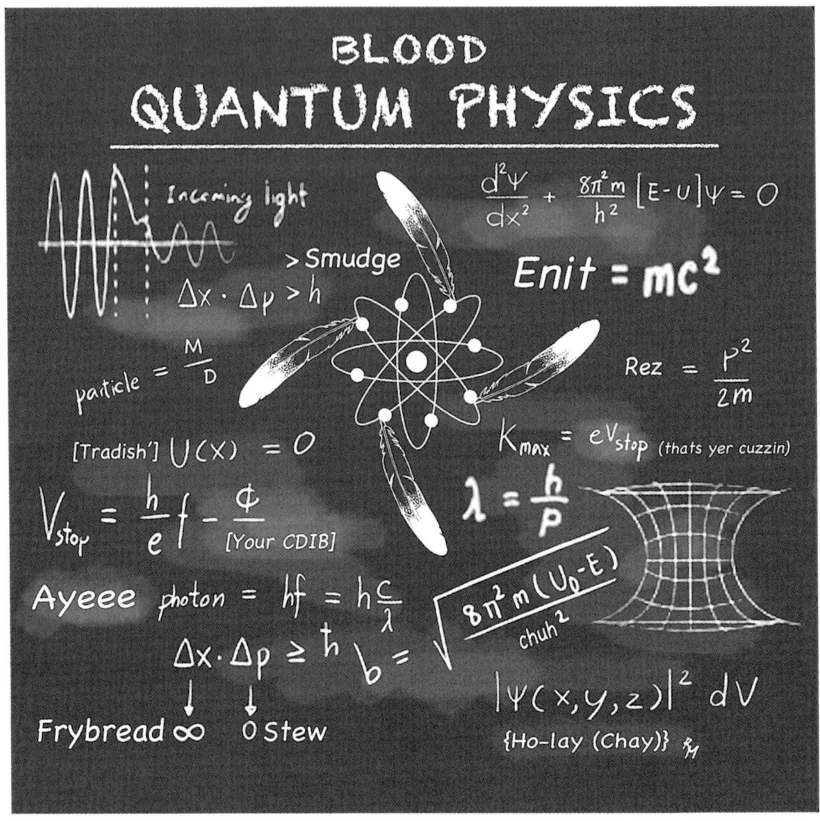

FIG. 1.15 Robert Martinez, "Blood Quantum Physics," designed for T-shirt, 2019. Courtesy of Robert Martinez.

light and the smoke of a smudging ceremony. In the middle whirls the emblem for the atom, which has become a shield with four feathers.

Fixed concepts of race, nation, tribe, and "blood quantum" leave no room for the far more fluid and inclusive categories historically embraced by most Native North American communities—including adoption of outsiders such as war captives as well as individuals with whom the community wanted to solidify diplomatic and economic relationships.[182] In the 1960s, the anthropologist A. Irving Hallowell proposed a name for this phenomenon—*transculturalization*: "the process whereby individuals under a variety of circumstances are temporarily or permanently detached from one group, enter the web of social relations that constitute another society, and come under the influence of its customs, ideas, and values to a greater or lesser degree."[183] But beyond transculturation, there is good reason, historically, to question the stability of even many tribal identities. The historian James F. Brooks, in a study of historical identity-making in the Southwest, writes, "Identities like Comanche, Kiowa, Apache, Navajo, Ute, Pueblo, Spanish-American and Hispano seem timeless and unquestioned in much historical literature. The intergroup economic, cultural, and biological exchanges across the centuries show that ethnicities in the Southwest were often a matter of biological exchange, strategic reconstruction, and political invention."[184] Of course, "biological exchange, strategic reconstruction, and political invention" describes the nature of identity in general, not just identity formation in the Southwest. But because Native nations have fought so hard for some measure of recognition and sovereignty, these sorts of analyses are not always welcome. Indeed, too much is at stake in terms of daily well-being—from health care to tribal voting roles—for Native people to fully subscribe to a freewheeling postmodern notion of unfixed identity.

In this book, when considering the question "What is 'real' Native American art?," it is important to remember that very old-fashioned paradigms still underpin the assumptions of much of the buying public concerning Native American art, as the Painter quotation illustrated. Chapter 2 considers the Great Plains of North America, the quintessential site of nostalgia for non-Natives searching for what we might term a "usable past," a phrase coined over a century ago by the literary critic Van Wyck Brooks. He observed that the past "has no objective reality" and asked, "*What is important for us?* What . . . ought we to elect to remember?"[185] The term has often been invoked by American historians and art historians to discuss the way Americans make what they will of their history in relation to what is needed in any particular cultural moment, and the voluminous literature in critical heritage studies over the past few decades has expanded and sharpened such questions.[186]

In recent years, it has become clear that these issues are far more than topics of academic interest, as toppling of Confederate monuments and the right-wing foment about the teaching of critical race studies indicate.[187] In the past three decades, proprietary actions regarding the circulation and use of objects and images outside of indigenous contexts have been at the forefront of postcolonial struggles concerning representation.[188] These include repatriation of objects, censorship of particular imagery, and the withholding of illustrative research materials from scholars. Sometimes the rhetoric surrounding objects and their repatriation, or sensitive images and their replication, is offered in terms that starkly separate a supposedly correct Indigenous position from a non-Indigenous stance seen as abrogating Native sovereignty. But there is seldom one "Indigenous position" on such issues, but rather a variety of complex responses. For example, in some Native communities, whether a person is Christian (or what variety of Christian), or follows customary Indigenous religious practices, influences the point of view they take. So does one's status as a person who makes money as an artist or holds a position in a clan, ceremonial society leadership, or tribal government. Moreover, Native American art history is filled with examples of cross-cultural collaboration that complicate such a one-dimensional story, as some of the following chapters demonstrate.

2

Cultural Cross-Dressers

A Long History of Imitating Indians

In September 1987, the Denver Museum of Natural History (now the Denver Museum of Nature and Science) hosted a powwow as its contribution to the sixth meeting of the Native American Art Studies Association, held that year in Denver. The anthropology curator Joyce Herold, then president of the association, invited Reginald and Gladys Laubin to attend the powwow as all-expenses-paid guests of the museum and to raise their own tipi as part of the festivities.[1] While the Laubins did not bring their tipi, they danced in the powwow. He was eighty-three and she was eighty-one. They wore their Plains-style regalia, as they had been doing for more than sixty years (figure 2.1). At the time, I was a thirty-seven-year-old scholar making the transition from studying pre-Columbian art to studying North American Indian art. There was a lot I still did not know, but I did know one thing with a visceral intensity: these ancient, wrinkled, white people dressed as Indians were freakish, fossils of an earlier time. Embarrassing, really.

Now what embarrasses me is my own quick dismissal, which was rooted in ignorance. But it is also a good example of how the barometer of cultural acceptability shifted relatively quickly during the final decades of the twentieth century. Herold was a distinguished colleague, but we were a generation apart—she was in college when I was born in 1952. To her, a Coloradan who had experienced many events at which Native and white people danced together in regalia, the authors of *The Indian Tipi* and *Indian Dances of North America* were worthy honorees. Their books were well known and often reprinted. I was too newly arrived in the embryonic subdiscipline of Native American art history to fully understand such things. As every generation seems to do, I judged something against my own ahistorical yardstick and

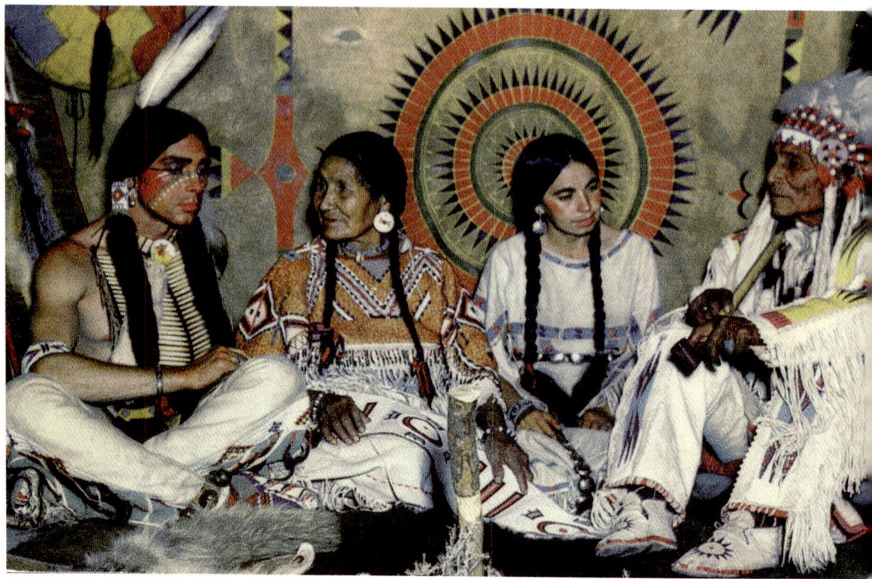

FIG. 2.1 Reginald and Gladys Laubin in their tipi in Grand Teton National Park, Wyoming, with a Blackfeet couple. Early 1950s. Postcard. Collection of Clyde Ellis. Photo courtesy of Clyde Ellis.

found it wanting. Now I seek to understand the nuances of how a white couple from New England found a measure of fame as proxies for real Native people.

The historian Philip J. Deloria has taught us that to understand the ways that playing Indian is fundamental to the American cultural imaginary, we have to go back to the colonial era, when, as Deloria puts it, "colonial crowds often acted out their political and economic discontent in Indian guise."[2] The colonial rebels who dressed as Mohawks and dumped hundreds of cases of tea into Boston Harbor on December 16, 1773, were simply the best-known example of this. But sometimes an apparent case of cultural cross-dressing is actually something quite different. In the eighteen century, some men—both Native and white—came together in a "middle ground" of shared material goods and clothing, and partly shared values, in which what they wore and how they acted was not playing Indian, or aspiring to be white men, but something else entirely.

Until I began researching this book, I was indifferent to the complex stories of those individuals—mostly men—who are historical reenactors. Many people are familiar with Civil War reenactors, but less visible in the public imagination are those who reenact the French and Indian War (1759), the American Revolutionary War (1775–83), and the War of 1812 (1812–15). I live eighty miles from Fort Niagara, New York, on the shore of Lake Ontario, where such reenactments take place every summer; since 2009, I have followed this phenomenon. I first went simply to see the remarkable works of quillwork and regalia worn by those who "played Indian." But I kept returning to try to understand their motivations. Are their motivations different from those of the so-called German Indians, those who set up tipi encampments in the Black Forest and elsewhere? Germans playing Indian live out a fantasy that holds respect for Native history and Native values as they understand them, but that also has its roots in German nationalism, class values, and historical encounters with real Native Americans. Another example, Mardi Gras Indians, are working-class African Americans (mostly male, like those in the previous categories) who labor all year in order to "mask Indian," as they call it.

Since the 1980s, Native scholars and activists have increasingly sought to educate people about how deeply offensive many Native people find "playing Indian" and related activities.[3] From the use of Native names and imagery as sports mascots to the pursuits of hobbyists who make and wear Native regalia, these actions are increasingly recognized by more members of the general public, too, as problematic. As mentioned in the introduction, the task of a historian of visual culture is to understand such practices, not simply to condemn them without seeking a nuanced understanding of their microhistories and motivations. The long-standing Anglo-American desire to recall and embody a mythic Native past is a troubling one, rooted in a deeply violent and racist past, as anyone with a cursory knowledge of American history recognizes. Yet it is more than this for its practitioners, and the spectrum of these practices, and the roles they play in people's lives, even those who may be unaware of some of the psychological subtleties, varies.

Chapters 2 and 3 are closely interrelated. This chapter examines the *actors* who "played Indian," or aligned themselves with Native people in some related way. Chapter 3 looks more closely at the *objects* that have arisen out of this compulsion and profiles some non-Native people who could not be characterized as hobbyists, but who make such objects for others.

Non-Native Guys in Indian Guise: Moments in a Long History

The impulse to own, bestow, make, or wear something associated with the legendary brave Indigenous men of the Great Plains has a long cultural history, going back to the time of George Catlin and Karl Bodmer. Less familiar to most readers is the adoption of Eastern Woodlands clothing by white men in the eighteenth and early nineteenth centuries, a topic explored here only glancingly.

MEN OF THE MIDDLE GROUND

The concept of "the middle ground" has become a defining metaphor of intercultural relations in the eighteenth and early nineteenth centuries in the Northeast and the Great Lakes. Proposed by the historian Richard White, the middle ground was a space for accommodation and hybridity and for the emergence of new cultures that conjoined Native and European ways.[4] To imagine a global, hybrid, world two and a half centuries ago, where men of radically diverse cultures came together as military comrades, trusted allies, traveling companions, and adopted kin is to overturn the view that later came to permeate US governmental policies toward Native peoples. That simplistic view was solidified in the second half of the nineteenth century, as part of the US government's policy of destruction of peoples on the Great Plains. While there was no shortage of people in the eighteenth century who had a one-dimensional view of Native Americans as "bloodthirsty savages," there was also a much smaller world of cross-cultural understanding, in which European and Native men sought similar political objectives, wore the same items of clothing, and used the same material objects. This section introduces some of these intercultural actors to provide a window onto the complexities of their hybrid worlds. A global economy was expressed in the dress and accoutrements of men who, while operating out of small communities in the Mohawk or Ohio River valleys, made decisions that reverberated across the Atlantic world.

No one in eighteenth-century North America understood better than William Johnson (ca. 1715–1774) that men who sought influence and alliance across cultural boundaries needed to meet each other halfway visually and sartorially, as well as in their actions. The historian Timothy Shannon observed of the illustrious Johnson that "among colonial Americans of his era, only Benjamin Franklin was more famous."[5] Born in Ireland, Johnson arrived in the colonies around 1738, making his home near what is today the eponymous Johnstown, New York, about 160 miles northwest of New York City. He eventually became Britain's most important intermediary with the Iroquois Confederacy and, finally, superintendent of Indian affairs for the Colony of New York (1756–74). A master of cross-cultural understanding, Johnson constructed what one biographer has termed a "polyglot and porous world."[6] He quickly realized that, among the Natives who interacted with Europeans, a subtle language of hierarchy and diplomacy was played out through material goods. As a trader, he sought to provide his Native consumers with exactly what they wanted, from lengths of cloth to ruffled shirts, ribbons, pipe hatchets, and so forth.[7]

Famous for his fluency in intercultural relations, Johnson recognized that he would be most successful in diplomacy if he used the visual and verbal languages of those he was trying to influence. So he wore what his high-ranking Native counterparts wore, manipulated wampum in the visual language of diplomacy, and spoke with great rhetorical flourishes, as was (and still is) valued among Haudenosaunee people. At a meeting with New York governor George Clinton in Albany in 1746, Johnson arrived with a contingent of Mohawks. As one observer wrote at the time, "Mr. Johnson put himself at the Head of the Mohawks, dressed and painted after the Manner of an Indian War-Captain; and the Indians who followed him were likewise dressed and painted as is usual with them when they set out to war."[8] At Fort Johnson, the stone house he built in 1748, and at Johnson Hall, which he built in 1763, Johnson entertained Mohawk leaders and European travelers. Native war councils were held in the courtyard behind his house, and contemporary accounts describe Johnson Hall and its grounds as often occupied by dozens or even hundreds of Native people feasting, making speeches, and receiving diplomatic gifts.[9]

No painting of Johnson in his intercultural garb exists, but the well-known portrait of Johnson's nephew Guy Johnson (1740–1788) by American artist Benjamin West (1738–1820) is surely an accurate representation of this family's intercultural garb (figure 2.2). Guy Johnson sailed to America in 1755 and joined his uncle in the Mohawk valley the following year. He worked as a captain of the Indian troops and eventually became his uncle's successor as Indian superintendent. He often traveled in the company of Mohawk warriors, most notably on trips to Canada and England in 1775. While in London, Guy Johnson and David Karonghyontye Hill (Mohawk, 1745–1790) posed for their double portrait. While the dress of both men is intercultural, Johnson's apparel is a remarkable amalgam of British clothing and that of the Indian trade. Over his white buttoned vest, he wears a beaded finger-woven sash around his waist. Over his red wool frock coat is draped a painted fur robe. His silk stockings are upheld by beaded garters, and on his feet are quilled moccasins. In his right hand he clutches what appears to be a British military hat that has been embellished with quillwork and beads. When European men wear such garb, scholars usually refer to it as "Indian dress."[10] Yet it is important to remember that this dress is polyglot, hybrid, and new. The men who wore it—British and Native alike—recognized it as a kind of sartorial Esperanto. It is, literally, a material expression of the middle ground.

High-ranking Native men expressed their intercultural fluency sartorially as well. Some wore British frock coats and other gentlemanly attire, as numerous eighteenth-century accounts describe.[11] From a twenty-first-century vantage point, this seems oddly confusing, or anachronistic; shouldn't Indians look like the barefoot, seated, tattooed figure in West's famous painting *The Death of General Wolfe* (1770)?[12] Ordinary warriors did look like that; their leaders decidedly did not.[13]

Native people, since first contact, had folded into their daily lives foreign manufactured goods. By the eighteenth century, the visual culture of the middle ground was quite inventive. The indigenous world of hide, hoof, quill, and shell was transformed into a world that included cloth, china, silver, and glass beads. Trade and treaty goods were a lexicon of globalization: metal goods, firearms, and cloth from England and France; beads from Venice; silver mined in Mexico, shipped to Spain, and shaped into ornaments in Albany, Montreal, and Quebec; packets of vermilion from China; and tobacco from Brazil by way of Lisbon.[14] Some of these manufactured goods were part of diplomatic exchange, but generally they served as payment for the pelts and skins that the British and French shipped to Europe.

Johnson and Hill posed for West, holding a musket and a calumet, respectively. These items bracket the figures as strong vertical elements of the composition, and they are key symbolic elements. The calumet, or peace pipe, was the crucial instrument in public diplomacy. Its use had both metaphorical and contractual implications. To "smoke the peace pipe" with others was to recognize them as allies and kin rather than enemies or strangers. To carry such a pipe, as Hill did, was to present oneself as a man of peace rather than a warrior. Such pipes, with wrapped and braided quillwork attached with bast

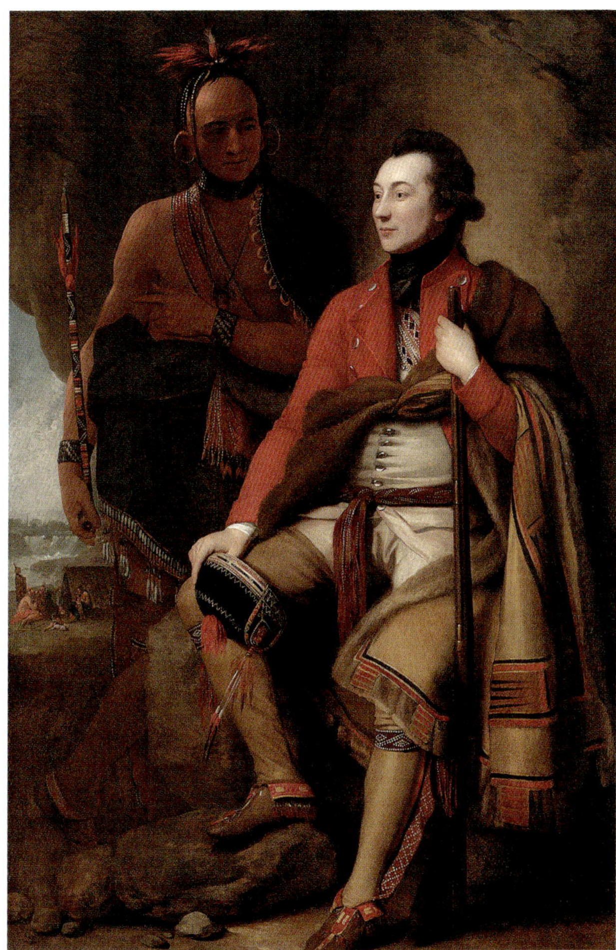

FIG. 2.2 Benjamin West, *Colonel Guy Johnson and Karonghyontye (Captain David Hill)*, 1776. Oil on canvas, 79 × 54 in. Andrew W. Mellon Collection, National Gallery of Art, Washington, DC, no. 1940.1.10.

fiber, were made all across the Eastern Woodlands to the Great Plains and were prized objects of diplomatic exchange.

Cloth and clothing was by far the largest category of trade goods distributed, ranging from lengths of wool and calico to linen and cotton shirts and ribbons, yarns, and threads.[15] One of the most important items was red, blue, and black stroud cloth, produced in the town of Stroud in the Cotswolds, a sheep-raising region of southwest England. By the eighteenth century, its most famous export was "Stroudwater Scarlet," a durable wool used in military jackets and highly prized by Native consumers in northeastern North America.[16] While its distinctive undyed selvedge was cut away in the manufacture of British clothing, Native buyers valued this feature, and it makes the cloth instantly recognizable. William Johnson, in his accounting entry for 1746–48, records distributing more than sixty-four ells of stroud (a British ell being approximately forty-five inches), plus numerous other lengths of linen cloth, silk ribbon, and finished shirts. Cloth was embellished with silk ribbons, metal cones, and rings. Natives and non-Natives alike used beaded woolen sashes, as is evident in the portrait of Guy Johnson. Both Native men and white ones wore beaded or quilled garters, as Johnson does in West's portrait.[17] Men are dressed in similar fashion in other eighteenth-century portraits as well.[18]

Twenty-first-century scholarship has not looked kindly on those who "play Indian," because of the twentieth-century legacy of impersonation of Indians in disrespectful and unflattering contexts, as much of this chapter recounts. But it is important to recognize that Guy Johnson and others like him were not, in fact, part of that history. Like their Native counterparts, such as David Karonghyontye Hill, Joseph Brant (Mohawk, 1743–1807), and a host of others, they were forging a new hybrid identity in a complex changing world.[19]

HOBBYISTS

Philip J. Deloria, Shari Huhndorf, and Alan Trachtenberg have dissected the peculiar American predilection for "playing Indian" or "going Native." They have judged it to be a symptom of the anxieties generated by modernity and by the unresolved violence of the nation's origins in the dispossession of Native people.[20] I will not recap the arguments of their well-known books here, except to briefly indicate how the practices of making and wearing Native regalia came about. These authors (respectively, a historian, a cultural studies scholar, and an Americanist) are less interested than I in the material culture of this phenomenon, but my work rests squarely on their shoulders.

The widespread mimicry of Indigenous dress began at the start of the twentieth century. In 1901, Ernest Thompson Seton (1860–1946) created a club for boys called the Woodcraft Indians, and, in 1910, he cofounded the Boy Scouts of America.[21] Indian lore and material culture were fundamental to these enterprises. As the historian Clyde Ellis has written, within a year of Seton's first encampment at his Connecticut estate in 1902 where boys dressed as Indians, "sixty tribes of 'Seton Indians' were organized." "In 1906, Seton claimed fifty thousand adherents; by 1910, one author put membership at an astonishing one hundred fifty thousand; and in 1922, the New York Times reported there were two hundred thousand Seton Indian tribes, making it one of the nation's largest youth movements."[22] When one imagines some two hundred thousand "tribes," the vast scope of the enterprise of making Native-style garb across North America becomes apparent. Seton's book *Two Little Savages* (1903) offered the first instruction on such things.[23] Other publications soon followed, as did other smaller groups copying the Boy Scout "Indian" experience.

Another figure central to this aspect of Scouting was Ralph Hubbard (1886–1980), who held a leadership role in the Boy Scouts from its earliest years. Starting in 1913, he taught Indian crafts and dancing in Boulder, Colorado. In 1920, he developed an Indian program for the first Boy Scout World Jamboree in England and, for years after that, in American jamborees in which Scouts performed in full Plains regalia. His Scouts performed at the Pageant of Progress at the Century of Progress International Exposition (sometimes called the Chicago World's Fair) in 1933–34. Notably, the boys with whom Hubbard worked did not always make their own costumes; he says that by 1928 they were wearing "genuine Indian handcrafted items" that he had collected over the years.[24]

While much was amateurish in such Boy Scout endeavors, there were also serious adherents who went to great lengths in their search for "authenticity" in both dress and actions. On the May 1947 cover of *Boys' Life* (the official publication of the Boy Scouts of America), a boy wears a huge feathered headdress, a floral-style beaded vest and breechclout, arm and leg bands, and moccasins (figure 2.3). He is a "chief," the highest rank in the internationally known Koshares, as the members of Boy Scout Troop 230, of La Junta, Colorado, are called, taking their name from the sacred clowns of Pueblo peoples. James "Buck" Burshears (1909–1987) founded this troop in 1933, developing an ambitious program of interpretive Indian-style dancing and shepherding his troop to national acclaim for decades. The troop has toured widely, dancing at rodeos, national Rotary events, football games, and other public venues. Every summer, even now, they dance at their "kiva"—a large replica of a Pueblo ceremonial room with a log roof. The article in *Boys' Life* outlines the arduous requirements for advancing through the ranks: among them, good character, good grades, and serious dancing and regalia-making ability. Notably, all of

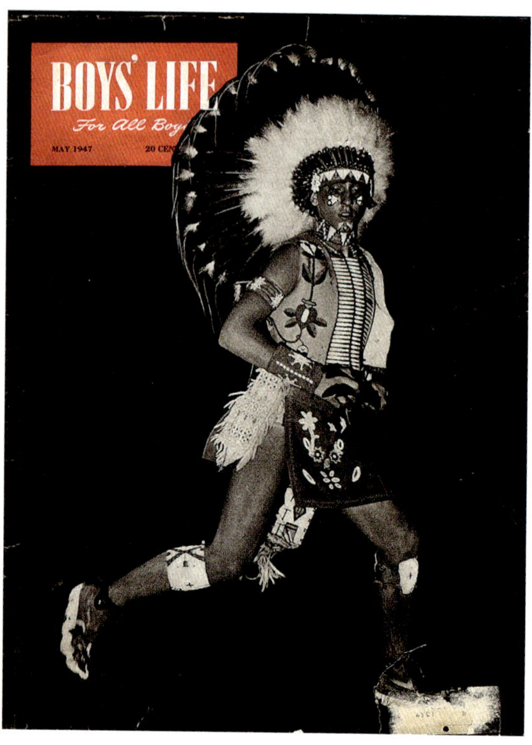

FIG. 2.3 *Boys' Life* magazine cover, May 1947, depicting Eagle Scout Lee Walters, head chief of the Koshares. Author's collection.

the highest-ranking members (inevitably called "chiefs") are also Eagle Scouts, the highest rank in Boy Scouting.[25] So this is a very different kind of "playing Indian" from many others.

Today, of course, most Native people (and their allies) find a photo of white boys dancing in full Native regalia deeply offensive. On the Great Plains, the wearing of a feathered warbonnet is limited to those singular men who have legitimately earned the highest military honors, repeatedly proving themselves in warfare. (Of course, this is contradicted by the thousands of photos taken for more than a century in which Native people from all over North America have strategically worn the Plains feathered headdress so that their white viewers will see them as "real" Indians.)[26] Nonetheless, to see such headgear on an adolescent white boy is as insulting to Plains men of high rank as would be the case for many in the US military if such a boy made and wore replicas of the accoutrements of a five-star general.[27]

Boy Scouts learned "Indian craft" at summer camp, and within their local troops, though few had someone with the expertise of Burshears as their leader. His home had a basement workshop for his Koshare troop, where his collection of real Plains regalia was available for examination. Boys also learned through their Scouting magazine. For example, "Indian Moccasins," a two-page spread inside another issue of *Boys' Life*, offers explicit moccasin-making instructions. Twenty-four illustrations and captions carefully show the steps, from tracing a foot pattern on brown paper to choosing and cutting a hide, punching it with an awl, and sewing the pieces together with linen thread.[28]

Milford Chandler (discussed in chapter 1) and Richard A. Pohrt (1911–2005) were notable figures who, in the early to mid-twentieth century, carried their boyhood hobby into a serious adult obsession. Their significant collections and modes of collecting were chronicled in an exhibition catalogue that bears their names, *Art of the American Indian Frontier: The Chandler-Pohrt Collection*.[29] They tell a familiar tale of childhoods reading *Boys' Life* magazine, as well as any other sources on Native peoples they could get their hands on. Chandler was a generation older, and for fifty-four years he shared his knowledge of Great Lakes and Plains material with Pohrt. Chandler made replicas and pastiches (see figures 1.1 and 1.8). His inspiration, as Pohrt describes, "came from objects that he had seen but could not acquire—specimens in museum collections and items pictured in old photographs and paintings. Usually he would make minor changes from the Indian original. . . . He never offered this work for sale."[30] In the 1920s, Chandler was a casual employee of the Field Museum of Natural History, and with other like-minded men he organized powwows at the Chicago Historical Society. In 1966, Pohrt bought his collection. These two individuals had a great influence over the next generation of men who became hobbyists and experts, including Benson Lanford, F. Dennis Lessard, Richard Conn, and Norman Feder.

Some who "played Indian" in Scouting became the Indian hobbyists of the mid-twentieth century, a topic that Ellis covers in far more detail.[31] It was the hobbyists who further codified and explained to an overwhelmingly white audience the making of Native garb, especially that of the Great Plains, in their magazines. The anthropologist William K. Powers (himself a former hobbyist) dates the movement to the creation of the *American Indian Hobbyist* magazine started by Feder in 1954, though such groups existed before then.[32]

Magazines such as the *American Indian Hobbyist* and *American Indian Crafts and Culture* were primarily "how-to" guides to correct costuming. For example, in 1957, the *American Indian Hobbyist* published Feder's detailed article "Old Time Sioux Costume," with fifteen drawings and explanations of different male clothing styles.[33] Other articles cover topics such as particular headgear, bustles, and moccasins. Several notable hobbyists and authors in such publications became the museum professionals of the 1960s and 1970s: Feder and Conn were both curators of Native art at the Denver Art Museum, for example, and the authors of numerous scholarly works.[34]

"THE INDIAN'S DANCING ENVOYS"

When I saw Reginald and Gladys Laubin dance at the 1987 Denver powwow, I did not approach them, but kept my distance, with the dismissive arrogance of a young, progressive scholar regarding something unspeakably outdated. And I certainly did not recognize the irony inherent in the fact that at the conference I was the discussant for the session "Replicas and Revivals in Native American Art," despite being ignorant of the Laubins' role in such activities. A dozen years later, I noted with interest Reginald Laubin's obituary in the *New York Times*, complete with a studio photo of him from 1936.[35] Only when I began this book did I discover that theirs was not a simple story of playing Indian, but a complex saga of their relationship not only to the Indian lore movement but also to the development of world dance on the concert stage in the early twentieth century.

Clyde Ellis has ably focused on the Laubins' career within North American hobbyist circles, so I will provide only highlights of that.[36] I will offer a brief look at their place in a modern dance movement that, in the first years of the twentieth century, sought to domesticate the exotic and bring it to audiences worldwide, usually by having non-Natives be stand-ins for real Native people. Because Reginald Laubin was photographed far more often than his wife, and was their spokesperson, I am focusing principally on him.

Reginald Laubin (1903–2000) was perhaps the most high-profile of those who made and wore Plains Indian dress during the twentieth century, particularly from the 1930s through the 1960s, when photos of him, and sometimes his wife, appeared in many publications documenting their dance performances across North America and Europe (see figure 2.4). It is worthwhile considering his role as a dancer as well as a maker of objects. He was born in Detroit and grew up in Lima, Ohio. As a child, he tried to fashion his own Indian garb.[37] This led him to the Boy Scouts, where many boys learned how to make Native-style things, as we have seen. Laubin often recounted the story of being mesmerized by two Native dancers (Gray Wolf, a Sioux, and Red Dog, a Cherokee) whose job it was to dance on the sidewalks of Lima one summer to drum up interest in a documentary film about Indians. He copied their moves and coveted their regalia, immersing himself in every book on Indians he could find in order to make his own apparel.[38]

Orphaned at sixteen, he took up residence with his uncle in Hartford, Connecticut. While attending the nearby Norwich Art School, he met fellow student Gladys Tortoiseshell (1906–1996), who came to share his passion for all things Native.[39] After their marriage in 1928, they drove west in their Ford Model T, spending the summer honeymooning in their tipi, on the land of Ralph Hubbard's Camp Ten-Sleep, in Elbert, Colorado. When Laubin was an Eagle Scout performing in an Indian pageant in 1921, he had first met Hubbard, who, according to Laubin, admired his talent.[40] By 1928, Hubbard was internationally known in the world of Scouting for his work on regalia making and dance performance, so surely the Laubins learned from him.

All their adult lives, the Laubins made their own Plains-style clothing and paraphernalia.[41] In 1996, they donated a collection of some nineteen hundred objects (both Native works and their own Native-style objects) to the Spurlock Museum at the University of Illinois Urbana-Champaign and their personal papers to the university's archives. Some of their work preserved in the museum is well made, though much is just adequate. In some cases, Reginald's work could be characterized as pastiche or collaboration. For example, he might do the beadwork and ribbon work on a purchased pipe stem or make a stem that was then quilled by his Sioux mentor and friend Harriet Iron Bull.[42] He made a mountain lion–skin quiver with arrows, on which he used, in the traditional manner, animal-skin glue on the fletching; his friend from Standing Rock Reservation in Fort Yates, North Dakota, Frank Benjamin Zahn Sr., provided the quilled and beaded rosettes to ornament the quiver.[43]

In the spring of 1934, deciding that they wanted to visit the Sioux reservations to study real Native dress and dance, the Laubins sought advice from the author Walter Stanley Campbell, who had just published a well-received book on Sitting Bull.[44] He suggested which reservations they might visit and the protocol for doing so: bring meat and Bull Durham tobacco, "show good nature and respect," and do not "ask too many pointed questions on short acquaintance." He advised that they look up Zahn at Fort Yates: "a most excellent interpreter, who worked with me and with Ernest Thompson Seton and others."[45]

As a result of this advice, they packed up their car and traveled to Standing

Rock. The Laubins' stature there was achieved accidentally—because of a shield cover Reginald Laubin had painted some years before, one with a lone buffalo head on it. The elderly Oscar Henry One Bull apparently was impressed by the fact that the young man's dance shield bore his own pictographic name. Moreover, according to Laubin, One Bull found the young man's Native-style garments equally impressive, and within days he publicly adopted both Reginald and Gladys, giving Reginald his own name (Tatanka Wanjila) and giving Gladys his mother's name (Good Feather, Wiyaka Wastewin).[46] While specious claims to aboriginal adoption abound in American narratives, this one is hard to question. The Laubins had a long and close relationship with One Bull, sending his family gifts and money and visiting often. In the Laubin Papers is a letter from One Bull. Dated February 9, 1941, and telling him about the death of One Bull's wife, it reads in part, "My dear Son, I'm sorry to say but your mother my wife has died. . . . Your mother had loved you son and also daughter-in-law. She really had taken you as her really son and daughter. . . . I am sending my best regards and a hearty hand shake to you son and daughter. I am your father."[47] Being adopted by One Bull was indeed a lucky break, for this was a most eminent Sioux family. One Bull (ca. 1853–1947) and his older brother White Bull (1849–1947) were born into a Miniconjou family but adopted by the illustrious Hunkpapa warrior Sitting Bull (1831–1890), certainly the most famous Native man at the turn of the twentieth century. So this placed the Laubins in an enviable genealogy, and this "fictive kinship," as anthropologists call family relationships based on affinity rather than consanguinity, underpinned their claim about the authenticity of their work; they always highlighted it in press releases, publications, and flyers about their performances.[48]

Reginald Laubin freely gave credit to One Bull for teaching him about the Sun Dance, the Strong Heart Society, and other matters.[49] Yet in his writings, Laubin was often cagey about where he learned certain skills. It appears that he never liked to admit having learned something from another white person.[50] In contrast, he was often self-congratulatory in recounting how so many Native people he met in the 1930s and 1940s were amazed at what the Laubins knew how to make, and he quotes them as offering tributes, such as "Your skins may be white but your hearts are Indian" and "Our friends, they come up to us and say, 'Are they your relatives from up north who visit you?' They think you are *real* Indians."[51] Such praise is a well-known trope in the story of those who "played Indian."

How did the acclaimed New York dance critic Walter Terry come to call Reginald and Gladys Laubin "the Indian's dancing envoys"?[52] In the late 1920s, the Laubins plotted a way to make their dancing more than a hobby. They developed Indian dance routines, performing in town auditoriums, schools, and eventually on the concert stage.[53] In 1933 and 1934, they danced at Chicago's Century of Progress International Exposition. In the fall of 1934 (just months after their fateful meeting with One Bull), they began to be accepted in the world of concert dance performances, dancing at the Wadsworth Atheneum in Hartford, Connecticut, on November 2, 1934. The Laubins had been dancing professionally for only a few years, so this booking was a pivotal moment for them as they sought to position their work for the concert stage. As many of the printed programs for their events promised: "Many beautiful, rare, and hitherto nearly unknown costumes are used in this performance. These are either genuine Indian articles or exact reproductions made by Mr. Laubin."[54]

Advertisements offering them for bookings were published in many magazines that announced the latest in dance ensembles, singers, and other acts for the stage. Their images, in face paint and long braided wigs, graced the cover of *Program: The Magazine of the American Platform* in January 1948.[55] Billed as "a magazine for program directors and entertainment committees," *Program*, along with *Musical America*, for example, often highlighted the successes of traveling acts such as the Laubins. A full-page ad in the February 10, 1940, issue of *Musical America* is quite typical (figure 2.4). It includes a pose of the Laubins costumed for action, as well as a more natural portrait, with encomia from Boston and Philadelphia newspapers. In February 1940, they were booking for the 1940–41 season, and their popularity is attested to by the announcement "Over 200 Engagements from September, 1939 thru April, 1940."

In the 1940s and 1950s, they continued to dance at many small venues, but in 1947, they also danced at a mecca for modern dance, Jacob's Pillow, in western Massachusetts. The critic Terry pronounced that "Mr. Laubin's closing 'hoop dance,' in which he moved two hoops about his feet, arms, and body while maintaining flawless foot rhythms and highly demanding motor patterns, was as virtuosic as anything I have ever seen, including the ballerina's thirty-two fouettés, and infinitely more beautiful."[56] Laubin typically danced with two to four hoops; in the professional photograph illustrated here, he uses four (figure 2.5).

Advances in motion picture technology after World War II had made filmmaking equipment accessible to a wider (yet still technical) audience;

FIG. 2.4 Reginald and Gladys Laubin, promotional advertisement published in *Musical America*, 1940. Courtesy of the Redpath Chautauqua Collection, Special Collections and University Archives, University of Iowa Libraries.

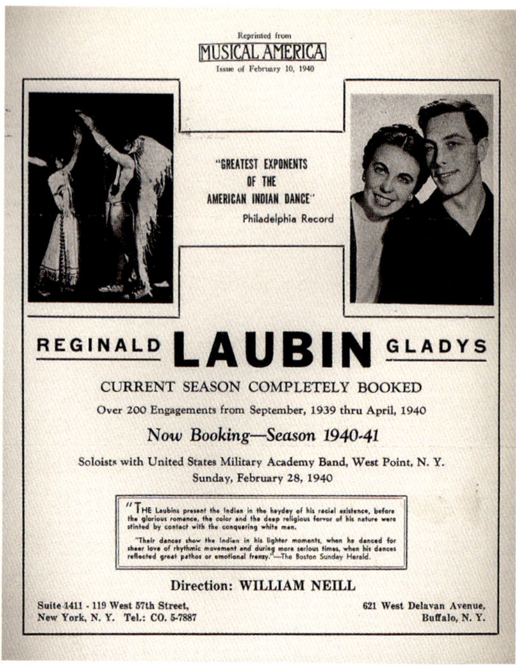

universities were beginning to see educational filmmaking as an outreach initiative. The University of Oklahoma produced three short documentaries featuring the Laubins. A still shot of the making of these shows the filmmakers consulting with them in an open-sided mock-up of their tipi. They wear dramatic face makeup and full Plains garb (as they do in figure 2.1). Behind them, a reproduction of a painted hide forms the backdrop, and a mixture of Native-made objects and their own creations are arrayed around them. The resultant films, *The Old Chief's Dance*, *Talking Hands*, and *War Dance*, varying in length from nine to twenty minutes, were advertised in a 1955 brochure titled *Three Important Films: Plains Indian Culture*.[57]

In the winter of 1953–54, the Laubins, for the first time accompanied by Native performers, gave more than 120 performances in nine countries: Norway, Sweden, Finland, Belgium, France, Italy, Spain, Israel, and Morocco.[58]

FIG. 2.5 Reginald Laubin performing the hoop dance, 1954. Photo by Lewis Benjamin "Squire" Haskins Jr. (1913–1984), Reginald and Gladys Laubin Collection, Spurlock Museum, University of Illinois Urbana-Champaign. Used with permission of Squire Haskins Photography.

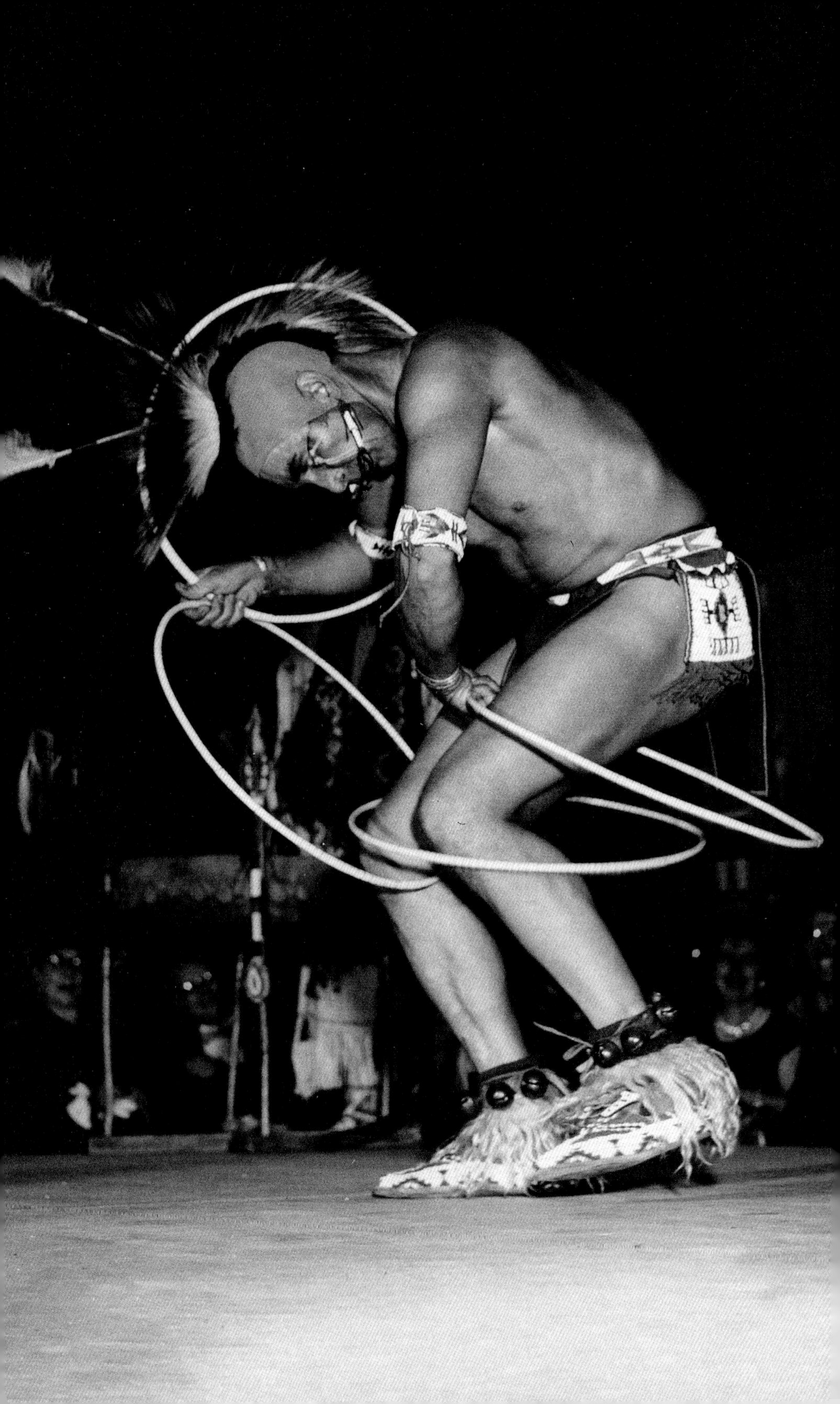

Their schedule for France gives a feel for its hectic pace: they performed on twenty-eight evenings of the month, and on nearly one-third of the days there were matinees as well. About two-thirds of the numbers featured the entire troupe of seven Crow dancers and the Laubins, but Reginald Laubin usually performed at least two solos, including his always well-received hoop dance.

In 1955, the Laubins began a long-running series of summer dance concerts at the newly built Jackson Lake Lodge in Grand Teton National Park, some twenty-five miles north of their log cabin in Moose, Wyoming. Because this park was an important tourist destination, and only a few miles south of Yellowstone, audiences were guaranteed. In the early years, they performed three times a week all summer, "to standing room audiences most of the time at the Lodge and sometimes actually turning people away," as Reginald wrote to a friend.[59] By the 1980s, they performed every Friday evening during July and August. The Laubins danced at Jackson Lake Lodge for thirty-three summers, retiring in 1988 only because Reginald, at eighty-four, felt he no longer had enough stamina in his legs for a vigorous dance program.[60]

The Laubins were such a familiar sight at Jackson Lake Lodge even in the 1950s that popular postcards were sold for decades. In figure 2.1, they pose with older Native friends, Wades in Water and his wife, Julia, a distinguished and well-known Blackfeet couple. Indeed, until recently, an enormous framed photo of the Laubins in their regalia still adorned one of the public rooms at the lodge.[61]

During the 1960s and 1970s, they also continued to perform at schools, museums, and universities and worked on their most ambitious book, *Indian Dances of North America*, published in 1977. Unfortunately, it was outdated by the time of its publication; a new wave of scholarship on Native cultural arts was forming, led by a younger generation, including Native performers themselves. They found value in the changing artistic manifestations of the contemporary moment, rather than reifying the arts of the past as the best and most authentic. Most of the book focuses on the Plains, and most of the twenty-five color plates are of the Laubins themselves. In the conclusion, they do seem to recognize that the days of white people as the exemplars of Native dance are over: "Although we have been doing Indian dancing professionally for years, we do not feel that it is a career to be recommended to non-Indians. In the future, if Indian dancing is to be preserved, the Indians must be encouraged to do it themselves."[62] "The Indians must be encouraged"? The paternalism that always underpinned their work remains in that final exhortation.

"INDIANTHUSIASM" IN GERMANY

Thousands of Germans, mostly male, participate in what the scholar Hartmut Lutz has termed "Indianthusiasm": an essentializing "ethnic identity that ossifies into stereotype" and "tends to historicize Indians as figures of the past."[63] In this way, it has much in common with the actions of American hobbyists and reenactors, but how is it different?

Most scholars who discuss Germans playing Indian in the twentieth and twenty-first centuries simply invoke the best-selling novels of Karl May (1842–1912) to explain the German fascination with Indians of the West. In contrast, the historian H. Glenn Penny has fully documented more than two hundred years of German interest in North American Indians, noting that since the first translations of James Fenimore Cooper's *Leatherstocking Tales* in 1826, Germans have been fascinated with Native North Americans.[64] This was amplified after the publication in 1839 of Prince Maximilian's accounts, with Karl Bodmer's accompanying plates (see figure 3.9). Other nineteenth-century German travelers followed, including Balduin Möllhausen (1825–1905), whose explorations in the West led him to publish not only popular travel accounts but also forty-five novels and sixty-two novellas about the American West that were popular in Germany, and Rudolf Cronau (1855–1939), who spent time with the Standing Rock Sioux in the 1880s and wrote popular books and articles and gave lectures focusing on his special friendship with Sitting Bull.[65]

So by the time May (already a best-selling serialized author with his Orientalist adventure novels of the 1880s, set in the Middle East) began publishing his novels about the Apache chief Winnetou and his white blood-brother Old Shatterhand in 1893, German fascination with the American West was firmly entrenched.[66] May's main talent, according to Penny, was to simplify the many versions of Native identity to which Germans had been exposed before him.[67]

Buffalo Bill's Wild West and other such entertainments were wildly popular in Germany. His company toured the country in the summers of 1890 and 1891; in some venues thousands of people queued every day, for weeks on end, to fill five thousand seats. This tour was repeated in 1906.[68] Other impresarios such as Carl Hagenbeck and Hans Stosch-Sarrasani employed Plains performers, many of them Lakota. The Sarrasani Circus, for example, played across Europe both before and after World War I. Therefore, lodged in the German imagination were not only the fictional Natives of nineteenth-century storytellers but also the real Plains Indians who performed in Germany at the turn of the twentieth century.[69] Out of this grew the modern Indian hobbyist movement, with many regional clubs, some of which convene in national summer camps with thousands of participants and hundreds of tipis set up.

As Penny has demonstrated, Germans have "instrumentalized" American Indians for their own uses in a number of ways. In the 1930s, the National Socialists endorsed May's tales as appropriate for Hitler Youth and embraced Native beadwork and other arts depicting the ancient Native sun sign (the swastika).[70] After the defeat of the Nazis, when large numbers of American servicemen were stationed in Germany, US Army initiatives reached out to citizens in numerous gestures of friendship and cross-cultural understanding. These included powwows, rodeos, and meetings with hobbyists.[71] In figure 2.6, US military men and German hobbyists wear Plains regalia at a meeting of the Heidelberg Ogalala Tribe. Large canvas tipis and replicas of nineteenth-century painted hides are in the background. In the center of the image, an American GI of Native heritage presents a pipe to Chief Willie Linder, a German hobbyist.[72] Compared to the excellence of some of the regalia worn by such hobbyists in the past thirty years, some of what is worn in this photo is quite amateurish. Today, in some clubs, in both Germany and the Czech Republic, the level of skill—especially quillwork skill—is extremely high. Apparently, some contemporary Czech quillwork made within such clubs has even been sold as nineteenth-century originals in Wyoming and elsewhere.[73]

When Lakota artist and scholar Arthur Amiotte (b. 1942) conducted lecture tours in Germany between 2002 and 2010, he encountered many hobbyists. In Dresden in 2002, a man proffered a beaded bag and asked Amiotte to tell him what tribe it was from. Inspecting the bag with the eyes of someone who had studied Plains beadwork for more than four decades, Amiotte replied with his usual quick wit, "I think it was made by a German Hidatsa." "But how could you know this?" the man asked in astonishment, admitting that he had made it. He went on to introduce himself as "chief" of a particular "tribe" of hobbyists. In recalling this man and his beaded bag in 2021, Amiotte said that there are always anachronisms in this kind of work and that the maker had mixed several types and sizes of beads and used colors that would not have been used by a nineteenth-century Hidatsa.[74] Amiotte met two types of hobbyists. He found the first type "ethnological in their precision, giving rise to many fine achievements in beadwork and quillwork." But he went on to note that their work existed in a kind of "ethnographic present," that is to say, the time when Karl Bodmer was on the Great Plains. The second type are die-hard hobbyists.

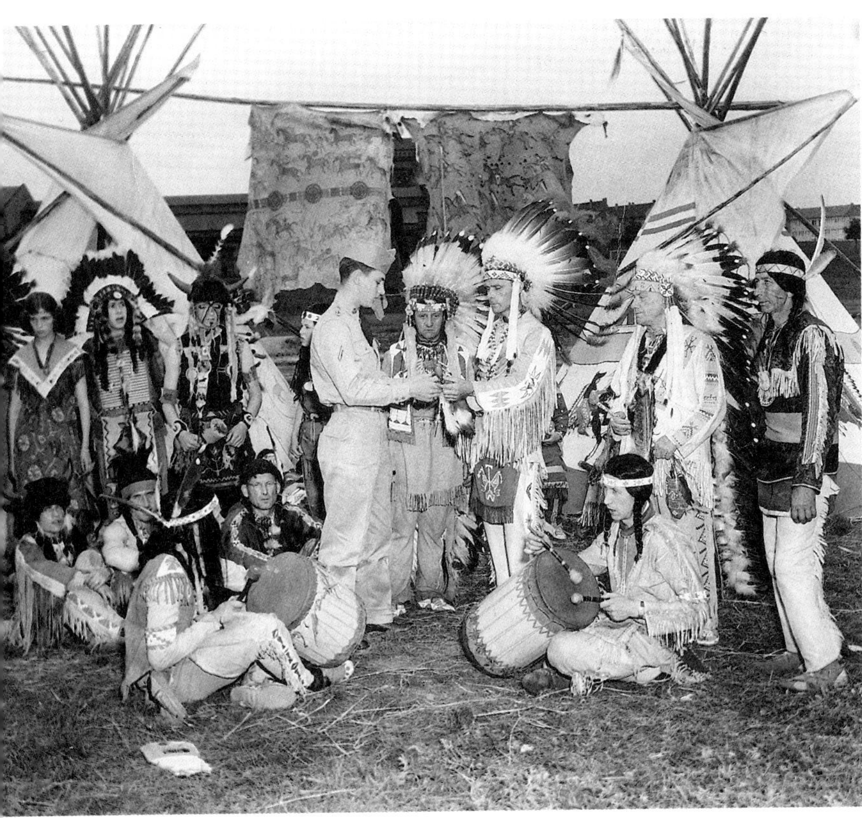

FIG. 2.6 Chief Willie Linder of the Heidelberg Ogalala Tribe presents a peace pipe to a US GI at an Indian jamboree in Mannheim, West Germany, 1956.

"Some of them truly think they are Indians," Amiotte explained. "They take very seriously the idea of having 'an Indian name.' Some recounted to me how one of their forebears had known the Indians in Buffalo Bill's Wild West, or the Sarrasani Circus, as if this gave them some sort of pedigree or credibility." He found this group particularly enamored of writings about Plains spirituality by people who were neither scholars nor Natives. "They love the work of Richard Erdoes and Thomas Mails. They love to do pipe ceremonies and give speeches about their names and their lines of descent."[75] When asked if he found such hobbyists infuriating, Amiotte said that, in fact, he found them entertaining: "But then, I'm not that judgmental, and I have had lots of experiences with American hobbyists. It's clear they respect Indian traditions, and they admire the ideals of Lakota culture. When I did consulting at the

Karl May Museum, the hobbyists took me to the grave of Edward Two-Two, who is buried in Dresden. He was a Lakota with the Sarrasani Circus. I found it noteworthy that those local hobbyists pay the annual fees for his grave site and do the upkeep on his grave."[76]

Penny insists on a complex reading of German hobbyists, noting that not only are they simply mocked or treated in the most superficial fashion by journalists but that even scholars demonstrate a lack of understanding of the complexities of their motivations, how these have changed over time and are different from region to region. The men he interviewed did not consider their activities a "hobby," arguing instead that they are an ethnological association devoted to practical ethnology rather than theoretical anthropology, and, as such, they sought to correct the typical misunderstandings about North American Natives held by ordinary Germans.[77] This echoes Amiotte's observation.

Penny offers the term *surrogate Indigeneity* as a way to understand German Indianthusiasts, suggesting that they act as surrogates not only for the Lakota and other performers who worked in Germany at the beginning of the twentieth century but also for those Natives who have come more recently to work with them as cultural experts and honored guests.[78] The best informed of the German hobbyists have engaged in useful acts of preservation of knowledge and artistic traditions for an audience some five thousand miles from the American West. Since they perform far from the originating point of these traditions, should they be held to different standards than American reenactors such as those examined in the previous section?

Penny's use here of *surrogate* seems apposite. It is a term I used in chapter 1, in relation to a machine-made surrogate of a Tlingit original clan hat (see figure 1.9), which serves to educate Smithsonian visitors about an original object sent back to its legitimate owners in Alaska. Gwyneira Isaac registered her concern about the need for social relationships to be forged when such surrogates are made and used: "Do we replicate the social relationships and obligations embodied by the original?"[79] It seems that some "German Indians" do forge social relationships: they invite Native experts to their meetings and care for the grave of a Lakota who died abroad more than a century ago, for example. One way that some German hobbyists seem quite different from their North American counterparts, in terms of maintaining alliances with Native people, is that not only are many well informed about the political problems besetting contemporary Natives but some seek to help with these problems. This impulse began in the 1960s, when they saw the analogy between American military imperialism in Southeast Asia and the country's internal imperialism toward its indigenous inhabitants. Notably, the American Indian Movement (AIM) opened an office in West Berlin in 1975, and some hobbyists have consistently showed their support for contemporary Native political causes. The novelist Liselotte Welskopf-Henrich (1901–1979) served as a leader in this regard; those who read her very popular novels (an audience that included many hobbyists) were educated about both historical and contemporary issues.[80] Her first series of six books, *Die Söhne der großen Bärin* (Sons of the Great Bear), published beginning in 1951, was set on the Great Plains in the nineteenth century. The second series of five, *Das Blut des Adlers* (Blood of the Eagle), considered problems of twentieth-century Native life and came up to the present, covering its fictional character's involvement in Wounded Knee.

In terms of the relationship of German hobbyists with their country's Nazi past, Lutz posits that Indianthusiasm "provides an ahistorical and guilt-free ideological realm, far removed from the more depressing aspects of German reality past and present. Moreover, it allows Germans to identify with the victims of history, rather than with the victimizers."[81] Yolanda Broyles-González offers a variant of this, based on her years of fieldwork with the Cheyenne Indian club in southwest Germany: she analyzes their actions as a "symbolic response to a situation of social breach and crisis within German society."[82] This is not the Nazism of the Second World War, and Germany's resultant identity crisis, but the crisis of modernity in industrialized Germany today. She describes the predominantly working-class members of the club, who are part of a traditional regional culture (and who speak Allemansch rather than Standard German), as feeling a sense of otherness: "It is the drama of one marginalized people giving expression to that marginalization by re-enacting the experience of another marginalized and subordinate people. The Germans' reenactment of the Cheyennes offers a 'distanced replication' of their own status in greater society and represents, as such, a symbolic action."[83]

Dutch anthropologist Petra Kalshoven is the only scholar writing in English whose work seriously engages with the material world of the Indianthusiasts. Rather than simply using the phrase "playing Indian," she considers theories of play and their deep immersion in making things. To her, their world represents a case study in an "anthropology of the senses," in which they engage deeply and physically with material culture, "exploring sensory realms of the past through the artifice of the replica."[84] Notably, these replicas do not simply exist in museum cases, but live on in new social contexts. Moreover, hobbyists and

FIG. 2.7 Members of the Munich Cowboy Club, photographed by Charles Belden, 1950s. Buffalo Bill Center of the West, Cody, Wyoming, no. P67.1653.3.

replica makers repeatedly told her, using German, Dutch, and French variants of the phrase, that they made "authentic replicas." She found that "the skill of making authentic replicas conferred authority to their makers."[85]

While today reenactors might seek such authority, it was not always so. In the 1950s, Wyoming photographer Charles Belden took photos of the Munich Cowboy Club.[86] It is clear from the photos that the reenactors were buying items of their attire far more often than they were making them. In figure 2.7, two men wear cloth trousers that they may have made themselves. The one on the left wears a fringed buckskin jacket with bands of beadwork on it, of uncertain origin. The two beaded bags at his waist (a small one that is clearly visible and a long pipe bag near his left hand) seem to be real Lakota beadwork. Beneath the beadwork, the pipe bag has bands of Lakota-style wrapped quillwork, which a German man in the 1950s was extremely unlikely to know how to make. The man on the right also wears a long Lakota beaded bag. Both wear Crow-style looped beaded necklaces. The man on the right wears a feathered bonnet with buffalo horns, which is likely Native-made, as are his beaded cuffs. Both the dark-colored bag with floral-style beadwork and the similarly embellished dark vest on the man on the right are likely velvet bags of Great Lakes origin. Where did such regalia come from? Clyde Ellis notes, "There was a pipeline for this material established by any number of trading posts in the U.S. in the 1920s–1940s, and they did a big business with European hobbyists. You could buy fully beaded moccasins for $3.50, whole golden eagles for $12.50, or even full 'chief' costumes."[87] A 1932 catalogue from Pawnee Bill's Indian Trading Post in Pawnee, Oklahoma, lists many such items offered for sale, from warbonnets, war shirts, and buckskin fringed coats to breast plates and beaded cuffs.[88] While scholars writing in the past two decades about German hobbyists stress their working-class backgrounds, the clothing in the 1950s photos makes it seem likely that, in that era, far more prosperous German men engaged in this hobby.

In 1988, the acclaimed folklorist Rayna Green (of Cherokee descent, b. 1942) wrote the first widely cited essay on whites playing Indian, "The Tribe Called Wannabee." She called playing Indian not only "an illness" but "an epidemic," asking rhetorically, "What would Americans or Germans play, if they could not play Indian?"[89] Notably, her essay was published in America's

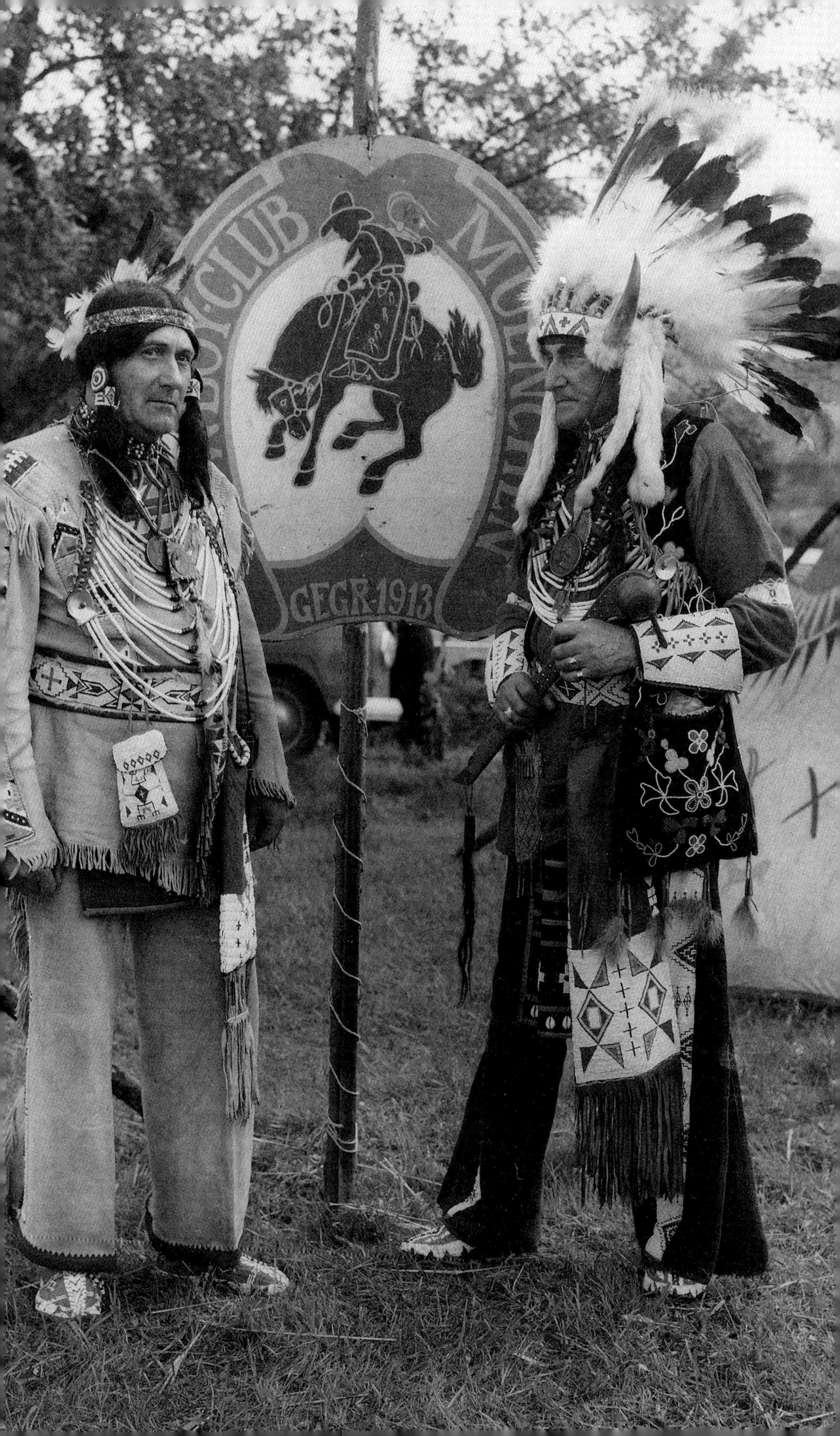
CLUB
GEGR·1913

premiere journal of folklore. Playing Indian might not seem to fit within a popular definition of what folklore is, yet the American Folklore Society defines folk traditions as things that people believe, do, and make that are vernacular rather than "high culture" and that are specifically valued as not modern.[90]

More somber to ponder is Green's assertion that playing Indian is the obverse of genocide.[91] One of the definitions of *obverse* is "the counterpart of a fact or a truth." If, like Reginald Laubin, you believe that there are no Indians who can dance as you can, so you find it easy to proclaim yourself "more Indian than the Indians," is this a form of cultural genocide? If, in your mind, authentic Indians are ones who live in tipi encampments, wear quills and feathers, and look as if they emerged from a Bodmer watercolor, you implicitly believe that real Indians are gone; therefore, you have the right to stand in for them. Is this a form of psychological genocide? Many would argue that this is so.

I end this section with an image from the world of contemporary art photography. Andrea Robbins (American, b. 1963) and Max Becher (German, b. 1964) completed a photo series in 1997–98 called *German Indians*. Shot at the annual celebration of the novelist Karl May's birthday in Radebeul, Germany, the series documents what the artists call a "transportation of place"—the uncanny desire that people have for making identities across temporal and geographical dislocations. Their photos of aging German men dressed as Lakota chiefs and middle-aged blond women in beaded hide dresses have garnered praise in the art world.[92] But I was drawn to the more modest image reproduced here—an open suitcase as an emblem of this "transportation of place" (figure 2.8). In this image, the idea of transportation is literal. The regalia of a man who plays Indian is carefully packed in a battered leather suitcase, which sits open on trampled grass in front of a canvas tipi. His large beaded moccasins with calico trim are at left, next to a red wool trade cloth blanket. The fringes of a hide shirt peek out from beneath the blanket. At the front, a pipe stem, studded with metal brads, fits tightly in the case. Equally fascinating are the printed materials adorning his suitcase. A business card from the Karl May Museum is taped at right, inside the lid. The outside of the case bears a host of stickers. Prominent among them are ones proclaiming, *Nimm's leicht, nimm mich* (Take it easy, take me) and *Nimm mit mich* (Take me along). The year before this photo was taken, Austrian pop singer Jazz Gitti had a best-selling album, *Nimm's leicht*.

The diverse identities of the suitcase's owner collide in this poignant photo. He is likely a late middle-aged man with a taste for the light pop music favored

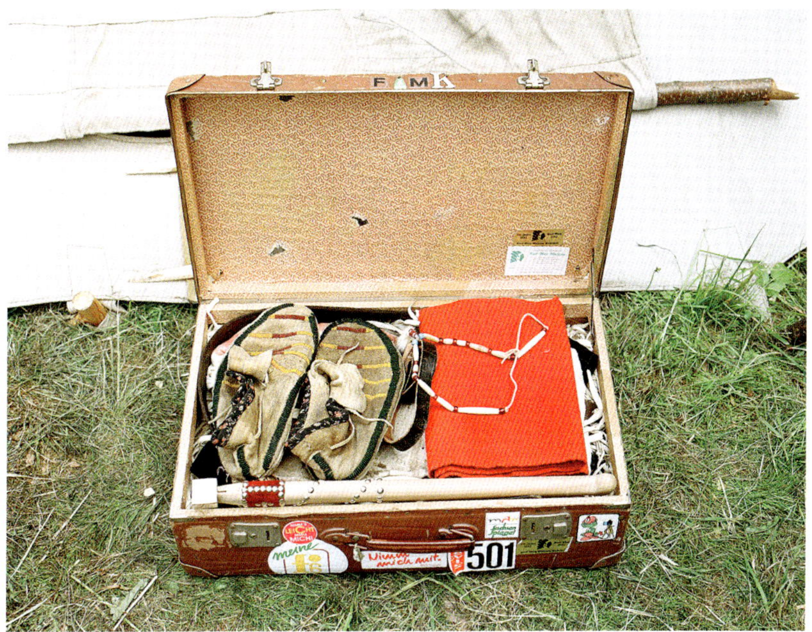

FIG. 2.8 Andrea Robbins and Max Becher, "Suitcase," from the series *German Indians*, 1997–98. Chromogenic print, 35 × 30 in.

by his generation. He probably has "played Indian" every summer for decades. But one can also read the stickers as the suitcase itself proclaiming to its owner, "Take me along," that is, take your alternative identity in this battered case and enjoy being transported to another century and another continent. One ineluctable fact about Indianthusiasm is also captured in this photo: when this identity becomes inconvenient, it can be tucked away in a suitcase. German Indians need not worry about racism, prejudice, or casual violence against them because of their skin color. This skin is easily shed. Like the American blackface of white performers a century ago, it is an identity easily inhabited and just as easily denied.

PLAYING INDIAN IN NEW YORK STATE IN THE TWENTY-FIRST CENTURY

Since the American bicentennial, many Americans have engaged in the hobbyist movement of historical reenactments. This involves scrupulous attention to the most minute aspects of dress, food, and other aspects of material culture to give both participants and onlookers a feel of authenticity.

The North American subculture of reenacting is a large one. Civil War reenactors are the best known and the largest, but thousands of people take part in eighteenth-century reenactments, though these have not given rise to a corresponding analytical literature by scholars or encyclopedic literature by practitioners.[93] In July 2009, I attended my first reenactment, where some two thousand participants (mostly men) assembled for several days on the shore of Lake Ontario to commemorate the 250th anniversary of the siege of Fort Niagara near Lewiston, New York. For a scholar of Native American art history, this was a rare opportunity to see replicas of objects well known to me from books and museum cases. But here, they were worn, carried, traded, and well used. Men like those in West's painting of Guy Johnson walked the pathways within the walls of the fort. Vendors in period dress sold cloth, buttons, finger-twined sashes, wampum, unworked cow horns, and finished powder horns. They eagerly shared their knowledge of how to make such things. Decades ago, it had been ingrained in me to value knowledge gained by years in the library or in fieldwork. More recently, I have come to value the deep knowledge of Indigenous makers and scholars. But white car mechanics and high school teachers who impersonate Indians and have deep knowledge of the objects they made? My world was decentered, yet I was intrigued.

The long legacy of impersonation of Indians in disrespectful contexts, as chronicled elsewhere in this book, makes many people extremely leery of the idea of white men performing reenactments in Native guise. Their motives are questioned: Do they know what they are doing? Where do they get their information? Is it accurate, or do they succumb to the same uninformed fantasies about Native peoples that the rest of American culture falls prey to? At the reenactments I have attended since 2009, I certainly have met the occasional white man who falls into stereotyped behavior, but most do not. Paradoxically, not only are many of the white men who engage in such practices well versed in Native material culture, but they are also extremely knowledgeable about the central role of Native peoples in American history (as are the reenactors of Native heritage; see chapter 5).

Fort Niagara was a pivotal place for relations between Haudenosaunee, French, British, and then American peoples, from the late seventeenth to the early nineteenth century. The French first built there in 1679 and sought permission from the Seneca to build a stone trading post in 1720. The British gained control in 1759, during the French and Indian War, and then it went back and forth between the British and the Americans until 1815.[94] All of this rich history offers many opportunities for reenactment, and participating in events there as a reenactor is carefully controlled.

Participation is by invitation of the Old Fort Niagara Association, and participants must live up to the association's rigorous standards of authenticity, which forbid anachronisms in dress or accoutrements. These were outlined in a document available online before the French and Indian War Encampment (July 5–7, 2019) that I attended as a paying visitor. Participants attending as Native reenactors (regardless of their ethnicity) had to scrupulously follow standards ranging from "best" to "unacceptable" in categories including clothing, hairstyles, accessories, and weaponry. For breechclouts, for example, the standards were as follows: "*Best*: Breechclout of stroud or wool broadcloth, light decoration with silk ribbon and ring brooches acceptable, in red, blue, black, or green. Clouts should end at midthigh. *Discouraged*: Excessively long clouts, over-decorated clouts, clouts in other colors, breeches. *Unacceptable*: Trousers, leather breechclouts."[95]

During prime reenacting season (May through October), one can crisscross New York State and Pennsylvania, attending numerous reenactments of eighteenth- and early nineteenth-century historical events. Some reenactors do so, devoting most of their leisure time to their historical pursuits. On August 24, 2019, I attended a reenactment of the Battle of Newtown, which commemorates one of the decisive victories in the infamous Sullivan Campaign of the summer of 1779. Best known for its "scorched earth" attack on some forty Haudenosaunee towns in which homes, cornfields, and storehouses were destroyed and entire orchards cut down, this genocidal campaign routed many Haudenosaunee from New York. They then fled to British territory across the border. Unlike Civil War reenactments, which often stage battles in which tens of thousands of men died, the numbers of dead here were quite small, yet the battle was key to the success of George Washington's plan to exterminate the Six Nations. As he unequivocally wrote to Major General John Sullivan at the start of the summer: "The immediate objects are the total destruction and devastation of their settlements and the capture of as many prisoners of every age and sex as possible."[96]

The main event that most visitors come to see at this reenactment, held near Elmira, New York, is the skirmishing in the woods between British Loyalists and their Haudenosaunee allies and the New York and New Hampshire brigades of the American revolutionary forces. The loud report of muskets and rifles and the smell of gunpowder made for a realistic display.[97] I was far more interested in the encampment, where one could talk with the individual participants. While I spoke with several, I focus here on just two: Jack Andrus and Duane Saxton (figure 2.9), both of whom play Haudenosaunee men in the annual reenactment of the Battle of Newtown.[98] Both are too old to fight in the woods; they leave that to the younger men.

I interviewed Andrus at this reenactment shortly before his eighty-seventh birthday. Like many reenactors I interviewed, he claims a distant Native heritage; he told me that his grandfather's birth certificate said "baby boy Wabanaki." He has been doing reenacting for more than three decades, using the Native moniker "Bark Eater." Tremendously knowledgeable about colonial and Native histories, Andrus taught history in public schools as a young man and then had a long career in the military, teaching about nuclear, biological, and chemical warfare. Part of the French Creek Living History Association (named for French Creek, a tributary of the Allegheny in northwestern Pennsylvania

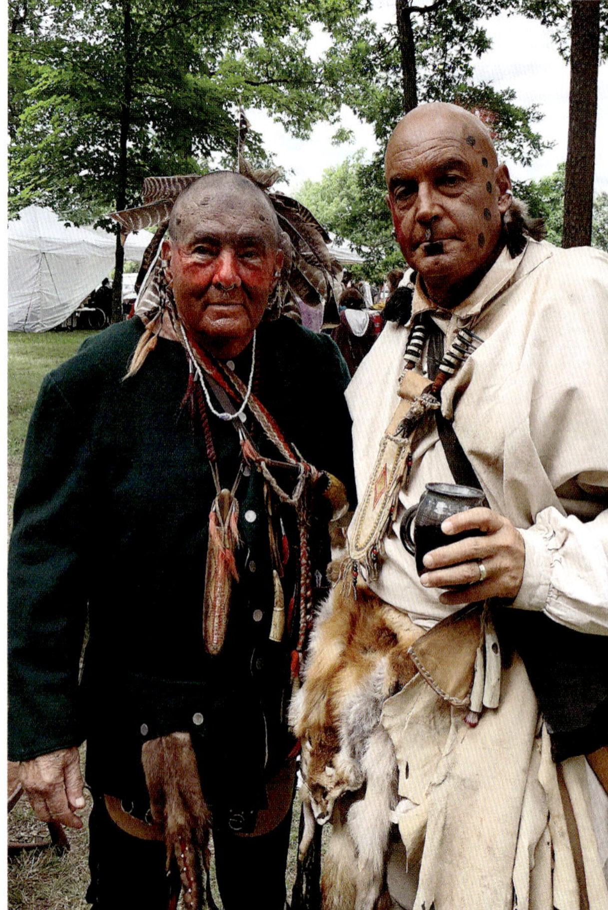

FIG. 2.9 Reenactors Jack Andrus and Duane Saxton, reenactment of the 1779 Battle of Newtown, August 24, 2019. Photo by author.

and western New York State), for years he typically would participate in reenactor events almost once a month, but now, in his late eighties, he does far less. Andrus's mostly bald head was shaved, and red pigment painted across his upper cheeks, eyes, and nose. He wore typical intercultural garb: wampum knee garters, a wool cloth tailored coat, and feathers in the small hank of hair at the back of his head. Like almost all his peers, he wore a quilled knife sheath, and his etched powder horn was of the type used by both Native and white men in the eighteenth century. Surprisingly, he was one of the few reenactors I interviewed who did not make his own regalia, but bought it from others.

More than two decades younger, Saxton described Andrus as his mentor; both live near Elmira. Saxton began reenacting in the mid-1980s, when his five-year-old son was so impressed with a Civil War reenactment that he said, "Daddy, let's do this!" Saxton found being part of a reenactment, such as that done at Gettysburg, to be awe-inspiring: "There were historical-era tents as far as the eye could see, and it was amazing to be part of history like that." He is involved in the Chemung Valley Living History Center, in Elmira, and reported that about twenty years ago one of the organizers told him, "I have a hide tanner, and an artillery guy, but I don't have a Native reenactor," so he decided to focus on that and to learn all he could about it.[99] He was particularly interested in hide tanning and in woodland cookery; as we talked, he served me some tasty woodchuck stew, bubbling over a campfire. His ornaments featured animal parts more than elaborate artistry. His knife had an antler handle, and the necklace holding its sheath was decorated with deer antler beads and bear claws.

A close friend attended some of the events at Fort Niagara and Newtown Battlefield State Park with me in 2019. More than twenty-five years earlier, he had visited an encampment of German Indian reenactors while motorcycling across Germany. His take on all these scenes was that of an astute viewer, but not a scholar: "All these guys remind me of an American Camaro Club, where the members happily debate the merits of a 1971 car or a 1972 car, and which bits were different."[100] He observed that it did not seem to matter what the "bits" in question were; the participants held in common a type of classificatory mind in which each aspect of the material world that fascinated them was carefully catalogued and endlessly discussed. In the case of the reenactors, to this we can add that the items were enthusiastically reproduced and worn as well.

"MASKING INDIAN": BLACK MARDI GRAS PERFORMERS IN NEW ORLEANS

A world apart from white American hobbyists and reenactors or German Indianthusiasts are the African American men who "mask Indian" for Mardi Gras in New Orleans. In 2016, Monk Boudreaux (Joseph Pierre Boudreaux, b. 1941) was honored with a National Endowment for the Arts National Heritage Fellowship for his work as a Mardi Gras Indian performer, craftsman, and musician (figure 2.10). Such fellowships recognize "master folk and traditional artists who have made significant contributions to our nation's traditional arts heritage."[101] Boudreaux is the "big chief" of the Golden Eagles, one of several dozen "tribes" of Mardi Gras Indians active in New Orleans since at least the end of the nineteenth century. Featured on National Public Radio, in several popular documentaries, and in the hit HBO television series *Treme*, Mardi Gras Indians today surely are the best-known non-Native group that "plays Indian." They also seem to be the least criticized, for their performances are in no way recognizable as mimicry of real Native art or experience. Nor can their dress be seen as appropriation of real Plains regalia. How did a late nineteenth-century adaptation of Plains Indian garb effect a transformation a century later into "traditional heritage" of African Americans in Louisiana?

While the performances of Mardi Gras Indians were documented in New Orleans newspapers as early as the beginning of the twentieth century, it was not until the 1980s that they received widespread attention by scholars, museums, filmmakers, and photographers.[102] It was clear to scholars that the flowering of a local carnival practice that featured feathered headdresses and intensely beaded garments was a response to the daily performances of Buffalo Bill's Wild West in New Orleans from December 1884 through April 1885. In addition to regularly scheduled performances for which spectators had to pay admission, mounted cowboys and Plains Indian warriors took part in some free street parades.[103] Moreover, the documentary photographer Michael P. Smith states that fifty to sixty Indians from the Wild West entourage, "including four chiefs," were "on the streets in their native dress during the Mardi Gras of 1885," though he cites no source for this assertion.[104]

Photos from the first half of the twentieth century reveal "suits" (as they are called by their wearers) of far less complexity than those of recent decades.[105] In the earlier suits, turkey feather headdresses and beaded and fringed items of dress still revealed the shape of the body. Within the past half century, those

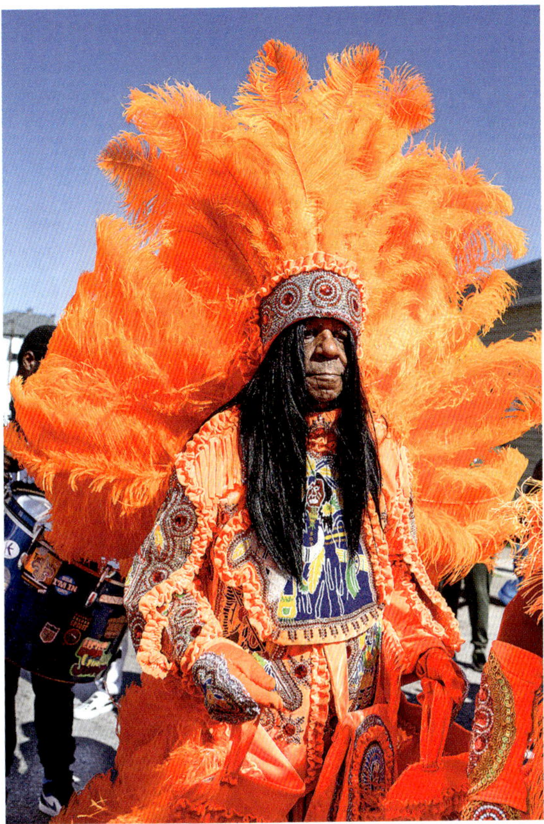

FIG. 2.10 Monk Boudreaux "masking Indian" at New Orleans Mardi Gras, March 2022. Photo by Robert N. Brown.

who "mask Indian" have been putting on a visual spectacle as impressive as anything seen at carnival in Rio de Janeiro or Port of Spain, though as the masker Larry E. Bannock told the filmmaker Karen Morell on the day before Mardi Gras in 1986, "In Brazil, the costumes are beautiful, but in each group, mostly all the suits [are] alike. Tomorrow morning, you not going to see no two Indian suits alike."[106] To make a resplendent suit involves hundreds of dyed ostrich feathers affixed to the outfit, as well as numerous beaded and sequined patches sewn to headgear, vests, aprons, leggings, boots, fans, wings, artificial hair braids, shields, and staffs.

Resplendent in bright saturated reds, yellows, blues, and purples, or even just dazzling white, the troupes include a big chief, often accompanied by his queen, a "spy boy" (who functions like a Plains Indian scout, clearing the way of danger), and others, which may include children and grandchildren also splendidly dressed. Spy boys wear remarkable costumes, too, and some go on to become big chiefs—the ones getting the most attention and garnering the most fame. Boudreaux recounted how he began by helping his father don his suit and then started sewing his own suit by age twelve.[107]

In 2022, Boudreaux favored bright orange as the color of choice for his costume (figure 2.10) and those of his retinue. Sequined panels adorned his headgear, arms, and gloves. The beaded panel on his chest was one he had worn before: a Native man in feathered headgear and dance attire. Men traditionally make their own suits and criticize those who do not. To put on a fine show, it is imperative always to appear in something new. Beaded panels may be recycled: what was on the chest one year may appear on another part of the body another year.

Suits often weigh more than one hundred pounds and represent a financial investment of several thousand dollars. The jazz musician Jelly Roll Morton (born Ferdinand LaMothe, 1890–1941) served as a spy boy in his youth, an era when violence and bloodshed sometimes broke out between rival tribes. But even then, aesthetic competition was paramount. He said that the main objective was "to make the enemy bow down."[108] When the rival tribes come marching down the street, swaying and swirling, and singing in a typical African American call-and-response pattern, rival big chiefs come right up into each other's faces, improvising rhymes and new riffs on their songs and challenging who is the "prettiest." The rival tribe will then "bow down" before the winner. Surely an insufficient term for these dazzling sartorial displays, "pretty" is the compliment of choice. In the film *All on a Mardi Gras Day* (2019), Big Chief Demond Melancon says, "Who prettier than pretty? You gonna kill 'em with that needle and thread!" and "You gotta be disciplined to learn the needle dance." Or, as Melancon states, "Needle and thread, kill 'em dead! A needle and thread, that's my gun."[109]

While images of Plains warriors, tipis, eagles, and the like are most common, not all of the imagery on the beaded patches is Plains related; it is up to the imagination of the creator. Sometimes Native imagery of the Southeast or African imagery appears. Designs can arise in the imagination, from books, or from a visit to a museum, where a real Native art object might inspire a new patch, as Bannock said of one of his patches in 1986.[110]

Just as many whites who play Indian claim "a bit of Indian blood," so do some of the urban Black residents of New Orleans who "mask Indian," as they call it.[111] It is indisputable that the lives and fortunes of Native and African peoples were intertwined in the lower Mississippi River area for centuries. These maskers could possibly be drawing on a cultural heritage that harks back to situations in which runaway slaves sought refuge with Native nations in southern Louisiana. Some scant few early images as well as some of the names these maskers gave their groups in the twentieth century (Black Cherokee, Seminole Hunters, Choctaw Hunters, Wild Tchoupitoulas) suggest that local Indigenous peoples were on the minds of these masqueraders when they began donning "Indian" regalia. Yet it seems clear that the Mardi Gras Indians are an "invented tradition" (or, more specifically, that they feature an invented genealogy of a tradition), using a term popularized by British historians Eric Hobsbawm and Terence Ranger.[112] Well known throughout the world, this involves the making of a backstory that legitimizes one's actions, and ultimately believing that story, irrespective of other compelling evidence.

The contemporary popular narratives of Native and Black history that accompany the Mardi Gras Indians are too often one-dimensional. In interviews, some maskers note, "We honor our ancestors and also the Native Americans who helped our ancestors."[113] A version of history in which dispossessed Indigenous people and enslaved former Africans conspired against white oppressors belies the complexities of more than three centuries in what is today southern Louisiana. As the historian Daniel Usner has demonstrated, alliances were ever shifting. Some Native people were enslaved or enslaved others. Sometimes enslaved Africans fled to Indian communities and were sheltered there. In other cases, Natives allied to the colonial powers hunted and returned fugitive slaves for reward money, and enslaved Blacks were sometimes recruited to attack Indigenous villages.[114] Some Native nations, including the Choctaw, maintained strong diplomatic and economic relations with the ruling class of colonial Louisiana until the removal era of the 1830s, but by 1904, fewer than one hundred Choctaw remained in Louisiana.[115] It seems unlikely that the Mardi Gras Indians were drawing from visual elements of local Native culture at the end of the nineteenth century, when few such visual elements remained. In contrast, what a revelation the mounted Plains warriors in feathered headgear and beaded vests and moccasins who paraded through New Orleans in 1884–85 must have been! Nonetheless, many maskers today resent the narrative that attributes their visual splendor to Buffalo Bill's Wild West, as if it somehow takes away from their own creativity and legitimacy.[116]

Mardi Gras Indians perform at carnival and on the Catholic Feast Day of St. Joseph.[117] Some are also well-known musicians who perform in their regalia;

others are hired for notable occasions, from the opening of new bookstores to jazz festivals and sporting events. And, of course, in true New Orleans tradition, they come out for the funerals of big chiefs.

A Mardi Gras Indian is far more of an "Imaginary Indian," so to speak, than most non-Natives who don Native regalia.[118] Were it not for the iconography of the beaded patches, some viewers might be hard-pressed to connect these visual extravagances to Plains Indians. The look is part of an aesthetics of abundant and exuberant display characteristic of carnival costume across the Caribbean, as well as in New York, in London, and elsewhere that carnival is inflected by Afro-Caribbean visual schemes.[119]

Unlike American hobbyists and German Indians who seek out precise historical information and living Indigenous people as advisers, the "Indian" in Mardi Gras Indians is just the seed of an idea that has germinated into a true New Orleans folk cultural expression rooted in the working lives of generations of Black men who have suffered racial oppression. It strikes me as significant that although the term *masking Indians* is common, no faces are masked here, and few are painted. The masking is of every other part of the body *except* for the face. It is important that the individual visages of these African American performers are visible, for the performance is principally about acclaim for and recognition of the "prettiest" big chief and his tribe. Just as I quoted Broyles-González as characterizing German Indianthusiasm as one marginalized group reenacting the life of another, it is evident that the original impetus for the Mardi Gras Indians—and perhaps their staying power as a distinctly working-class African American experience—is that the North American Indian, and most specifically the Plains Indian warrior, is an idealized surrogate. This surrogate was popularized worldwide by Buffalo Bill's Wild West, but it was also promulgated in the movie and television westerns of a twentieth-century American childhood, including that lived in working-class segregated neighborhoods in New Orleans. Perhaps the example of a proud Native people who also suffered and fought oppression at the hands of whites gave voice to that which otherwise could not be voiced. The Plains Indian is a proxy for the oppressed African American. And the spectacular version of Indigeneity (in both senses of the term, in its beauty and its extravagance) parading, drumming, and singing in the streets of Black neighborhoods is a way of saying "we will not bow down," not to rivals, and not to oppressors.

Conclusion: Cultural Cross-Dressing as "Benign Colonialism"?

In 1996, Chicano performance artist Guillermo Gómez-Peña (b. 1955) wrote that, in addition to blatant and malignant forms of colonial oppression, "Americans and Europeans have often performed *involuntary* colonialist roles. In their desire to help, they often unknowingly become ventriloquists, impresarios, *flaneurs*, messiahs, or cultural transvestites. Though painful, these forms of benign colonialism must be discussed openly . . . but without accusing anyone."[120] Such discussions, he exhorts, must form part of the "heroic project of forgiving and therefore healing our colonial and post-colonial wounds." This is a generous assessment of the actions of performers, reenactors, and others who have "played Indian" in various ways. In this chapter, I have examined cultural cross-dressers ranging from the white performer of Native dances to the white historical reenactor of Native personae to the Black Mardi Gras Indian. I have shown that while their motives are diverse, none of the modern or contemporary figures seem to be doing anything remotely like the complex, nuanced intercultural exchanges of the eighteenth-century "men of the middle ground." Moreover, I find it hard to reconcile the joy they express in their knowledge, their regalia, and their hobby with the fact that many Native people find their actions to be offensive. The one exception seems to be the exuberant Mardi Gras Indians, whose representation has morphed into something so distant from its origin in Plains imagery that it stands somewhat apart from all the others, in its recognition of the shared centuries of oppression at the hands of the dominant culture.

In 1992, Gómez-Peña and Coco Fusco (Cuban American, b. 1960) performed a piece about two indigenous Americans behind bars, *The Couple in the Cage: Two Undiscovered Amerindians Visit the West*. It was widely celebrated—and widely misunderstood—everywhere it was performed during the American quincentennial. Some viewers thought it was an actual display of Native people, like those so common during the nineteenth century. Gómez-Peña and Fusco have talked about the ways that the piece touches on colonial wounds and "stands in a place between ethnography and pornography."[121]

They, too, were playing Indian—but were taking on fictional personae that never existed—except in the minds of Euro-Americans. The reason that white men playing Indian in whatever context—halftime sports performances, the concert stage in the mid-twentieth century, the Black Forest today—enflames colonial wounds for Native people is that such performances provide a collective trigger for five centuries of cultural trauma of which most non-Native people have little understanding. Today, many people are sensitive to the notion of "triggering trauma" on a personal level, but the concept of a *collective* cultural trauma is equally important and has been theorized in psychiatry, sociology, and history. The sociologist Jeffrey C. Alexander provides a succinct definition: "Cultural trauma occurs when members of a collectivity feel they have been subjected to a horrendous event that leaves indelible marks upon their group consciousness, marking their memories forever and changing their future identity in fundamental and irrevocable ways."[122] What is the solution when cultural cross-dressers believe that what they do is not only harmless but also educational, despite the fact that some members of the groups they are impersonating find their actions painful?

Another way to characterize playing Indian is by the notion of "ethnic drag" espoused by German scholar Katrin Sieg, who defines this as "the impersonation of ethnic others by a subject that stages and conceals its dominance." She suggests that while such actors may invoke "multiculturalism" (or perhaps, as Gómez-Peña would put it, a "benign colonialism"), what they do "excludes the material bodies of cultural others, and subsumes the markers of difference (turban, skin color) under 'universal meanings.'"[123] The men who play Indian in the twenty-first century, whether in New York State or in Germany, are doing something that is outside the mainstream. They are often mocked or censured, though in this case the censure is by progressive scholars or Native peoples, or both, rather than by forces of cultural conservatism. Taking on these personae is no doubt liberatory for these enactors, but at what cost to others?

One feminist critique of drag has something to offer here: it argues that drag does not actually subvert constricting gender roles, but rather provides a sometimes cruel reification of women's experience that actually reinforces gender stereotypes; in other words, it might be entertaining and freeing for those who practice and view it, but it is alienating and offensive to many women.[124] So, too, ethnic drag, of the sort practiced by non-Natives playing Indian, actually reinforces the dominant cultural belief that Indians are in the past and cannot speak for themselves. They require white interlocutors who perform a kind of cultural ventriloquism in which they take a lifeless dummy—the nineteenth-century image in the popular imaginary of the Indian chief—and breathe life into it. This is quite different from the Mardi Gras Indians and, as I discuss in chapter 5, Native people themselves making and donning historical regalia in order to animate the past and educate others.

The performance studies scholar Diana Taylor, in her influential book *The Archive and the Repertoire*, challenges us to seriously examine the important relationship between embodied performance and the production of knowledge. While the post-Enlightenment West places a higher value on archival ways of knowing (books and documents), she defines the repertoire as "a non-archival system of transfer." Performance is a very effective episteme (a way of knowing) and a very effective system of producing and transferring knowledge.[125] Enactment makes certain stories highly visible, as well as attractive to those who may not otherwise encounter them. Embodied memories are long-lasting and visceral. But Taylor urges us to recognize that embodied performance "transmits as many layers of meaning as there are spectators, participants, and witnesses."[126] To this list I would add "scholars who seek to turn them into archival knowledge." Taylor examines case studies in which performance can encourage a false identification with certain scenarios that then gets used politically. Indeed, performance readily participates in the transmission of traumatic memory, both in the case of keeping holocaust history relevant and alive, for example, and in the case of perpetuating and reenacting a cultural trauma, as I have argued is the case for performances of Native identity by non-Native people.

Here, we might consider the seemingly inflammatory insights of two Indigenous commentators: Gómez-Peña's striking remark about a type of performance that stands between ethnography and pornography, and Rayna Green's comment cited earlier that playing Indian is the obverse of genocide. Pornography? Genocide? Most participants and onlookers in various sorts of enactments of Indianness would be shocked by such characterizations, but perhaps these are not far from the truth. The theater historian Joseph Roach, in his magisterial book *Cities of the Dead: Circum-Atlantic Performance*, reminds us that the function of the surrogated aboriginal is to disappear.[127] The long-lived American trope of the Vanishing Indian allows others to step in, to perform acts of surrogate performance, ventriloquism, and artistic reproduction, until it looks like the original actors, makers, and users have all but disappeared. But, of course, they have not.

Coda: The Hoop Dance on the World Stage

I end this chapter with an image that talks back to all these cultural cross-dressers. While Reginald and Gladys Laubin may have been the first to perform

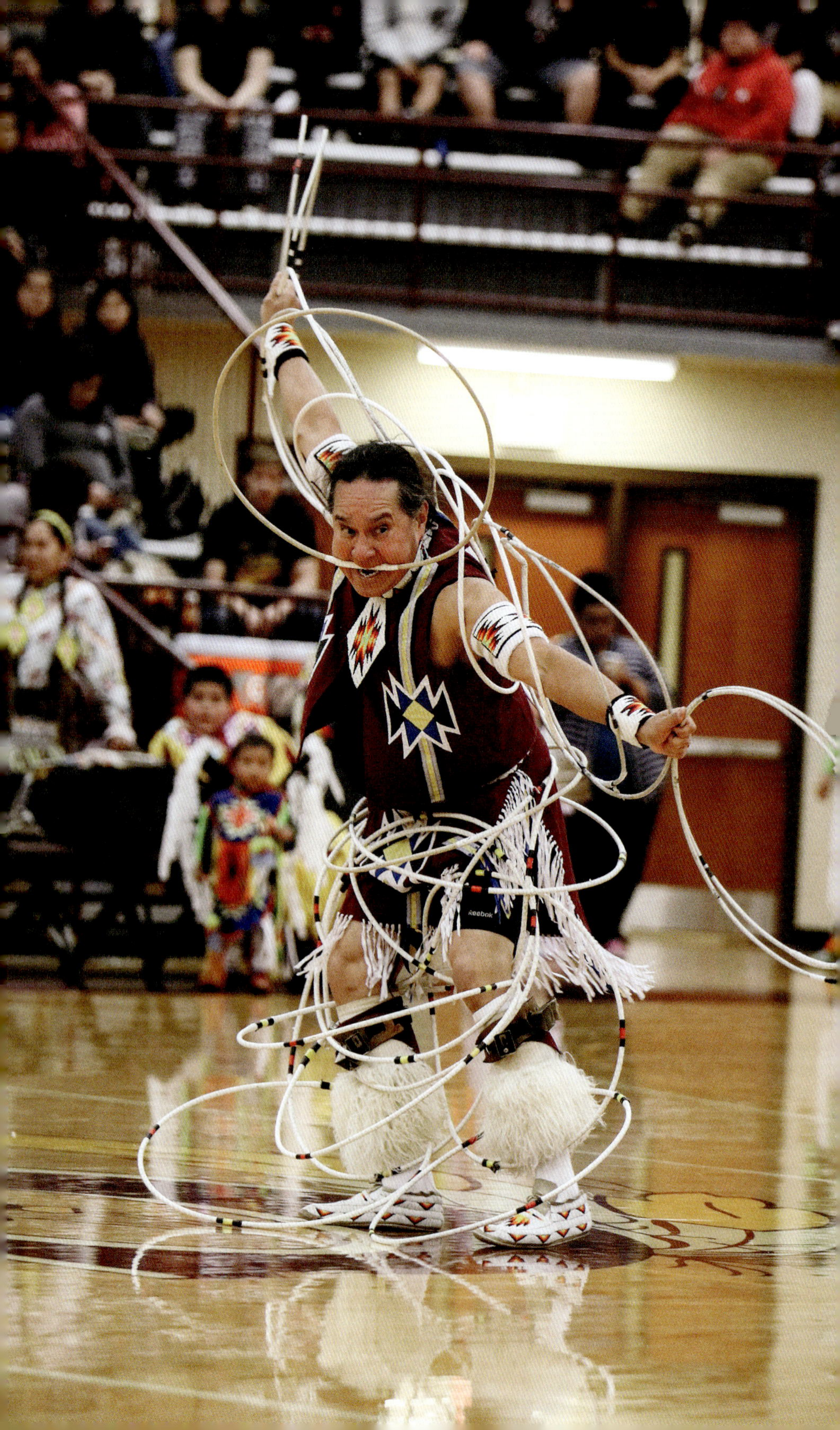
Reebok

FIG. 2.11 Eddie Swimmer, Cherokee hoop dancer, 2017. Photo by Scott McKie Brings Plenty, *Cherokee One Feather*.

Native dance at Jacob's Pillow, they were by no means the last. In August 1995, American Indian Dance Theatre was on the program, and Eddie Swimmer (Cherokee, b. 1961) performed the hoop dance, as Reginald Laubin had done nearly fifty years before.[128] Swimmer, a member of the group's inaugural company in 1987, won the first World Hoop Dance Championship in 1991 and was the model for the hoop dancer in the US Postal Service's Native Dance series in 1996. Whereas Laubin (and most early hoop dancers) used just a few hoops, Swimmer is renowned for his ability to dance with some three dozen hoops (figure 2.11).[129]

Writing that the origin of the hoop dance is unclear, and that different regions have historically used one, two, or four hoops, the Laubins remarked disparagingly, "Nowadays dancers use ten, twelve, or even fifteen hoops, so the dance has now merely become a stunt, and the symbolism as well as the style and beauty of movement has all but disappeared. We just heard of a hoop dancer who is using twenty-four hoops!"[130] Those who treasure the memory of Hopi-Tewa hoop dancer Nakotah LaRance (1989–2020) and those who admire the artistry of Swimmer would classify Reginald Laubin's two-hoop dance as a stunt and the work of Swimmer and LaRance as supreme, cosmopolitan Native artistry, equally alive and at home in the powwow arena, on YouTube, or at Jacob's Pillow.[131] The authentic Dancing Indian lives on.

3
Replication and Reproduction on the Great Plains of Nostalgia

In the spring of 1996, on my way home from visiting my dear friend Lakota artist Arthur Amiotte in Custer, South Dakota, I sought to bring my then husband a small memento of my trip. Its selection was more fraught than would ordinarily be the case, for while I was traveling, his long-ailing father had died. On the way to the airport in Rapid City, I stopped at Prairie Edge and Sioux Trading Post, a well-known source for contemporary Northern Plains art, replicas of historic pieces, and better-than-average souvenirs. In a pedantic gesture acknowledging—if only to myself—the role of the miniature in the circuits of tourist art worldwide, I bought a tiny painted shield (figure 3.1). Simplistically and hurriedly, I thought, "a tiny war shield for my courageous guy." This gesture implicated me in a long history of nostalgic appropriations of male emblems of Plains Indian culture, all of which are saturated with romantic ideas about bravery, stoicism, and masculinity in the minds of those who seek to use them as their own.

The miniature, as many scholars have noted, shrinks a symbol down to a manageable size. The distinguished anthropologist Claude Lévi-Strauss, in his classic essay "The Science of the Concrete," says that by such actions we exercise power over an alien thing; to shrink it down is to render it "less formidable." Similarly, for the literary critic Susan Stewart, the miniature is "manipulatable" and "domesticated." And the art historian Ruth B. Phillips demonstrates that from the era of eighteenth-century cabinets of curiosity to contemporary tourist items, the miniature has always been a metonym for Indianness itself, giving "the *illusion* of a complete understanding" (emphasis mine).[1]

While this shield is a true miniature, most of the examples in this chapter are metaphorical miniatures of one sort or another. Their makers seem to want to represent the essence of a noble Plains identity—to distill the courage and nobility from one version of the past and re-present it in a nostalgic form for their own use. While this may not always be a conscious aim, I believe that, in so doing, they are trying, in a small personal way, to redeem a violent and messy history of American aggression against Native people.

I seek to understand how replication and proliferation have unfolded in transcultural contexts. Nowhere is the appropriation and romanticization of Native imagery and attributes more widespread and deeply entrenched than with regard to the Lakota, Crow, Kiowa, and other nations of the American West. The Plains Indian is *the* stereotype of Native people in the American imaginary.[2] An entire book could be devoted to the replication and circulation of Plains imagery in North American culture; I focus on particular shields and shirts to highlight connections and repetitions across temporal and geographic realms and to demonstrate that certain replicative impulses have remained robust in American culture for over two hundred years.

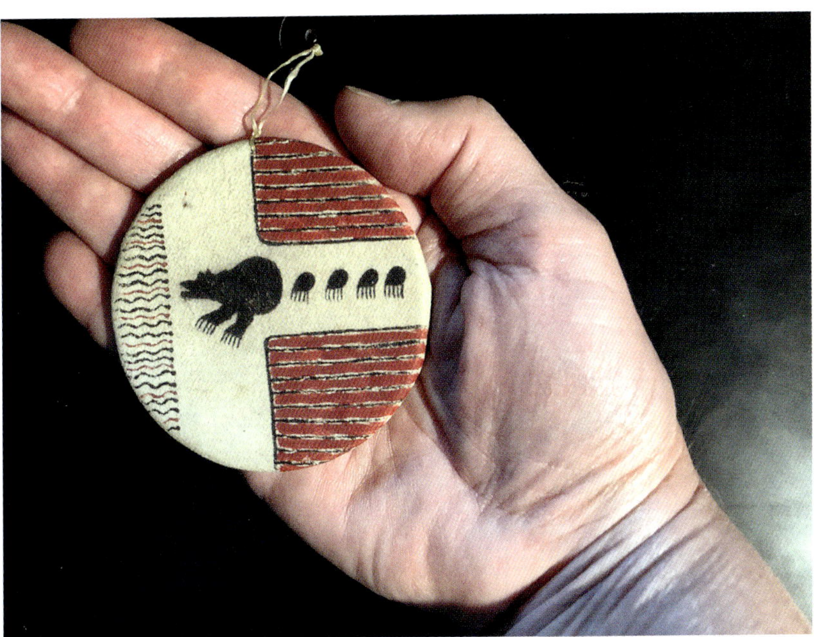

FIG. 3.1 Miniature shield painted with Crow bear design. Painted buckskin sewn with commercial sinew. 2⅞ in. diameter. Purchased at Prairie Edge, Rapid City, South Dakota, 1996. Author's collection

FIG. 3.2 Crow shield cover, ca. 1860, Montana. Tanned deer hide and pigments, beads, wool, flicker feather. 21½ in. diameter. Courtesy of the Buffalo Bill Center of the West, Cody, Wyoming, no. NA.108.105.

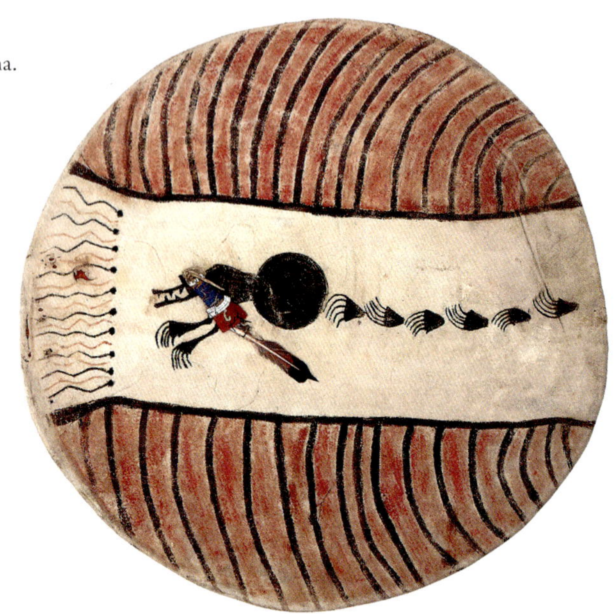

Big Bear's Shield and Its Progeny

When I purchased the miniature shield at Prairie Edge (figure 3.1), I recognized it as a replica of one I had seen in exhibition catalogues, but I thought little more about it until I was outlining this chapter more than fifteen years later. Then I discovered that it is one of many multicultural progeny of a Crow shield that perhaps originated in the eighteenth century. All of these offspring, each in its own way, sought to draw from the power of the original.

In 1901–2, Stephen Simms (1863–1937) undertook a collecting trip to the Crow Reservation in Montana, to gather a collection of Crow shields for the Field Museum of Natural History in Chicago, where he was curator of ethnology. He acquired some sixty-eight painted shields and shield covers from individual Crow people. Some are plain, or modestly painted, while others feature bold figural designs.[3] On one that had belonged to the Crow warrior Big Bear, a grizzly bear faces a fusillade of bullets. The bear is squeezed between two painted areas of the shield's surface, one red, one green, each with ten curving rib-like brown lines.

Simms collected at least three versions of this shield. A second depicts the bear emerging from a striped enclosure and rushing at a fusillade of thirty-two bullets.[4] A third, collected from a man named Plain Owl, is today in the Plains Indian Museum at the Buffalo Bill Center of the West in Cody, Wyoming.[5] The upper and lower thirds are both painted red, and the bear faces ten flying bullets (figure 3.2). While today we think of museum collections as sacrosanct (except for deaccessioning for repatriation), it was not uncommon before 1960 for museums to sell objects out of their collections or to exchange so-called duplicates with other institutions, thus adding a noteworthy detour to biographies of certain objects. Nearly one-third of the Field Museum's Crow shields were sold to private collectors or traded to other museums.[6] When Milford Chandler worked briefly for the Field Museum in the early 1920s, he bought Plain Owl's shield and later sold it to Richard A. Pohrt.[7]

Why three versions of what was essentially one shield image? In Crow practices, the idea of making replicas—or alternative versions—was acceptable even before white collectors came and offered money for such items. The anthropologist Robert Lowie, who worked very closely with elderly Crow men from 1907 to 1917, reported on Crow medicine objects in general, of which shields were one category: "Though sacred objects were almost uniformly derived from revelations ultimately, many individuals owned medicines which they had merely bought from the original visionary or even second-hand from another purchaser. When a person saw another man prospering on the acquisition of some medicine, he would be tempted to acquire the medicine also in order to share the owner's success. In such cases, the visionary made copies for the buyers to the number of four; with the fourth replica he lost his property rights."[8] This suggests that, according to Crow belief, limited power abides in a visionary object, power that fades with too much replication, or the further away that the object moves from the original dreamer. While some of the shields Simms purchased showed signs of wear, and some were said to have been handed down through families, it is likely that others were new. In 1988, members of the Crow cultural commission who saw the Field Museum shields thought that some may have been made specifically for sale, because of their vivid colors and unworn condition.[9]

The right to replicate Crow shield designs took an intertribal turn in the late eighteenth century, when the Kiowa lived in the Black Hills of South Dakota and were neighbors to the Crow. Typically on the Plains, captured enemy regalia became the new owner's property, with the right to wear and

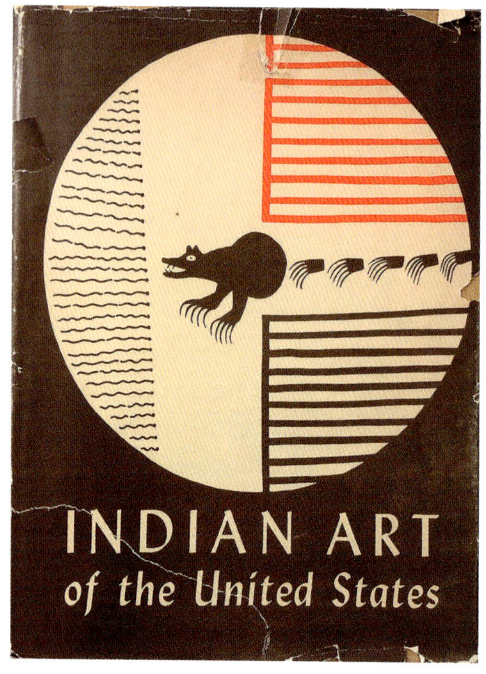

FIG. 3.3 Dust jacket of *Indian Art of the United States* catalogue, Museum of Modern Art, New York, 1941. Illustration by Miguel Covarrubias. Author's collection.

display it. So perhaps during one battle, a Kiowa warrior earned the rights to replicate and carry this bear design. More than a century later, in 1904, the ethnologist James Mooney commissioned from his Kiowa consultants in Oklahoma several shields, among them the Crow bear shield. This one gained national attention when it was displayed at the Museum of Modern Art in its acclaimed 1941 *Indian Art of the United States* exhibit and a drawing of it graced the catalogue's dust jacket (figure 3.3). Here the colored and striped portion of the background is limited to the right-hand side of the shield, and the bear faces many more bullets. The Kiowa understood this to have originally been a Crow shield and noted that they had "captured it before they had been removed to the south."[10]

Illustrations of all these versions have appeared in important publications. Big Bear's shield from the Field Museum was illustrated in Norman Feder's *American Indian Art* in 1971, in the influential 1972 exhibit catalogue *American Indian Art: Form and Tradition*, and in *Visions of the People*, a major traveling show in 1992.[11] Books and catalogues of museum exhibitions are a key visual source for those who replicate (and fake) art objects, of course. Yet hobbyists made replicas long before the publication of lavishly illustrated books. Reginald Laubin made a copy of the Crow bear shield in 1933 modeled after Big Bear's shield in the Field Museum. Not particularly well crafted or painted, it is a studio prop, made to be used in onstage dance performances and seen from a distance.[12] To the original design, Laubin added feathers wrapped in leather thongs and tied to the edges. I do not know if Laubin ever examined the shields in the Field Museum, but he did know Chandler and most likely handled and copied the one that Chandler had bought from the Field Museum.

In 2011, when first researching this chapter, I googled the Prairie Edge website (something that did not exist, of course, in 1996 when I made my purchase) and discovered that my little shield, still in stock, was one of a dozen "mini shields," many recognizable as famous war shields of the past now held in museums or published in exhibition catalogues.[13] The explanation on the website for the bear shield read at that time: "Bears were honored as a lordly spirit, noted for their bravery and fighting strength. By putting the bear on his shield, the warrior received the bear's attributes in battle. This design shows the bear at the entrance of a cave protecting his family from the attack of its enemy. This mini shield is based on a Kiowa design."[14] Moreover, the website was careful to indicate the ethnicity of the makers ("Dan and Lynelle Chapman, Sturgis, SD, Non-Native"). The information that it is "based on a Kiowa design" suggests that in the genealogy of images, the makers had looked at the Museum of Modern Art catalogue, the most prominent place to illustrate and list it as Kiowa. I find it noteworthy that the "artist" of such a small item is noted. In 2019, as I finished this chapter, Prairie Edge no longer sold the miniatures, but a full-size replica of the Kiowa shield, also by Dan Chapman, was offered for $250. It is embellished with red wool trade cloth, and a bead and piece of deer antler hang from a medicine bag containing "buffalo hair, sage, sweetgrass, and a buffalo tooth," reminiscent of the small medicine bag amulets that grace some of the original Crow shields.[15] Imitation eagle feathers hang from the bottom.

This examination of the bear shield as an object type reveals its incredible social mobility: first within Crow society and then beyond—with the Kiowa and then to white imitators for use variously as an object in dance performance, an object of admiration to hang on a collector's wall, or a miniature token of affection. Each successor finds a way to draw spiritual power, cultural capital, status, economic gain, or aesthetic pleasure from the way the shield mirrors either the original or one of the others in the chain of replication. The Crow bear shield continues to generate diverse offspring. For example, Choctaw artist Marcus Amerman, best known for his beaded portraits, made a full-size fused glass version of this shield, which was exhibited at the Brooklyn Museum in 2011.[16]

Nostalgia's Emporium: Prairie Edge Trading Company

The lure of Plains object-types on the non-Native imagination is nowhere more evident than at Prairie Edge and Sioux Trading Post, in Rapid City, South Dakota. Just a quick detour from Interstate 90, it is a well-known tourist destination. The building sports a twelve-foot hand-lettered sign on its east facade proclaiming: "Buffalo skulls and robes, beadwork, jewelry, books, tapes, gifts, cards, craft supplies, hide paintings, world's largest collection of Italian glass beads, quillwork, original art, prints, posters." Yet this litany hardly captures the flavor of its interior, for in its Native American Gallery, the largest and most dazzling part of the first floor, the visitor is overwhelmed by scores of re-creations of past glories of Plains Indian art (figure 3.4). Well lit, with a two-story ceiling, it manages to convey both the spaciousness of an art gallery and the exuberant overflow of a department store. Here, objects reflecting the apogee of Plains Indian glory are within reach of middle-class collectors, who can feed their acquisitive hunger engendered by too many museums with quilled war shirts locked in glass cases, too many old western movies where mounted warriors wear feathered headdresses, and too many Edward Curtis photos of noble Sioux in beaded regalia.

The requisite feathered warbonnets, replete with imitation eagle feathers (usually painted turkey feathers), are always on display. During my first research visit in 2011, a series of painted and beaded hides were mounted on the west wall. These included a forty-two-inch-long deer hide robe embellished with beads and ermine skins, a bearskin robe ("commercially tanned with all parts intact including the claws"), and the magisterially named "Seven Generations Buffalo Robe," which extended almost eight feet in length.[17] Ranging in price from $799 to $3,300, each offered the artist's name and cultural affiliation in the supporting documentation. Prairie Edge carries work by both Native and non-Native artists. As is required by the Indian Arts and Crafts Act of 1990, each work of art is labeled with the tribal affiliation (or lack of it—"non-Native artist") of its maker. Prairie Edge—unlike some stores in other tourist

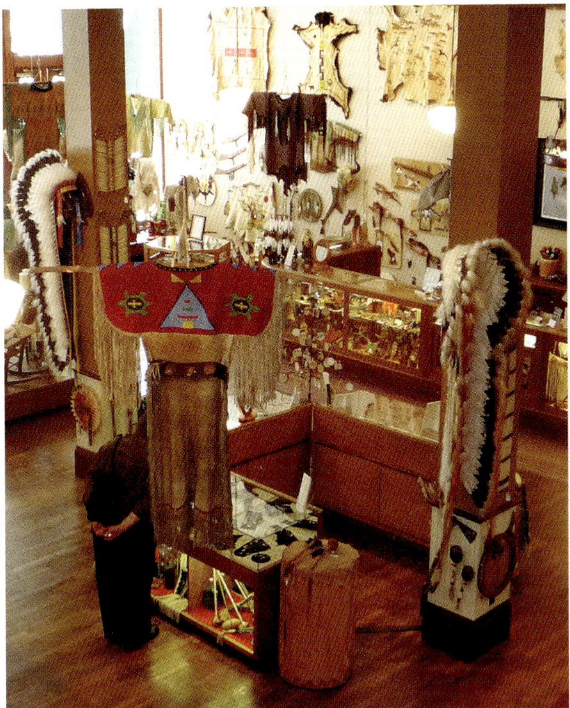

FIG. 3.4 View of Native American Gallery from mezzanine, at Prairie Edge Trading Company and Galleries, Rapid City, South Dakota, June 2011. Photo by author.

destinations, such as Santa Fe and Scottsdale—has always been scrupulous about adhering to this protocol.

Prairie Edge has grown to be the largest and most respected venue for Plains regalia destined for home display. All of it is contemporary, and much of it is made by Native artists. The store provides a livelihood for many Native artists who live in the area, which has long been economically depressed. But rather than focus on the sales venue for such artists, and the economic boost given to downtown Rapid City by a store as successful as Prairie Edge, I seek to elucidate the canny marketing that plays to modern nostalgia and romance about the Plains Indian undergirding this enterprise. To do so, I focus on the works made by non-Native artists, one of whom, Dan Chapman, was the founder of the business that became Prairie Edge.[18]

In 1979, Chapman was one of two men in Sturgis, South Dakota, who started a mail-order company to wholesale buffalo skulls.[19] This developed into Prairie Edge. In 1993, Ray Hillenbrand (1934–2019), a wealthy entrepreneur

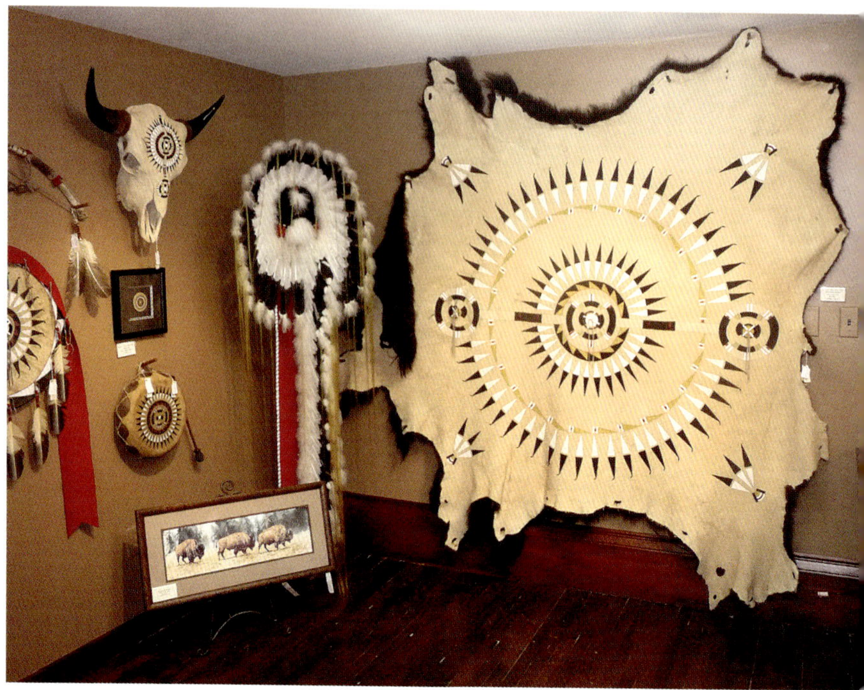

FIG. 3.5 Black War Bonnet Society Collection, Prairie Edge Trading Company and Galleries, June 2011. Photo by author.

and ranch owner, purchased the store, providing the capital to substantially enlarge the enterprise. Hillebrand had noted that there were numerous national outlets for the sale of Southwestern arts, yet nothing comparable existed for Northern Plains arts. He sought to provide such a venue for high-quality work, both one-of-a-kind pieces by Native artists and work by non-Natives who adhered to Native traditions.[20] Today, his daughter Mimi Hillenbrand owns the store.

The various components of Prairie Edge offer something for every price range. On the first floor is an affordable shop featuring T-shirts, cards, jewelry, and mugs. Behind that is the Sioux Trading Post, where many Native people come to buy beads, jewelry findings, hides, thread, and other materials, and the Native American Gallery, already described. Upstairs, a mezzanine and second floor offer books, CDs, and DVDs on Native American culture and the West, as well as a remarkable glass bead library.[21] Two-dimensional works of art are also sold upstairs, including prints, collages, and contemporary "ledger art," that is, drawings made on historical ledger pages in the style of this late nineteenth-century genre. Nothing is avant-garde or daring; nearly everything bears a relationship to historic arts of the Great Plains.

In the reception area and conference room of the private second-floor office suite, objects from Prairie Edge's permanent collection (not for sale) were on display. The Native Art Gallery manager characterized the permanent collection as a way to illustrate to prospective artists the level of quality Prairie Edge expects. These works of art also enhance the corporate, upscale ambience of the offices. Among the works in the permanent collection on display in 2011 were painted hides by contemporary Native artists and a hide robe and woman's dress quilled by Chris Ravenshead, one of the most accomplished non-Native masters of contemporary quillwork.

In addition to its retail store, Prairie Edge has a robust internet presence, serving customers worldwide. A glossy brochure for the store is found in hotel, restaurant, and highway information racks across South Dakota. In the first sentence of the brochure, Prairie Edge positions itself: "Some think of this place as a Native American art gallery. Others see it as an authentic trading post reminiscent of days gone by." Its use of a passive, distancing language ("some think of it . . .") suggests an omniscient third person, rather than a marketing team. The all-important word *authentic* occurs repeatedly, and the potential visitor is promised "an experience that lasts forever."

Not all of the artwork offered at Prairie Edge is, strictly speaking, "traditional" in medium or subject matter. As the hybrid art of the reservation era has become more well known among the buying public, and has achieved higher prices at auction, so too have contemporary replica makers taken up those hybrid forms, including ledger drawings, beaded chairs, and quilled valises.

Representatives from Prairie Edge make annual buying trips to the Crow Reservation in nearby Montana. Native artists passing through Rapid City, perhaps on their way to a powwow or to the annual Crow Fair, stop in to offer their work. Some of the works by artists represented by Prairie Edge for many years are remarkable, such as the fine beaded cradles by Kevin D. Fast Horse, which sell for as much as $4,000 apiece. But far more interesting from the point of view of the cultural politics of nostalgia are the somewhat less costly replicas made principally by non-Native artists such as Dan Chapman and Dan Skinner. Lynn Thomas, manager of the Native American Gallery, referred to these as the "baseline collections," from which I inferred that they could be replicated multiple times; having been featured for years in the widely distributed print catalogue (no longer issued), they were best sellers.[22] These are not marketed as multiples on the internet, where each seems to be offered as an individual work of art. In the store, however, the pieces of each collection are displayed together, in a manner that suggests the furnishings of a western-style room. Three of the baseline collections that were popular in 2011 were the Black War Bonnet Society, the Crazy Horse, and the Ghost Dance Collections. I will focus only on the first of these.

In 2011, the Black War Bonnet Society Collection was arrayed handsomely in a corner (figure 3.5). In a restrained black-and-white color scheme, the collection consisted of a large buffalo hide ($1,910), a shield ($355), a drum ($212), and a bison skull ($380), all painted with radiating feather designs. (These items, at slightly higher prices, were still available a decade later.) There is a miniature shield as well ($28), which can also be purchased in a black shadow box frame ($95). A trailing feather headdress completes the installation.

All of the pieces in this collection listed Chapman, often in conjunction with Skinner, as the maker. In 2011, the manager of the Native American Gallery seemed uncomfortable with my use of the word *copies* to characterize these pieces, reminding me that each was painted by hand. "They represent stories," she insisted.[23] She did admit, of course, that they are reproduced over and over and can be made to any size that the customer needs.

In 2022, Dan Tribby, general manager of Prairie Edge, emphasized that today he hires mostly young Native people who want to be artists and trains them. For example, Chapman would give them a beginning skill set: how to make a shield out of willow hoops and rawhide. Once they had mastered that, they were on their own to come up with a memorable design. "The decoration is what makes it special," Tribby observed. "We recognized a long time ago that we have to invest in the artists. Whether they are Native or non-Native, they come to Prairie Edge because it is a cool environment. No one here will subject them to racism or disrespect."[24]

In the ubiquitous marketing parlance of twenty-first-century "boutique capitalism," as we might call it, commercialization veils its inexorable force by means of personalization: the Martha Stewart Collection at Kmart, the Franklin Mint Collection, or the Thomas Kinkade Collection. But even reproductions engender knockoffs. When I asked the manager of the Native Arts Gallery about copycats, she was elusive, saying only, "It is always flattering to be copied."[25] But on other websites I found Black War Bonnet Society hides and shields that looked remarkably like those made by Chapman, all at competitive prices. No scholar or Lakota of my acquaintance has ever heard of such a warrior society among any Indigenous group on the Plains. So these are replicas of replicas of a nonexistent original.

As a private company, Prairie Edge's annual sales are not made public. The Hillenbrands are among Rapid City's most prominent citizens, whose family holdings and investment partnerships are significant. For many years, Ray Hillenbrand was also chairman of the board of Destination Rapid City, and he developed a rundown property east of Prairie Edge into a park, Main Street Square. Its vision statement promised that Main Street Square would be "the keystone for revitalizing the city as well as a destination on The Great American Road Trip."[26] Today it is the site of many events, including Native POP: People of the Plains, a juried art show.[27] Marketing nostalgia is big business. And the great American road trip is not complete without a stop at an emporium of Native nostalgia, in a stunningly apt location, on Main Street, in the heartland of the United States.

The long-held desire to "play Indian" by appropriating Native customs and donning Native-style garments is deeply engrained in the national psyche of the United States. To own a piece of Indian art, even at second or third remove, as in the apparently specious Black War Bonnet Society Collection, or a miniature replica of a bear shield, is to be invested in a recuperation of America's sad history—seemingly to show oneself as a proponent of Native culture. But for some, knowing and owning is not enough. Keeping alive the means of making Indian art is central to their mission.

Nostalgia's Master Craftspeople

"QUILLWORK BUILT THIS HOUSE": THE ART OF CHRIS RAVENSHEAD

While prowling the Prairie Edge website in 2011, I came across a remarkable Métis coat, ornamented with quilled designs (figure 3.6). Arising from the relationships of eighteenth- and nineteenth-century French fur trappers and Native women across the Northern Plains and the Great Lakes, Métis art conjoined the quill- and beadwork techniques of aboriginal women and the tailored clothing styles of their white consorts.[28] The maker of the coat was identified as "Chris Ravenshead, non–Native American, Custer, SD." I was traveling to Custer just six weeks later and was eager to interview the man who made this coat (figure 3.7).

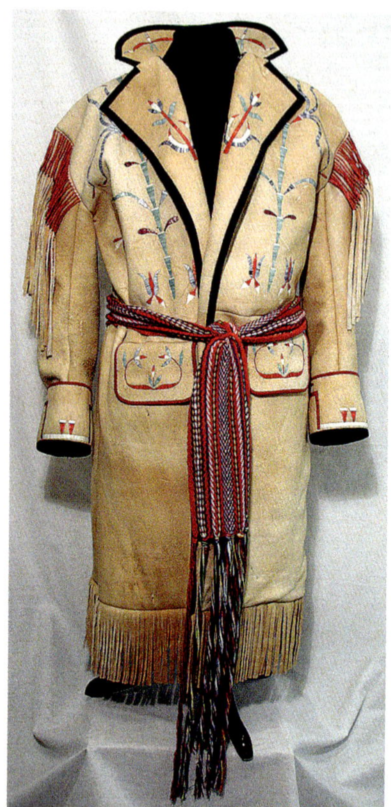
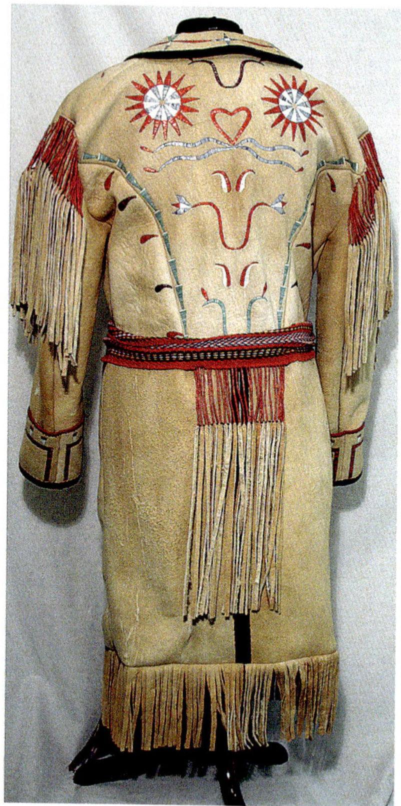

FIG. 3.6 Chris Ravenshead, Métis coat offered for sale at Prairie Edge Trading Company and Galleries, 2011.

Ravenshead lives in a modest home on a gravel road some twenty miles south of Custer.[29] In 2011, the household included his wife, Dayneta "Neta" Bald Eagle; their three adolescent daughters; and a menagerie of dogs, cats, ducks, and other animals. Born in 1957 in Belgium, Ravenshead is Walloon (a French-speaking subgroup in Belgium) and grew up in Rochefort and Brussels. While serving in the army in 1976, he came on vacation to South Dakota to visit a Belgian friend, Josee Kesteman, who had married David Bald Eagle (1919–2016), a prominent Miniconjou Lakota living on the Cheyenne River Sioux Reservation. Fascinated by life in the American West, Ravenshead went home to finish his military service, came back to South Dakota "for a three-month visit," and never looked back. He married one of Bald Eagle's daughters, and they lived at first on the Cheyenne River Reservation. There he found old people still using traditional materials to make art, but few of the young people were interested in that. "I studied with a woman who was so traditional, she didn't even like to use a needle. She preferred to use an awl [to pierce the hide for beadwork or quillwork]. I told her 'You could use a needle, you know,' and she said to me, 'It's not the Lakota way.'"

Ravenshead learned not only quillwork and beadwork from his teachers but Lakota and English as well. "Lakota is easier for a French speaker—a lot of the sounds are the same," he says. When Neta Bald Eagle teases him that he speaks English like an old Lakota lady, he smiles and says softly, "Well, that's where I learned it." He started by making small, contemporary, touristy items, but increasingly became interested in historic clothing and regalia. He has been making items to sell at Prairie Edge "almost since the beginning of that store," he says. One of the most accomplished non-Native quill workers, Ravenshead makes his living fashioning replicas of shirts, bags, robes, and other items and doing restoration work on old garments and regalia. The day I spoke with him, he was restoring a nineteenth-century beaded calf's-head bag. When my questions about his work apparently suggested doubts about its economic viability, Bald Eagle proudly told me, "Quillwork built this house."

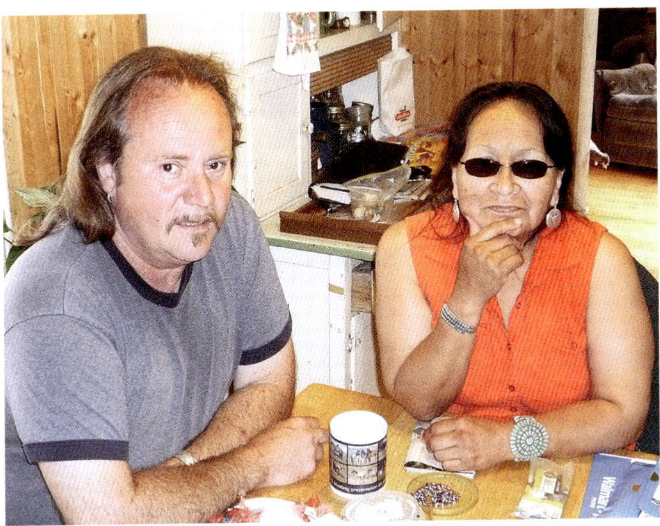

FIG. 3.7 Chris Ravenshead and Neta Bald Eagle in their South Dakota home, 2011. Photo by author.

When inexpensive beads came into widespread use on the Great Plains in the second half of the nineteenth century, quillwork diminished in importance; in many places it was almost an unknown art by the mid-twentieth century. Some Lakota women continued to do it, and Ravenshead was taught by those women. There has been something of a small renaissance of quillwork on the Northern Plains in the past few decades, and he is clearly part of that movement.[30] If beadwork takes patience and dexterity, quillwork demands these qualities in spades. It begins with shooting a porcupine and plucking its quills. "I harvested porcupines when I lived on the Cheyenne River Reservation," Ravenshead recalled. But in his current home in southwest South Dakota, there are no porcupines. So he buys quills from trappers now. Ravenshead dyes them himself, principally with aniline dyes, as Lakota women have been doing for about 150 years. Occasionally, in his museum replica work, natural dyes are requested for older pieces, and he knows traditional dye methods too.

Ravenshead is skilled at all of the quillwork techniques. Most often he uses spot-stitching: the hide is stitched with long parallel rows of sinew thread, and the flattened quills are wrapped beneath the two rows of threads, with the points tucked and neatly hidden. He is also adept at plaiting quills to produce a diamond-shaped woven design. Proud of the fact that his work is sinew sewn, Ravenshead remarked that most bead workers and quill workers use commercial thread: "Not very many take the time to use sinew." He harvests sinew from deer he shoots himself. He mischievously asks me if I know how to tell when the sinew is dry enough. Not waiting for a reply, he says, "I do like the Lakota ladies taught me—stick it against the fridge. When it falls off, it is ready." He demonstrated how to separate a strand of sinew from the dried deer tendon: first the tendon must be twisted and crumpled with the hands to separate a strand, then the strand needs to be worked with the fingers to remove the flaky membrane. Noting that saliva is far superior to water for moistening the sinew, he passes a strand through his mouth and then works a twist into the strand by rubbing it across his thigh, using the same gesture that Navajo spinners use to twist their yarn.

Ravenshead's Metis-style coat is a tour de force of the quill worker's art, with floral, sunburst, and other designs on its back, front, collar, and cuffs and quill-wrapped hide fringe hanging from each shoulder (see figure 3.6). It is a slightly simplified version of one published in *Art of the American Indian Frontier*.[31] Ravenshead said that he often has to simplify things when he offers them for sale through a store such as Prairie Edge, or the cost would be prohibitive. This coat, made of smoked brain-tanned elk hide and lined with calico fabric, was listed for sale at $11,400 in 2011. It was the third such Metis coat he had made for the store, and another, at the same price, was featured online in 2019. Sometimes the inspiration for Ravenshead's quillwork comes from nineteenth-century pictorial beadwork or ledger art. He showed me a bag with a scene of a courting couple quilled in six colors that looked like it had been adapted from a ledger drawing.

Collectors who buy historic garments know Ravenshead's work, and because of his marriage into the large Bald Eagle family, many Native people know him as well. Some might be inclined to criticize him as a non-Native doing Native art or to say that a male should not do quillwork—an art that, according to Lakota teachings, was specifically given by the supernatural Double Woman as a woman's art.[32] Yet, for people such as he, who fit within a matrix of Lakota kinship bonds, the policing of an idealized set of cultural boundaries—and even gender boundaries—concerning who has the right to make quillwork seems, in my opinion, to be misguided. Ravenshead came to the American West decades ago, seeking relief from the crowded urbanism of Europe. He made a new family, took the time to learn from willing teachers, and has devoted himself unstintingly to this work. Neta Bald Eagle said, about her husband's work, "He's got so much knowledge. He's taught me more about my culture than I learned from anyone else."

I asked Ravenshead if he knew whether any of his old-style work had ever been misrepresented after it had left his hands. He said that a pair of Comanche-style moccasins he had made were offered at auction in the early 2000s as historic moccasins and sold for $10,000. Similarly, a pipe bag he had sold for $800 was advertised in Santa Fe as "an Old Cheyenne Pipe Bag, $20,000." The most egregious example he mentioned concerned a quilled box-and-border robe he sold in the 1980s. He claims it was entered by another artist at a prestigious national competition for tribally enrolled Native artists. Without any apparent anger in his voice, Ravenshead told me, "My robe won multiple prizes under someone else's name." If what he alleges is true, this represents a veritable "through the looking glass" experience—an inverted world of anti-authenticity, where nothing is as it seems and everything has been turned inside out. Not Native American art has become Native American art and has even won prizes for doing so.

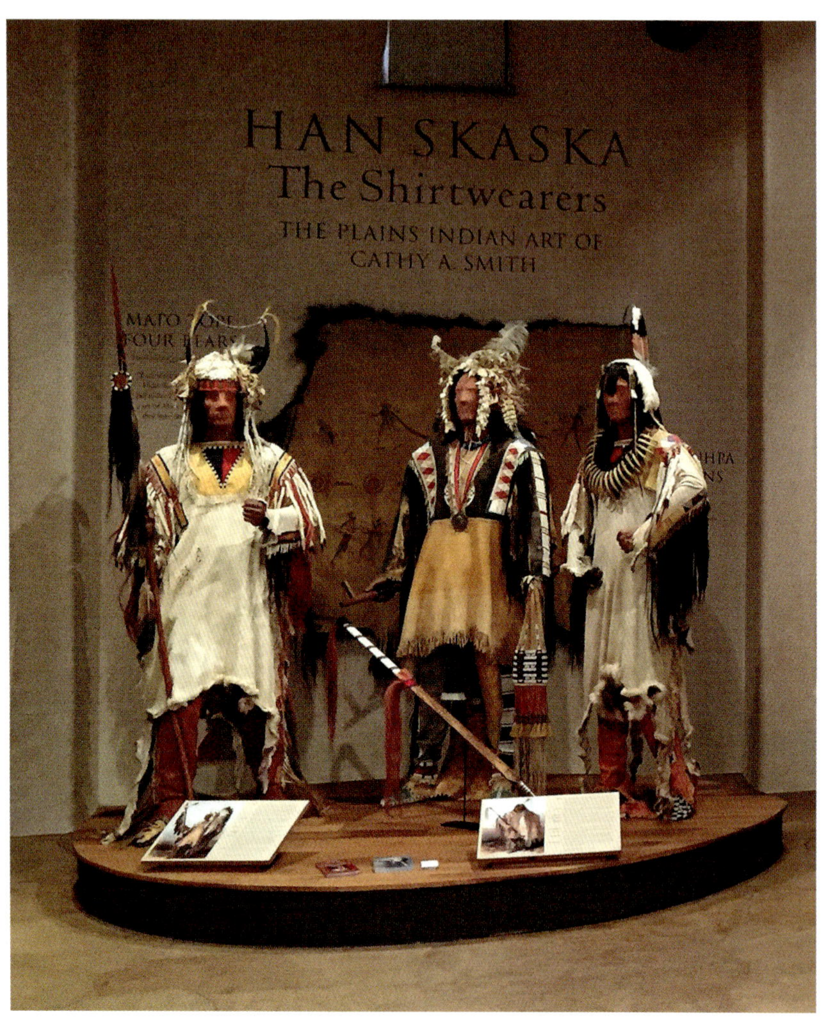

FIG. 3.8 *Han Skaska—the Shirtwearers*, by Cathy A. Smith. Photo by author taken of its installation in a private home in Santa Fe, New Mexico, April 2017. Permanent collection, Booth Western Art Museum, Cartersville, Georgia.

MAKING THE NINETEENTH CENTURY COME ALIVE: CATHY A. SMITH AND "THE SHIRTWEARERS"

In 2017, I visited a grand private home on the southern outskirts of Santa Fe, where a spacious room contained astonishingly detailed full-size replicas of the garments and regalia of twelve distinguished Native leaders of the nineteenth century, among them Mató-tópe (Mandan, ca. 1784–1837); Red Cloud (Oglala, 1822–1909); Kicking Bear (Miniconjou, 1846–1904); and Little Chief (Northern Cheyenne, ca. 1820–1904) (figure 3.8). The wall bears the title *Han Skaska—the Shirtwearers*. Even without the accompanying labels, many scholars would recognize these men by the superbly crafted replicas of their famous war shirts and other accoutrements. This labor of more than six years is the work of the artist and costume designer Cathy A. Smith. Though not Native, Smith has been involved in Native artistic practices and ceremonial life since her youth; she has received an Emmy and other honors for her work replicating nineteenth-century Plains material culture, using scrupulously accurate historical processes and materials.[33]

Some of the costumes are worn by life-size mannequins, including that of Mató-tópe (figure 3.8, the figure at left). As mentioned in chapter 1, Mató-tópe is well known from the letters and drawings of George Catlin as well as the shirt that Catlin claimed belonged to that Mandan chief (see figure 1.3), the watercolors and aquatints of Karl Bodmer (figure 3.9), and the daybooks of Prince Maximilian. These visitors gave Mató-tópe artistic materials and collected objects from him. During the winter of 1833–34, which the European visitors spent at Fort Clark, Mató-tópe was a welcome and frequent guest.[34] Catlin noted that Mató-tópe's garment was made of two mountain sheep hides, and his split-horn headdress was worn only by those "whose exceeding valour, worth, and power is admitted by all the nation."[35]

Smith's re-creation of Mató-tópe's garments brings Bodmer's famous portrait of this man to life. It demonstrates Smith's deep knowledge of materials and cultural practices, as well as her artistry. The mannequin's mountain sheep hide shirt is adorned with beadwork, quillwork, painting, and ermine tails. The split buffalo horn bonnet is covered with ermine hide strips and has a full trailer of eagle feathers, along with owl feathers, red stroud cloth, and brass Hudson's Bay Company buttons. Smith has even included the wooden replica of the knife that Mató-tópe wore in his headgear and spoke about when he recounted his war exploits.[36]

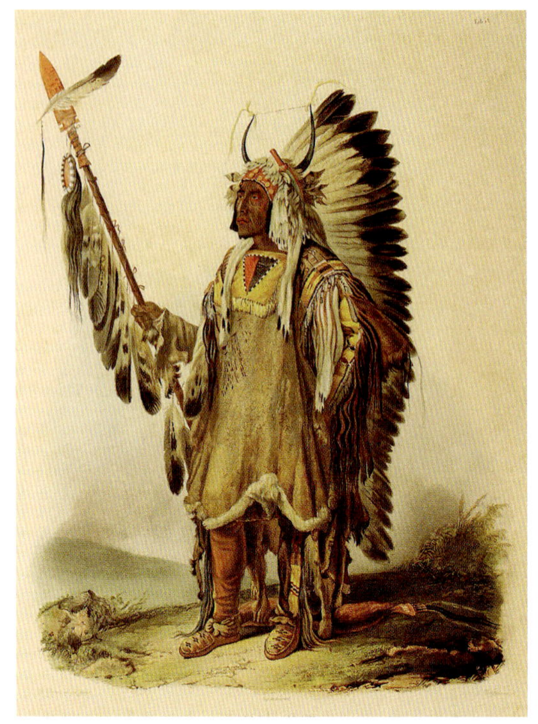

FIG. 3.9 Karl Bodmer, 1839. Aquatint after his watercolor *Mató-Tópe (Four Bears), Mandan Chief*, 1834, from the book by Prince Maximilian of Wied-Neuwied, *Maximilian, Prince of Wied's Travels in the Interior of North America, during the Years 1832–1834* (London: Ackerman, 1839).

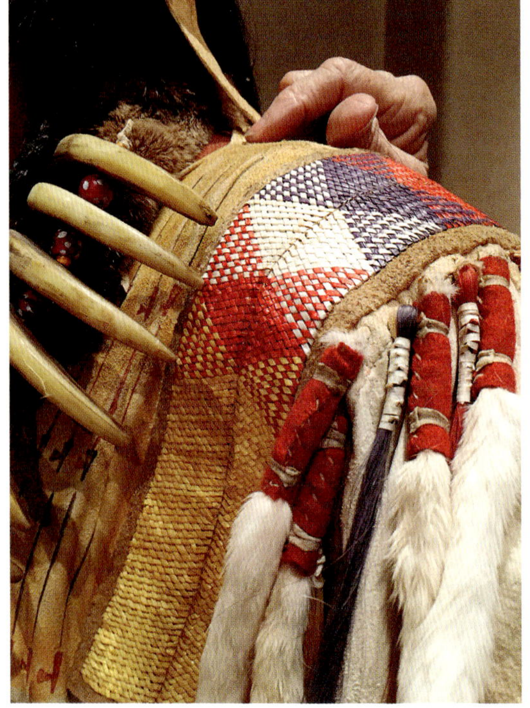

FIG. 3.10 Detail of quillwork on shoulder of costume for Pehriska-Ruhpa figure. *Han Skaska—the Shirtwearers*, by Cathy A. Smith. Photo by author taken of its installation in a private home in Santa Fe, New Mexico, April 2017. Permanent collection, Booth Western Art Museum, Cartersville, Georgia.

As we examine each constellation of garments and accessories, Smith recounts the challenges of making historically accurate replicas. "To figure out the details for each character required a treasure hunt," she says. For the bear claw necklace for the figure of Pehriska-Ruhpa (Hidatsa, early nineteenth century; exact dates unknown), she needed more than two dozen grizzly bear claws, but that animal is nearly extinct on the Plains. She borrowed one original claw from the collector Benson Lanford and had multiples cast in resin. Pointing to the intricately plaited quillwork on Pehriska-Ruhpa's shoulders (figure 3.10), she remarks, "The quills from the back of the neck of the porcupine are the only ones long enough *and* thin enough to do this kind of plaiting. You can't use the long fat tail quills—they aren't pliable enough. You have to skin and pluck about six porcupines to get this many long quills."

This commission was a once-in-a-lifetime opportunity for Smith to marshal decades worth of deep cultural knowledge and to display her many artistic skills. In Santa Fe, she met the media mogul R. Michael Kammerer Jr. (1940–2007), who collected memorabilia associated with US presidents. He was fascinated by the lives of great men, and when he saw some of the war shirts that Smith had created for films, he realized that these, too, were memorials to great men. Since they were not for sale, he proposed a commission of twelve shirts of Native leaders. Smith encouraged him to expand the commission to include lances, headgear, jewelry, moccasins, leggings, and other items, in order to present a fuller picture of each individual. Kammerer displayed them in the conference room of his newly built home in Santa Fe.[37] After his death, the house remained empty for several years, and the collection was loaned to the National Cowgirl Museum and Hall of Fame.[38] When German billionaire Joachen Zeitz bought the home, he chose to keep the collection intact. For several years, these meticulous replicas shared space with African contemporary art, works by Warhol and Fritz Scholder, and original Plains artifacts. In 2022, Zeitz donated this collection to the Booth Western Art Museum in Cartersville, Georgia, where it now shares space with other arts of the American West, both Native and non-Native.

In 2016, Zeitz allowed a German film crew to rent Mató-tópe's costume and use it, under Smith's supervision, for scenes they shot at the reconstructed Mandan earth lodges of On-a-Slant Village in North Dakota. In the documentary *Ein Prinz unter Indianern: Die Reisen des Maximilian zu Wied* (A prince among Indians: The travels of Maximilian of Wied), the actor Marty Young Bear of the Three Affiliated Tribes of Fort Berthold, North Dakota (Mandan,

Hidatsa, Arikara), played Mató-tópe, and Smith was technical adviser for the costuming, making all of the costumes and props.[39]

How did a white, self-identified "cowgirl" come to such a profession? Born in Deadwood, South Dakota, in 1950, Smith grew up on her grandparent's ranch on the edge of the Cheyenne River Sioux Reservation. She describes a childhood that combined great freedom with adult skills and responsibilities: by the time she was ten, she owned her own .22 long rifle and could sew her own clothes. After a short stint at Colorado State University and a brief early marriage to a Native man who competed on the Indian Professional Rodeo circuit, she and her young daughter moved back to her grandfather's ranch in 1972. She resumed long-standing friendships with her Lakota, Mandan, and Hidatsa neighbors and describes herself as the adopted daughter of Kenneth and Darlene Young Bear (since deceased), who were respected elders and medicine people of the Cheyenne River Sioux. Already adept at beadwork, Smith told the Young Bears that she wanted to learn quillwork. To undertake this, they required her to follow correct Lakota protocol: she had to fast and undertake a vision quest, and if she dreamed of Double Woman (the Lakota supernatural who in ancient times is said to have taught quillwork to one young woman to share with others), it would be fitting for her to pursue this traditional art.[40] Darlene Young Bear also brought Smith to visit Bertha Hump, who, according to Young Bear, was "the last of the Double Woman dreamers," and whose permission must also be sought. As the elderly woman had only sons, and no one else had evinced interest, she agreed to teach Smith, ultimately entrusting her with a most valued possession: a well-worn buffalo horn awl used for piercing hide in order to insert quills.[41]

In 1989, Smith moved to Santa Fe to pursue her arts. She had already been restoring artifacts for Jim Aplan (1931–2018), a gunsmith and seller of western memorabilia in South Dakota, as well as for other collectors and museums. Aplan had sent her to the annual ethnographic arts fair in Santa Fe to run his booth. There she came into contact with the world of high-end collecting of Native American art. When staff of the movie-in-progress *Dances with Wolves* came to Santa Fe to do costume research, they hired Smith as a technical adviser for her deep knowledge of nineteenth-century dress on the Northern Plains. While she was not credited as costume designer, she both designed and created all the Native garments used in the film, overseeing a small staff of helpers.

"Most costume designers think they can learn a new historical era in two weeks and then design the clothing," she said. "But you can't do that with Plains garments. The knowledge is too specialized." She gives the director Kevin Costner credit for mostly allowing her to do things accurately, within the constraints of his budget. "I had to acquire six hundred hides at a moment's notice, and we had to make each costume in duplicate or triplicate, since shooting can't stop just because a hide shirt is ripped or soiled." She hired two Lakota friends and two relatives to help with this extraordinary feat. "We worked twelve to fifteen hours a day, since everything had to be completed in the ten weeks before shooting started."

Smith considers the commission of *Han Skaska*—encompassing some sixty handmade objects—her greatest artistic achievement. In recent years she has been asked to replicate other notable historical works. For example, in 2011, a Lakota war shirt known to have been owned by Black Bird, a high-ranking Oglala Lakota warrior, was auctioned at Sotheby's for $2,658,500, at that time a record price for Native American art.[42] The underbidder for this impeccably beaded shirt, with hair locks attached to the shoulders and sleeves, commissioned Smith to make him an exact replica. "I have six months of work in that shirt," Smith recalled in 2017. Smith defends her replica making for wealthy collectors: "Increasingly I think it's not appropriate for some rich guy to own an important nineteenth-century war shirt; it should either be repatriated or it should be in a major museum where people can see it. That's where my reproductions come in. An individual can commission such a reproduction for a private home."

Smith and her daughter, Jennifer Jesse Smith, run Nambe Trading Post, in Nambe, New Mexico. There, alongside authentic Navajo rugs, Pueblo silver jewelry, Plains beaded moccasins, and her daughter's line of silver jewelry, Smith displays and sells her own replicas of nineteenth-century ledger drawings, painted hide robes, and quilled and beaded garments. The Emmy she won as costume designer for *Son of the Morning Star* (1991), a two-part TV miniseries, is displayed there, along with some of the garments worn in *Dances with Wolves* and in Netflix's *Longmire* (2012–17), for which she served as a consultant, renting for the series many items from her warehouse of historical props and costumes.

Though both Ravenshead and Smith were taught by Lakota women, Smith had a far more ritually correct training. When asked about the appropriateness of a white woman making Native-style art in the twenty-first century, Smith says, "It is only in Santa Fe that I hear these criticisms. No one criticizes me back on the reservation in South Dakota, where they know me, and where I go for ceremonies every year. In fact, I'm sometimes asked to teach the young girls and to make ceremonial items for medicine people."

In researching this book, I interviewed some Native people, such as Trevor Isaac, mentioned in chapter 1, who will buy ceremonial regalia from white artists; to them it is the correctness of the object itself, not the ethnicity of the maker, that is important. Others feel strongly that no non-Native person should be making a living from Native-style art. While I understand the reasoning behind their point of view, such an analysis suggests that it is a zero-sum game. In my opinion, the realm of historical replicas is quite different from the realm of contemporary art in this regard. There are certainly a small number of Native artists who make superb replicas of historical materials—one thinks of Navajo weavers who make so-called revival-style first phase chief's blankets, the originals of which sell for upwards of $100,000. But does Smith's incredibly exacting, high-priced, and specialized artistry really take work away from Native artists? When one criticizes her practice, is it important to be able to cite exact Native individuals who could step in and do such ambitious commissions, or is it enough to say idealistically that such work "should" be given to some unspecified Native artist?

The curator and cultural resource specialist Joe D. Horse Capture (A'aninin, b. 1963) is one critic of the practice of non-Native artists making such things. He says, "It is understandable that at a certain time, a couple of generations ago, Native people who lacked certain objects would rely on white people's knowledge. But now that we have Native people who have brought back these historical practices, we don't need this anymore. The question I always ask about such people is this: Are they just profiteering, or do they give back to Native communities? Do they pass on their skills to Native people directly? How are they benefiting Native people by using traditional knowledge?" He goes on to give the example of Richard A. Pohrt, the collector and Native art expert discussed earlier, who was a good friend of his father, George Horse Capture Sr.: "The old-timers look at these relationships in a different way than we do today. Pohrt was adopted into my tribe. In the middle of the twentieth century he was one of the few who were listening to the old stories. He would come and bring gifts for this privilege, as was appropriate. He made things for his own use or to give to Indian people."[43]

The sorry history of broken promises, genocide, "playing Indian," and all the rest has made many Native people extremely skeptical of non-Natives who participate in Native culture or make Native-style arts. Smith is unapologetic about her right to do such things, saying,

> My great-grandmother in the *Hunka* way [i.e., adoption as a particularly valued child] was Maza Win, Iron Woman, a part Lakota woman who married a Hidatsa man, Young Bear. I lived with Kenneth Young Bear (Iron Woman's grandson) and his wife Darlene Knife for some years at Eagle Butte, South Dakota, apprenticing with Kenneth. They took me as their daughter in the *Hunka* ceremony. I gave a horse, a war bonnet, a buffalo robe, and tobacco to Kenneth as an offering to "put me on the hill" (i.e., *hanbley cia*). To pursue such a vision quest, I was required to do the appropriate "sacred business." The vision quest preceded my activities of doing quillwork and beadwork to make a living.[44]

For more than three decades, Smith has participated in ceremonies with her Lakota relatives on the Cheyenne River Sioux and Rosebud Reservations, sometimes in ways that outsiders would be surprised to hear were open to a non-Lakota woman. This has included participating in the Sun Dance and sweat lodge ceremonies.

Conclusion: Nostalgia, Sites of Memory, and the White Fixation on a Romantic Past

People often use the term *nostalgia* in statements such as "My mother is nostalgic for her early years in rural Quebec" or "I'm nostalgic for my childhood in Indiana in the 1950s. It was like a Norman Rockwell painting." Of course, such nostalgia conveniently elides the sexism, social rigidity, and racism of small-town life decades ago. Nostalgia presents a backward-looking idealism, conveniently manifesting only feelings of comfort, safety, and belonging. It is a common human emotion, and research psychologists claim that nostalgic thoughts about the past "bolster a sense of continuity and meaning in one's life."[45]

But nostalgia's range is far greater than personal feelings for one's singular past. Groups of people coalesce around their collective longing for a particular slice of the past, be it medieval craft fairs, the battlefields of the Civil War, or Native lifeways on the Great Plains in the nineteenth century. Such nostalgia is inherently illogical, for no one literally seeks a return to an era before penicillin, anesthesia, or reliable contraception. But such collectivities provide an identity that contrasts markedly with twenty-first-century modernity. It is useful to try to unpack nostalgia's variants, especially when it comes to the fictive nostalgia that people feel for cultures and time periods that are not theirs to claim, but for which they feel an affinity. Notably, nostalgia was first conceived of as a medical condition.

NOSTALGIA: DISEASE OR DIS-EASE?

The word *nostalgia* was coined in 1688 as a medical term for the physical symptoms brought on by the homesickness of Swiss mercenary soldiers for their alpine land while they were fighting abroad.[46] By the nineteenth century, nostalgia was more clearly understood as a whole bundle of inchoate feelings that people have not only for their own pasts but also for earlier times in general, when life was supposedly easier, less alienated, and less fast-paced. Such feelings of nostalgia, when widespread, can give rise to social and artistic movements. Following the industrial revolution, for example, it fueled the British Arts and Crafts movement; medieval craftsmen's guilds were idealized, and the handmade was highly valued. The so-called heritage crusade in Europe in the late nineteenth and twentieth centuries, and the colonial revival in the United States, stoked by the centennial of 1876, caused people to take stock of rapidly disappearing buildings, customs, skills, and objects and to re-create them.[47]

During the past four decades in particular, many cultural critics have written about nostalgia and theorized the complexities of its meaning. The literary theorist Svetlana Boym has pointed out that "the nostalgic [person] desires to turn history into private or collective mythology."[48] Susan Stewart goes so far as to characterize nostalgia as "a social disease," and for many it may well be.[49] The historian Michael Kammen has written that "nostalgia . . . is essentially history without guilt."[50] Yet I have found that some collectors of Native American art *are* quick to invoke the tragic and violent history of the United States concerning its Native inhabitants, as if their collection is a form of personal reparation, an expiation of the sins of their ancestors.

As with all cultural manifestations, nostalgia is marked by gender, age, race, class, and nationality. When I look at the Great Plains of nostalgia, I see in its North American manifestation an engagement predominantly by white, middle-aged, middle-to-upper-class men, men whose childhoods were formed by an identification with Indians in Boy Scouts, for example. (Cathy A. Smith is a clear exception to this gender generalization.)

It is impossible to look at this phenomenon without invoking the anthropologist Renato Rosaldo's classic essay "Imperialist Nostalgia," which cogently outlines the way that all of us in the Western world who benefited from imperialism are, in fact, complicit with it and that if we are nostalgic for what has been "lost," we must recognize our complicity in this loss. He locates the origins of imperialist nostalgia in the agents of colonialism (among them soldiers, missionaries, and even early anthropologists) who express "a longing for the very forms of life they intentionally altered or destroyed."[51] So the cultural descendants of men who sought to wipe out Plains tribes through warfare, smallpox, and religious proselytization are the ones who choose to collect symbols of the civilizations that were critically destabilized and traumatized. When Kammerer commissioned Smith to make "the Shirtwearers," he saw it as a tribute to the "great men" of Indigenous America whose histories and cultures had been all but obliterated by Euro-American "great men."

For some, the nostalgic impulse also reflects a dis-ease with their own cultural background or era. Chris Ravenshead described feeling disillusioned with late twentieth-century urban life in Belgium And I cannot help but see a dis-ease with modern American male culture in Reginald Laubin's obsessive insertion of himself into another time and place. In the twenty-first century, in contrast, most culturally sensitive people feel a profound dis-ease at the actions of those who seek their identity in ethnic groups to which they have no legitimate claim.

THE MATERIALITY OF NOSTALGIA

I do not believe that Smith and Ravenshead undertake their work because of a simple nostalgia for an alien past; this stands in contrast to what I have observed in many white collectors and reenactors. Everyone who makes art knows well that the lure of materials is deeply seductive. For those who work with traditional Native materials, the satisfaction of dyeing quills, sorting beads and stringing them on sinew, or cutting, stretching, and rolling fringe for a deerskin dress provides both tactile and visual pleasure.

Petra Kalshoven, in her study of European hobbyists making replicas while "playing Indian" ("Indianists," in her terminology), has written of their deep love of materials, calling their avocation "a sensuous practice."[52] Part of the materiality of nostalgia is an unflagging search for the authentic and the correct. This is evident in Smith's narratives about beads, mountain sheep hides, and grizzly bear claws. Vast amounts of money sometimes change hands for authentic materials, and when they are not available, realistic simulacra such as cast bear claws are employed for the right look. Today some materials are harder to obtain because of their rarity; others are far easier, because of the long arm of the internet. Moreover, patience with materials and techniques is the hallmark of those who re-create historical objects. Makers talk about the laborious process of smoking a deer or moose hide properly, for example. Smith spoke of testing the mettle of those who wanted to learn quillwork, by insisting that they undertake the whole process, from hunting the porcupine to plucking, washing, dyeing, and sorting the quills. She found that many non-Natives were too squeamish to kill the animals, and few wanted to do the labor-intensive work. Admittedly, some of the work can be streamlined: pre-dyed quills and brain-tanned hides can be ordered online. Moreover, the internet can make technical learning easier, for there are YouTube videos on all of these practices. In chapter 4, I profile a Euro-American couple who painstakingly replicate eleventh-century Mimbres bowls. The search for the proper clay sources and the use of yucca-leaf brushes and natural pigments are all part of the joy of their endeavor. This is a very specialized kind of material nostalgia indeed.

SITES OF MEMORY

When I first described Smith's Shirtwearers project to Joe D. Horse Capture, he chortled—not at the maker but at the collector: "White people! I'll never understand them. Why would someone want these figures in his home?"[53] Indeed, Native people seem variously perplexed, amused, or outraged at the hold that the "romance of the West" has on the white imagination. I believe that the work of the distinguished French historian Pierre Nora (b. 1931) provides insight. From 1984 to 1992, Nora oversaw the publication of an ambitious reference work, *Les lieux de mémoire*. It sought to examine "sites of memory" that elucidate French culture and history. Nora used the word *lieux* (translated as "sites") not just for literal geographic spaces, but for many topics—buildings, people, cities, and novels—that constitute national memory for the French.[54] I believe that in the American psyche, shields, feathered headdresses, and war shirts from the Plains form a constellation of *lieux de mémoire* denoting a troubled relationship to American history—and an attempt to achieve distance and absolution from the real historical record. Most Americans have not been taught the full extent of the horrors perpetrated against Native people over the past several centuries, having only a sketchy understanding that brutal military campaigns were waged against Plains peoples and that their lands were stolen outright. But to keep this from troubling their psyches, Americans have constructed a mental template of the ecological Indian, the spiritual Indian, and the noble Indian, and all of these are formed in the image of the warrior of the Plains.[55] They choose to celebrate this image, acknowledging inchoately that "we treated the Indians badly." Moreover, for the heroism of the American past to be truly satisfying, a worthy foe is necessary—and the Plains warrior provides such a foe.[56]

In chapter 1, I used the term *surrogate* to label the three-dimensional digital replication of a Tlingit clan hat. But we might expand the idea of surrogacy in terms of the emotional, psychological, and cultural needs of individuals or collectivities at particular historical moments. The need to replay the ennobling bits of Native American cultural history, with white men wearing the garb of the people their ancestors vanquished, suggests the working out of a deeply held cultural trauma, a topic beyond the scope of this book.[57]

The image of the Plains warrior as a *lieu de mémoire* for North Americans is the focus for guilt, admiration, and reparation. But this seldom results in any palpable gesture of reparation to the descendants. It is merely an internal emotional reparation: the sentiment that by esteeming and romanticizing what our ancestors thought to destroy, we make it live on. But true catharsis cannot be achieved through this fetishization of the warrior of the Plains. Neither the guilt, nor a deep study of the events that gave rise to it, nor the full extent of what genuine reparation would entail is fully acknowledged and admitted. No active political and social solutions are sought. So all that is left is a sense of admiration, which has played out repeatedly and inadequately over successive generations.

Coda: Woodcraft Indians in the Twenty-First Century

While finalizing this chapter, I conducted a last internet search on the Hillenbrand family, owners of Prairie Edge. Ray Hillenbrand's obituary led me to other articles. I discovered that both he and his daughter had attended Culver Military Academy in Culver, Indiana (class of 1952 and 1980, respectively). Moreover, in 2018, Hillenbrand gave the Crisp Visual Arts Center at the academy a collection of thirty-seven works by Native artists from Prairie

Edge, works that would be used by the visiting Miniconjou scholar Donovin Sprague, with Culver Woodcraft Camp staff and campers, in the Indian Lore, Indian Dance, and Indian Crafts classes. Before this, I thought I was principally doing *historical* research; I had no idea that Woodcraft Indians still existed. The website for Culver Academy's six-week-long Woodcraft Camp for boys and girls ages nine to fourteen shows that in addition to academics, horseback riding, and water sports, the classes listed above—sounding exactly like those offered a century ago by men such as Ernest Thompson Seton and Ralph Hubbard (discussed in chapter 2)—persist. And a YouTube video of the camp shows events that take place at the Woodcraft Council Fire every summer weekend, complete with children dancing in Indian garments. Indeed, the Woodcraft Council Fire at Culver has an impeccable genealogy, the firepit having been laid out in 1917 by Sir Robert Baden-Powell himself (British founder of the international Scouting movement).[58]

Seeds are still being planted to ensure that the Great Plains of nostalgia will be harvesting followers for decades to come.

4

The Deliberate Forgery, the Accidental Fake, the Visual Fiction, and the Replica

From July 1986 through July 1987, I was acting curator of the Pre-Columbian Collection at Dumbarton Oaks, Harvard's research center in Washington, DC. The storage vault in my office at "D.O.," as scholars call the institution, held many small-sized treasures: Costa Rican gold jewelry, Olmec jades, and Maya painted vases, among them. But one suite of objects held particular fascination for me: a group of whistles, pipes, and wands inlaid with delicate circles of shell beads. Occasionally, on a quiet afternoon, I would lay them out on my desk just to relish the beauty of their workmanship. A couple were made of steatite, a soft easily worked stone (figure 4.1); others were bone, one topped with a crystal, another with a whorled shell (figure 4.2). All were adorned with shell beads of various sizes. "Chumash," their labels said. I knew this to be a California tribe, but I had never seen anything like these elegant specimens.

At that point in my career, I was moving away from the study of pre-Columbian Mesoamerica and beginning to publish on North American Indian art. Intrigued by the beautiful Chumash objects, I sought to learn more. Oddly, they were not included in the major early publications on the Bliss collection, and only a few other catalogues had Chumash stone items, generally steatite whales and other small animal sculptures, sometimes with a bit of modest shell inlay—nothing like these richly embellished objects.

As I dug into the files, I discovered that the "Chumash" objects there had recently been denounced as forgeries, as recounted below. My love of unusual objects—and my ignorance of California archaeology—had led me to admire these artifacts, and I was disappointed that they were spurious. More than thirty years later I returned to D.O. to study them again for this book, armed with far deeper knowledge about fakes and about Native American art and archaeology.

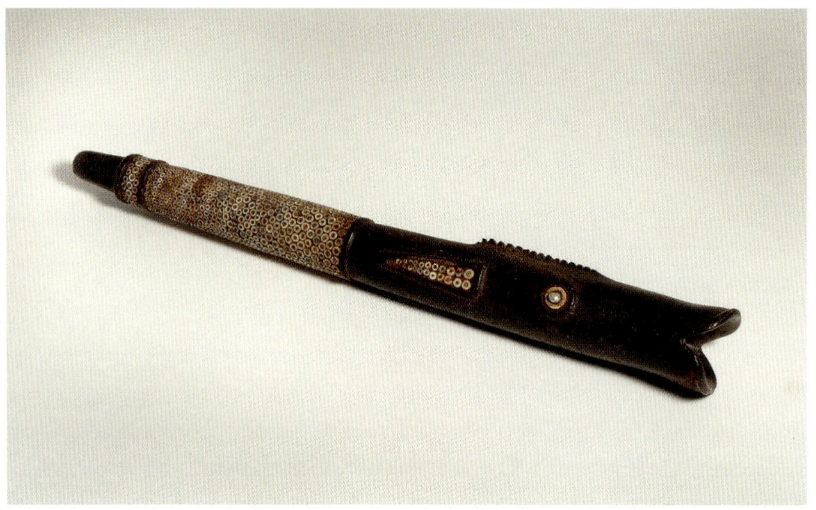

FIG. 4.1 “Cloud blower” in the shape of a fish. Steatite, shell, and pearl. Ancient Chumash, California, with modern additions. No. PC.B.N.005, 40 × 51 cm. © Dumbarton Oaks, Pre-Columbian Collection, Washington, DC. Photography by Joseph Mills.

A decade after my sojourn at Dumbarton Oaks, when I was immersed in studying Plains ledger drawings full-time, the American Indian art specialist at Sotheby’s sent me superb color slides and photocopies of a book of so-called Hidatsa drawings that she hoped to offer for sale and sought my scholarly opinion. Having looked closely at Plains drawings in collections all across the country, I knew these were by a modern hand as soon as I opened the envelope. I was not the first to tell the Sotheby’s expert that these were decidedly not drawn by a nineteenth-century Plains artist; nonetheless, they were sold in Sotheby’s June 1997 auction for nearly $80,000. So this became the second instance of Native North American fakes to catch my attention (though in the world of pre-Columbian art that I moved in during the 1980s, fakes had been much in the news).[1] As I researched them further, I came to believe that they were “accidental fakes.”

During the 1970s and 1980s, ancient Mimbres painted bowls were increasingly in the limelight: in auctions, books, and museum exhibits. Meanwhile, looters were busily bulldozing Mimbres archaeological sites in southern New Mexico. Some collectors wanted to showcase in their homes Mimbres vessels that were as immaculate and pristine as the decor around them. This led to the "restoration" of hundreds of pots in a manner that was not up to the rigorous standards of museum conservators, an issue that I began researching in 2010 and that I have come to call "visual fictions." Concurrently, I was fascinated with the range of Mimbres replicas available in the marketplace, from those of the greatest faithfulness to the ancient works of art to those that were merely distant cousins—cousins from Nicaragua. This chapter takes up these four topics—what I have termed the deliberate forgery, the accidental fake, the visual fiction, and the replica.

With a few exceptions, most anthropologists and so-called dirt archaeologists who study Native things have not been trained to look at art objects as individual works of creativity or to carefully compare their visual aspects with other individual objects. After all, that was long the purview of art history.[2] Ironically, the rise of the social history of art in the 1960s, and the so-called New Art History since the 1980s, has meant that most art historians who teach in universities today (including me), and even many among a younger generation of curators in art museums, have turned away from the material and connoisseurial aspects of the field. Instead, we have embraced a transdisciplinary approach, finding far more to excite us in pursuits such as gender studies and postcolonial critique. The inadvertent fallout of this turning away from the material aspects of works of art is legion. For example, scholars may be seduced by unusual iconography that, although corroborated by the ethnographic literature, is at odds with the style of the objects. Moreover, wealthy collectors have too often trusted the dealers and auction houses to know what they are selling and to be ethical about their transactions. The three case studies in this chapter demonstrate that the legal principle *caveat emptor*—let the buyer beware—remains important when art is treated as merchandise. Finally, as questionable objects bought by private collectors with more enthusiasm than knowledge, and objects restored according to the whims and desires of private collectors, have entered art museums, there is an increasingly urgent need to identify works that may egregiously misrepresent the cultures from which they are purported to come. The kinds of objects examined in this chapter do, however, tell fascinating tales about how objects from the past are used, misused, copied, and transformed. As the anthropologist Igor Kopytoff has argued, it is important to tell a full cultural biography of an object as it moves through time, space, and different cultural realms.[3]

"Tops in Exquisite Workmanship": Fake Chumash Objects in the Rarified World of Art Dealing and Collecting

The Chumash pieces are tops in exquisite workmanship.
Yes, you both should really be a little excited.
—*Letter from the art dealer Earl Stendahl to Robert Woods Bliss, February 16, 1947*

In recent decades, most art historians and art museum curators, if asked about Chumash art, would invoke the masterful baskets made by Chumash women who had been brought forcibly into the mission system around 1800.[4] These beautifully wrought objects, with images of Spanish coins and sometimes the maker's own name twined into the basket, are reminders of both the chilling history of colonization and the indominable spirit of the Native artist. But archaeologists know a different Chumash world. For some thirteen thousand years, the Chumash lived on the Channel Islands off the coast of Santa Barbara, California, and on the mainland between Santa Barbara and Los Angeles. Divided into small chieftainships, they maintained a robust trade of goods between the islands and the mainland. Spanish explorers as early as 1542 began to report on the Chumash. Two centuries later, Spanish missionaries began the inexorable drive to subdue them. A cultural holocaust ensued.

EXCAVATIONS, LICIT AND ILLICIT

Ancient Chumash artists made steatite sculptures, mostly of marine animals. They worked bones—principally deer tibiae—into whistles and other forms. They also wore and used shell beads by the thousands. The work of professional bead makers of the Channel Islands was traded up and down the Pacific coast, and even as far inland as the Great Basin.[5] Long before the scientific practice of archaeology took hold in North America, people were looting or haphazardly "excavating" Chumash graves, sometimes in the name of "science" and sometimes simply to amass collections, with a lot of blurring between these pursuits. In the 1870s, casual collecting expeditions were mounted by the Smithsonian and the Musée de l'Homme in Paris, both of which found the types of objects that would soon come to be common in Chumash excavations: stone mortars, steatite tubes, shell ornaments, bones, beads, and crystals.[6] As early as 1875, one archaeologist complained that the mounds had been, in his words, "pretty well picked over by collectors and amateur curio-hunters."[7]

With our twenty-first-century sensibilities, which are far more cognizant of the ethical implications of digging up other people's ancestors, it is shocking to read the early reports that casually announce the plundering of scores of graves at a time.[8] By the beginning of the twentieth century, many Native villages and burials on the mainland were uncovered, bulldozed, and looted during the building of roads and homes as the immigrant population of southern California grew. Looters and amateurs remained far more prevalent than trained archaeologists.[9] In fact, the distinction between them blurs in some so-called scientific expeditions, such as those funded by George Heye (1874–1957), the founder of the Museum of the American Indian. The excavation and accumulation of objects that he financed from 1939 to 1941, in particular, resulted in a publication featuring what all Chumash archaeologists recognize to be an egregious number of fakes and doctored specimens. These include many shell-encrusted stone and bone implements probably made by a small number of Californians who participated in the looting of real objects, as well as their subsequent elaboration and sale.[10] To understand how this unfolded, it will be instructive to look at how the foremost collector of pre-Columbian art in mid-twentieth-century America came to buy some outlandish yet beautiful objects from southern California.

THE BLISS COLLECTION, EARL STENDAHL, AND ARTHUR SANGER

The Pre-Columbian Collection at Dumbarton Oaks is displayed in the Philip Johnson–designed pavilion, built in 1963. The main building had been the home of Robert Woods Bliss (1875–1962) and Mildred Barnes Bliss (1879–1969), ardent art collectors.[11] After amassing substantial collections of Byzantine and pre-Columbian art, and nurturing an ambitious garden designed by the famed landscape architect Beatrix Farrand, they gave their house and grounds to Harvard in 1940. Eventually, their collections followed. The Blisses established a tripartite mandate for their collecting: Byzantine art, pre-Columbian art of Latin America, and a library on the history of landscape architecture. These were offbeat choices for a patrician couple in the mid-twentieth century. Their collecting was informed principally by aesthetics and facilitated by Mildred Bliss's wealth as heiress to the Fletcher's Castoria patent medicine fortune. Though they owned a Degas and an El Greco, today they are remembered principally for their extraordinary collection of pre-Columbian art, an area that very few art museums—or collectors—paid attention to in the 1930s and 1940s.

The Blisses were especially enthusiastic in their hunt for ancient art of the Americas, particularly Mesoamerica and the Andes. Robert Bliss was aided by one of the foremost dealers in this new field: Earl Stendahl of Los Angeles. Stendahl (1888–1966) was better known for selling European modernist paintings, but he also sold what was then called "primitive art" to Bliss, as well as to Nelson Rockefeller, Walter Arensberg, and other prominent collectors.[12]

In 1947, Mildred Bliss, in particular, was charmed by photos of some archaeological objects from California that Stendahl had sent, and she wanted to own them. Perhaps she reasoned that they could legitimately be part of a collection of what was at that time sometimes called ancient American art or medieval American art (though the Blisses never bought any works from the ancient Southwest or from Mississippian cultures, for example).[13] The works illustrated here are three of the eight Chumash objects that they bought from Stendahl.[14] Never having been displayed or published, these works are unknown outside a small circle of scholars.

The steatite object inlaid with hundreds of small olivella shell beads (see figure 4.1) is called a cloud blower because objects of such shape—albeit far plainer—are known to have been used in shamanic curing rites in which clouds of smoke were blown over the bodies of the ill. Here the wide end is formed in the shape of an open-mouthed fish with a serrated dorsal fin. The eye is depicted with a shell ring and inset pearl. Professional archaeologists have excavated steatite cloud blowers and sucking tubes (also used in shamanic rites to suck an illness from the patient's body), but have found none as elaborately ornamented as this one.[15]

Two lavishly decorated bone whistles are among the most elaborate Chumash fakes at Dumbarton Oaks (see figure 4.2), and similar examples are found in other American art museums. One bone is plain, while the other is incised with bands and cross-hatching filled with red pigment. In the illustration, the mouthpiece for the whistle is at left, with a transverse sound hole on the side. These are surely authentic precontact bone whistles recovered from burials and "improved on" in the forger's studio. Chumash ceremonial whistles made of deer tibia are well known from all periods of Chumash culture, and their use is described in the ethnological literature. Most of the large whistles date from around 900 CE and into the historic period; their average size is about nine inches long.[16] Most have simple asphaltum plugs filling the stop at the wider end, whereas the objects illustrated here are crowned with shell and crystal that have been set into the asphaltum matrix.

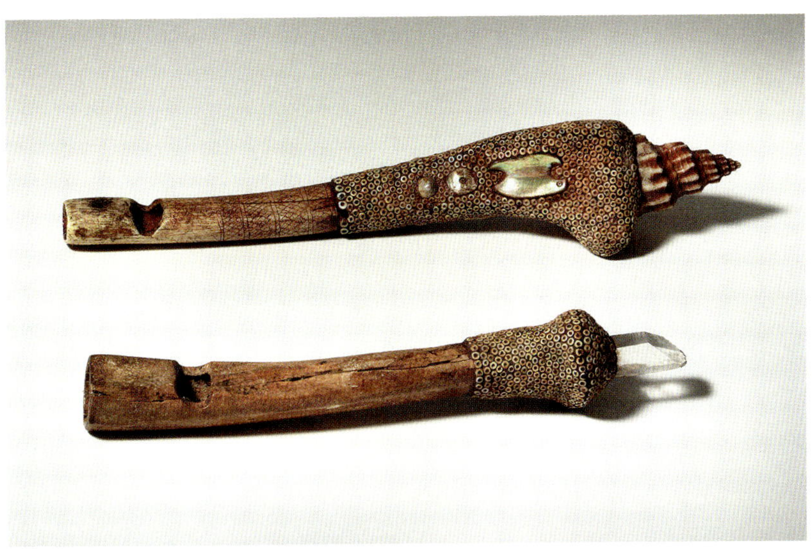

FIG. 4.2 Two whistles. Deer tibia bone, shell, pearls, crystal, asphaltum. Ancient Chumash, California, with modern additions. No. PC.B.N.007, 24 × 3.6 cm; no. PC.B.N.002, 29.8 × 5.6 cm. © Dumbarton Oaks, Pre-Columbian Collection, Washington, DC. Photography by Joseph Mills.

Scores of small round bead disks and some larger pearls and shells are set into the asphaltum as well.[17]

Asphaltum is a naturally occurring tar substance found in clumps on southern California beaches as well as welling up from springs or in seepages.[18] The Chumash heated asphaltum and used it to waterproof boats and baskets, to affix arrows to shafts, and to serve as a matrix for beads on stone and bone objects. But nowhere in a controlled archaeological excavation has anything as elaborate as the Dumbarton Oaks pieces been uncovered.

In 2002, the archaeologist Lynn Gamble, one of the foremost experts on Chumash material culture, studied the many bone and steatite forgeries in the Heye Collection at the National Museum of the American Indian, observing that in these objects the inlaid beads represent Chumash bead technology from widely varying time periods, suggesting that they had been aggregated in the construction of these objects; in some cases, she found microscopic evidence that the beads and asphaltum were mechanically ground down after the beads were set.[19] The use, within one object, of beads that may have been made a millennium apart suggests a looter who owned a large collection of beads, and mechanical tools to grind the surface to a smooth finish. Unquestionably, some components of the Dumbarton Oaks objects are real Chumash artifacts. But under what circumstances were they fashioned into elegant impostors that traveled from the hands of a forger to a dealer, to wealthy collectors, ultimately to find homes in major American art museums?

The correspondence between Stendhal and Robert Bliss, now held in the archives at Dumbarton Oaks, illuminates the ways that art dealers can tantalize collectors as they drop tidbits of information. The first letter from Stendhal concerning Chumash objects is dated February 16, 1947.[20] It is obvious that he and Bliss had had ongoing conversations about these items: "The Chumash pieces are tops in exquisite workmanship. Yes, you both should really be a little excited." Bliss replied, expressing his interest, and on March 20, 1947, Stendahl reassured Bliss that he did not sell any of the Chumash material to another collector: "I have decided to hold all and sell as a collection. You will receive some Kodachromes of the new things just acquired. Never have I seen such pieces. I have had my men out scouting the country for any material and now I think pretty near all available is in this group of about 114 pieces with many cases of shell beads, pendants, and necklaces. Perfectly beautiful material." Shortly thereafter, he sent photographs of two Chumash whistles now in the collection (see figure 4.2), about which Bliss replied: "Mrs. Bliss has been captivated by the two whistles and insists that you send them on here. . . . Also she would like to see the pipe [i.e., the cloud blower (see figure 4.1)]." At the end of the letter, Bliss expressed possible interest in the whole collection that Stendahl had mentioned earlier. In reply, on April 5, 1947, Stendahl used the time-honored method of mentioning that another important collector might be interested:

> Mr. Arensberg has the refusal [i.e., rights of first refusal] of some of the pieces. . . . I would not sell the collection for less than Mrs. Maitland paid for hers, which was $15,000. There are many more pieces in this collection and I would say some of them are as high a quality and many of finer workmanship.
>
> This collection was formed from a few private parties who had found them years ago. People along the highway gathered some objects when the bulldozers cut through the burials and some of this material will come on the market eventually, but I feel this about finishes the important pieces from the Chumash.[21]

Later in the letter he casually dropped some additional information: "The whistles have really caused a lot of excitement. . . . Four of the Board of the Minneapolis Museum will have a meeting in my home next Tuesday to make a very large selection. I will, however, hold out the things that you are interested in." This is a classic means of getting an indecisive collector to make a decision: not only is a rival collector interested, but members of the board of an art museum may soon pounce! Nonetheless, a year later the objects were still available: on February 13, 1948, Bliss mentioned that he and his wife were "still talking about the two Chumash pieces that Mrs. Bliss liked so well," and four days later he sent Stendahl a check for several objects. A subsequent letter from Stendahl, on March 8, 1948, made it clear that $2,000 was the portion of the bill for "two bone whistles inlaid with shell beads and one sailfish." On June 21, 1954, Stendahl sent a bill for several more pieces, including a "Fish Pipe, steatite, from Arroyo Sequit, $1000" (see figure 4.1).

The Blisses made an investment of what today would be $30,000 for four of the eight Chumash objects they purchased, without anything to back up this purchase other than their own aesthetic sensibilities—no comparative research, no examination of objects in museum collections, and no advice other than that of the dealer who sought to make a sale. These were very high prices for objects of American Indian art in the 1940s and 1950s.[22] Captivated by the beauty of these unusual items, Robert and Mildred Bliss's famous "connoisseurial eye" failed them.[23]

Stendahl's statement that the collection was formed from private parties, and material gathered along the highways after bulldozers uncovered it, accurately characterizes the state of Chumash archaeology from the mid-nineteenth century to the 1940s. What Stendahl does not mention is that he was getting these objects from one man: an unsavory character named Arthur Sanger (1880–1971).

The archaeologist Henry Koerper has characterized Sanger as a "grifter extraordinaire" who made and sold egregious fakes.[24] He owned a yacht on which he often sailed to the Channel Islands to dig for artifacts. He also participated in excavations funded by institutions, had a large collection of Chumash material in his home, and, according to the most reputable archaeologists in southern California, was the source for much questionable material, including that sold by Stendahl. Two publications in 1930 illustrated Sanger digging on San Nicolas Island as part of a group providing material to the Los Angeles County Museum of History (now the Natural History Museum of Los Angeles County) and other institutions; the author noted that Sanger "ha[d] been digging for Indian relics on all the Channel Islands for the past twenty years."[25]

In 1993, the archaeologist Georgia Lee laid bare the issue of Chumash fakes and who was responsible for them. Sanger's name and, secondarily, that of O. T. Littleton (both of whom worked on the excavations Heye sponsored in 1939–41) are prominent. Among those quoted was an archaeology master's student who interviewed Sanger in 1951 and asked him about Chumash objects, to which Sanger admitted "fixing it all up to make it sell."[26] One of the scholars quoted was Arthur Woodward (1898–1986), curator of history and archaeology at the Los Angeles County Museum of History, who wrote that Stendahl bought items from Sanger and others, and he stated, "All of these [spurious] items that have appeared on the market . . . have passed through Stendahl's hands."[27] The scholars involved in this correspondence agreed that it was telling that no elaborate objects like those sold by Stendahl "turned up during the sixty or seventy years of excavations." "Why are they only found by the commercial dealers?" they asked. One commented, "I think it is unusual that no one but Sanger finds them."[28]

In 1984, the curator Elizabeth Boone queried the archaeologist Travis Hudson about the Chumash pieces at Dumbarton Oaks. Hudson (1941–1985), curator of anthropology at the Santa Barbara Museum of Natural History, was one of the foremost scholars of Chumash material culture. In his five-page, single-spaced reply to Boone, he explained, "Starting with documented pieces, we have over 100 years of archaeological work in this region. . . . All of the effigies, pipes, whistles, etc. from controlled situations, the documented pieces, are nothing like those which relate in various ways to Sanger. . . . One should be careful of very elaborate effigies when such objects can be traced back to only one man, despite the archaeological work of hundreds of scholars over 100 years. Why should Sanger be the only one to find these things?"[29] Hudson went on to point out that steatite is easy to carve and that shells, beads, and tar are easily acquired by looters. He also noted that beads from different periods were used; in particular, beads from about 500 CE were applied to bone whistles that likely dated from a millennium later.[30]

Robert and Mildred Bliss were not the only major collectors who became enamored of the "Chumash" pieces that Stendahl had for sale. In 1955, Nelson Rockefeller (1908–1979), one of the twentieth century's foremost collectors of tribal art, bought a whistle almost identical to those in figure 4.2. It was displayed in the Museum of Primitive Art that he founded in 1954 and then became part of the Metropolitan Museum.[31] Jay C. Leff (1925–2000), a Pittsburgh banker who amassed a notable collection of the arts of Africa and the Americas, also bought one. Published in a 1959 catalogue of his collection, it was later given to the Carnegie Institute in Pittsburgh.[32] The founding director of the Seattle Art Museum, Richard Fuller (1897–1976), who gave some seventy-five hundred objects to the museum, bought an almost identical whistle inlaid with beads and topped with a whorled shell. The acquisition records say he bought it from Stendahl Galleries in 1962 for $1,200.[33] These objects are not on exhibit, and most remain little known.

As with other objects in this book, including the catlinite pipes and Zuni vessels in chapter 1, it might be surprising to realize that even in the late nineteenth century, experts were warning about the rash of Chumash fakes on the market. Writing in the *American Archaeologist* in 1898, the archaeologist Horatio Nelson Rust (1828–1906) published a short, cautionary note:

> The very desirable soapstone cooking vessels and other stone relics, found about Santa Barbara, California are so perfectly counterfitted that sometimes experienced archaeologists are deceived by the imitations. The soapstone from which they are made is taken from Santa Catalina Island, and the serpentine from Point Piedras Blancos. By smearing them with grease, then burning and smoking them, they are made to look like the best prehistoric specimens. And Santa Barbara does a flourishing business in these frauds. I think it is the duty of every archaeologist to expose the frauds as promptly as they would the making of counterfeit money.[34]

California archaeologists in the 1940s and 1950s were actively writing to each other about such fakes even as Stendahl was selling them. The unanswerable question is, how much did Stendahl know? Was he in cahoots with Sanger to create and provide the most elegant-looking Chumash objects to the monied gentleman-collectors of Los Angeles, New York City, and Washington, DC? Stendahl's biographer acknowledges his active complicity in the looting of Jaina Island and other Mexican archaeological sites—a common event, practiced openly before the United Nations Educational, Scientific, and Cultural Organization's (UNESCO) 1972 Convention concerning the Protection of the World Cultural and Natural Heritage.[35]

Not all fakes are made with an intention to fool collectors and make money for their makers. Some fakes are accidental.

Codex Covarrubias—an Accidental Fake

How can a fake be accidental? Makers of shell and pottery replicas of Southwestern archaeological material have shared anecdotes that reveal a number of possibilities. For example, one described selling a Hohokam-style carved shell ornament and another an Ancestral Pueblo–style pot (each with initials or a signature etched into the material), only to have each item presented for sale within the local antiquities market some months later, dirtied and slightly battered, with the initials sandpapered off. Of course, this "new find" is accompanied by a tall tale of a recent discovery in a cave or burial. In these instances, the maker did not intend to deceive when he made the object. Its transformation was effected after it left his hands. I believe this to be the case with a book of ledger drawings sold at Sotheby's New York auction house in June 1997.

Many of us who study Native American art are approached occasionally by auction houses seeking our expertise in evaluating and authenticating works of art. It happened to me with some frequency in the 1990s. In July 1996, the head of the American Indian art department at Sotheby's telephoned, requesting that I examine a book of ledger drawings that it planned to sell that fall. I was then in the second year of a two-year Getty Scholars Grant, during which I traveled across North America looking at hundreds of Plains Indian drawings in both private and public collections; the major traveling exhibit of such drawings resulting from my research was opening in New York that autumn.[36] My opinion was apparently a matter of some urgency, for Sotheby's wanted to feature the book in its fall 1996 auction of American Indian art. Color photocopies and slides of all the images were shipped to me overnight.

Sotheby's had good reason to be excited by the possibilities offered by this book of drawings: it was substantial—more than six dozen images in ink and colored pencil, executed in a nineteenth-century ledger.[37] From the 1860s to the 1920s, many men on the Great Plains drew their personal exploits and tribal stories in discarded ledgers and other notebooks. Starting in the late 1970s, scholars' and collectors' interest in this genre grew in tandem, with books being written and facsimiles of ledger books full of drawings being published by galleries before the individual pages were sliced out and sold.[38]

In 1994, Sotheby's had set auction records when a book of seventy-six drawings by the Lakota artist Black Hawk achieved a price of $428,750, the second-highest price achieved by an American Indian work of art up to that time.[39] I knew immediately that this drawing book, in contrast, was not a Plains work of art. The drawings were too modern in style, and in some cases too unusual in content, to have been made in the nineteenth century (see figure 4.9). Yet as I studied it further, I came to believe—and still believe today—that it was not an outright forgery. Enough time has passed that I can tell the story of my own brief involvement with this work that the sales catalogue characterized merely as "drawn in an atypical stylized manner."

The information accompanying the images indicated that the book had come from the library of Miguel Covarrubias (1904–1957), a well-known Mexican artist and writer. My immediate shock at the bizarreness of the images turned to a hunch that Covarrubias had drawn them. (Because of my years as a scholar of pre-Columbian art, I was familiar with his work.) After several days of research, I wrote back to Sotheby's saying that, in my professional opinion, this was not by a nineteenth-century Plains artist, but by Covarrubias himself, giving numerous reasons for my assessment.[40] My detailed reply was never acknowledged and Sotheby's never again contacted me for my professional opinion on works offered for sale.

Covarrubias's considerable role in Native North American art history in the middle of the twentieth century is little known today. It is important to understand his expertise in this, as well as his versatility as an artist, caricaturist, and scholar, in order to understand how it might be possible that these drawings came from his pen.[41]

MIGUEL COVARRUBIAS AND NATIVE AMERICAN ART

This Mexican polymath wrote books on pre-Columbian art, indigenous Mexican cultures, the island of Bali, and North American Indian art. He traveled in sophisticated circles in Mexico City, New York, and Paris from the 1920s until his death. But most importantly, Covarrubias was a talented artist who excelled at cartoon, at caricature, and at book illustrations of all sorts. He illustrated his own publications as well as those written by others on topics ranging from African American folklore to Bernal Díaz del Castillo's *The Conquest of Mexico*.[42] In everything that he did, his mind synthesized reams of data, and his eye refined and distilled visual material to its essence. I believe that Covarrubias himself created this drawing book I have come to call Codex Covarrubias.[43]

Covarrubias lived in New York City off and on for many years, from his arrival at age nineteen in 1923 until 1950.[44] His understanding of Native American art was shaped by the attitudes of other avant-garde intellectuals and artists, his close relationships with anthropologists and archaeologists, and his own prodigious research. Throughout his cosmopolitan and peripatetic life, he encountered many curators, artists, and scholars interested in Native art, both in the United States and in Mexico City. But it was surely his friendship with René d'Harnoncourt that was most influential.[45] He worked with d'Harnoncourt on *Twenty Centuries of Mexican Art* (1940) and on the influential blockbuster *Indian Art of the United States* (1941), both at the radical new Museum of Modern Art. Soon thereafter, he was awarded a Guggenheim grant to tour North American museums to study Native American art and to choose objects for an exhibit of such art he staged in Mexico City in 1945, with an accompanying book, *El arte indígena de Norteamérica.* While these have remained almost unknown in North America, they set the stage for Covarrubias's most substantial contribution—the writing of *The Eagle, the Jaguar, and the Serpent: Indian Art of the Americas.*[46]

He was an indefatigable scholar who read everything he could on the Native North American arts and cultures before writing *The Eagle, the Jaguar, and the Serpent.* The collections of the American Museum of Natural History and the Museum of the American Indian were well known to him, and objects from their collections illustrated his book. A perusal of the book's bibliography suggests that Covarrubias had surveyed nearly everything published on the archaeology and ethnology of North America, from the early ethnographies of the Plains to recent archaeological monographs on Alaska and portfolios on contemporary Native painting. Moreover, the book's illustrations demonstrated Covarrubias's familiarity with the major museum collections of Native art. He executed some 124 drawings for the book himself. After studying Covarrubias's publications, it was clear to me that, for him, to draw was to think; words followed.

Before Covarrubias's 1954 volume, the most ambitious coverage of the art of indigenous North America—and the only one written by an art historian—was the Spanish scholar José Pijoán's *Arte de los pueblos aborígenes* of 1931. Devoting some two hundred pages to North America, it is a thorough examination of the major art forms, from ancient pottery to modern painting, written at a time when the primary sources on such materials were limited.[47] Pijoán's volume is far less well known in North America than it should be, but as a native Spanish speaker, Covarrubias was undoubtedly familiar with it. In the 1940s, there was not the wealth of publications on ledger drawings that became available by the late 1980s. Yet in 1938, the scholar Hartley Burr Alexander had published a portfolio of Sioux drawings, and the following year John Ewers of the Smithsonian published *Plains Indian Painting*.[48] Ledger drawings in museum collections in New York, Boston, Chicago, Washington, DC, and elsewhere were known to some scholars. Covarrubias illustrated Inuit drawings from the American Museum of Natural History; perhaps he also examined the numerous Cheyenne and Lakota drawings in that collection.[49]

"A RARE HIDATSA BOOK . . . DRAWN IN AN ATYPICALLY STYLIZED MANNER"

In the June 4, 1997, Sotheby's catalogue *Important American Indian Art*, the description and illustrations of Lot 96 took up nine pages.[50] Many of the drawings, done with a bold confident hand, depict subjects common in Cheyenne, Lakota, and Kiowa drawings from the last third of the nineteenth century: courtship, horsemanship, hunting, and ceremony. Yet not one of these drawings "looked right"—the art historical shorthand for something that does not appear to be authentic.

One half-page image and fifty-one small-scale images emphasized the work's importance in the eyes of the auction house, for seldom is a work in an auction catalogue afforded more than a couple of images. The lengthy essay described the drawing book as illustrating the exploits of "Lion Boy" (apparently so designated because several pages depict the protagonist hunting a mountain lion). Moreover, it was called a Hidatsa book "of early date."[51] While sometimes Sotheby's commissions scholars to write brief, signed essays about significant works of art for its catalogues, this one was unsigned, though cited opinions offered by Mike Cowdrey.[52] The likely price range for the work was recorded as $75,000–$125,000. It sold for $79,500.

Many drawing books contain wonderful scenes of courtship in which males and females are paired up within blankets. But nowhere else in the huge corpus of ledger drawings have I ever seen one that uses x-ray vision to reveal sexual play occurring within the blanket (see figure 4.9). Overt sexual content is never seen in Plains drawings, though explicitly sexual monikers appear in Plains men's nicknames for each other.[53] To my mind, this reflects a twentieth-century urbanite's sense of humor, *not* a nineteenth-century warrior-artist's. Another

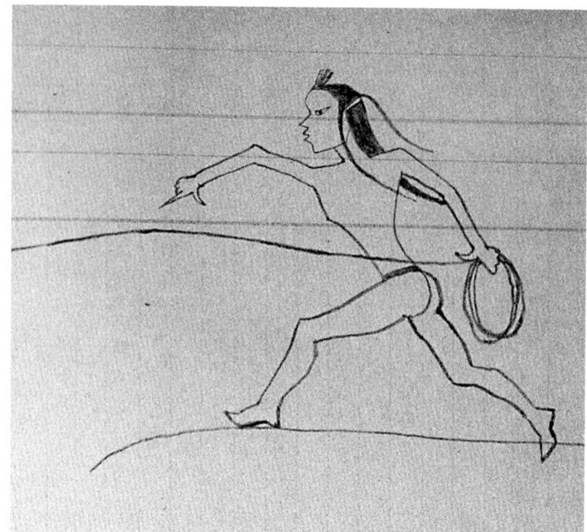

FIG. 4.3 Man lassoing an elk (detail). Codex Covarrubias, image no. 39. Ink and colored pencil on ledger paper, 10 × 7⅞ in. Photo courtesy of Sotheby's.

aspect of physiognomy that is anomalous compared to the corpus of Plains drawings is the way this artist draws the curvaceous bare buttocks and legs of his male figures (figure 4.3). This exact body type is ubiquitous in 1920s and 1930s Art Deco, including the doors of Rockefeller Center, constructed when Covarrubias was spending time in New York City.[54]

Codex Covarrubias also features many iconographic anomalies—things that those of us who have studied ledger drawings for decades have simply never seen. Indeed, their existence was used by the writer of the Sotheby's catalogue entry as evidence of the book's authenticity, for the drawings depict activities well documented in the ethnographic literature on the Northern Plains in general and the Hidatsa in particular. In 1928, the anthropologist Gilbert L. Wilson's report of eagle-trapping practices among the Hidatsa, as explained and illustrated by Hidatsa artist Edward Goodbird, was published. It described that a hunter would dig a pit where he could lie in wait, a bloodied white rabbit placed above for bait (figure 4.4). The text described that a lid of latticework and brush covered the opening, allowing the hunter to reach out and seize the eagle's legs.[55] In the ledger drawing version, the hunter sits up on his knees, ready to pull the cord when the eagle alights on the rabbit (figure 4.5). Then the hunter would take it to the eagle-trapping lodge for ceremonial use. Wilson's text says that bears were the first to conduct such ceremonies in their lodges, though Goodbird provides no illustration. The Sotheby's ledger does.[56]

Although Covarrubias appreciated North American Indian art, his great love was the pre-Hispanic art of his homeland. So it is not surprising that a couple of the drawings in Codex Covarrubias display a central Mexican sensibility. In the *Matricula de tributos* (a sixteenth-century manuscript depicting the tribute levied on numerous municipalities by the Aztec state), the items of tribute are laid out in neat rows: regalia and shields, woven blankets, and so forth (figure 4.6). Curiously, the final page of Codex Covarrubias, too, is laid out as if to render such a tax to a Hidatsa chief: horses, peace pipes, guns, knives, bags, and trade blankets (with pre-Columbian codex-style tally marks beside the blankets) (figure 4.7). This is the ultimate in artistic bricolage: a sixteenth-century Aztec codex, as translated through the pen of a twentieth-century Mexican artist, in tribute to the nineteenth-century artists of the American Plains.

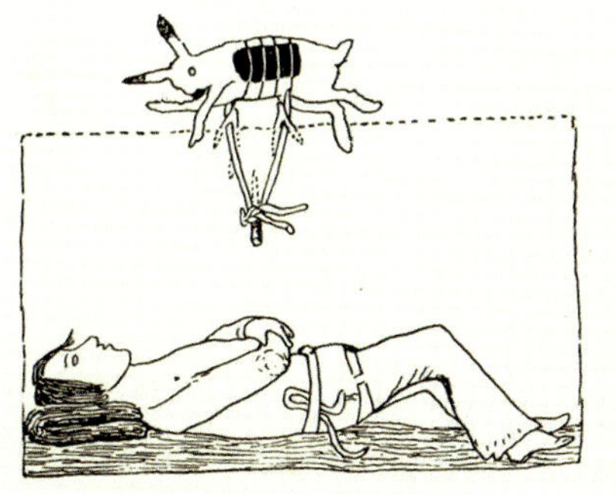

FIG. 4.4 / RIGHT Illustration by Hidatsa artist Edward Goodbird of hunter lying in wait to trap an eagle, drawn after figure 6c of Gilbert L. Wilson, *Hidatsa Eagle Trapping*, 1928.

FIG. 4.5 / BELOW Eagle trapping. Codex Covarrubias, image no. 21. Ink and colored pencil on ledger paper, 10 × 7⅞ in. Photo courtesy of Sotheby's.

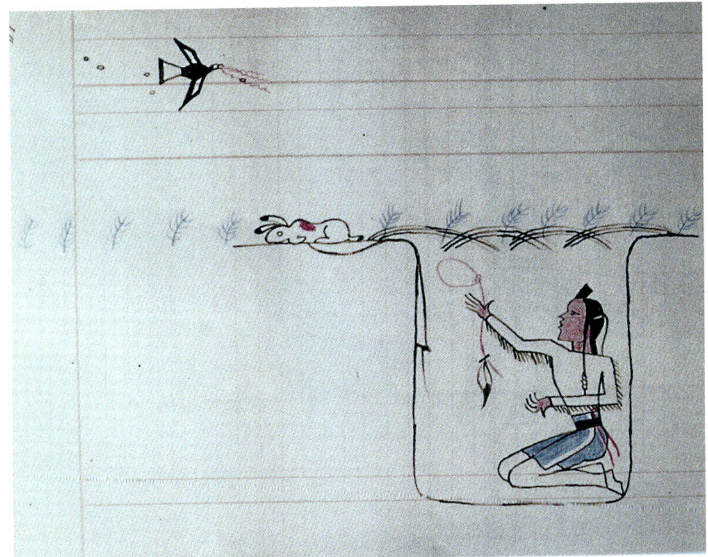

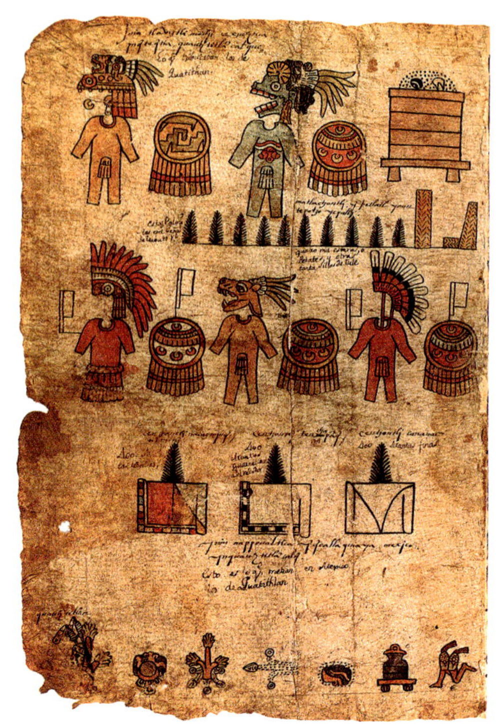

FIG. 4.6 / RIGHT Page from the *Matrícula de tributos* (Aztec tribute roll, ca. 1525). Pigment on amate paper, 29 × 42 cm. Collection Instituto Nacional de Antropología e Historia, Mexico City.

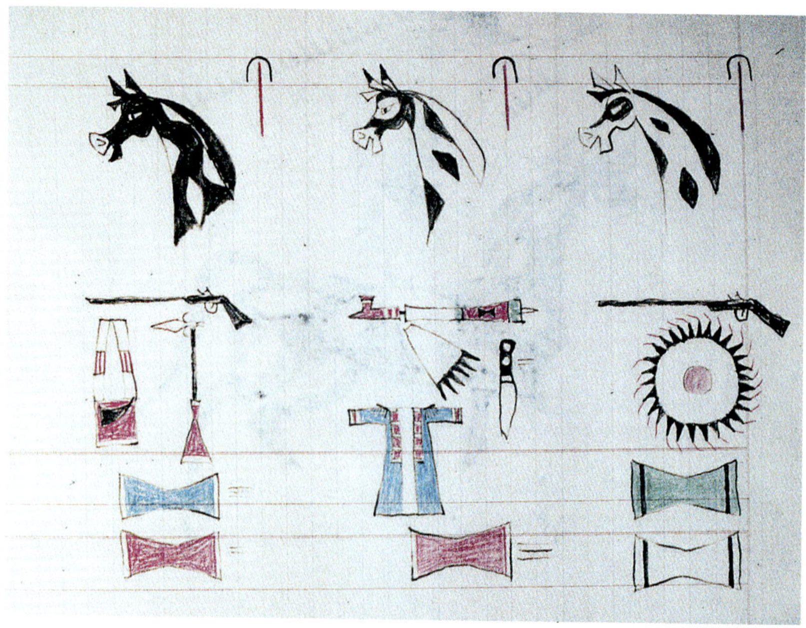

FIG. 4.7 / BELOW Spoils of an enemy raid. Codex Covarrubias, image no. 135. Ink and colored pencil on ledger paper, 10 × 7⅞ in. Photo courtesy of Sotheby's.

I do not believe that Covarrubias—so finely tuned to the stylistic specificities of the arts he studied and reproduced—meant to deceive when he drew in this book, which apparently was kept as part of his library, rather than as a work of art in his collection. Instead, it was a handful of late twentieth-century scholars of Plains culture who were blind to the basic stylistic characteristics of Plains drawings, combined with the greed of the modern marketplace, that led to the absurd conclusion that the drawing book offered by Sotheby's, with its cartoon-faced horses and priapic young men, is part of the same grand artistic tradition as well-known drawing books by Black Hawk, Silver Horn, Howling Wolf, and other artists from the Great Plains.

Trying to demonstrate that the drawings in the Covarrubias ledger were done by the Mexican artist himself is not as simple as performing a basic Morellian stylistic comparison between these works and others by his hand, for Covarrubias was a master of mimicry and caricature, moving fluently among different drawing styles.[57] I am confident that if Covarrubias wanted to make a Plains ledger book that would fool viewers, this versatile artist could easily have done so. But I believe he was playing, drawing this for his own amusement, and for that of his circle of intimates, for the drawing book evinces a cosmopolitan reach—from the sexy Art Deco buttocks of its male figures to its horses prancing on tippy-toes like equine Nijinskys.[58] I find Codex Covarrubias of interest principally as a cultural document revealing much about the art market, as well as the politics and circulation of images both in the mid-twentieth century and in its closing decade.

While researching these drawings in 2007, I corresponded with Bill Holm about them. In addition to his work on Northwest Coast art (see chapter 1), he was quite knowledgeable about the arts and cultures of the Northern Plains. When Holm first saw pictures of these so-called Hidatsa drawings in 1997, he was sure they were legitimate, for he was, as he wrote to me, "bowled over by the range of subjects, the details, the exquisite drawing, and the accuracy of the depiction of Hidatsa culture, mythology, and history."[59] But as he studied them more closely, he began to doubt their authenticity, principally because of what he saw as the unwitting use of one-point perspective in some details, as well as the sophisticated rendering of some humans and animals. Holm believed that Covarrubias could not have made these ethnographically detailed drawings, because *The Eagle, the Jaguar, and the Serpent* does not evince a detailed enough understanding of Northern Plains culture and art. It is true that the book's passages on the Plains are cursory, as Covarrubias was being pressed to send his long-overdue manuscript to his publisher.[60] Holm also believed that the drawing book could not have been created by Covarrubias because so many details of Hidatsa cultural practices were published only after his death. Yet as I have demonstrated, some of these details were published in readily available scholarly sources in the 1920s.

Why would Covarrubias have gone to the trouble to create such a suite of drawings? It might make more sense to us that such a work would be circulated among an academic in-crowd today, as a means of poking fun of an art world that would pay $428,750 or even $79,500—for a book of modest drawings by hitherto-unknown Native artists. But in fact, like Covarrubias's droll drawings that reach out across time to touch an audience decades after they were published in *Vanity Fair* or the *New Yorker*, these Plains-style drawings probably seemed as timely then, within his circle of intimates, as they do now. René d'Harnoncourt, who drew personal cartoons for Covarrubias, and the artist Wolfgang Paalen, who lived in Mexico from 1939 through the 1950s and who collected Native North American art, would certainly have appreciated the humor in such a notebook, as would their friends who were curators and collectors.[61] I believe that it would have seemed unthinkable to them that these would ever be mistaken for nineteenth-century Plains drawings and that Covarrubias did this for his own amusement, as a way of amalgamating the vast visual knowledge he had of Plains iconography, Aztec tribute rolls, and a host of other topics—all rattling around in his head like loose change in a pocket.

Cutting-edge scholars and artists in the 1920s and 1930s easily transgressed borders in their work. For example, in the United States, early twentieth-century scholarship on American art was enlivened by an interest in African American and Native American visual culture and folk art, before retreating into canonical narratives of Anglo-American artistic traditions in the 1950s. Today, scholarship in American art history has been invigorated once again by close analysis of various cross-currents, from encounters within competing American cultural traditions to transatlantic ones.[62] As scholars chafe at various canonical strictures, we seem always to rediscover that we are not the first generation to do so.

Covarrubias's work on Native North American art aligns with his focus on modernism and indigenous Latin America. And his light-hearted bricolage of Native iconographic and stylistic features, as evidenced in Codex Covarrubias, is part of this transgressive modernity as well. For me, Codex Covarrubias serves as a curiously real (if not technically "authentic") talisman—a vision of an integrated history in which a lively, all-encompassing, and playful modernity is lodged in an unlikely place—between the covers of an old, discarded notebook.

"Less than What They Were": Mimbres Visual Fictions

In the short period between 1000 and 1150 CE, women in villages along the Mimbres River valley and nearby areas of southwestern New Mexico created the painted pottery bowls that came to be so valued in the twentieth century.[63] What has attracted everyone from early hobbyists who dug up pots to serious archaeologists, artists, and others is the singularly captivating imagery painted within the convex surfaces of bowls. Complex geometric designs swirl around the rims or fill entire surfaces. Beguiling humans and animals with both naturalistic and conventionalized traits rotate around the bowls' interiors. For their makers, these painted bowls were useful both in life and after death. Evidence of daily wear marks their surfaces, and the centers of many were ritually pieced with a "kill hole" before being placed over the heads of the dead buried beneath the floors of their houses.[64] Mimbres culture grew out of the traditions of Hohokam people to the south and west and was part of an intercultural network that extended into the Ancestral Pueblo region to the north.

A SHORT HISTORY OF INTEREST IN MIMBRES ART

Since its first discovery in the late nineteenth century, Mimbres painted pottery has fascinated archaeologists, looters, collectors, commercial designers, and, more recently, art historians. Mimbres imagery has inspired modern Native artists, too. But this section is concerned with the "embellishment," "restoration," and "conservation" of Mimbres vessels. Each of these is a loaded word.

Smithsonian archeologist Jesse Walter Fewkes published his first paper on Mimbres painted pottery in 1914. By the mid-1920s, he was buying Mimbres bowls for the Smithsonian's vast collections.[65] Harriet and Cornelius B. Cosgrove, who lived in Silver City (a town in the Mimbres region), started informally excavating Mimbres sites in the mid-1910s. The Cosgroves were so professional in their work that Harvard archaeologist A. V. Kidder invited them to direct the excavations at the Swarts Ruin for the Peabody Museum.

In four field seasons (1924–27), the Cosgroves excavated hundreds of bowls, and they documented many more from private collections and other sites.[66]

In the publication *The Swarts Ruin*, Harriet Cosgrove's meticulous renderings of the vessels from her excavations and from other collections captivated the larger world. In more than 732 individual drawings of painted bowls, Cosgrove rendered the diversity and exuberance of Mimbres iconography in a manner than was graphically far more legible than the distorted photos of curved wall bowls (figure 4.8). Simultaneously, Mimbres designs appeared in more popular venues. Both the *Illustrated London News* and the popular magazine *Art and Archaeology* published articles on Mimbres art between 1929 and 1932.[67] Mimbres pottery was featured both in the influential *Exposition of Indian Tribal Arts* in New York City in 1931 and in the 1939 Indian arts

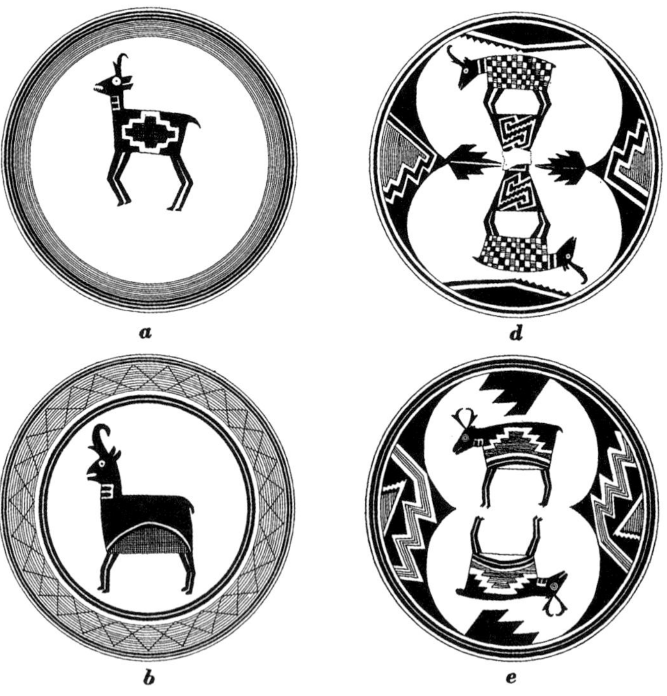

FIG. 4.8 Drawings of Mimbres bowls by Harriet Cosgrove, from *The Swarts Ruin*, 1932, plate 224.

and crafts exhibit in San Francisco.[68] Seen by more than a million people, the latter exhibit was, in effect, an aesthetic trial run for the ambitious exhibition that took over the entire Museum of Modern Art in 1941, *Indian Art of the United States*. At the art museum, opening the section on ancient arts, eight painted Mimbres bowls were displayed in the neutral Plexiglass vitrines that have become the stereotype of the "white box" museum installation but which were, at that time, bold and unusual.[69]

During the first half of the twentieth century, while scientific excavations were being conducted and published, many other Mimbres sites were being dug by pot hunters; later, the looting got even worse. The 1970s and 1980s, in particular, were a horrific time, with looters' bulldozers and backhoes destroying everything else in the search for painted pottery.[70] The publication of the art historian J. J. Brody's *Mimbres Painted Pottery* in 1977 signaled a new era of interest in these wares.[71] Brody began his groundbreaking study with an anecdote, recounting that, in 1963, New York art dealer Julius Carlebach sent a buyer to New Mexico with the instructions to buy ten thousand Mimbres pots.[72] In his characteristically acerbic way, Brody remarks: "Only his principal knows what the order was, or whether it was filled. It is certain that large numbers of pots were bought, including several forgeries. Most were eventually sold to collectors and some found their way into public museums."[73] While the story may or may not be apocryphal, the number invoked certainly is. What Carlebach likely meant was that these bowls were aesthetically so compelling that he could sell every single one that came into his gallery. The prominent collector Nelson Rockefeller bought ten Mimbres bowls from another New York City dealer in 1964 for his Museum of Primitive Art.[74]

Such interest at the highest levels of collecting is both the result of looting and something that encourages more looting. Prominent exhibitions and publications gave this ancient American aesthetic tradition the attention it deserves, but this went hand in hand with greater looting, greater interest in private collecting, more action in auction houses, and a concomitant rise in prices.[75] The most influential exhibit, *Mimbres Pottery: Ancient Art of the American Southwest*, toured the country in 1984–85, closing at the Metropolitan Museum in the autumn of 1985.[76] While Mimbres bowls had been glued back together and overpainted in early decades, in the second half of the twentieth century, collectors' lust for the finest vessels with figural designs led to a crisis in embellishment, over-restoration, and fakery.

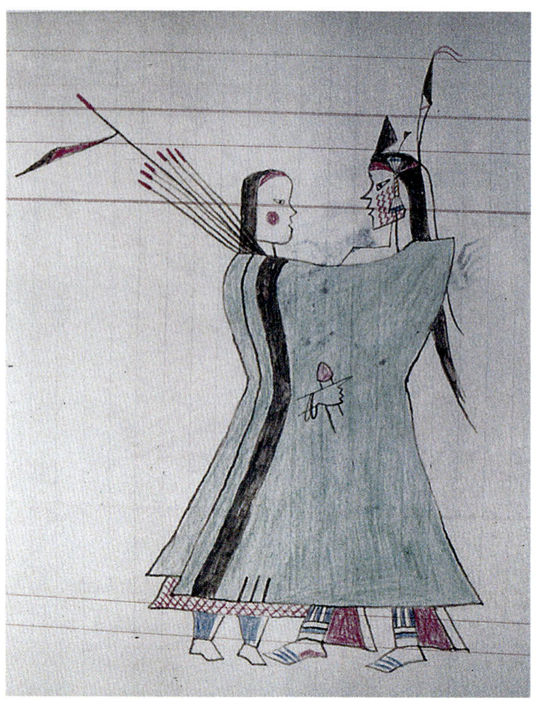

FIG. 4.9 Courting couple. Codex Covarrubias, image no. 135. Ink and colored pencil on ledger paper, 10 × 7⅞ in. Photo courtesy of Sotheby's.

THE PROBLEMATICS OF ARTISANAL RESTORATION

Looking at a Mimbres painted vessel with a well-trained object conservator is the art historical equivalent of driving through Wyoming with a geologist. In the latter case, instead of seeing scenery, one sees five hundred million years of historical stratification. In the former, instead of seeing simply a beautiful painted pot, one sees a thousand years of history and one hundred years of desecration. In 2017, I interviewed Dale Kronkright, head of conservation at the Georgia O'Keeffe Museum, about the restoration of Mimbres vessels.[77] Before then, I had interviewed people who made replicas and duplicates and individuals who restored Mimbres bowls for private collectors. Kronkright incisively critiqued an early draft of this section, causing me to substantially rethink it, for he taught me that the gap between conservation and what he terms "artisanal restoration" is vast.

The two "restorers" of Mimbres vessels whom I interviewed have worked in this area for decades. I spent two intensive days with one and an afternoon with the other. Each was extremely forthcoming with me about the work he did, and each saw himself as an ethical professional. As with other interviews for this book, I told each one that I would write up an initial draft and submit it to him for approval and correction. After seeing my draft, one said that he did not want his name used in my book, fearing it might compromise his standing with his numerous private clients. For this reason, I have omitted both names. Everything I write here is true of at least one of these men, though I have protected their identities by omitting certain details that might identify them, such as educational background and publications.

Through our conversations, I came to admire the painstaking work that they did for their private clients, though I understood that it did not conform to the highest standards of museum conservation. Each seemed to have a photographic memory and could easily recall details about scores of vessels. One had substantial notes and photos documenting his work, though he said that none of his clients seemed interested in having such data; at my prodding, he admitted it would be useful, should such pieces end up in museum collections.

It surprised me that Kronkright dismissed their work, suggesting that if I called them restorers, and their work restoration, I should put those terms in quotation marks (as I shall do henceforth). For the most part, he judged their craft harshly: "They are not part of the scientific community; they are part of the entertainment industry, for their job is to make things pretty, to make them socially desirable objects for collectors."[78] While I am sure that each of these artisanal "restorers" would vehemently object to this characterization, both clearly understood that the collectors called the shots. "My clients want excellent fine art," one said. "They don't want blank spaces, like in restored Greek vases."[79]

To set this discussion of restored Mimbres vessels in context, it is important to recognize that art museums display many objects that are seemingly pristine. In the field of Native American art, for example, ancient pots with apparently perfect painted surfaces and mid-nineteenth-century Navajo blankets with impeccable unfrayed wefts are often on exhibit.[80] In rare cases, these objects may have been treated so carefully that they truly are untouched by the vicissitudes of time; far more likely, they have been subject to alteration. This can range from simple cleaning and stabilization to what one of the Mimbres pottery "restorers" calls "extreme restoration," as discussed below. There is a fine line between Native American art and "not Native American art" in the realm of restoration, something that is seldom written about in this field.[81]

Contemporary codes for museum restoration hold that the "principle of reversibility" is paramount. Repairs done to an object should be easily undone, for newer and better methods and materials are sure to arise.[82] Conservators often cite the 1964 Charter of Venice, article 9 of which states, "The process of restoration is a highly specialized operation. Its aim is to preserve and reveal the aesthetic and historic value of the monument and is based on respect for original material and authentic documents. *It must stop at the point where conjecture begins*" (emphasis added).[83] Nonetheless, museums are full of objects that have been poorly restored, overly restored, or irrevocably changed by the restoration process.[84] A 2004 conservation project concerning Mimbres vessels at the Museum of Indian Arts and Culture / Laboratory of Anthropology in Santa Fe found that, around 1930, archaeological staff at the museum had "restored" Mimbres bowls recently excavated at Cameron Creek using materials as diverse as "animal glue, shellac, cellulose nitrate, linseed oil paints, natural resin varnishes, and early synthetic resins," as well as plaster of paris.[85] This conservation project removed the dark, disfiguring resin stains and some overpainting but chose not to remove the plaster of paris holding the bowls together.

Private collectors, of course, are unhampered by professional or institutional standards of restoration, or even simple record-keeping. Some of them may be unaware of the rigorous standards of contemporary museum conservators, while others seek to show their collections in the most impeccable condition possible, making aesthetic concerns paramount. Some pots no longer resemble thousand-year-old objects.

Both of the artisanal "restorers" I interviewed have worked on thousands of archaeological vessels from the American Southwest over the past four decades. Each varies in how interested he is in the archaeological aspects of the work—one is deeply interested, the other less so. Notably, both were trained in studio pottery before turning to artisanal restoration. To watch each at his craft is to see someone who looks closely, handles gently, and describes carefully. Like many artists, each has formidable powers of visual recollection. Unlike the people who make "authentic replicas" from scratch, such as Paul and Laurel Thornburg, who are discussed in the next section, these men use mostly modern materials in restorations of Mimbres bowls, aiming for structural soundness and aesthetic "completion" of painted images, not accuracy in materials. A restoration job in one of their home studios may start with sherds encrusted with salts and other organic matter. Or the task may be to disassemble a vessel that was glued using inferior materials forty years ago. After cleaning the pieces, a bowl-like support may be fashioned out of clay to cradle the sherds in proper relationship to each other. Then the gaps are filled with Hydrocal, a gypsum cement that is of higher tensile strength than ordinary plaster of paris. Acrylic paint, sometimes mixed with wood ash to give the paint a texture that mimics the eroded surface found in an archaeological bowl, completes the work.

If a vessel has been badly glued by a previous owner, it may take an hour to remove old adhesives and break it down into its component pieces. About three more hours are needed to clean the pieces, which may include bleaching and soaking. Plastering takes four or five more hours, as does painting the base coat and matching the white slip. Painting the missing portions of the design adds several more hours to the process. If the cracks are going to be carved back in, and a bit of antique patina added, three to five more hours may be required. Both men stress that this can be very tedious, but care and precision are central. One said, "Every step has to be perfect. If the cleaning is not perfect, the glue job won't be perfect. If the glue job is not perfect, the surface won't be right, and then the painting won't be right."

As the Charter of Venice succinctly states, restoration stops "at the point where conjecture begins." And the ethical line between restoration and forgery blurs when a restorer accedes to the wishes of an art dealer or a collector who wants a finer pot with a more complex iconography, thus transforming a geometric Mimbres bowl into one that features figural elements, for example. Both men stress that they refuse to embellish a bowl's painting; if unable to find the logical points of departure for linking visual elements (feet, tools, animal parts, geometric designs), they will not add them. Yet both have done "extreme restoration," as one of them calls it, at the request of private collectors. Perhaps the most extreme example involves the potsherd that was transformed into a bowl depicting a standing woman who carries a burden basket on her head and a staff, as the drawing in figure 4.10 indicates.[86] When the artisanal restorer built this bowl around one figural potsherd, he did not knowingly do it for the art market; the collector who owned the potsherd asked him to make a pot out of it as a present for his mother. I saw the photographs documenting the process; as the drawing shows, the fragment clearly depicted a woman's belly, her small breasts drawn in typical Mimbres fashion. Enough was visible, he says, that he extrapolated: "A woman would have the fringed belt that Mimbres women on painted bowls wear. And it's clear from the sherd that

FIG. 4.10 Mimbres bowl "restored" from one original central piece, drawing by Kendall DeBoer, 2022.

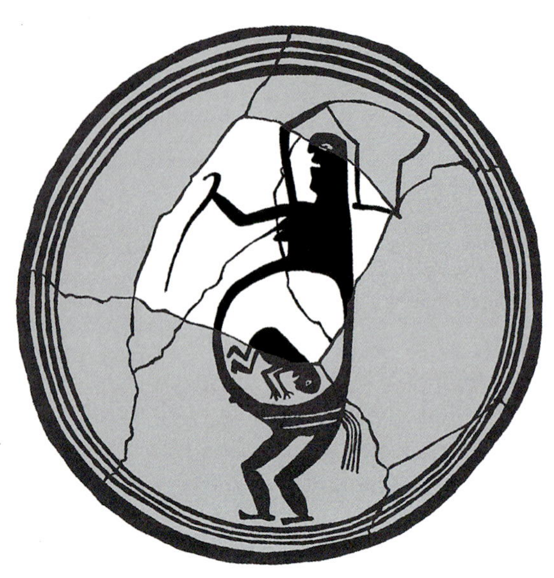

FIG. 4.11 Mimbres bowl used on cover of J. J. Brody, *Mimbres Painted Pottery*, 1977. Museum of Western Colorado, Grand Junction, Colorado, no. G495.

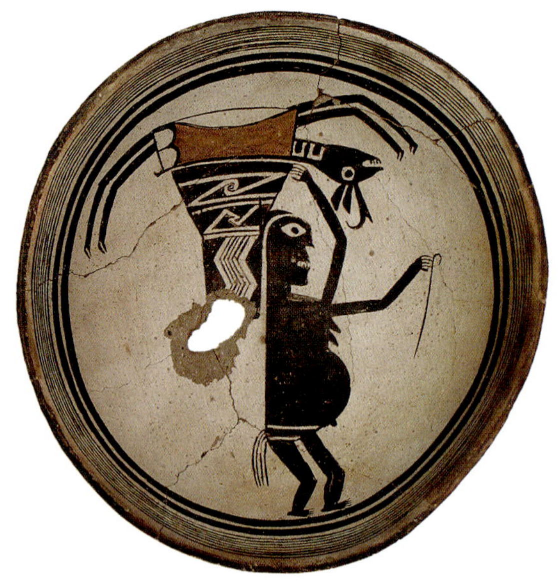

she is carrying something on her head shaped like a burden basket, with one arm up to hold it. So I drew a burden basket." Pointing to the Mimbres bowl depicting a pregnant woman carrying a burden basket pictured on the dust jacket of Brody's 1977 *Mimbres Painted Pottery* (figure 4.11), he said, "That same pot provided the model for the lower body, legs, and feet."[87] He observed that such x-ray visions of pregnancy occur in Mimbres paintings of animals as well as women, so that his depiction of the fetus is based on real paintings.

Compared to some bowls, the scene is not complex, and the "restorer" asserts that he did not embellish the iconography beyond what was discernible from the fragment with which he started. He did not give the pot an elaborate geometric rim pattern—though it may have had one—he just painted a simple three-line stripe and a black rim. Yet, if in some future study of Mimbres iconography, a researcher is counting attributes and adds this vessel to the sample, it will skew the sample concerning everything except the pregnancy, the basket, and the breasts—for the other attributes are borrowed from more complete bowls.

When finished with this exercise in "extreme restoration," the "restorer" wrote on the underside, "This is a hypothetical reconstruction, based on this sherd unit," and drew on the convex surface what is still visible on the concave interior: the outlines of the original central sherd. He also signed his name. This bowl has changed hands several times, and the inscription and signature were, at some point, removed. The collector who owns it now apparently knows its history. But if this vessel is ever sold again, a subsequent owner, if he neglects to perform "conservatorial due diligence" as we might call it (having an expert look at the pot under a black light, performing thermoluminescence testing, and swabbing the painted surface with acetone, for example), might be surprised to find that he has essentially paid for a potsherd surrounded by Hydrocal.

The artisanal "restorers" I interviewed were dismissive of some of the imagery embellishing Mimbres bowls done by an earlier generation of forgers. Indeed, some are quite nonsensical. In the Mimbres Pottery Images Digital Database (MimPIDD) there is a photo of a bowl depicting the zany antics of what I would call a "mock-Mimbreño."[88] This seeming conflation of a Hindu snake charmer and a Hopi snake dancer has rattlesnakes coiled around his limbs, as another snake arises from a trapezoidal basket. Nowhere in the corpus of scientifically excavated Mimbres painted vessels is there anything remotely like this.[89]

Mimbres pottery occasionally appears on eBay. Potsherds sporting recognizable figural details might sell from $200 to $400, dubious-looking bowls for hundreds more. Occasionally a beautiful plain bowl is on offer, of the sort used by the thousands in Mimbres daily life. This would be called a "blank" in the world of machine tooling, that is, something that is ready to be customized. Some forgers see these plain bowls in the same terms: an impeccable old surface on which to paint figural designs in an effort to have an extraordinary "story bowl" to sell. While some of the most beautiful Mimbres bowls are geometric, these vessels with human and animal designs are particularly sought after and bring the highest prices. In part, this is because the short-lived narrative style of Mimbres pottery was relatively rare in Native North America, and in part it relates to the elemental and ubiquitous human curiosity about story. How do we know that forgers actually do this? Because the artisanal "restorers" I interviewed have removed figural designs from bowls with authentically painted rims.

Another action that artisanal "restorers" are asked to do by high-end private collectors is to fill in the "kill hole" found on most Mimbres bowls taken from burial contexts. Clearly, some collectors are not interested in the complex histories that these bowls tell or in their ruggedly beautiful and shabby materiality. They seek only the most elegant version of an ancient object. (When I asked permission of two different pairs of dealers and collectors to illustrate such a bowl in its before and after states, both refused.) Exhibition catalogues are full of such vessels, for the high-end art collector prefers beauty to truth, the illusion of perfection to the veracity of a thousand-year-old object.

The professionalization of conservation as a science beginning in the 1960s has made clear how deep the divide is between artisanal "restorers" of works of art (who are sometimes self-taught or taught in the time-honored tradition of informal apprenticeship) and conservators. The former sometimes characterize conservators as bureaucrats who would prefer that objects be untouched and displayed under such controlled conditions that museumgoers must peer at them in virtual darkness. Conservators, in comparison, have been taught in their professional training to be wary of the work of so-called nonprofessionals. Moreover, often the work of museum conservation requires them to undo or redo work by artisanal "restorers" who did not use the most up-to-date materials or abide by the most stringent standards.

Professionals thoroughly document their treatment of objects. One "artisanal restorer" told me, "It is not my job to be the archivist of what has been done to Mimbres pottery," though he does have vivid recall of the vessels he has worked on, saying things such as "That one was just reconstruction—getting rid of the old glue from a poorly assembled vessel, cleaning it and regluing it with Duco cement."[90] About other pieces we examined in books, he remarked, "I replaced the whole bottom half of that one," or "That one is definitely a fake—you can tell the hand of a particular faker, just as you can tell the hand of some ancient Mimbres pottery painters."

Reversibility, as mentioned, is fundamental to the modern science of conservation. A modern scientifically trained conservator, when introducing new materials into ancient ones, always uses a subordinate material—something with weaker tensile strength and lesser cohesion than the materials one is preserving. As Kronkright told me, "It has been standard since the 1970s that the repair materials should give way first. That's why conservators would never use Hydrocal. Hobbyists love it. It is strong, easy to work with, and easy to paint. We use weaker repair materials, so if the object breaks, it will break at the repair, not at the original material."

He went on to say that what the artisanal "restorer" does is not preservation. "The conservator's job is to slow the rate of deterioration, not to change the object. The cleaning these so-called 'restorers' do alters the temper, and the paint. It extracts soluble components. Basically, they are messing with the original. Their techniques are about improving the appearance, but sometimes the materials they use accelerate deterioration."

He explained that in scientific pottery conservation, the subordinate fills, as they are called, are meant to fit into an empty space but not to adhere to the original pot. "It is meant to be less in every way than the original, and completely removable." Using thin epoxy putty, not even as thick as cardboard and faced with Japanese paper, the subordinate fill should be painted to look like the background of a painted pot. This technique is most often seen in the classical Greek painted pots in museums. "It is meant to look visually subordinate," he stressed, "not to fill in what is not there." Kronkright ended our interview by saying that unless what has been done to these vessels is easily reversible *and* documented, they become "less than what they were," providing the title of this section of the chapter.

The urge to perfect the past should not be surprising. People in all cultures seek to clean up the messy and shameful realities of their histories, as professional historians know all too well. The first decades of the twenty-first century have been filled with efforts to sanitize the American past, for example, an activity that professional historians have been studying for decades. The historian David Lowenthal demarcated the differences between heritage and history: while "testable truth is history's chief hallmark," heritage "uses historical traces and tells historical tales, but these tales and traces are stitched into fables that are open neither to critical analysis nor to comparative scrutiny."[91] So, too, the differences between an appreciation of the realities of the past on the part of professional art historians and the search for the noble, cosmetically altered version of the past sought by too many collectors are all too evident.

A Tale of Two "Mimbres" Bowls

As mentioned above, numerous publications in the 1970s and 1980s brought greater attention to Mimbres painted bowls, engendering widespread commercial appropriation of this imagery as a metonym of the Southwest. It also caused one Anglo couple to begin experimentation in making what they call "authentic replicas" that follow in every aspect the way that Mimbres bowls were made in the ancient world. To call something an "authentic replica" is seemingly a contradiction in terms, but even replicas have degrees of veracity, as discussed in chapter 1. This section examines two versions of replication, both of them cross-cultural and cross-temporal. One seeks to mimic the past with the most painstaking accuracy in materials and iconography. The other seeks to use the modern interest in "Indigeneity" (as defined in the broadest possible terms) to make links between the ancient American Southwest and modern Central America without too much effort at material verisimilitude.

"AUTHENTIC REPLICAS" IN SOUTHERN ARIZONA

To find the most convincing replicas of Mimbres pots, one must travel to southern Arizona, to a small community about thirty miles from the Mexican border. Off a dirt road in the rolling hills, Paul and Laurel Thornburg live in a modest adobe house. Next door is their pottery studio—a well-insulated yurt containing a couch, shelves stocked with the labors of their hands, a table for working clay and forming pots, a well-lit pottery painting table, and a small kitchenette and bath. The Thornburgs estimate that in the past twenty-five years they have made some five thousand replicas of ancient pots of the Southwest; more than three thousand of these have been Mimbres bowls.[92]

To visitors familiar with the great collections and publications on Mimbres

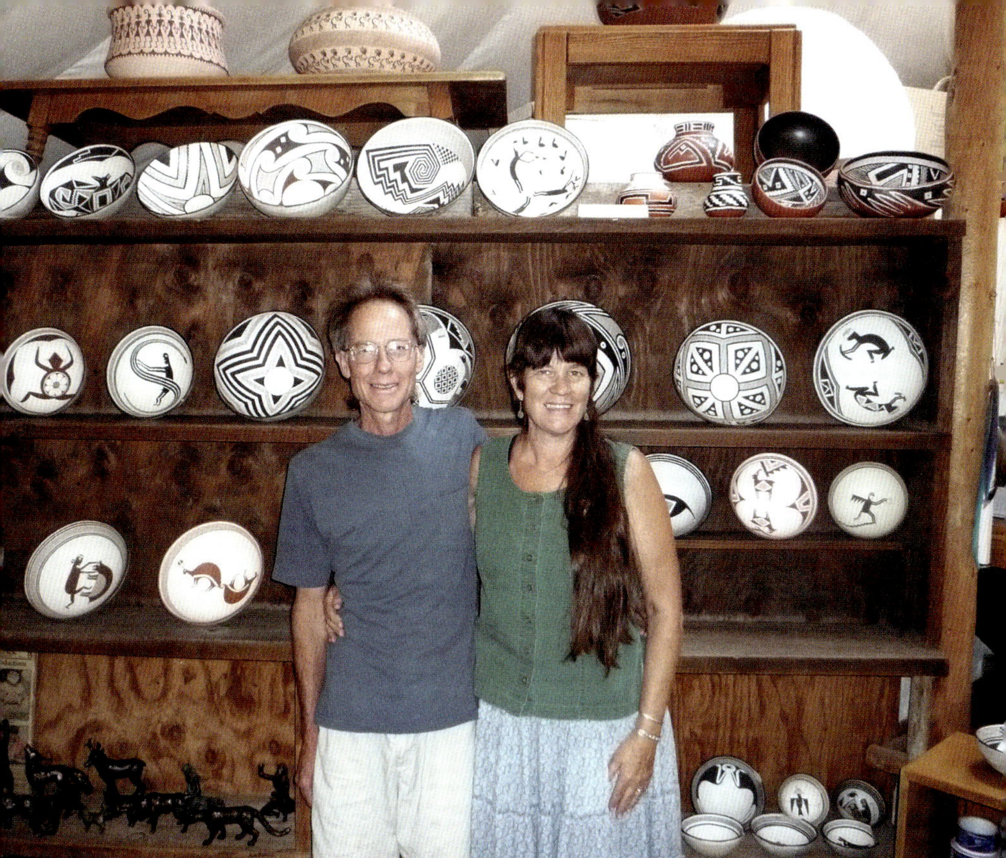

FIG. 4.12 Paul and Laurel Thornburg in their pottery studio and showroom, June 2011. Photo by author.

painted pottery, their shelves are full of familiar objects (figure 4.12): a graphically complex scene of rotational symmetry featuring three long-legged birds; a bat whose body and outstretched wings are filled with ornate patterns; a bowl with quadripartite geometric designs and circles.[93] To hold these beautiful objects in one's hands, without museum guards or storeroom protocols, seems almost transgressive, until one remembers that they were made within the past decades, not a millennium ago.

Both free spirits born in the 1950s, the Thornburgs describe an array of jobs (among them, dancer, costume designer, beekeeper, and ranch worker) leading up to their vocation as makers of high-quality replicas of Mimbres pottery. In his youth, Paul was an apprentice to a stoneware potter. While the modern production techniques he learned had little applicability to his current work, the apprenticeship provided insights into clays, tempers, and firing temperatures, giving him a good foundation for his subsequent practice. In 1987, the Thornburgs were experimenting with making replicas of Hohokam pottery. They had been using clays indigenous to Arizona, but in what they fondly call their "claymobile" (a pickup truck), they traveled to the Gila River area of southwestern New Mexico in search of appropriate clays and tempering materials to make Mimbres bowls. There, a tip from a forest ranger who remembered seeing a "white mineral deposit" led them on a search for a source for fine white clay, which they have since used as the slip for their bowls. To speak with these two resourceful individuals is to recognize the remarkable knowledge that they have extracted—quite literally—from the earth. Like all artists who are fully in command of their craft, they have an admirable intimacy with their tools and materials. Almost nothing they use is of commercial manufacture. Centuries of ethno-scientific experimentation is condensed in a quarter century's work: how ancient Salado and Hohokam potters may have wrapped grass awns (stiff bristles) with agave fibers and used a drop of piñon or juniper sap to secure these natural bristles to a grass handle; how a slim strand of yucca laden with iron-ore pigment hugs the concave curve of a Mimbres bowl to produce narrow, even lines that cannot be reproduced with modern hair fiber brushes. The Thornburgs have performed intensive experiments with how different clays fire in open pits, or in a cliff-face tunnel, and the advantages of oak over cottonwood as a fuel.

The word *authentic* frequently crops up when the Thornburgs discuss their work. Every aspect of their craft (except for its execution in a Mongolian-style yurt) conforms as closely as possible to ancient Mimbres practice. They dig both clay and stone temper from sources in the Mimbres region. They grind temper and iron oxide pigments with a stone mano and metate. The bowls are shaped and coiled meticulously by hand. They find that sherds of their own broken Mimbres-style bowls provide the most durable scrapers. Several favorites have exceedingly smooth edges, having been in use for more than a decade. Cotton and leather cloths smooth the surface of the bowl before it is polished with smooth agate stones. A creamy slip of white clay is poured into the interior of the vessel; when the excess drips down the side of the exterior, Paul does not wipe it off; he points out that they have seen such drips on the exteriors of ancient Mimbres bowls they have examined in museum storerooms, giving them confidence that the ancient potter poured her slip in the same manner.

Though the literature on indigenous pottery painting usually cites Rocky

Mountain bee balm as a binder for pigments, the Thornburgs have found that gum from the deciduous mesquite (indigenous to the Southwest) is an excellent binder. Small chunks of the dried gum or sap (resembling amber-colored rock candy) can be ground up with pigments to ensure that a viscous paint will be easy to apply. "It's basically the gum arabic of the New World," Laurel says.

The deep knowledge gained from years of experimentation and refinement of technique provides many such insights. Of the clay they have dug in Mimbres territory, Paul says, "The clay prefers the bowl form. It's not as easy to make ollas (jars) out of this clay. It's just not plastic enough. When we try to make ollas with this clay, they often crack during firing." Both of them stress that every stage of the process must be done exactly right. The clay must be properly prepared to be malleable in just the right way. The temper must be ground, and ground again, and then folded into the clay in a manner reminiscent of a French chef folding butter into *pâte feuilletée* until it is perfectly blended. The coils must be shaped with precision and shingled just right, one over another, to avoid air pockets. Infinite patience is required for each step. "I'll do about six hundred rotations on the metate to grind a small batch of pigment," Paul says, with no trace of impatience at the tedium of this task.

After more than three thousand bowls, Laurel says, "Our hands know how to follow the lines." The results of all of their experiments are carefully documented in both photos and voluminous notes. They plan to donate their detailed archive of notes, maps, photos, and instructions to the Arizona State Museum at the University of Arizona in Tucson, which has a comprehensive collection of Southwestern pottery. There it will take its place as a valuable source of information about the ancient American past, with all the other data such museums gather.

They have assembled a singularly important record (both written and photographic) about their clays, tempers, and pigments, as well as processes of construction. "We have lots of notes and pictures of our observations during the six hours or so that it takes to fire," Laurel says. "Notes on weather, wind direction, stacking technique, and number of bowls in the chamber." She talks about watching the pots as they fire—seeing the color change from red hot to orange, to yellow—the hottest phase. She notes that the size, type, and condition of the wood is always a factor and that even the wood's age seems to have an effect on the results. But as all potters acknowledge, a successful firing is a combination of deep knowledge, long practice, and serendipity: "It is still always a letting go and accepting 'whatever the fire decides,'" she says philosophically.

The first publications on their work, some thirty years ago, highlighted the fact that to collect such replicas was to strike a blow against the looting of archaeological sites.[94] Such admiration has been reiterated in a popular book on Mimbres archaeology: "The Thornburgs' delicate, detailed work has had a great effect on Mimbres archaeology, stirring public interest in Mimbres culture and giving people who want to own a Mimbres bowl a beautiful, legitimate, and legal alternative to illegally acquired, or 'pothunted,' artifacts."[95] Hopi artist and designer Ramona Sakiestewa admires their work: "No one else replicates Mimbres pottery the way they do, with such great thought and research."[96]

While they want their work to be thoroughly authentic, Paul and Laurel Thornburg understand that their scrupulous authenticity in production methods might allow others less scrupulous to pass off their work as real Mimbres pieces from a thousand years ago. They have always signed their pieces, but since the late 1980s, the Thornburgs have made it even harder for their work to be subsequently sold as archaeological pots. Their friend Rukin Jelks, a mineral collector, suggested that the tungsten ore scheelite would provide a solution.[97] Almost invisible to the naked eye, scheelite fluoresces to a bright white under a shortwave ultraviolet light. At first, they embedded scheelite crystals right into the surface of the vessel, but now they paint the date in scheelite in large scale on the underside of each bowl, which they also sign with their Thornburg logo, listing the source for the design.

The gift shop at the Arizona State Museum has carried their vessels. Former shop manager Martin Kim admired the fine craftsmanship in their work and their ethical stance concerning the replication process.[98] In Mimbres territory, their work has been carried at the Western New Mexico Museum gift shop. In each case, proceeds from sales support the work of the museum. The pots are reasonable enough in price—$100–$1,000—that some are impulse purchases by museum visitors. But there are also collectors who buy in bulk or in quantity over time. "One collector in Texas ordered a pot a month for about four years," Laurel recalls.

They evince no interest in transgressing the boundaries of Mimbres iconography. "Someone asked us to paint a dinosaur and a man on a bowl once, and someone else wanted a Mimbres Mickey Mouse. In both cases, the answer was no," Laurel says. "We only replicate real bowls in museums or private collections. We would never 'make up' a Mimbres bowl or alter the design of an original."

While some cultural critics might be quick to condemn copies of ancient Native vessels made by non-Native people, it is worth investigating the situation a little more closely. Unlike contemporary silver jewelry made in the style of Navajo work, or katsinas made by non-Hopi people, there are no Native people making this work in this fashion that painstakingly seeks to replicate the production processes of the past; it takes no livelihood away from a Native artist. Moreover, in their ceaseless search for the most authentic means of production, Paul and Laurel Thornburg have contributed a great deal to the scientific and technological knowledge of the material expression of ancient Mimbreños.

After my interview with the Thornburgs, I bought an inexpensive plastic bag of potsherds that they assured me could be assembled into a complete bowl (figure 4.13). (They occasionally broke a bowl that was not up to their standards. This one had fired imperfectly; one side of the interior was a smoky gray, and some of the rim decoration was obscured.) I wanted to have the experience of assembling it myself with Duco cement and then to use it in my teaching about such issues. In the concave interior, a man stands with a gigantic fish held over his head. Twelve thin lines and three wider ones form the inner rim design—the lines that Paul forms so adeptly with his yucca-strand brush. Painted on the bottom of the exterior are the words "Thornburg / American Museum of Natural History / NM [i.e., New Mexico] circa 1000–1150 AD." And of course, under the slip of the bowl's exterior, unseen, is the modern date of its making, in scheelite that will fluoresce, should anyone years from now need to determine if it is an ancient Mimbres vessel. Over the decade that this book was in progress, this bowl became a metonym for the entire project and the many layers of artifice, talent, research, and yearning that underpin so much of what is "not Native American art."

A "MIMBRES" OUTPOST IN NICARAGUA

While trolling the internet in 2011, to determine the global reach of Mimbres imagery, I came across a website selling Mimbres-style bowls made in Nicaragua. Because of its genealogy, one particularly appealed to me: a replica of a mountain lion bowl copied by Julian Martinez, as I discuss in chapter 5 (figure 4.14; for comparison, see figure 5.4). The website guaranteed that

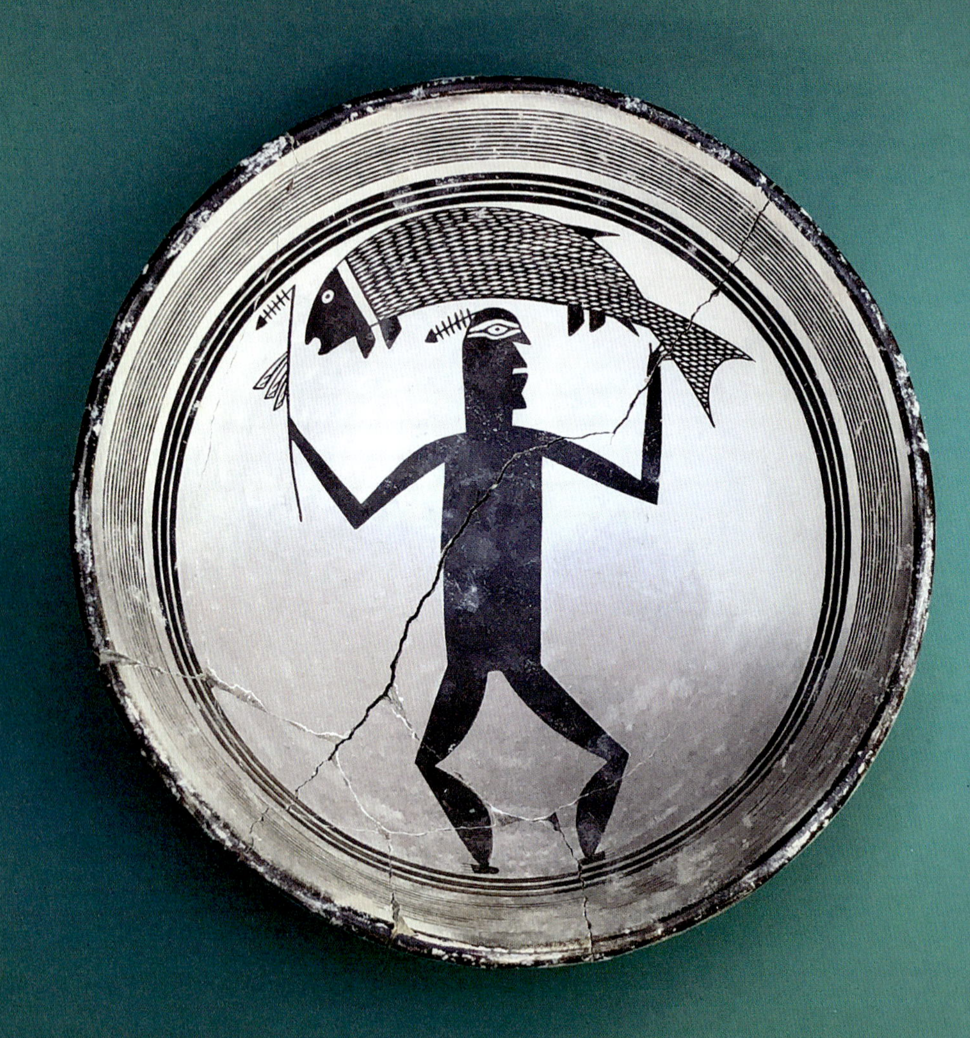

FIG. 4.13 Replica of Mimbres bowl reassembled by author from potsherds provided by Paul and Laurel Thornburg, 2011. Collection of the author.

it was "a great collectible piece, made in a very limited series exclusively for Mayta Clay" and "signed by the widely-respected artist Gregorio Bracamonte." I promptly ordered it. At eighty-nine dollars, it was a bargain, compared to the Thornburgs' "authentic replicas," to contemporary Acoma vessels, or to ancient Mimbres bowls.

A few potters working in San Juan de Oriente, near the capital city of Managua, use Mimbres imagery in their work. Many inhabitants of this small community (some thirty-five hundred people) are descended from the indigenous Nahuatl population that migrated from central Mexico about a thousand years ago. Notably, one of their legacies is fine pottery making: ancient Nicoya polychrome was one of the great ceramic traditions of Central America. North American venders of contemporary artisanal pottery from San Juan de Oriente love to stress such cultural continuities: the clay is local, the pottery tradition is ancient, and the colonial Spanish overlords nicknamed this village San Juan de los Platos (San Juan of the Dishes) because of its reputation

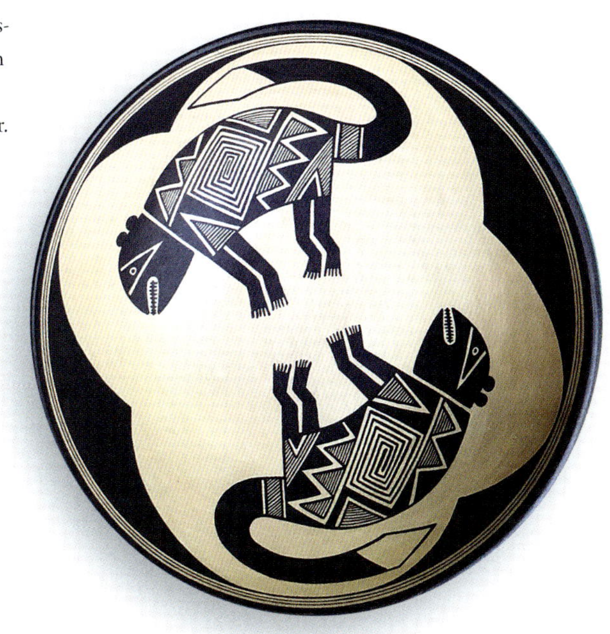

FIG. 4.14 Bowl with Mimbres-style mountain lions, San Juan de Oriente, Nicaragua, ca. 2010. Collection of the author.

as a pottery-making center.[99] With help from potters in North America and Europe, there has been a resurgence of pottery making here since the Sandinista revolution in 1979, accompanied by development of craft schools and co-operatives to market the local wares. This is seen by local people, governmental authorities, and aid workers as a means for economic development and self-determination. Potters for Peace and other North American groups have worked to develop microenterprises among extended families and women's groups in villages such as San Juan de Oriente.

Potters here, as in every other tourist-based craft industry in developing countries, adopt changing fads and see what sells. They have long produced a range of styles: ancient Nicoya forms, an international folk-art vocabulary of floral and animal forms, and Classic Maya iconography from Guatemala. The use of Mimbres designs by a few potters came about through the efforts of one importer, a man named Reese Guth.[100] After traveling to this village several times, this former potter decided to start an import business, surmising that there might be a market for earthenware pottery with Mimbres designs. Guth went back to Nicaragua with an old paperback, *Art of a Vanished Race: The Mimbres Classic Black-on-White*, which he gave to the master potter Gregorio Bracamonte; other books followed.[101] All of the designs in *Art of a Vanished Race*, in turn, were copied from and credited to drawings in the early publications by the Cosgroves and Fewkes cited above, so for the most part the Nicaraguan potters are replicating well-published bowls from museum collections.

Since Bracamonte had long been adapting complex Maya and Nicoya designs into his vessels, the Mimbres style was not a difficult challenge. Since about 2000, the Bracamonte family has produced a small repertoire of bowls with Mimbres designs.[102] Most are signed by Bracamonte and affixed with a sticker that says "Made in Nicaragua." But, as anyone who knows the history of pot signing at San Ildefonso Pueblo will recognize, the signing of a pot and the making of a pot can be two different things.[103] In San Juan de Oriente, pots are made in family workshops, with numerous apprentices. The master signs a pot that any number of apprentices may have shaped, fired, slipped, and painted.

Having done research on the history of pottery making in Nicaragua, Reese Guth talked about such enterprises as being opportunities for families to "pull themselves up, not by their bootstraps, but by their ceramic heritage."[104] He sold many types of collectible ceramics made in San Juan. The Mimbres bowls were but a small part of his inventory and sales. No one could ever mistake these vessels for Mimbres originals: the walls are thick, the clay is heavy, and the background color is a dark beige rather than white. Nor could this work be mistaken for contemporary handmade Pueblo pottery from the Southwest.

Marketing such works necessitates framing them with an ennobling story. Many purchasers seek to support efforts that foster self-determination and sustainable, local enterprises based on heritage. The language of this web-based marketing stresses heritage: "The continuance of their ceramic tradition . . . has become one of the strongest links to the pre-Columbian heritage of the Nicaraguan people. The potters are still using designs and techniques handed down from one generation to the next, reaching back centuries before Europeans ever set foot in the New World. The fact that this village . . . produces such extraordinarily talented artists is a testament both to their skill and to the ancestral gifts left by generations past."[105] All of the pots sold on MaytaClay.com were identified by the artist's name (i.e., the name of the head of a family workshop). The descriptions also characterize these works as "some of the finest examples of contemporary indigenous ceramics in all of the Americas," "an outstanding addition to any collection of Native American pottery," "done in a limited edition and signed by the artist," or "signed by Gregorio Bracamonte, perhaps the leading talent in pre-Columbian reproduction work in all of Central America."[106] For buyers knowledgeable about recent trends in pottery, MaytaClay.com positions the work of San Juan de Oriente as "comparable to the Mata Ortiz region of Mexico twenty or more years ago in terms of its importance in the world of collectible pottery."[107] In other words, the implication is that the price of this pottery will only rise, as it becomes better known.

Mimbres-style pottery is just one small part of the handmade pottery industry of San Juan de Oriente. This situation is analogous to the replicas of Navajo rugs made in Oaxaca, as discussed in chapter 1. Just as handmade American quilts have been replicated in Chinese factories for sale to those for whom "the real thing" is out of their price range, so, too, Zapotec replicas of Navajo rugs and Nicaraguan knockoffs of ancient Mimbres ceramics provide a way for the less affluent to have a version of what they admire. Yet, in contrast to the Chinese example, made in a textile factory in which workers are paid a pittance, in Oaxaca and in Nicaragua, Mestizo and indigenous entrepreneurial families make these items at least partly on their own terms.

If viewed in a short time span, Mimbres-style vessels made in Nicaragua may seem an absurd appropriation. When viewed across lengthier temporalities, it makes more sense. A thousand years ago, the ancestors of the inhabitants of San Juan de Oriente traveled hundreds of miles from their central Mexican homeland, bringing a new pottery style to southern Central America. That pottery style, in turn, was traded across ethnic boundaries for several hundred years. Spanish colonial incursions brought new styles and new markets, as does the global marketplace of the twenty-first century.

Conclusion: "It's Not Right"—Connoisseurship and the Veracity of Objects

While an undergraduate at the University of Massachusetts Amherst, I had been entertained by the reminiscences of a professor of decorative arts who, early in his career, had worked briefly for Bernard Berenson (1865–1959), the legendary scholar/dealer/connoisseur of old master paintings. My professor liked to tell anecdotes of seventeenth-century paintings being carted into Berenson's study at I Tatti, his villa in Florence, for his evaluation. Sometimes, before a painting had even been carried all the way through the door, he would have determined that it was an egregious fake and would say, in his Lithuanian accent, "Take it away! Take it away!" The implication was that his connoisseurial eye was so good that he could spot a fake from fifty paces. The only time in my life when I knew what this felt like was when I opened the expressed package from Sotheby's that summer day in 1996 containing the images of the "rare Hidatsa book of drawings." Having spent nearly two years researching and examining real Plains drawings full-time, my reaction was just as instantaneous.

Art dealers and curators use a shorthand phrase for such a gut instinct: "It's not right." By this they mean that perhaps it is not authentic, or it is over-restored, or it is not by the artist in question. This first response is then necessarily followed up by a great deal of research. It is easy to make fun of that kind of connoisseurship, for it can seem like nothing more than a hunch. As a graduate student in the history of art at Yale in the late 1970s, I scorned the heavy suitcase full of assumptions that, in my mind, the word *connoisseurship* carried: Old. Male. Elitist. Eurocentric. Tedious. Yet fifteen years later, I found myself setting up five slide projectors in a row as I carefully examined the Morellian details of drawings made by nineteenth-century Kiowa and Cheyenne warriors with names such as Chief Killer and Making Medicine. I found that attributing a name to formerly anonymous Plains Indian artists was a legitimate and satisfying task. With experience, I realized that connoisseurship is merely a tool; like any other tool, it depends on the skill of the hand that wields it.

The distinguished historian Carlo Ginsburg offers my favorite insight into the meaning of connoisseurship. He characterizes it as "interdisciplinarity from within," remarking that it has "a cognitive richness which is unsuspected by its detractors as well as by some of its practitioners."[108] Ginsburg points out, for example, that to conduct research on just one material object—a German still life painting of flowers—requires inquiry into botany, archival sources, paleography, and watermarks, as well as art history. True connoisseurship means understanding the full range of information an object can tell us.

Nearly four decades' worth of cultural studies, postcolonial critique, and feminist critique has demonstrated that all art historical, historical, anthropological, and archival data must be used critically. Moreover, they must be approached as constructions that are contingent, growing out of particular historical circumstances in which blinders of race, religion, gender, and class, among other things, set limits on what queries scholars thought to make, and what answers they listened to. But connoisseurship can ask—as well as answer—numerous questions that are still highly pertinent for a twenty-first-century history of art.

Nonetheless, the case studies in this chapter led me to reflect that in other areas of art history, it would be unthinkable to consider only connoisseurship, as in the case of the Chumash objects, or iconography and not style, as in the case of the book of ledger drawings, when determining the veracity of an object. Having given talks on Codex Covarrubias perhaps a dozen times during the twenty-five years between its sale at Sotheby's and the publication of this book, I have found that, in each instance, artists and art historians in the audience who may know little about Native American art, but who have looked at lots of drawings from all time periods, readily agreed that these looked nothing like the authentic nineteenth-century Plains Indian drawings in my PowerPoint and that they clearly showed a hand influenced by Art Deco. In contrast, in audiences where the knowledge of Plains Indian anthropology ran deep, the viewers were so taken with the ethnographic verity of the depictions that they were unable to see that the stylistic elements were completely incongruous.

The recent "material turn" in art history and anthropology is likely to disappoint if we expect it to help address the issues that this chapter, and others, bring up. Far too often, the material turn is concerned principally with the theoretical and political aspects of the material world and not materiality itself.[109] In the twenty-first century, far too few art historians get their hands dirty understanding materials and the making of objects.

This book is a deep dive into the cultural biography of things. Igor Kopytoff, who made that phrase well known to academics, wrote that "a culturally-informed economic biography of an object would look at it as a culturally constructed entity, endowed with culturally specific meanings, and classified and reclassified into culturally constituted categories." He also noted that each individual's version of a cultural biography is different from that of others and "also shifts contextually and biographically as the originators' perspectives, affiliations, and interests shift."[110] Cultural biographies, too, can be occluded, falsified, and stuck together with too much Duco cement.

5

Cross-Cultural Replication and Native Revitalization

Techniques of Remembering

Driving from Santa Fe to Phoenix in November 2006, I detoured off Interstate 40 to the Walmart Supercenter in Gallup, New Mexico, to see with my own eyes what my friend Jennifer McLerran had described: large reproductions of Navajo sandpaintings hanging above clothes racks in America's largest retailer, right on the eastern edge of the Navajo Nation (figure 5.1). As I took a few quick photos, the chain of reproducibility of one of the continent's great Indigenous icons—the Navajo sandpainting—had seemingly arrived at its logical conclusion, for doesn't everything result in a version in Walmart? Notably, these reproductions had been made for the Museum of Navajo Ceremonial Art in Santa Fe in the 1940s, and they had been repatriated to the Navajo Nation, presumably because they did not belong in a non-Native museum. How did they end up in Walmart?

In this chapter, I investigate reproductions, replicas, and revivals made by Native people themselves. In the first example, collaboration between a Navajo ritual specialist and a white woman produced images that were circulated, published, and exhibited in a variety of non-Native contexts. I present intellectual issues concerning artistic replication of long-standing interest within art history as well as ethical issues concerning the replication of sacred iconography as perceived by Navajo today and as enacted by Navajo and non-Navajo collaborators in the early to mid-twentieth century, principally on the Navajo reservation. Sometimes the rhetoric surrounding culturally sensitive images and their replication is offered in terms that starkly separate a supposedly correct Indigenous position from a non-Indigenous stance seen as abrogating Native sovereignty. There is seldom one correct "Indigenous point of view" on such issues, but rather a variety of complex responses. Moreover, Native

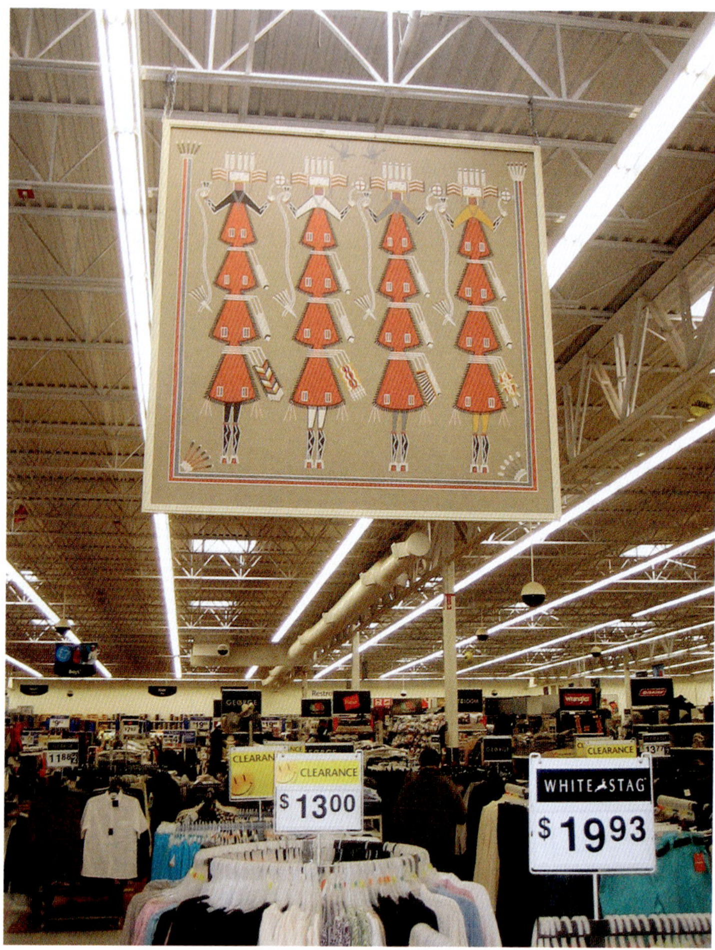

FIG. 5.1 Replica of "The Long Bodied Goddesses in the Lodge of Dew." Gouache on Masonite, 6 × 6 ft. Created at the Museum of Navajo Ceremonial Art, ca. 1937, as installed at Walmart, Gallup, New Mexico, summer 2006.
Photo by author.

American art history is filled with examples of cross-cultural collaboration that complicate such a one-dimensional story.

In a briefer example, I consider ancient Mimbres pottery, discussed in chapter 4, but here the focus is on the way its imagery has been adopted and adapted by Pueblo potters on vessels made for sale. The Seneca Arts Project (SAP), an initiative of the national Works Progress Administration (WPA) of the 1930s, is well known in terms of its paintings and sculpture, but the revival of Seneca-style beadwork by women as part of that project is seldom discussed. Yet it is a brilliant example of the replication of a historical tradition, a "technique of remembering," in the memorable phrase of British sociologist John Urry.[1]

Native artists make replicas for a multitude of reasons. The impetus may be principally economic, and arise from outside the community, as in the case of the Seneca people of western New York who engaged in a program replicating their ancestral arts during the Great Depression, under the auspices of a government program. The motivating factor may be principally aesthetic, or have to do with pride in heritage. (Of course, motives can be multiple. Aesthetic pride in the work of the ancestors is not incompatible with a desire to earn a living through one's art.) Such cases tend to flower during eras when the ancestral arts have been achieving widespread recognition or when there is a critical mass of people in the same place interested in the same historical objects. The revival of Iroquoian-style quillwork on items of personal adornment is a recent development, flourishing in small numbers among Native people in the Northeast principally since the beginning of the twenty-first century. I profile two such Indigenous replica makers.

This chapter differs from the others, in that the ethnicity of the makers is not in question. They are indisputably Native (aside from the one non-Native collaborator, in the first section). Their rights to use ancestral imagery in their work is a given. This chapter serves as a small corrective to all of the Native-style art in other chapters, mostly made by non-Natives. Perhaps here the emphasis posed by the book's title differs: instead of "not *Native American* art," I am asking the reader to consider "not Native American *art*." That is, strictly speaking, is it *art* when one is making multiples for sale? Is it *art* when it is also a replica? Is a replica different from a revival?

Sandpainting as an Act of Cross-Cultural Replication

For more than a century, the Navajo art of sandpainting has been acknowledged as one of the great arts of the indigenous Americas, and it has been included in every major exhibit and book surveying Native North American art.[2] Ceremonial practitioners called medicine men, singers, or chanters (or, in Navajo, *hataałii*) draw on expertise resulting from years of apprenticeship. On a bed of packed earth, the *hataałii* and his assistants, almost always male, carefully drop from their fingertips ground minerals and plant pollens of different colors, creating anthropomorphic images of supernatural figures and their activities that occurred within specific sacred locales in the mythic past. Sandpaintings, or dry-paintings as they are sometimes called, illustrate and actualize harmonious relationships among the Diyin Dine'é (the supernaturals, or Holy People), Dinétah (the Navajo land), and the Dine'é (the Navajo themselves, literally "Earth Surface People"). The making of such images is part of a multi-night ritual involving singing, praying, and the use of herbal medicine, in which a person who seeks physical or psychological healing, or both, sits within this image. To be ministered to and sung over by the *hataałii* while surrounded by the healing force field of such a cosmogram is to embody and make manifest the central ideal of Navajo culture: *hózhó*, rendered in English as a combination of harmony, goodness, wellness, and beauty.[3]

In 1884, US Army physician and amateur ethnologist Washington Matthews (1843–1905) was the first to open the window on one of the great intellectual, religious, artistic, and literary cultures of the world, shedding light on what the literary scholar Paul Zolbrod has called "the deep intricacies of Navajo creativity."[4] Matthews described the making of a sandpainting in a way that most subsequent observers would recognize: several men worked for hours, supervised by the *hataałii*.[5] Both in the nineteenth century and today, the candidate for healing is led into the sandpainting and sits upon it, thus partially disturbing the carefully arranged images. When the patient leaves and the ceremony is over, the *hataałii* obliterates the image and the materials are returned to the desert.

In the Navajo creation story, the original supernatural makers, the Diyin Dine'é, generated such images using the transitory materials of the universe, unrolling a sheet of clouds and making images with rainbows and lightning.[6] This accounts for the tradition of ephemerality of all subsequent renderings. Since there was no precedent for making them out of more permanent materials, might we posit that the only "originals" (in the art historical sense of the term) are those that the supernaturals made out of the materials of the universe? Since every instance of ceremonial art is an attempt to perfectly reproduce the actions of the supernaturals in ancient times, how can we reconcile what happens when replicas of such reproductions enter the picture?

It is noteworthy that the first white man to see and write about sandpaintings was also the first to engage in cross-cultural replication of these images. Matthews made notes and sketches at ceremonies in the early 1880s. This was not unproblematic then, and it has continued to be problematic in various ways. As Matthews wrote in his preliminary paper in 1885, "I obtained unrestricted access to the medicine-lodge, saw the hieratic figures drawn, and was given permission to sketch them, much to the horror of the large majority of the assembled multitude."[7] This "horror" derived from the belief that such an art was to be rendered only by a ritual specialist and his helpers for use in ceremony. One of the first sandpaintings that Matthews recorded depicts the "Long Bodies," four tall female supernaturals (figure 5.2). Each is so tall that it takes four hide garments, rather than one, to clothe her. The Long Bodies tell the hero, who has entered their dwelling place, "Look at us well and remember how we appear, for in your ceremonies you must draw our picture."[8] While replication of these images is a sacred duty, so is their eradication. Yet the *hataałii* must be able to precisely re-create an image the next time he is called on to perform a ceremony. *Hataałii* are known for their prodigious feats of memory, for they have to memorize hundreds of songs and dozens of paintings for each chantway in which they specialize. Some have been known to keep small notebooks to help with this process.

In *The Shape of Time* (1962), the art historian George Kubler coined the phrase "prime object" for truly original works of art. Using as his examples the Parthenon and Raphael's Vatican frescoes, Kubler wrote, "Prime objects and replications denote principal inventions, and the entire system of replicas, reproductions, copies, reductions, transfers, and derivations, floating in the wake of an important work of art." Kubler terms all of these the "replica-mass."[9] Kubler's insights seem applicable, in part, to this situation in which the only prime objects are those that the supernaturals made out of the materials of the universe. However, when looked at in that light, is it the inevitable conclusion that every sandpainting made by a Navajo ritual specialist is no more than a replica? And what of replicas of these replicas? Framing Kubler's words by Navajo epistemology, do all human-made versions—whether ceremonial or

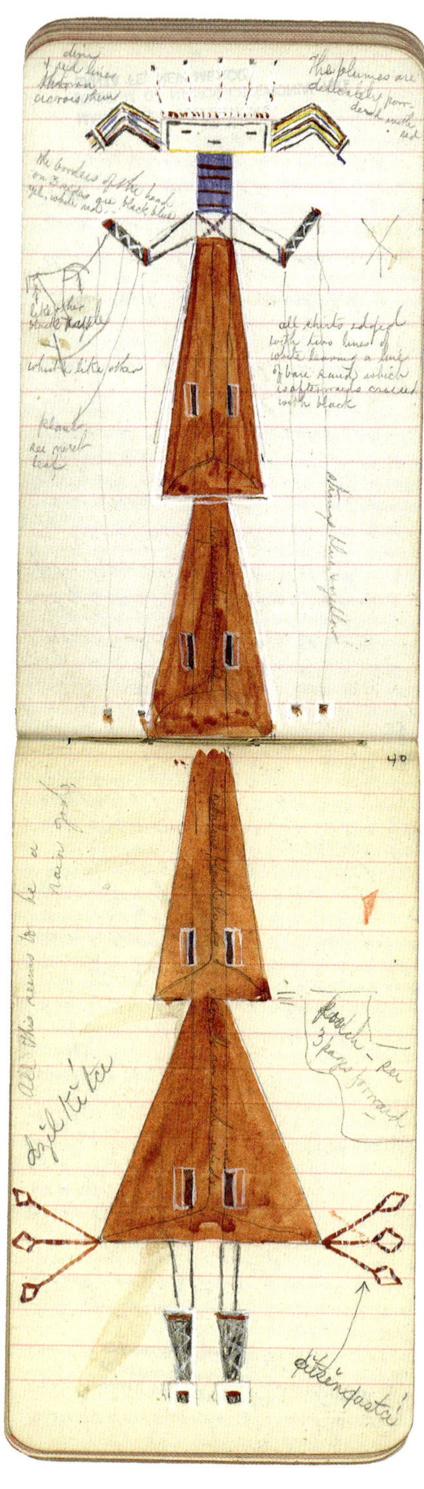

FIG. 5.2 Washington Matthews, notebook sketch of one of the "Long Bodies," 1884. Washington Matthews Collection, Wheelwright Museum of the American Indian, Santa Fe, New Mexico.

commercial or scholarly—simply "float in the wake of the original" and form a "replica-mass"? This is more important than it seems, because for more than a century sandpaintings have been replicated in many ways, in numerous media, and by Navajo and non-Navajo alike. In addition to the ubiquitous bandanas and beach towels on which such imagery is reproduced, there is a large category of works made by entrepreneurial Navajo themselves in which colored sands are glued to Masonite to make items for sale. These range from inexpensive magnets and plaques to finely crafted works sold in galleries. This phenomenon has been well studied, and most Navajo accept that the imagery on such commercial objects has been altered in some way so that aspects of its ceremonial correctness have been concealed, making it lifeless in terms of its ceremonial efficacy.[10]

One glimpse into Navajo beliefs about imitation at the beginning of the twentieth century is provided by an early source, in regard to the imitation of Navajo masks used in ceremonial performance: "Owing to the elaborate ritual connected with the construction of the masks and their dedication very few sets are extant. These are, therefore, disposed of only with extreme reluctance, though the courtesy of their use is readily granted to a friendly shaman. For purposes of barter, and also for prestige, imitations of the genuine masks are made of other than ceremonial hide."[11] The writer goes on to explain that an imitation made of horsehide rather than "ceremonial hide," for example, might be sold to the neighboring Zuni tribe for their use. Here, the idea of some sort of substitution is introduced, so that the ceremonial item is not authentic but is an "imitation." Some contemporary *hataalii* have observed mistakes or omissions in some sandpaintings replicated on paper and in other media. Scholars and ritual specialists alike have speculated that perhaps this is a way of ensuring that they are ritually inactive. Should all of these, then, be called imitations and fall into the same class as the commercial replicas? If so, does intentionality play no part in distinguishing these various representations? One is reminded here of Hopi doll carver Wilson Tawaquaptewa, discussed in chapter 1, who altered the details of the figures he carved so that he was not sharing sacred imagery in his commercial activities (see figure 1.10).

FRANC JOHNSON NEWCOMB AND HOSTEEN KLAH

While many anthropologists and other cultural interlocutors have collaborated with Navajo artists and intellectuals since the time of Matthews, one white woman, Franc Johnson Newcomb (1887–1970), and the esteemed *hataałii* Hosteen Klah (Left-Handed) (1867–1937) are the paradigmatic example. These individuals who were anomalous within their own cultures came together in a liminal space between Navajo and Anglo worlds. For twenty years they collaborated on the making of sandpaintings in permanent form because of their shared interest in understanding and preserving a religious imagery of enormous eloquence and beauty. Newcomb also wrote Klah's biography—a classic of the anthropological genre.[12]

Klah was born to a family wealthy in sheep and horses. He was an intersex individual (*nádleeh*). For the Navajo, this is a sign of extreme power, for it combines the powers of both sexes.[13] As a child, when he accompanied his uncle, a medicine man, to ceremonies, Klah's unusually accurate memory soon became apparent. He could recall the many complex chants sung in multi-night rituals, a trait fundamental to being a ceremonial practitioner. He mastered more ceremonial chants than almost anyone and was sent to different parts of the reservation to learn from different chanters. Although Navajo is today a written language, the individual with a keen memory and powers of song and oratory is still recognized as a consummate resource for ceremony, protocol, and history.

When Franc Johnson married the trader A. J. Newcomb in 1914 and moved to her husband's remote trading post in northwestern New Mexico—a location now called Newcomb—Klah and his sister were the first visitors. They welcomed her by bringing a fox pelt as a gift.[14] When they met, Newcomb was twenty-seven, and Klah was twenty years older. She wrote, "With Hosteen Klah, the powerful medicine man of this section as our sponsor, we were invited to attend many of the social functions and religious rites held in our valley." The "beautiful sandpaintings drawn on the floors of the various ceremonial lodges" greatly interested her.[15]

Around 1917, Klah took her to a three-day ceremony, and during the breaks she tried to make sketches of the multiple sandpaintings, but got things confused.[16] When Klah saw that her designs were jumbled, he asked if she would like him to paint them for her.[17] So she cut squares of heavy brown wrapping paper from the trading post and they worked together: "When two figures were alike, he drew one and I copied it for the other. He made the intricate designs and I drew the rainbows and the plants. It took a couple of weeks of our spare time, but finally I had my first four sketches of Navajo sand paintings."[18] Newcomb came to be renowned among the *hataałii* for her prodigious memory and ability to accurately transcribe what she had seen during the ceremony, as she drew in her notebooks outside the hogan. Moreover, because she visited Navajo households with the castor oil, cough syrup, and bandages provided by the health supervisor in Washington, DC, she soon was recognized as a healer, that is to say, someone whose status paralleled that of the *hataalii*. So, despite her gender, she was respected in this realm.[19] She and Klah became collaborators and friends.

These collaborators were unusual people. Newcomb did not conform to ascribed gender roles of either Navajo or white women. Moreover, she healed with medicines, far more likely to be a male role among the Navajo. She was named for her father, Frank, who died when she was three; even her first name is ambiguous in its gender implications.[20] While Klah transgressed European gender categories—both in his physical body and in his prodigious talents—the idea of the *nádleeh*, though rare, was foundational in Navajo thought. He was unusual for a man and unusual for a woman, as one who combined the talents of a renowned ritual specialist and a weaver of uncommon technical ability.[21]

Newcomb accompanied Klah to ceremonials all over Navajo territory. Due to his power and influence, she was allowed to watch and record. Many non-Native scholars used her images in their publications, and Newcomb often collaborated with the anthropologist Gladys A. Reichard.[22] Mary Cabot Wheelwright, who in 1937 founded the Museum of Navajo Ceremonial Art (now the Wheelwright Museum of the American Indian) after years of planning and collaboration with Klah, hired Newcomb to collect and make replicas of even more sandpaintings. Several hundred are in the archives of the Wheelwright Museum. Another hundred were collected by Wendell T. Bush, a professor of religion at Columbia University, to be part of the Bush Collection of Religion and Culture (figure 5.3).[23] Klah used this image in his Shootingway ceremony. It depicts one of the Hero Twins of Navajo cosmology dressed for war in his flint-studded clothing and holding five white arrows of lightning. Lightning shoots from his feet and crisscrosses his body. The blue orb within which he stands represents his father, the Sun, who has girded him for war and sent him out to slay the powers of evil and destruction in the world.

Newcomb signed some of these and left others unsigned, while a few were signed by Klah. This gives rise to another unanswerable question in considering Navajo replicas: Does the signature of an artist (Native or non-Native) on the small-scale rendering in tempera paint of part of an ephemeral ceremonial performance carry any legitimacy?

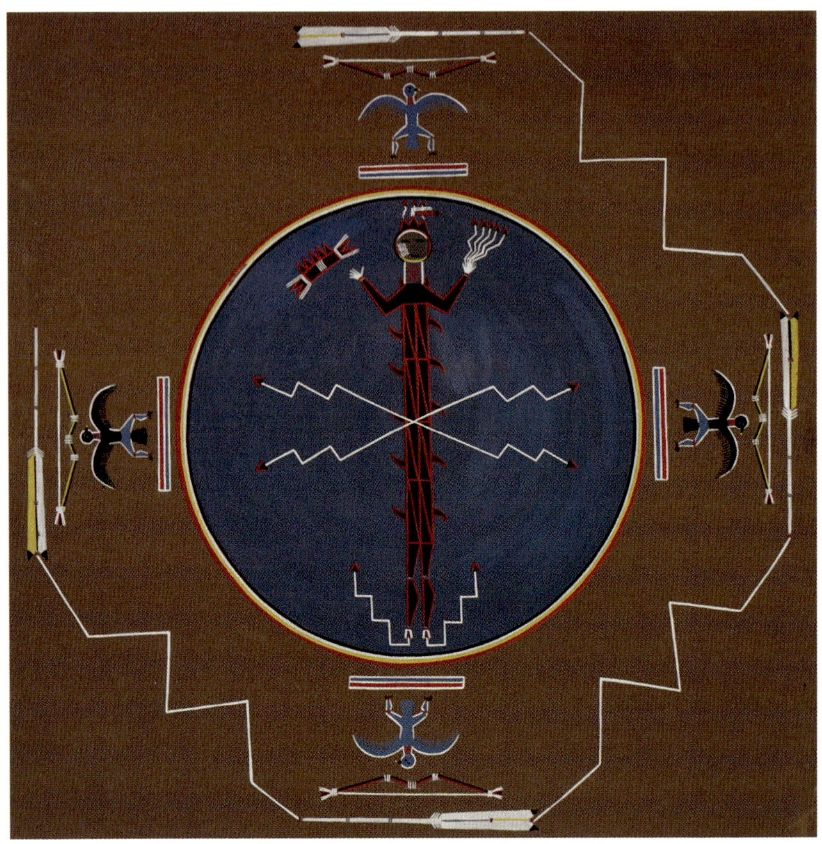

FIG. 5.3 Franc Johnson Newcomb and Hosteen Klah (unsigned), *Monster Slayer n the House of the Sun*, 1930s. Poster paint on cardboard, 22 × 22 in. (55.9 × 55.9 cm). Art Properties, Avery Architectural and Fine Arts Library, Columbia University, Bush Collection of Religion and Culture, no. C00.1483.63.

After publishing Klah's biography in 1964, Newcomb wrote partial drafts for other books, never published.[24] In one, "In Quest of Navajo Chanters," she recounts that because of the death of a medicine man in the Chuska Mountains region, an important healing ceremony, the Mountain Chant, had been lost: "The family knew his prayers, songs, and rites, and I had the sandpaintings, so I was asked to sit in as one of the medicine men."[25] It is important to recognize that this seemingly unorthodox collaboration took place, that both Native and non-Native people who worked to preserve this knowledge were consulted not only by scholars but also by practicing ritual specialists. In today's political climate where calls for sovereignty, and in some cases for the isolation of cultural knowledge from outsiders, are numerous, it is crucial to understand how such intercultural collaborations flourished in the past, just as some continue to do so in the present.

SANDPAINTING AS CROSS-CULTURAL PERFORMANCE

Ritual sandpaintings are one act in a protracted performance involving medicine, song, and ritual paraphernalia. Simulacra of such performances have occurred repeatedly over more than one hundred years. There were populist displays and demonstrations of sandpainting at hotels, world fairs, museums, and other tourist destinations. The Navajo, of course, provide just one example among many of how people of color, for generations, have been expected to perform their culture for the general public—a topic of much recent interest in cultural studies and of ongoing interest to contemporary Native performance artists.[26]

In 1893, Klah was part of the Navajo contingent to the Chicago World's Columbian Exposition, where he demonstrated weaving by daily completing a few inches of work in front of crowds of observers. Some forty years later, in 1933, the sixty-seven-year-old Klah traveled with two other Navajo to the Century of Progress International Exposition in Chicago, where daily he demonstrated the art of sandpainting to crowds that gathered in the New Mexico State Building.[27] Newcomb recalled, "Klah had a square about twelve by twelve feet fenced so that curious spectators could not crowd too close to him while he was working, or step on the painting when it was finished."[28]

New England philanthropist Mary Cabot Wheelwright (1878–1958) opened the Museum of Navajo Ceremonial Art in Santa Fe in 1937, shortly after the death of Klah. It was conceived as a tribute to their friendship and his formidable knowledge in particular, as well as the many other *hataałii* she had met over the years. Wheelwright characterized him as "one of the most remarkable persons" she ever knew.[29] Klah also allowed Wheelwright to make wax cylinder recordings of his ceremonial songs. He introduced her to other ritual practitioners and taught her the appropriate way to pay for the knowledge she was recording: "They liked very much to have presents of things useful to their ceremonies, such as abalone shells, turkey feathers, turquoise, small white shells, tobacco, and crystal which stands for truth. I always paid them for the time they gave me and usually provided transportation to and from their homes. I always told them exactly why I wanted to record their myths."[30] The octagonal interior of her museum, replicating the shape of a Navajo hogan, was replete with large sandpainting replicas, made by the museum's own designers and installers based on instructions left by Klah and others.[31]

During the months of 1941 when the strikingly modern and unprecedented *Indian Art of the United States* was installed at the Museum of Modern Art in New York, Navajo sandpainters performed simulacra of their ritual work in the gallery every day, an event familiar to subsequent generations through an often-reproduced publicity photo. A press release for this event named the *hataałii* and stated which chants they would draw imagery from, going on to explain, "Some of the traditional restrictions imposed for the actual healing ceremony will not apply. For example, it will not be necessary to finish the sand painting and destroy it within a single day. The making of one painting will continue several days, at the end of which it will be destroyed. The following day a new painting will be begun."[32] The art historian Jessica Horton has insightfully documented the *hataałii* Fred Stevens's (1922–1983) demonstration of sandpaintings as part of a government initiative in the United States, Europe, Turkey, and Latin America in 1966–68. Rather than focusing on the "colonial gaze" most scholars find intrinsic to such performances, Horton suggests that Stevens transformed sandpaintings from "ceremonial to geopolitical agents" and stresses the "relational potential" of such demonstrations. Though these were sponsored by the US Agency for International Development, Horton finds that they diverged from the "propaganda" fostered by such government programs and, instead, "incorporated damaged land and bodies into international relations and created a path for collective rebalancing."[33] A few *hataałii* continue the practice of sandpainting demonstrations as a form of cross-cultural education, akin to that performed by Tibetan monks worldwide over the past few decades.[34]

NAVAJO SANDPAINTING IN THE AGE OF ANTHROPOLOGICAL REPRODUCTION, OR "IT'S UP TO YOU"

This subheading, of course, plays on Walter Benjamin's famous 1935 essay, "The Work of Art in the Age of Mechanical Reproduction."[35] That German cultural critic pinpointed an essential conundrum for art in the modern era: that the endless reproducibility, via photography and film, of works of art calls into question the importance of the original, the lure of the authentic, and the "aura," as he called it, of the original work of art. Benjamin's famous insight is that "what withers in the age of the technological reproducibility of the work of art is the latter's aura." He goes on to point out that the reproduction "detaches the reproduced object from the sphere of tradition," substituting a mass existence for a unique one, and leads to "a massive upheaval in the domain of objects handed down from the past—a shattering of tradition."[36] Though referring to the art of modern Europe, Benjamin's insights are uncannily apposite here. He posited that the unique value of the authentic had its basis in ritual and that reproduction places the copy "in situations which the original itself cannot attain."[37] This makes sense to scholars of Native American art and to Native artists and ritual practitioners, though perhaps in different ways. Moreover, it helps explain why some (though not all) Navajo who closely observe the strictures of traditional spiritual practice are made uncomfortable by the countless reproductions of ceremonial imagery generated over the past hundred years and more. But it is inescapable that the era from the late nineteenth century to the late twentieth *was* "the age of anthropological reproduction." What was published, through the collaborative efforts of Navajo holy men and white interlocutors, cannot be unpublished. What has been reproduced and seen cannot be unseen. It is now part of humanity's collective knowledge and has formed part of the history of religion, of art, and of anthropology.

This study of transcultural replicas and copies complicates a one-dimensional narrative of Native art and anthropology that has arisen in the past three decades or so (one that circulates less in print than in dismissive conversations) that insists that information and objects have moved in just one direction—that they drain out of Native communities against their will. This is, verifiably, the principal story of the past 150 years, but it is not the only story. Because of this belief, a generation coming of age imbued with contemporary ideas of identity politics and collective cultural authority has not always credited their elders and ancestors with having and using considerable savvy and agency in the ways that they chose to interact with serious seekers of knowledge, such as Newcomb, Wheelwright, and others. Inevitably, a new generation of Indigenous cultural authorities has chosen to use, withhold, or position in a different context the objects of earlier collaboration and encounter, sometimes with odd results.

I have already mentioned Newcomb's experience of being asked to sit in as a *hataalii*'s assistant at a ceremony where she was the only one who knew the imagery. When I first read this in her unpublished notes at the Wheelwright

Museum, I was astounded that a non-Navajo—and a woman—was allowed to make a ritually potent image to be used in curing. But this should not be surprising, in light of an important tenet of Navajo culture. Some contemporary Navajo take offense that Hosteen Klah and others did these things or that, in 1992, the chanter Billy Yellow allowed his medicine bag's contents and one of his curing rituals to be published in a best-selling book and shown in a PBS television series.[38] This is all covered by one phrase central to Navajo ethics and social actions: *Aashi bi'bohlii*—"It's up to you."

Noted weaver D. Y. Begay recalls that her mother used to use this phrase in reference to her daughter's weavings.[39] Navajo culture has a strong predilection for individual autonomy. Add to this that sandpainters have always been the intellectual aristocracy, as well as very powerful in their influence and prestige, and it makes sense that a sandpainter can choose how to use and circulate knowledge. When he takes an apprentice, that apprentice pays to learn; when he makes sandpaintings to cure, or to be experienced in other contexts or distributed through the media, he is paid for his knowledge. Simply put—it is up to him how he uses his knowledge. Others may criticize, but it is ultimately his business.

At a time when a new generation of Native scholars, artists, and cultural workers are insisting on intellectual sovereignty, it is important to remember that in the first half of the twentieth century, these seemingly unorthodox collaborations and replications of sacred imagery took place. These transcultural collaborations that copied, circulated, and demonstrated the iconography of sandpainting helped to preserve the intricacies of one of the world's most complex epistemological and cosmological systems. Native and non-Native people worked together to preserve this knowledge. Moreover, they were on call to help practicing ritual specialists. Newcomb wrote about trying to persuade a chanter named "Yellow Hair" to provide more information about some sandpaintings she already had. At first he demurred, acquiescing only when she told him she did not want to ask him about anything that was private, but wanted a fuller picture of what she already had. "I think the thing that decided him in my favor," Newcomb wrote, "was when I told him that all the things I had were open to the young Navajo singers if they needed to learn something I had written down."[40] Today the Wheelwright Museum serves as such a source. For example, for many years, some archival materials have been open only to ritual specialists trying to verify certain protocols, a decision made in collaboration with Navajo cultural specialists.[41]

This is an ever-changing cultural terrain, however. From 2002 to 2006, the art historian Jennifer McLerran held consultations concerning the substantial collection of sandpainting textiles at the Kennedy Museum of Art at Ohio University. She relates, "The Navajo medicine men and officials of the Navajo Traditional Cultural Program I talked to (who were both apprentice medicine men) believed that recording of sandpainting designs by non-Natives did not help to preserve the practice because the traditional method of passing this information along is not through visual recording but through oral transmission and instruction by older medicine men."[42]

Tracing the cultural biography of the class of replicas of Navajo sandpaintings on paper that proliferated in the twentieth century reveals two fascinating narratives: a decades-long story of intercultural collaboration and a more recent tale concerning reclamation of cultural patrimony. Conversations about the proper ownership of cultural patrimony have been foregrounded in the decades since the passage into law of the Native American Graves Protection and Repatriation Act in 1990. And it brings up the question: How are we to understand the products of these collaborations? Are they Navajo art? Are they copies of Navajo art, no different from illustrations in a book? Are they, in today's more critical environment, cultural theft? Are they items that should be back in Navajo hands? And, if so, does this indicate that copies *do*, in fact, retain the "aura" of ceremonial originals? As the anthropologist Nancy Parezo has pointed out, the *hataalii*'s ritual sandpainting is not an object but an act—literally "a place where the gods come and go."[43] So what happens when an "act" is fossilized into a representation?

Navajo opposition to the fixing of these ephemeral actions into objecthood stems from many different positions. Some are based on a kind of "strict constructionist" view of Navajo cosmology: since the original supernatural makers created them of the transitory materials of the universe, there is no precedent for making them out of more permanent materials. Parezo notes that part of the prohibition about making them permanent is that those with malicious intent or simple ignorance could misuse them.[44] More than sixteen hundred such sandpaintings made in collaborative settings live on in archives and museums today. Many exist in a troubled relationship with archival standards of openness and access.[45] At some institutions, the scholar who seeks to study these items as documents of an intercultural intellectual enterprise may be told that they are off-limits to non-Navajo people.[46] In some cases, museums have returned these images to the Navajo Nation Museum and Cultural Center or to Diné College. Several years before the passage of the Native American Graves Protection and Repatriation Act, the Wheelwright Museum, as a gesture of collaborative goodwill, sent a series of large six-by-six-foot replicas to Diné College—the very sandpaintings that had filled the museum at its opening in 1937. This was an early example of recent efforts to decolonize knowledge and to follow the standards of each Indigenous community concerning esoteric knowledge.[47]

This brings us full circle—back to the sandpaintings exhibited at the Gallup Walmart early in the twenty-first century (see figure 5.1)—and asks us to consider Benjamin's dictum that "technological reproduction can place the copy of the original in situations which the original itself cannot attain."[48] The Walmart sandpainting replicas were the ones that the Wheelwright Museum had returned to Navajo custody, the category that the anthropologist Gladys A. Reichard termed in 1939 "authentic copies." Apparently, one of the educators at Diné College wanted to use them as publicity, for the college had established an information desk in Walmart where Navajo could enroll for classes.[49] So while some outsiders who know only a little bit about contemporary intercultural politics might agree that it is best if ceremonial knowledge and imagery is returned to its culture of origin, these same outsiders might be puzzled that such images ended up in Walmart. For as has been demonstrated in previous chapters, a fuzzy romanticism still obtains when many people think about Native spirituality and cosmological imagery: sure, they should have it back, but not to put in . . . Walmart! But the reality of repatriation is that such objects, once returned, can and should be used however the descendants of their makers choose to use them. That is the nature of sovereignty.

Perhaps there is another way to interpret the sandpaintings in Walmart in the early twenty-first century. Historically, Gallup has been an Anglo town where Navajo were, at best, tolerated and, at worst, abused. Perhaps, for a few years at the beginning of the twenty-first century, the local branch of the corporate behemoth Walmart was quietly claimed as Navajo space. Do sandpainting replicas lose their aura when so radically detached from their origins, or do they find a new vitality in an intercultural space where contemporary Navajo people can claim their own relationships to this imagery? When I informally queried Navajo employees in Walmart in 2006 about their opinions of the images hanging overhead, some said it made them proud of their heritage. When I returned in May 2013 and found no trace of the sandpaintings, I asked several Navajo employees if they missed them; some said they did, while others said they had not noticed their absence.[50]

It is not surprising that contemporary Navajo express a range of opinions about the replication of sandpainting imagery. Some weavers, for example, make their living by creating technically challenging sandpainting textiles, working by special commission, and earning a good wage.[51] Others come from families or regions of the reservation where the weaving of sandpainting designs has never been part of their practice. Some view such work with deep distrust because they follow traditional beliefs and are wary of possible misuse of the power of sacred imagery. Some Navajo practice Mormon, Mennonite, or fundamentalist versions of Christianity and eschew sandpainting imagery because it represents what Christian doctrine has taught them to reject. Finally, some are simply indifferent to this issue.

One *hataałii* expressed to me the viewpoint that if particular sandpainting imagery was "already out there on the internet," then it is fine to reproduce it again, but that the imagery, prayers, songs, and beliefs that have not been shared should remain private. In a number of educational settings off the reservation, he has made full-scale replicas of some familiar sandpaintings as they appear in ceremony, using crushed sands and minerals carefully spread on the floor. Yet he distinguishes these from the "real" ceremonial ones that he has constructed in certain off-reservation settings both in the United States and abroad. He agrees that when an individual becomes a medicine man "it is his choice" how to share his knowledge. Yet in discussion of the sandpainting replicas done by Klah, Newcomb, and others, as well as the commercial replicas in which ground minerals are affixed to Masonite, he left the door open to the possibility that such images, even if deliberately incomplete or "ritually incorrect," still might have some latent power and could harm the person who makes them.

Neo-orthodoxy is on the rise in the Navajo Nation, as elsewhere, as a way of expressing sovereignty and ownership of knowledge and practice while living surrounded by a large nation-state whose members have all too often appropriated Navajo imagery for profit and use in advertising, film, and other public media. While Navajo people generally exhibit personal generosity to outsiders, a vein of extreme skepticism also underpins such interactions. Many are suspicious of the dominant culture's attempts to gain, study, use, or publish Navajo knowledge, despite the long history of productive collaborations that

I have chronicled one small part of here.[52] This attitude is understandable, given the far more prevalent racism, control, and deprivation to which the Navajo have been subject for more than two hundred years. So for some, the flip side of the Navajo predilection for autonomy, "It's up to you," shades into "It's not for you."

One individual (not a medicine man) told me, while forbidding me to quote him by name, "I think all of those sandpainting rugs in museums should be unraveled, and the wool used for something else. I don't want them destroyed or burned, like some people do, but I do think they should be unraveled."[53] He, like most Navajo living on the eastern side of the Navajo Nation, shops in the Gallup Walmart at least once a week, and he acknowledged having seen the replicas there. His comments suggest that, for some Navajo, what Benjamin called "aura" is not degraded by reproduction—mechanical or otherwise. Instead, it persists through multiple iterations, from the ceremonial performance of sandpainting to the visual recording of iconographic aspects of that performance through painting, drawing, and weaving.

Anthropologists have long characterized Navajo people as unusually open to innovative use of the materials, techniques, beliefs, and imagery of others. Indeed, creative adaptation and mimesis are practically core values of Navajo epistemology, extending back to their initial relationships with Pueblo peoples some six hundred years ago, followed by their strategic use of aspects of Spanish and Anglo culture since first contact. Moreover, Navajo philosophy insists that the world is always in motion—indeed, the principal supernatural is named Changing Woman, and Navajo language strongly favors verbs of motion rather than those of stasis.[54] Navajo ceremonial art has long pivoted around the idea of replicating, copying, and translating the ideal "prime objects" created at the beginning of time by the Diyin Dine'é, who set all things in motion.

A Native Mimbres "Revival"

The Mimbres pottery examined in chapter 4—of keen interest to archaeologists, museums, collectors, and the public for more than a century—has been equally important to many artists. Many Pueblo artists, in particular, are deeply moved by this ancestral tradition that combines figuration and abstraction. Pueblo potters have adopted and adapted Mimbreño imagery in their work for a hundred years. Some, such as pottery painter Julian Martinez (San Ildefonso Pueblo, 1885–1943), sought to replicate these images exactly. Others, including a number of Acoma potters, have incorporated Mimbres iconography into their grammar of forms. Distinguished Hopi painter Fred Kabotie sought to understand how sacred concepts linked ancient Mimbreños with modern Hopi.[55] Other painters and designers have incorporated Mimbres designs into their twentieth- and twenty-first-century works in remarkably varied ways, deserving of their own book. Here I offer a limited number of examples, all of which are works by potters.[56]

PUEBLO POTTERS

It may seem to us that the earliest publications on Mimbres pottery would have been inaccessible to Pueblo artists, for they were published in arcane sources such as the Papers of the Peabody Museum series at Harvard. Yet even in the early twentieth century, many museums and libraries had subscriptions to such publications, and many archaeologists and anthropologists got them for free, just by writing and asking. Given that Pueblo artists such as Julian Martinez mingled freely with anthropologists and archaeologists in Santa Fe, at archaeological sites, and in their home communities, it is safe to assume that they had access to even the earliest publications. Martinez drew inspiration from pottery sherds he found while working as a digger on the Pajarito Plateau in the first decade of the twentieth century.[57] It is clear that the feather designs he executed on both San Ildefonso polychrome and on black-on-black ware came from ancient sources much farther south in New Mexico. Jesse Walter Fewkes's *Designs on Prehistoric Pottery from the Mimbres Valley, New Mexico* was issued in 1923 and contains what must be the inspiration for Martinez's early radiating feather designs.[58] A black-on-black ware plate made by Maria Poveka Martinez (San Ildefonso Pueblo, 1887–1980) and decorated by Julian Martinez, her husband, around 1930 depicts two mountain lions that radiate around the surface of a lobed design (figure 5.4). This exactly copies the geometric painting on the bodies and faces of the Mimbres mountain lion bowl drawn in Fewkes's 1924 supplement to his 1923 publication.[59]

Artists from all cultures reference the past. When done by Native artists of the Southwest, it is not the same type of appropriative gesture as when modern non-Native artists choose to use the inventory of Mimbres painted designs in their work. Because of cultural connections between ancient Mimbreños and modern Pueblo peoples, it is a recuperative gesture, a dialogue between past and present. Just as some Pueblo potters talk about using temper from

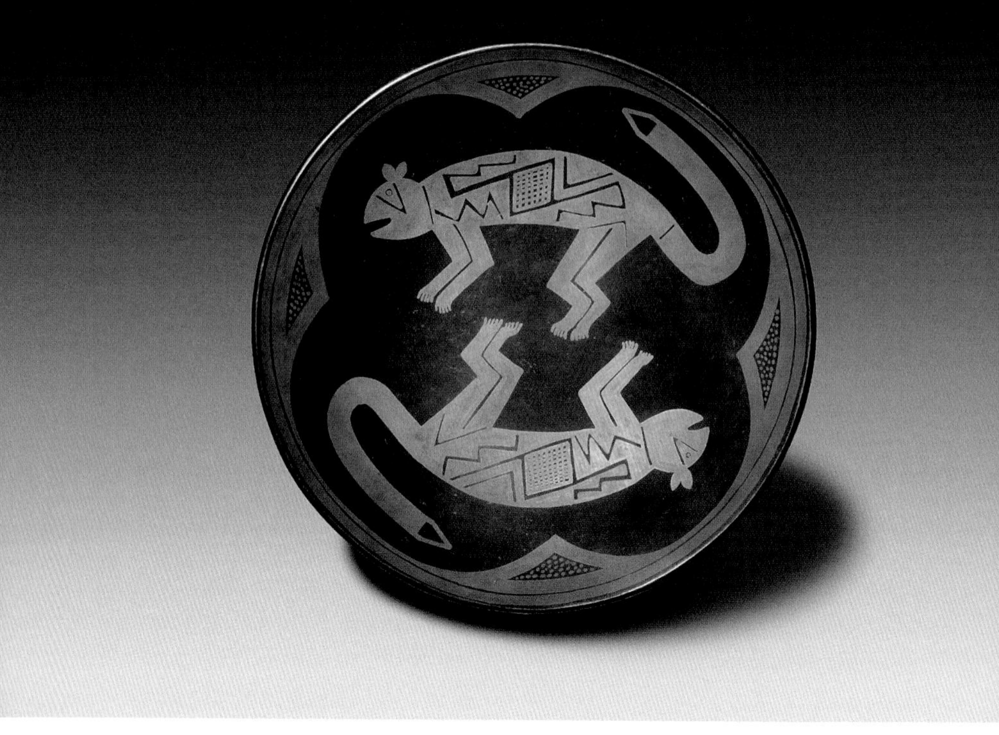

FIG. 5.4 Maria Poveka Martinez and Julian Martinez, plate, ca. 1930. Clay, 14¾ in. (37.47 cm) diameter. Estelle and Morton Sosland Collection, Nelson-Atkins Museum of Art, Kansas City, Missouri, no. 2009.41.24. Photo © Nelson Gallery Foundation.

ground-up ancient potsherds as a way of incorporating the work of the ancestors into their vessels, so too is Julian Martinez conducting a dialogue with Indigenous painters who preceded him by a thousand years in the desert southwest.

As the author Bruce Bernstein has observed, the archaeologist Edgar Lee Hewett and pottery scholar Kenneth Chapman hold principal responsibility for suggesting to Pueblo potters in the first half of the twentieth century the use of Mimbres and other ancient design motifs. He notes that these museum curators understood all too well the romantic views that buyers held about Native art and that encouraging the use of precontact designs on pottery helped maintain notions of authenticity and traditionalism, thus ensuring a robust market for contemporary wares.[60]

At Acoma, since the time of the famous potter Lucy M. Lewis (1898–1992), Mimbres designs have been taken up by many potters. The archaeologist

Steven A. LeBlanc says that sometime after World War II, the archaeologist Harry Mera gave a copy of the Cosgroves' Swarts Ruin site report, with its hundreds of drawings of vessels, to Lewis, and thus she added Mimbres iconography to her already celebrated fine-line designs.[61] On Lewis's first visit to Santa Fe in 1958, Chapman showed her real examples of Mimbres and Ancestral Puebloan pottery, and the collector Tony Berlant recalls seeing the well-worn and clay-spattered copy of the Cosgroves' book in her home when he visited Lewis at Acoma in the 1960s.[62] Many other Acoma potters followed Lewis's example and perhaps relied on her copy of the Mimbres book for visual inspiration. Her daughter, Emma Lewis Mitchell (1931–2013), who also used Mimbres imagery, told the potter Rick Dillingham: "I want to keep them [the Mimbres designs] alive by continuing to use them . . . as the Mimbres people painted them. I feel a spiritual connection to them."[63]

Today, one of the most interesting Acoma potters to experiment with Mimbres iconography is Charmae Shields Natseway (b. 1958), whose work is in many museum collections, including the National Museum of the American Indian and the School for Advanced Research. She comes from a family of accomplished potters, most notably her grandmother Dolores Sanchez (1888–1991) and her mother, Ethel Shields (b. 1926). Natseway grew up all over the Southwest, moving for her contractor father's work. After high school, she returned to Acoma and began to work more seriously on her pottery. Her husband, Thomas Natseway, from Laguna, is a potter as well, who specializes in miniatures, and they dig their own clay from local sources.

"I was always interested in Mimbres imagery, from the first time I saw it," Charmae Shields Natseway says.[64] Several collectors have shared their books with her, and she described well-known Albuquerque collector Ruth Schultz as having been her mentor for decades, encouraging her creativity and buying many of her creations.[65] In addition to learning from books, the artist says she also dreams the designs that she paints. Having experimented with abstract designs since childhood, she often combines abstract patterning with Mimbres figural imagery (figure 5.5).

Natseway's work has a striking contemporary feel, for she has broken out of traditional vessel forms to experiment with slab-built constructions, many of them quite small. The one illustrated here is a triangular vessel with abstract patterns around the sides and a pair of male and female figures on the top. These figures are adapted from a painted bowl excavated by the Cosgroves in the 1920s that has been much illustrated.[66] To make the slabs for her triangular,

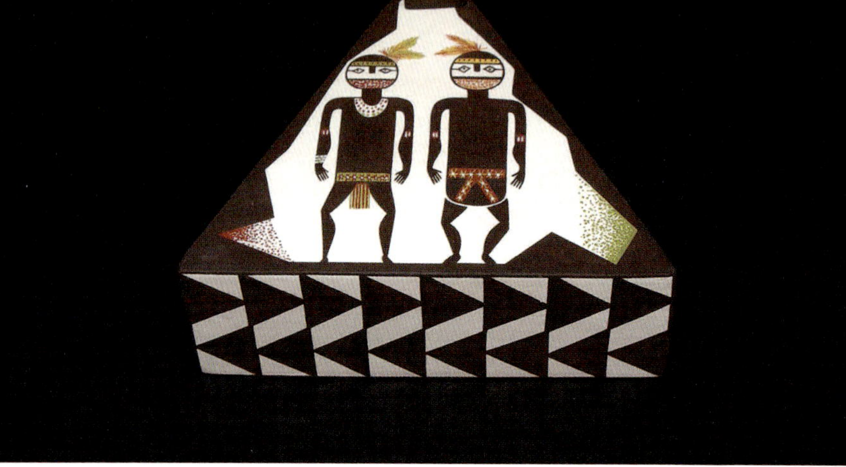

FIG. 5.5 Charmae Shields Natseway, triangular vessel with Mimbres imagery, 2011. Courtesy of the Andrea Fisher Gallery, Santa Fe, New Mexico.

pyramidal, and trapezoidal constructions, Natseway uses brass plates provided by her machinist brother-in-law in order to maintain exacting dimensions. She paints with traditional clay slips, with which she has experimented for years. She notes that "yellow slip is tricky—it is just clay and peels off if you put too much on the brush," whereas for other colors she uses iron oxides and beeweed as a binder (as do the Thornburgs, discussed in chapter 4).

Pueblo potters have been seeking inspiration from ancient Native wares for generations. Among the Haudenosaunee, keeping the arts of the past alive can be documented in successive waves since 1850.

Replicating and Reviving Seneca Beadwork, 1935–1941

A photo taken at the Seneca community of Tonawanda in 1936 chronicles a moment in a historic initiative in which Seneca people were paid with government funds to re-create nineteenth-century historical arts.[67] Four women sit on a bench, talking and holding beaded items they had made as part of the Seneca Arts Project (SAP), an endeavor funded by the federal Works Progress

Administration (WPA) to provide work during the Great Depression (figure 5.6). Rose Spring, Alice Poodry, and Melinda Skye sit close together, looking amiable. To the right, a bit apart, sits the older Martha Skye. When I came across this photo at the Rochester Museum and Science Center (RMSC), I had already examined the beaded skirts and sashes that the three young women had made, so I recognized the names. Suddenly, the human aspect of my intellectual project to study the beaded replicas made by women of the SAP came to the forefront.

These women wear the ordinary sweaters, dresses, and stacked-heel lace-up shoes of countless American women in the 1930s. What did they get out of this initiative of replicating the art of their nineteenth-century foremothers? What is their legacy for bead workers today? For decades, the creative work of their hands (and that of their neighbors and kin) has rested in numerous dark cabinets and storage boxes in the Rochester museum. (Established as the Rochester Municipal Museum in 1912, the museum's name was changed to the Rochester Museum of Arts and Sciences in 1930, and in 1968 it became the

FIG. 5.6 Artists in the Seneca Arts Project, Tonawanda, New York. (From left) Rose Spring, Alice Poodry, Melinda Skye, and Martha Skye, 1936. Photo by William G. Frank. Bill Frank Negative Collection, Rochester Museum and Science Center, Rochester, New York.

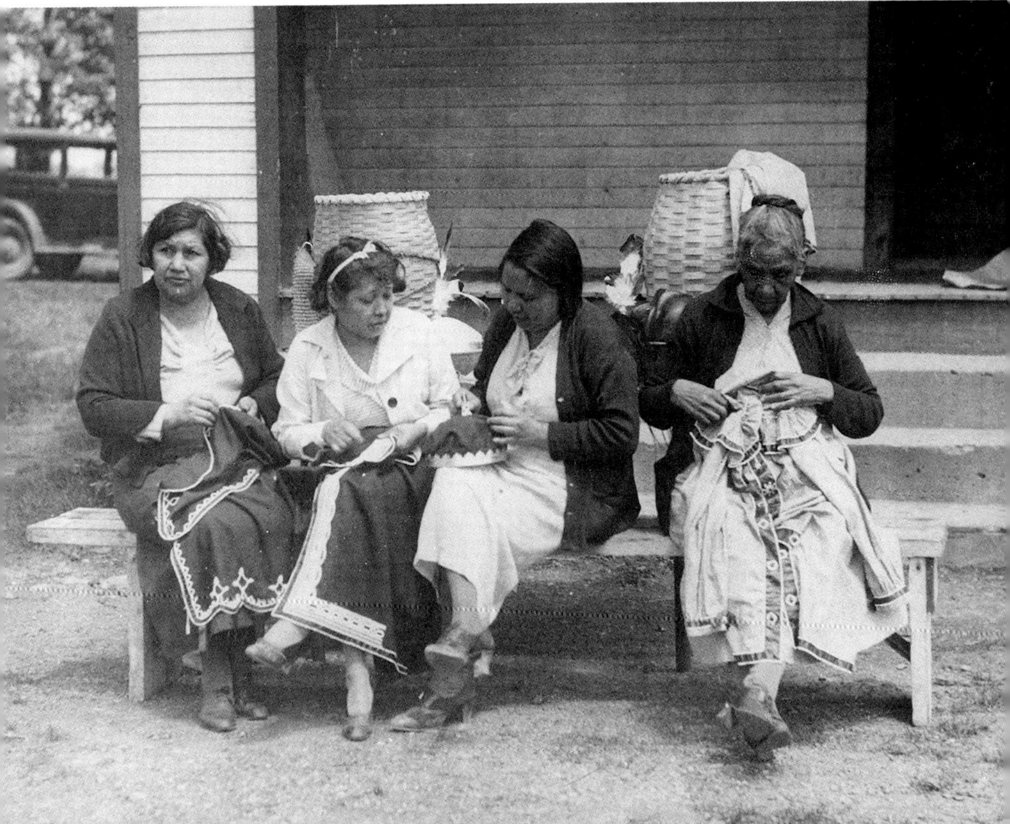

Rochester Museum and Science Center.) While their beaded wool garments were much exhibited in the 1930s and 1940s, today they are seldom seen. Were these women simply working for a wage of fifty cents an hour during an era when jobs were hard to come by, or was their work more meaningful to them than that? In published accounts of the SAP, only male names are invoked. Why had I never heard of Spring, Poodry, or the Skyes before 2019? Collectively, they made more than five hundred objects.

During the six years of its existence, the SAP provided work for more than eighty Seneca, who made between five thousand and six thousand objects, most of which are still at the RMSC.[68] The project was a prominent component of President Franklin Roosevelt's WPA initiatives for Native people.[69] In Native American art history, the best-known results of the project are dozens of paintings of Iroquois lifeways by Ernest Smith (1907–1975) and numerous "false face" masks (today more properly called medicine faces) carved by Jesse Cornplanter (1889–1957) and others.[70] Baskets, war clubs, moccasins, clothing, and other objects of traditional Haudenosaunee life made within the program have long been displayed in the Rochester museum, and some were used for decades in the museum's school programs. Every type of object made was represented in numerous traveling exhibits. Yet little art historical attention has been paid to the remarkably diverse and elegant skirts, leggings, ceremonial bibs, breechcloths, sashes, moccasins, hair ornaments, overdresses, head scarves, and other items made from cloth and painstakingly beaded by women in the style of their nineteenth-century foremothers. For this reason, I am focusing on those arts, specifically the beaded skirt.[71]

Notably, every work in the project is identified by the maker's name. Because this was a government program for which careful records were kept of hours worked and costs of materials used, it offers insight into the working habits of Native textile artists. Many of the names recorded still resonate with meaning and personal significance to Seneca and other Haudenosaunee today. Moreover, these objects provide a material bridge from Iroquoia in the nineteenth century to Iroquoia today. To understand how this project came about, and its significance in Seneca history in particular and in Native art history in general, it is important to know something of the genealogies—both familial and intellectual—of those who provided inspiration and impetus for it.

LEWIS HENRY MORGAN, THE PARKERS, AND SENECA MATERIAL CULTURE

The names Morgan and Parker are woven throughout the story of the SAP. Lewis Henry Morgan (1818–1881) was the founding father of American ethnology, whose entrée into Iroquois culture in the 1840s was occasioned by his acquaintance with Ely Parker (1828–1895), a young Seneca born at Tonawanda, west of Morgan's home in Rochester, New York. The two became research collaborators, and Morgan dedicated his first book, *League of the Ho-dé-no-sau-nee, or Iroquois*, to Parker, calling it "the fruit of our joint researches."[72] In 1848, Morgan sought to form a collection of traditional Iroquois clothing and implements.[73] He turned to Parker's parents, William and Elizabeth Parker, and sister Caroline Parker (ca. 1826–1892). Caroline Parker made items of clothing for the New York State Museum in Albany. Some of these, as well as works in the RMSC and daguerreotypes and engravings of her wearing such pieces, were the models for the SAP.

Born in the year of Morgan's death, Arthur C. Parker (1881–1955) followed in the footsteps of his intellectual hero. A well-known archaeologist and descendant of Ely Parker, Arthur Parker worked at the New York State Museum amid Morgan's collections from 1906 to 1924, taking up the directorship of the Rochester Municipal Museum in 1925.[74] Parker is best known today for his creation of the SAP. Using his contacts at both Cattaraugus and at Tonawanda, he sought to ameliorate Depression-era poverty there and to foster a renaissance in Seneca art. Parker was present at (and saved hundreds of items from) a fire at the New York State Museum in Albany in 1911 that destroyed much of the great collection of Haudenosaunee objects that Morgan had amassed (and those that Parker had collected, as well). With the remaining items, many books and photos, and some objects in the Rochester museum, he put together a resource collection to inspire the Seneca who would be "remaking" the works of their ancestors.

ART FOR REVENUE AND REVITALIZATION

General unemployment in the United States in 1933, during the Great Depression, was nearly 25 percent, and in Native communities the situation was far more dire. During 1933–34, approximately half of the Native people who lived on reservations in New York State (some 2,700 of 5,500) received relief aid from the State Department of Social Welfare.[75] In April 1934, Parker, as director of the Rochester Museum of Arts and Sciences, received notice that a proposal he had submitted to the Temporary Emergency Relief Administration (TERA) of the state of New York would be funded. This would allow him to hire workers for a number of initiatives, including a pilot project to teach and pay Seneca people at both the Tonawanda and Cattaraugus Reservations to revive their arts of wood carving, silver making, bead- and quillwork, basket making, and doll making, paying them thirty cents an hour to do so.[76] A few months later, Parker wrote to John C. Brennan, superintendent of the Thomas Indian School on the Cattaraugus Reservation, asking if he knew of any people at Cattaraugus eligible to receive relief aid who might have artistic talents. He outlined his vision for the program: "Briefly, our plan is to supply the material and instruction and have facsimiles of old Indian artifacts manufactured. These articles will come to our museum and be available for exchange or exhibition. As the relief worker acquires skill, he may voluntarily withdraw and manufacture these articles for his own profit. We shall attempt to provide a market or build a number of 'trading post souvenir stands.' We are hoping to develop a better type of New York Indian souvenir, based on the best in the old art and eliminating the crudeness of the degenerated art of recent times."[77] A year later, the TERA grant was superseded by annual funding from the WPA.[78]

Both in his applications to funding agencies and in published articles, Parker emphasized that this project, while ostensibly an economic relief measure, was also an opportunity for cultural revitalization: "Our arts project . . . seeks to capitalize the best in ancient art and to redevelop it as a racial contribution. We are saving the old arts and passing them on to the youth of the reservation and the very effort made to achieve this is reawakening interest in the native pattern of thought."[79] Today we understand this rhetoric of "original and pristine" Native art to be both inaccurate historically and deeply flawed conceptually. Haudenosaunee art, for centuries, had been altered every time its makers encountered the work and the materials of another Native nation, as well as the material goods of European interlopers. Beads, manufactured cloth, and metal ornaments, for example, had been integral to Seneca art making for more than two centuries when Parker wrote those words.[80] In keeping with many early twentieth-century initiatives involving Native arts, Parker's public rhetoric about the project was that little instruction was required: "Only in extreme cases has any instruction been given, it being believed that our function is to assist in bringing out the innate ability of our Indian workers themselves."[81] There were, in the early 1930s, some Seneca people skilled in wood carving, basketry, and the making of corn-husk dolls. At Tonawanda, the center for traditional religion, objects associated with healing, such as masks and rattles, were still in use and no instruction was needed. Silver-working skills had apparently dwindled to almost nothing. No one had worked with porcupine quills for many decades. Seneca-style beadwork, one of the great Indigenous art forms of the Northeast in the eighteenth and nineteenth centuries, was not much in evidence at the poverty-stricken reservations when the program commenced. On public occasions, some people wore Plains-style beadwork, for that was what the American public in the first half of the twentieth century recognized as "Indian."[82] Parker and his staff provided examples of nineteenth-century Seneca objects from which to learn. Some were original museum specimens, while others were simply photographs in the anthropological papers written by Morgan, Parker, and others.[83] Cephas Hill, the Tuscarora supervisor of the Tonawanda project, wrote in 1935: "Our sponsors, the Rochester Museum of Arts and Sciences, have provided us with work benches, carving tools, silversmith's tools, needles and thread, patterns photographs, line drawings and models with which to work. Besides, we have the guidance of a willing staff of museum workers who act in an advisory capacity to our Indian craftsmen. Materials are either furnished by the Museum, they are procured on the Reservation, or they are donated by our Indians." He goes on to say that some forms of ancient craft are remembered and that both drawings in scholarly publications and actual museum objects provided inspiration.[84] For the bead workers, of course, the great inspirations were the pieces collected by Morgan in 1849 and 1850, including a skirt in the RMSC collection attributed to Caroline Parker.

BEADED GARMENTS: FROM CAROLINE PARKER TO THE SENECA ARTS PROJECT

In 1849, Morgan commissioned Caroline Parker to make items of clothing, including the magnificently adorned skirt that she wore in daguerreotype portraits and that Morgan deposited in the New York State Museum (figure 5.7). Both her portraits and the skirt itself have been widely published.[85] The Rochester museum owns another skirt that has been attributed to her—the most elegant and ambitiously beaded item in the whole RMSC collection (figure 5.8). From the bottom corner blooms an exuberant tree of life with three

FIG. 5.7 / RIGHT Caroline Parker, ca. 1849. Daguerreotype. Arthur C. Parker Collection of Negatives, New York State Museum, Albany, no. RM2086A.

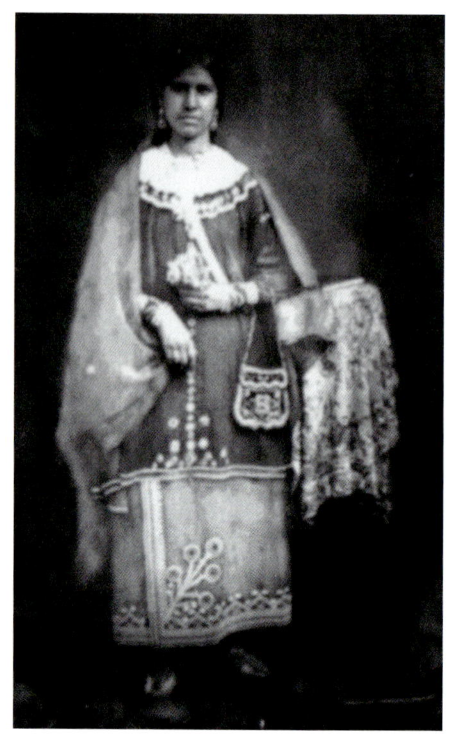

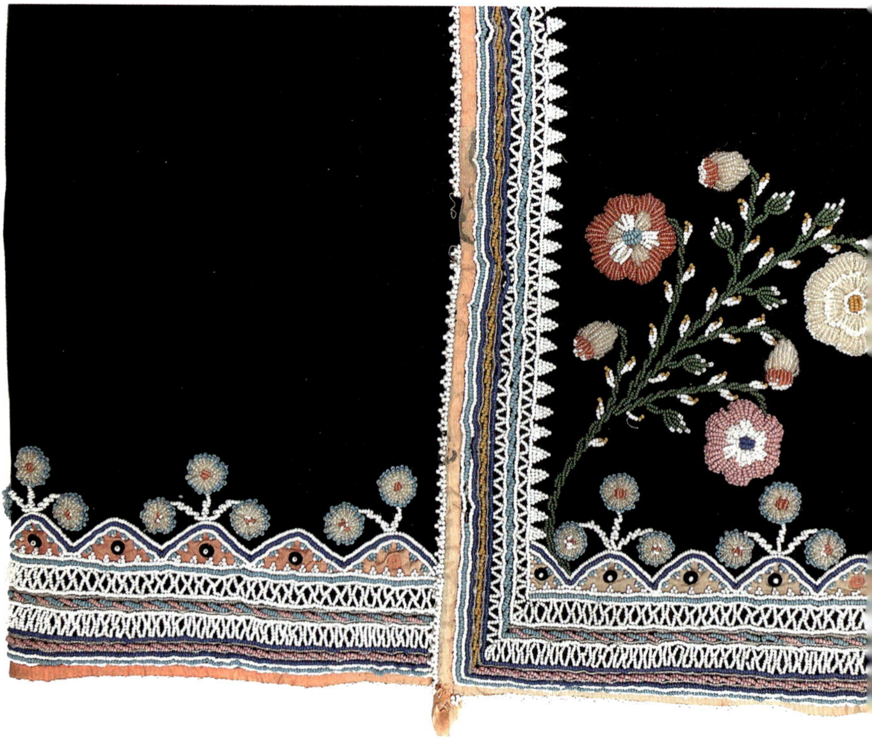

FIG. 5.8 / BELOW Detail of beaded skirt attributed to Caroline Parker, ca. 1850. Wool broadcloth, silk, glass beads. 23 × 48 in. Lewis Henry Morgan Collection, Rochester Museum and Science Center, Rochester, New York, no. 70.89.61. Photo by author.

raised beadwork open blossoms, three large buds, and numerous tiny white and orange buds. The vine itself consists of two lines of beadwork that cross over each other to make a raised design, a feature also seen in the dusky rose and light blue beaded portions of the borders. None of the beadwork replicated in the SAP rises to this extraordinary level of workmanship.

Parker and his staff obtained materials for the program from diverse sources. Complete records are lacking, but hints are provided in files, in correspondence, and in minutes of museum meetings. Satin ribbons and wool broadcloth could be purchased at almost any fabric shop.[86] Some of the beads came in hanks, wrapped in large brown paper bundles stamped "Made in Czechoslovakia." Others were packed in small glassine tubes, labeled "Walco 'Chief Brand' Beads," and surely came directly from the Walco store on Thirty-Seventh Street in New York City.[87]

Only fourteen Tonawanda women took part in the SAP from 1935 to 1941, yet their output was astounding, especially in the medium of beadwork on cloth.[88] In the photo taken at Tonawanda in 1936 (see figure 5.6), Rose Spring and Alice Poodry hold beaded wool skirts on their laps. Melinda Skye holds a beaded hat. At right, Martha Skye inspects a cotton overdress ornamented with silk ribbons, glass beads, and silver brooches.[89] (The making of such brooches was also part of the SAP.) The women have come outside to pose for the photo on the steps of the small building in which they worked. The three younger women created some of the finest beadwork of the project. Spring made twenty-five sets of leggings, fourteen overdresses, fifteen skirts, seven men's shirts, and a small number of sashes, ceremonial bibs, arm and leg bands, and a few other items. Poodry and Melinda Skye were among the most prolific workers. Poodry made some 157 objects between 1935 and 1939. These included about fifteen beaded skirts, thirty-six pairs of leggings, ten head throws, six overdresses, twenty sets of arm or leg bands, nine sashes, and other items. Skye, who worked from 1935 to the end of the project in the summer of 1941, made more than 250 objects, among them some thirty-five pairs of moccasins, seven skirts, thirty-two sets of leggings, eighteen head throws, fourteen ceremonial bibs, eleven overdresses, nineteen men's shirts, twenty sets of arm and leg bands, and thirteen hats. Martha Skye, though she only worked for the program until 1938, made twenty-one overdresses (like the one she holds on her lap), as well as a dozen sets of leggings and men's shirts.[90] She was also adept at making baskets and sieves; the ones on the stairs behind the seated women are likely hers.

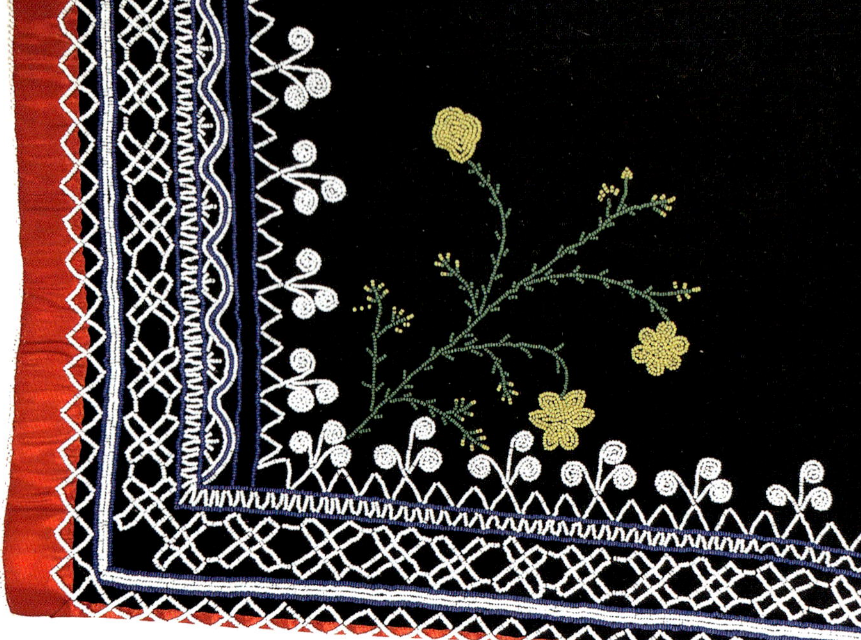

FIG. 5.9 Melinda Skye (Tonawanda Seneca, 1901–1963), detail of beaded skirt, 1938. Navy blue wool broadcloth, red satin ribbon, and white, green, yellow, and blue glass beads. Rochester Museum and Science Center, Rochester, New York, no. 37.510.9. Photo by author.

Only seven Tonawanda women made skirts for the project. None matches the beaded complexity of the nineteenth-century prototypes, yet many of the forty-four skirts bear lovely tree of life designs springing out of complex borders. One skirt Melinda Skye made is an exceptionally fine example (figure 5.9). On navy blue broadcloth edged with wide red satin ribbon, a four-and-one-half-inch band of geometric blue and white beadwork covers some of the red satin and moves up into the dark wool. The flowers and buds on the green tree of life are embroidered in bright yellow beads. Work records show that the artist spent approximately 123 hours on its making in January and February 1938, far more time than most women spent on beaded skirts. She made coordinating red-beaded broadcloth leggings with navy blue satin trim and beaded designs in white, blue, and yellow.[91]

REPLICAS OF REPLICAS

While images of Caroline Parker are always used to illustrate "traditional" dress of Seneca women (or Haudenosaunee women in general) (see figure

5.7), it is important to recognize that when this twenty-three-year-old woman from Tonawanda created exquisite examples of clothing for Morgan in 1849, she was not making examples of what an educated Seneca woman like herself wore. By this time, Parker had already attended a local Baptist school, as well as the Cayuga Academy in Auburn, New York, and was enrolled at the recently established Albany Normal School, on the other side of the state.[92] Such items were worn on ceremonial occasions within the longhouse among those who practiced traditional ways, but they actually reflected the clothing style of the first part of the nineteenth century—Parker's mother's generation—and the second part of the eighteenth century, when they were the latest in cosmopolitan fashion, featuring trade cloth of both wool and cotton, silk ribbon, beads, and silver ornaments. In 1849, when culture was changing dramatically, Parker was ensuring that the artistry of her foremothers would be remembered. Her artistic descendants in the late 1930s were doing the same.

ECONOMICS, EXCHANGES, AND INFLUENCES

All SAP workers earned the same hourly wage of fifty cents, even before a federal minimum wage was set at twenty-five cents per hour by the Fair Labor Standards Act of 1938.[93] It is noteworthy that their pay was twice the national minimum wage; even though the federal contracts list them as "unskilled laborers," clearly Arthur Parker recognized their skill. Though voluminous paperwork charts the precise costs involved in producing each item, we know almost nothing about the beliefs and motivations of the women who, for weeks, months, and sometimes years at a time, earned their livings by making objects of their cultural patrimony. Some of their work was innovative and elegant, while other pieces were merely serviceable. While a few women may have continued to make items for themselves and members of their communities, sadly there was no non-Native market in the 1940s for exquisitely beaded items, for which their makers were accustomed to earning a good wage in the SAP. Who would have paid fifty dollars, one hundred dollars, or more for such garments in the 1940s? Though Arthur Parker had envisioned at the start of this endeavor that "at the completion of this project the Indians [would] manufacture similar materials for sale," that happened in only a limited way, principally for men's carving and painting.[94] Is it blindness to the elegance of the exquisite beadwork that has kept the clothing of the SAP out of the limelight or the simple misogyny of twentieth-century American culture? Most articles, whether written in the 1930s or the 1980s, have focused on the masks and the paintings, either mentioning the clothing in passing or ignoring it completely.

Works from the SAP were loaned to diverse venues. Some traveled as part of larger WPA exhibits showcasing the results of this ambitious federal project. Others were part of educational and artistic exhibits mounted locally, nationally, and abroad. Not surprisingly, given how well known the project was, exhibits were held at both the New York World's Fair (1939) and the Golden Gate International Exposition in San Francisco (1940).[95] Materials went out to the Fleming Museum at the University of Vermont (1939); the Memorial Art Gallery in Rochester, New York (1949); the Syracuse Museum of Fine Arts (1951); the Montclair Art Museum in New Jersey (1954); and the San Diego Museum of Man (1957), among others.[96] Internationally, they were part of an exhibit of American folk art in Paris in 1937. In 1962, seventy-five items toured Israeli museums, in a program sponsored by the US Information Agency.[97]

Before the late twentieth century, museums often swapped objects of which they had a surfeit to other museums. There is no complete list of what museums received SAP items "by exchange," as it was called. Penciled notes on original accession cards or mention in the museum's annual reports indicate that a selection of items went to ethnographic museums in Belgium and Norway. Two groups of exchanges occurred with the Denver Art Museum, which already in the 1930s had perhaps the finest collections of Native objects in an American art museum. In 1936, thirty-nine items went to Denver, including a complete woman's outfit. In 1951, a Seneca skirt made by Rose Spring, as well as an overdress and leggings, augmented the Denver collection. Both this outfit and one sent in 1936 were used in the curator Frederic Douglas's famous Indian Fashion Shows across the country.[98]

Since 1989, two exhibits at the RMSC have drawn attention to the work of the project. *A Seneca Renaissance: The Indian Arts Project* (1989) displayed some one hundred objects in a 2,000-square-foot gallery.[99] SAP workers who were still alive were interviewed, and their perspectives brought into the narrative. No catalogue was published. In 2018, *Bridging the Gap: Seneca Art across Generations* featured work by Caroline Parker, the WPA women, and contemporary Tonawanda bead workers, who used materials left over from the WPA project that had been discovered in the museum's remote storage facility.[100] Some of the artists were direct descendants of the WPA workers and spoke about the importance to them of that era's beadwork. Melissa Smith, granddaughter of Melinda Skye, cherishes the fact that beadwork connects her to her grandmother, going on to say that while making things she has a "good mind"; this concept, central to Haudenosaunee philosophy, involves a benevolent awareness of all living things.[101] Another bead worker, Allison Smith, noted that, growing up, she had heard mainly about the WPA wood-carvers and that only recently had she seen the beadwork: "To be asked to make something using the material that my ancestors had used was exciting. As I was beading, I could imagine them all sitting in the workhouse, talking, beading, and laughing."[102]

When I asked Michael Galban, who works at the Seneca Art and Culture Center at Ganondagan State Historic Site and is himself a bead worker and quill worker, what he thought the lasting effects of the SAP were, he replied, "It solidified what people considered to be truly Iroquoian."[103] As mentioned above, in the 1930s many Haudenosaunee were wearing Plains-style regalia at public events. "Today, that would be laughable," Galban said.

As early as 1936, Arthur Parker knew that in the SAP he had generated something culturally significant. He wrote, "Like the specimens made for Lewis Henry Morgan in 1849, our results are destined to become of historic importance."[104] As the project ended in 1941, Parker reflected on the enterprise he had created, asking how, as an ethnologist, he should classify these "hundreds of recreated objects." He found himself in a quandary: "We are still perplexed in knowing just what to call these things. Shall it be '1935–1941 reproductions by Seneca Indians' presenting their own material culture; or, shall it be something else? Our choice is 'reproductions,' but it is hard to convince the Indians that the articles are not 'genuine' and as good as they make for themselves."[105]

The historian Laurel Thatcher Ulrich, in her magisterial study of objects of women's use and manufacture, remarks on how much objects reveal when they are "imbedded in the rich texture of local history."[106] In some ways, it is heartbreaking to think of thousands of beaded items of Seneca dress entombed in a museum vault. Their makers were paid well, but then they relinquished the work of their hands to the institution that had commissioned them. These elegant expressions of women's creativity did not live on in Tonawanda, the way that Navajo artist Gerald Nailor's 1943 murals still enliven the Navajo governmental chambers in Window Rock, Arizona, or numerous WPA-funded totem poles made by Tlingit and Haida men continue to animate the landscape of southeastern Alaska.[107] Increasingly the RMSC has reached out to the people of Tonawanda, encouraging them to come examine and learn from these objects, and, of course, it is astonishing to have such a rich resource in a near pristine state. What if Arthur Parker and the WPA were seen now to have maintained an unbroken lineage of Seneca culture, allowing twenty-first-century Seneca to reclaim a portion of these objects for their community?

Native Reenacting and Replica Making in the Twenty-First Century

As discussed in other chapters, most scholars and Native Americans today dismiss reenactors as "playing Indian" because of the long legacy of impersonation of Native people in disrespectful contexts. At the reenactments I have attended since 2009, I certainly have met white men who fall into stereotyped behavior, though many do not. But what about when Native people engage in such practices?[108] This section profiles two Native men, Michael Galban and Jamie Jacobs, who participate in eighteenth-century reenactments and make their own regalia, though my focus here is on objects rather than reenactments. My hope is that this will allow the reader to think about the ways that Native replication and reenactment may be different from or similar to the work of non-Natives discussed in previous chapters.

MICHAEL GALBAN: A WASHOE MAKER OF HAUDENOSAUNEE OBJECTS

Chapter 1 analyzed the work of Don Smith ("Chief Lelooska"), who made Northwest Coast–style objects and danced them both in Native ceremony and in performances of his own devising, though he was not of any Northwest Coast heritage. Moreover, his own claims to Native ancestry were suspect, at best. What about a man of Washoe (Wašiw), Mono Lake Paiute (Kutzadika'a), and Italian American heritage who is a foremost authority on eighteenth-century material culture of the Native Northeast, who makes historically accurate replicas, and who sometimes wears them in reenactments? Michael Galban (enrolled Washoe Tribe of Nevada and California, b. 1970) grew up both in rural Nevada and in Rochester, New York. He wrote in 2013 that, as a boy in Nevada playing cowboys and Indians, "I was always the Indian in that game, and in my eyes we were always the victors. Despite the popular misconceptions about the history of Native people, I consider my very existence a victory. As an adult, I find myself twenty years in the field of public history, focusing on the Native American colonial experience and challenging popular misconceptions of the past every single day."[109] How did Galban come to this work?[110] The answer reveals the complexity of Native identities in the twenty-first century, something that essentialist notions of Native nationhood do little to reveal. His Native father married his Italian American mother, and they raised their children mostly in Rochester.

Galban's bachelor of fine arts degree from the State University of New York at Geneseo, with concentrations in art history and anthropology, prepared him well for his life's work. Shortly after graduation, he took a summer job at the Ganondagan State Historic Site and never left. A National Historic Landmark in Victor, southeast of Rochester, its website describes Ganondagan as "the only New York State Historic Site dedicated to a Native American theme," "the only Seneca town developed and interpreted in the United States," and "the original site of a 17th-century Seneca town," which "existed there peacefully more than 350 years ago."[111]

In the mid-1990s, a bark lodge was being built there. Upon its completion in 1998, Galban was intent on filling it with objects of daily life appropriate to its era. One day a non-Native reenactor came to the park and spoke with him. "This guy actually had a clue," he said. "I was impressed!" The man encouraged Galban to attend a conference for reenactors and replicators. "There I found a world of dedicated people, and an audience really interested in the teaching materials I brought," he told me. He realized that there were, in fact, a number of people who had the skills that he had been trying to learn from books. Eventually, Ganondagan hired Brent Boyd, of Williamsburg, Ontario, a non-Native restorer who specialized in quillwork and moose hair restoration, to conduct a three-day workshop to instruct Native artists in these techniques. Galban said that the workshop did not, as he had hoped, reinject these techniques into the community of Native artists, but it gave him the skills he needed to start making objects. He made items to stock the longhouse and then began to seek out more information within historical collections and scholarly books.

Today, Galban's official title is director of interpretive programs at the Seneca Art and Culture Center, built in 2015 at Ganondagan; he also serves as curator and historian. In addition to these professional responsibilities, he is among the most talented makers of historic Haudenosaunee artifacts and a historical reenactor. Having pored over his family's stash of books on Native arts and culture as a child, he told me, he was prepared for this job in ways he did not quite understand until he was an adult. Galban married a Mohawk woman, and because of her matrilineal traditions, their three children are Mohawk: "So this is something I can give to them, to contribute to their understanding of their history." He has taught workshops in many Native communities in the Northeast, from snowshoe making to basket making to quillwork. As he made more and more historically accurate objects, he eventually sought to wear them and to use his formidable knowledge and skills to educate others through historical reenactment.

In his office in the summer of 2019, we looked at objects he had made, among them a *gustoweh* (Haudenosaunee male hat), quilled pouches, and intricately twined tumplines (figure 5.10). Part of the impetus for making such items is his own interest in owning them: "It's the collector in me. I see amazing things in museums and the only way I am going to own them is by making them myself." We examined two examples of his beautifully embellished tumplines, also called burden straps (figure 5.11). These are made in a technique called "closed twining." The bottom of the basswood warp cords are not attached to anything, and the maker nimbly uses his fingers to wrap finer basswood threads to make the weft. Moose hair is further wound around the weft strands so that it appears only on top. The example on the left is made principally with undyed moose hair; the one on the right has a supplementary weft of dyed porcupine quills. Both are edged with small white beads, a Haudenosaunee custom in much historical quill- and beadwork, as well as in the SAP. Holding these superb objects, I am reminded of Lewis Henry Morgan's observation in the middle of the nineteenth century that "in the manufacture of the several species of burden strap, more skill, ingenuity and patient industry are exhibited, perhaps, than in any other single article fabricated by the Iroquois."[112]

"Moose hair tumplines were the second most collected Native item from the colonial era, after moccasins," Galban tells me. "I got interested in making them from the Seneca Arts Project material at the Rochester museum. They used to have a video in the galleries and I watched it really carefully. I learned how to process basswood fiber from that video." He is referring to a 1936 film of SAP participant Everett Parker, who learned basswood fiber production and tumpline making from elder Sarah Hill.[113] Galban is writing a book on tumpline weaving and moose hair finger weaving. His historical replicas have been published alongside Haudenosaunee originals. He has done commissions for museums, has published on other historical artifacts, and writes occasional blog posts on such topics.[114]

Galban has long worked with the historical painter Robert Griffing to ensure the accuracy of Griffing's paintings: "I am the art director of the paintings. Both my wife, Tonia, and I have modeled for him and made some items that he uses." Galban wrote the text for a book of Griffing's paintings of historical

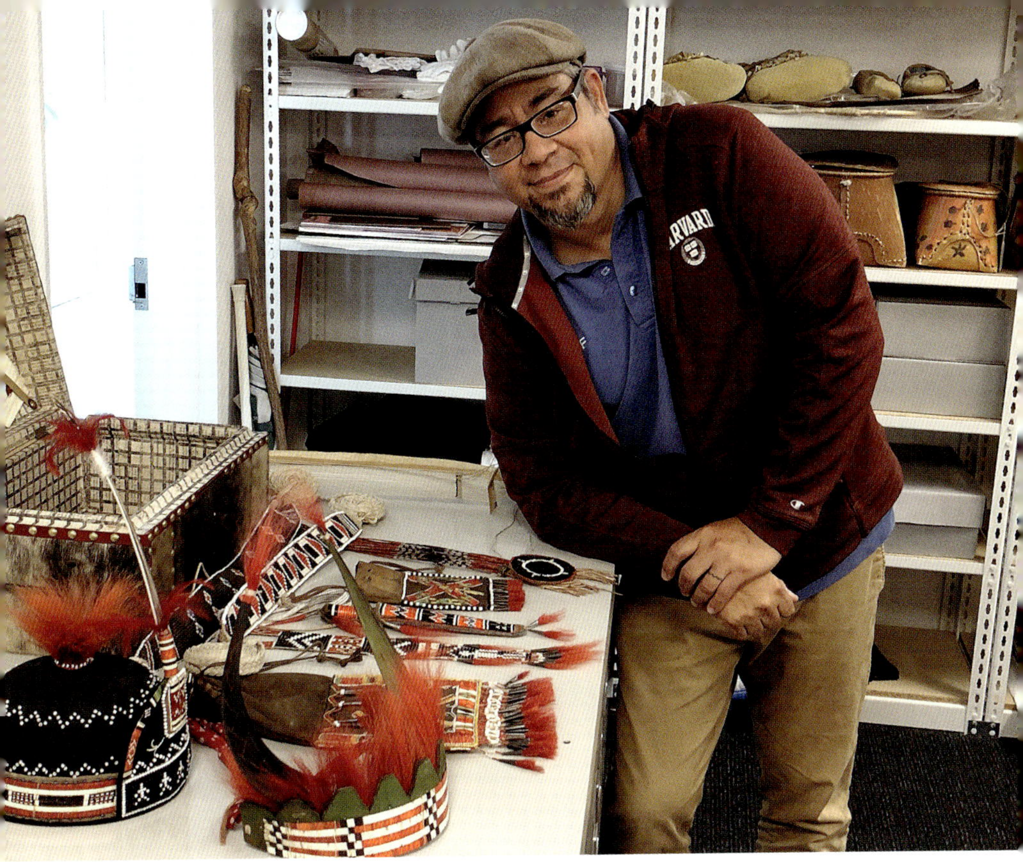

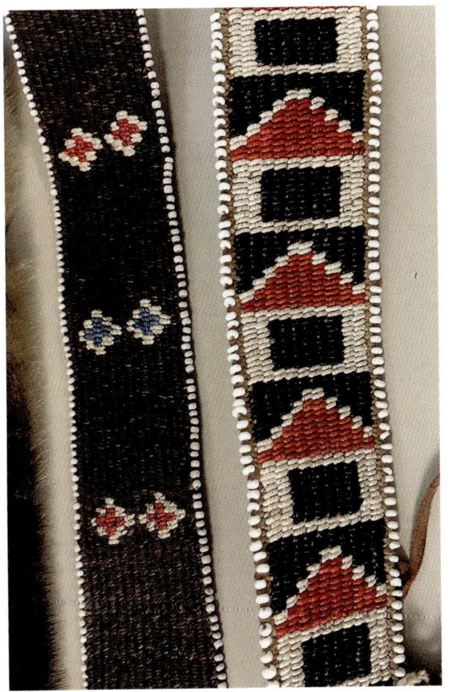

FIG. 5.10 / ABOVE Michael Galban and his historical replicas, Seneca Art and Culture Center, Ganondagan State Historical Site, Victor, New York, July 2019. Photo by author.

FIG. 5.11 / LEFT Details of two Iroquois-style tumplines made by Michael Galban, July 2019. Photo by author.

figures and events in the Native Northeast.[115] He has consulted on films, including *The New World* (2005), about the founding of the Jamestown settlement in what is now Virginia, and directed the Oneida exhibit at the Museum of the American Revolution, in Philadelphia. Galban has curated many exhibits at the Seneca Art and Culture Center at Ganondagan, including *Hodinöhsö:ni' Women: From the Time of Creation* (2017).

When people ask him why he does not make things that stem from his own cultural traditions, Galban replies, "My life is here in New York State. There are no materials here to do arts from the California/Nevada region—the plants and animals are different here. I can't find tule, or willows, or devil's claw, or antelope. I can't order bulrush and bear grass on Amazon. So, I use what's around me here in the forests. The place that my Kaniekehake wife and kids know as their homelands." Other Native peoples of the Northeast who have learned so much about historical arts and material culture from Galban surely are glad that this is so. He holds himself to strict historical standards in his replicas, writing: "My personal challenge when reproducing a historic object is to combine three forms of evidence. I like to have an image from the time period and region depicting the object in use if possible, a written description of the same, and finally an extant object of equal importance. This is not always possible in every instance but it is my goal none the less. I try and avoid 'building motorcycles from oil stains' to borrow a phrase."[116] Making historical items led to wearing them in reenactments. "Making things and showing them to people is great," Galban says, "but wearing them is a real joy." Galban formerly sold some of his creations, but seldom does now, for he has little time to make them and prefers to create them for his own use or occasionally to trade with other reenactors.

JAMIE JACOBS AND THE ART OF THE ANCESTORS

Jamie Jacobs (Tonawanda Seneca, b. 1981) has worked as collections assistant at the RMSC since 2006. Among his many duties, he has handled repatriation of objects and is a conduit to the Native communities whose collections are in the museum, including his own community. He is a Seneca speaker and cultural interpreter who is much in demand as a lecturer at museums and universities.[117]

Jacobs credits his interest in making things to his father, who gave him his first set of tools at fifteen, taught him how to use them, and instructed him on how to fix his first car. He went to school for motorcycle mechanics and still does motorcycle building and repair. But his finest work is on a far smaller scale. He is a master at seventeenth- and eighteenth-century quillwork artistry. His Onandaga father also taught him how to carve, and his Seneca grandmother taught him how to bead.

In his early years of working at the RMSC, he noticed quillwork in the museum labeled as Seneca. "I didn't know about this before I went to work here, but it interested me; I only knew about beadwork." Around 2012, he attended a reenactment of the French and Indian War at Fort Niagara and saw quilled items there. Soon thereafter, he took a workshop at the fort with Galban, and he speaks admiringly of Galban's talent and generosity. Jacobs has worked tirelessly to hone his skills, and today his quilled bags, moccasins, and knife sheaths are sought after by reenactors, private collectors, and museums. In 2019, he sold two pieces to the New York State Museum in Albany, which was endeavoring to bring its collecting of Native art (started by Morgan in the mid-nineteenth century) into the present. Jacobs's work is inspired by Eastern Woodlands pieces in museums around the world; in our conversations, he mentions objects in the Peabody Museum at Harvard, as well as ethnographic museums in Stockholm and St. Petersburg. "But I don't make exact replicas. I use the historic pieces as inspiration."

The bag illustrated here (figure 5.12) is based on one pictured in *American Indian Art Magazine* some years ago.[118] The vertical lines of folded quillwork are made by using two threaded needles and two quills (sometimes in contrasting colors) to create a sawtooth pattern. These are outlined by a thin single line of sewn quills. He hand cut and rolled the small pendant tin cone tinklers that are stuffed with red-dyed deer tail hair, and the bag's seams are ornamented with a delicate single line of white beads. While all artists are impatient when asked, "How long did it take you to make that?," he estimates that the bag alone was more than forty hours of work. Since the birth of his daughter, he has far less time to work on his artistry. He estimates that before he became a father, he worked nine to ten hours a week in the evenings. "Now it is maybe six hours every couple of weeks," he says.

While some replica makers, such as Chris Ravenshead and Cathy A. Smith (chapter 3) or the Thornburgs (chapter 4), seek to use only materials from the historical era, Jacobs wants to achieve a correct look but without the tedium of doing every step according to historical precedent. He uses only brain-tanned hides bought from expert hide tanners, but sometimes he overdyes the hide with walnut shell dye to achieve an even brown finish. He does not hunt

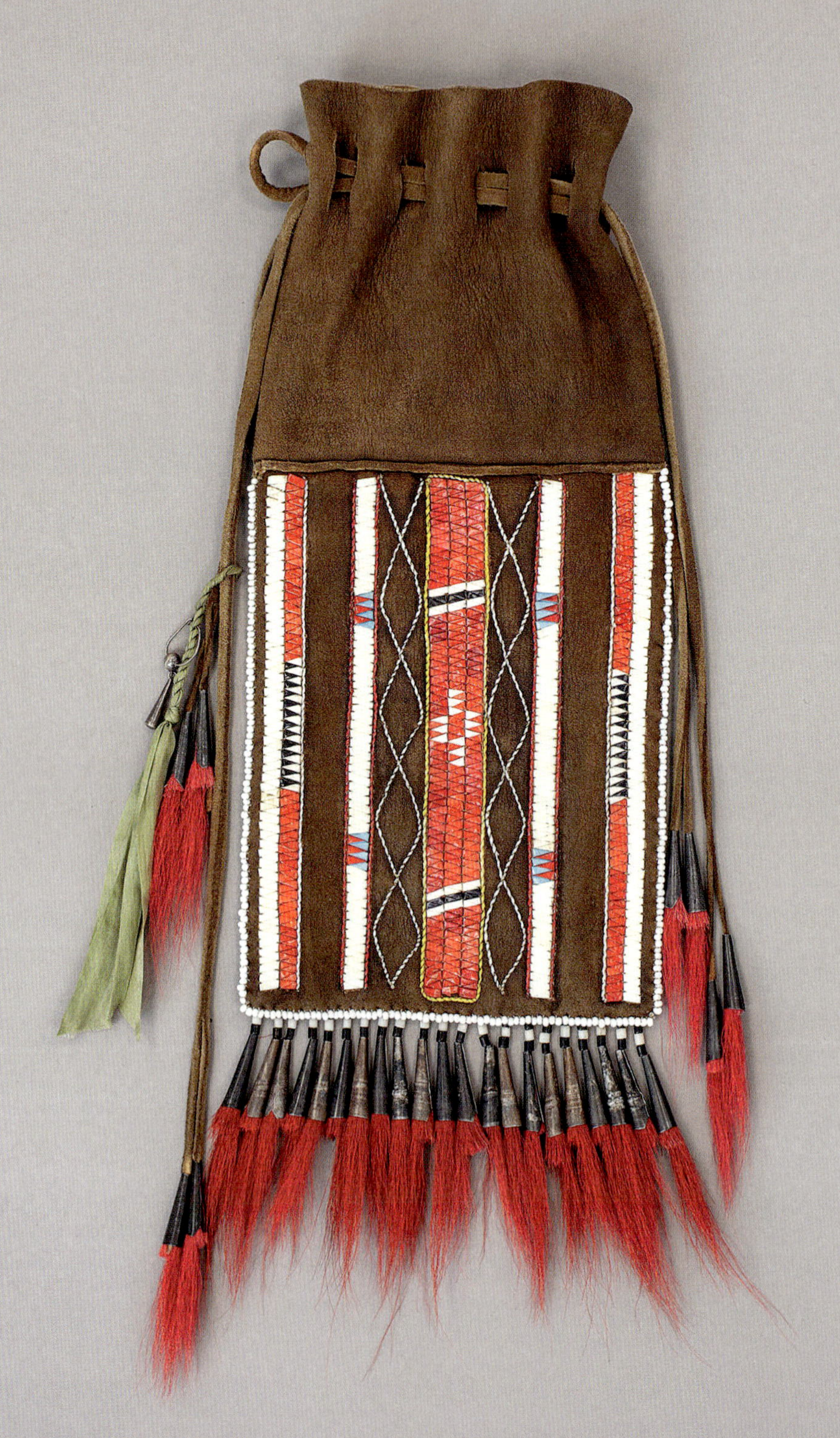

FIG. 5.12 Jamie Jacobs, replica of seventeenth-century quilled leather pouch, 2018. 21½ × 7 in. Collection of the New York State Museum, Albany, no. 2018.29.1.

porcupines himself. He tells me that there are not porcupines near Tonawanda, but they do live up near Watertown, New York, and down in Pennsylvania. "Sometimes I pick up roadkill," he admits, "but more often I get quills from hunters, or buy them on eBay." Aside from walnut shells, he is not interested in traditional dyeing with plant materials. "That's a whole other discipline," he says. "I use Rit dye." (I reassure him that most quill workers in the Dakotas use Rit dye too.) Neither does he use sinew or plant cordage to affix his quills; he uses nylon beading thread and Gold Eye embroidery needles. While some makers of historical or archaeological objects in any field are sticklers for doing it exactly as it was done centuries ago, others take a more expedient approach, recognizing that in the historical era people were eager for innovation and time-saving practices, and so it is fine for contemporary makers to use time-saving methods and materials as well. Moreover, some makers of historical objects do this precisely so that their work will not be resold as an ancient original. If a buyer takes a quick look inside one of Jacobs's bags, for example, the small knots in the nylon cording provide verification that this is a contemporary work.

Jacobs won Best in Show in the 2020 Ganondagan virtual juried Hodinöhsö:ni' Art Show for his eighteenth-century-style deer hide bag, quilled on both sides. One side depicts an abstract thunderbird in red, black, and white quills set against the plain hide background. The other is fully quilled in a bold geometric design in red, green, yellow, black, and white.[119] This bag is multi-referential, as is so much contemporary Native artwork. Jacobs describes it as representing both the contemporary and the historical. "It's an homage to Seneca women but with some contemporary style."

There is a certain symmetry in Jacobs having grown up some twenty miles from Fort Niagara, having been moved to learn quillwork by being impressed by the work he saw reenactors use there more than a decade ago, and now being an award-winning quill worker, teacher, and reenactor himself. I asked him what he thinks about the white men who don Native garb in the reenactments at the fort. "I don't have any problem with it, except when they try to do ceremonial things. That is not their business." Indeed, he says that the best conversations about historical arts and culture happen with other reenactors. "They are an amazing font of knowledge."

Conclusion: Replicating as a "Technique of Remembering"

The term *reproduction* covers everything from mechanical to photographic reproduction, and every Native nation has its own way of thinking about reproduction and replication. Yet, as Gwyneira Isaac has written about the Zuni, it would not be inaccurate to say that for most Native people, repetition is "an affirmation of the continuity of knowledge."[120] Both Caroline Parker and the SAP beadwork artists absolutely were affirming the continuity of knowledge. The twentieth-century bead workers sometimes used the electric yellow and orange beads available in their own era as accent colors, giving a modern touch to the customary white, red, and light blue beads used as the main colors. And while they used traditional Seneca motifs, they did not interpret the idea of replica as meaning an exact copy. They kept Seneca women's art alive; it became encoded in the fingertips and memories of a generation of Tonawanda women, and the objects in the RMSC persist in keeping it alive. The SAP was not an initiative that arose from within the culture. It was offered from outside the community, but as a well-paid and artistically satisfying program, during a time when jobs were scarce, it was embraced by the Seneca.

The sociologist John Urry has characterized various populist engagements with heritage, from touristic visits to historical sites, to heritage fairs and festivals, to reenacting, as worthwhile "techniques of remembering."[121] Every artist knows that to work materials with one's hands is to know them intimately in a way that is inaccessible to those who do not do such work. For Native practitioners, to use the materials that were central to life in the past, such as the quills, basswood fiber, and moose hair that Michael Galban manipulates so expertly, is to know history in a deeply satisfying way that book learning alone cannot provide. Cognitive knowledge, affective knowledge, and haptic knowledge form nearly unbreakable bonds in one's neural pathways, and the past revives through the work of one's hands. Of course, for Native makers such as those chronicled in this chapter, honoring one's heritage and one's ancestors is also to demonstrate that what is ancient is modern as well.

Acoma potters generally grind up old potsherds to use as temper; Lillian Salvador (b. 1944) not only used Mimbres imagery in her work but also sought ancient potsherds from her friend's land in the Mimbres region to grind up and temper her clay, forging both a material and an artistic connection with the distant past.[122] Many Pueblo painters have affirmed the continuity of Native culture over the millennia by incorporating Mimbres imagery into their paintings. The painter Fred Kabotie (Hopi, ca. 1900–1986) knew the archaeologist Harriet Cosgrove, for in the late 1930s, after leaving the Mimbres region, she worked on excavations at Awatovi, not far from his home. She shared her Mimbres drawings with Kabotie, and he won a Guggenheim Fellowship in 1945 to study and interpret Mimbres iconography from his cultural perspective; *Designs from the Ancient Mimbreños with a Hopi Interpretation*, a handsome volume published in 1949, was the result.[123]

The complexities of Mimbres figuration and abstraction have inspired a number of Pueblo modernist painters, most notably Tony Da (San Ildefonso Pueblo, 1940–2008) and Helen Hardin (Santa Clara Pueblo, 1943–1984).[124] Each completely absorbed Mimbres figuration and abstraction into their own private visual languages and demonstrated that these ancestral visual modes were congruent with modernist concerns. The artist and designer Ramona Sakiestewa (Hopi, b. 1948) has adapted Mimbres designs in works ranging from commercially made blankets to notecards. In 1995, she designed the Ancient Blanket series produced by Scalamandré.[125] One of the five designs, titled Gila, is based on Mimbres imagery of a men's gambling game.[126] Describing herself as having always been aware of Mimbres imagery, Sakiestewa talks readily about the excellence of Mimbres graphic design, with its sophisticated use of pictorial space, its rotational symmetry, and its superb quality of line. "Every artist who lives in the Southwest has to take on the challenge of Mimbres design eventually," she remarked.

Coda: Diego Romero: Mimbres Imagery for a New Millennium

The painted bowls and vessels of Diego Romero (Cochiti Pueblo, b. 1964) are well known for offering a clear-eyed, often humorous, and sometimes hard-hitting commentary on Native life in an era of greed, substance abuse, pollution, and casino gaming. He studied at the Institute of American Indian Arts in Santa Fe, the Otis Art Institute in Los Angeles, and the University of California, Los Angeles, where he earned a master of fine arts in studio pottery in 1993. His interest in the clear graphic possibilities of comic book art led Romero to use Mimbres pictorial style for depicting Pueblo life. Though raised in Berkeley, California, Romero's paternal ancestors came from Cochiti, and his grandmother Teresita Chavez Romero (1894–1991) was a potter. Romero's

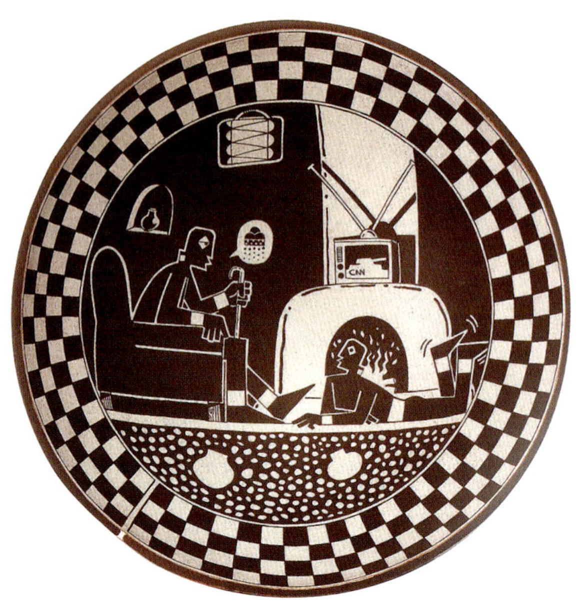

FIG. 5.13 Diego Romero, *Mo-Mo (Grandfather)*, ca. 2000. Ceramic, 6 × 15¼ in. Augustana Teaching Museum of Art, Rock Island, Illinois, no. 2008.22.

work is usually slab built over a mold, though he occasionally hand coils the whole pot or the top inch of the rim.[127] He generally paints a narrative scene on the interior of the bowl, with a geometric pattern on the rim.

In the bowl illustrated here (figure 5.13), a grandfather figure sits in an easy chair and talks to his grandson about rain, indicated by the cloud design in the speech bubble. They inhabit a Pueblo living room, with a drum on the wall, a fire in the fireplace, and CNN on the TV. Below the floor of the home, ancient vessels are buried. Romero's imagery takes on topics from the Pueblo Revolt of 1680 and the murder of the participants at the hands of the Spanish to the exploits of the "Chongo Brothers," who stand in for all modern Native men who are disenfranchised, though they sometimes seem to be about the artist and his brother Mateo, who is also an artist.[128] Romero's hip postmodern versions of Southwestern pottery have entered international museum collections and demonstrate the continuing appeal of the Mimbres style more than a millennium after its first appearance. He uses ancient imagery as a very effective technique of remembering, reminding young, hip Natives who admire his work of the many layers of their visual history as well as a history of genocide and resistance. His work affirms the relevance of ancient modes of artistic practice to twenty-first-century art making.

Conclusion *Vexed Identities and the "Destruction of Mimicry" in the Twenty-First Century*

I have presented examples ranging over two hundred years of the making of and trade in spurious Indigenous objects and the making of historical replicas by both Native and non-Native artists. My aim has been to demonstrate the complexity of each of these situations. I conclude with one final, long-lived, and multifaceted example, that of the unauthorized reproduction and circulation of the visages of Zuni *kokko* and Hopi "friends," or what outsiders have called katsina "masks," an imprecise term, as I discuss below.[1] Many of the themes of this book come together in examining the vexed issue of the making, display, sale, and repatriation of possibly fake sacred images. Yet this example also demonstrates that views of the authentic, the copy, and the fake that arise from a positivistic post-Enlightenment meaning of these terms do not fully reckon with some Native views on this subject.

And I give the last word—-and the final images—in this book to one of the most creative and prolific Native North American artists of the twenty-first century, Nicholas Galanin, who has critiqued the commodification and appropriation of Native culture by outsiders. I have chosen his work to stand as a final commentary on all I have presented, for he turns these issues on their heads and asks us to look at them anew.

Hopi and Zuni "Masks" and Their Replications

At the beginning of the twentieth century, the anthropologist Matilda Coxe Stevenson wrote of how customs had changed at Zuni in the twenty years she had been working there: "In 1879 no amount of money could have purchased a genuine Zuñi mask, and not for the world would they have manufactured a bogus specimen, so great was their dread of offending their gods." She goes on to say, "At present the less orthodox men will manufacture almost anything a collector may desire. Spurious ancient fetishes are made by the sackful and passed off as genuine. So it is also with masks and altars. Any number of fraudulent objects may be obtained at the prices set by the clever Indians."[2] Until about 2015, I thought the making of fraudulent Zuni masks to be a thing of the past. Now I am not so sure.

SACRED MASKS AT AUCTION: REAL OR FAKE?

Most scholars of Native art are familiar with the international outcry that resulted in April 2013 when the French auction house Néret-Minet, Tessier et Sarrou published the catalogue for an upcoming sale, *Masques katsinam des indiens Hopis de l'Arizona*.[3] I attended that auction, which took place on April 12, the day that I arrived in Paris for a vacation. I did not schedule my trip to coincide with the auction, but when I realized the serendipity of my arrival—just hours before the sale—it felt imperative to go directly from the airport to bear witness.

Survival International France, Comité de Solidarité avec les Indiens des Amériques (Committee of Solidarity with the American Indians), and other French human rights groups had issued statements and were protesting outside the auction house as people were entering.[4] The American embassy's cultural affairs officer in Paris, Phillip Breeden, had requested that the auction be delayed to allow inquiries into the possibility that these were stolen items. A legal challenge filed by French lawyer Pierre Servan-Schreiber on behalf of Survival International and the Hopi people was determined in favor of the auction house just two hours before the sale.[5]

Newspapers across Europe and North America had covered the controversy, including photos of the auctioneer Gilles Néret-Minet with the masks, proclaiming, "This sale is not just a business transaction but a homage to the Hopi Indians" and "I think the Hopis should be happy that so many people want to understand and analyze their civilization."[6] Though I had followed the press coverage in the weeks before arriving in Paris, and had seen photos of the masks on display, it was profoundly shocking to walk through the protesters, enter the building, and take a seat in the salesroom. Only those who bought auction catalogues in the foyer, and their companions, were allowed to enter the salesroom. Moreover, it seemed that the guards were trying to determine who might be a protester, based on stereotypes about comportment, age, and looks. In this instance, it was to my advantage to be a woman of a certain age, with an elegant scarf wrapped around my neck. They allowed us, one by one, through a single door, rather than through the wide double doors. For security reasons, the masks were in a well-guarded adjacent room. As each came up for auction, it was displayed on an overhead monitor, though it is customary in auctions of far higher-priced objects to actually bring each object onto the stage during the auction.

So I sat there, toggling between feelings of fascination as a scholar and revulsion as an ethical witness to a cultural travesty. I lasted as a quiet observer through the sale of nearly five dozen items, as a young Hopi man (exchange student Bo Lomahquahu, who, with his stylishly cropped hair, black jacket, and fashionable leather shoulder bag, apparently did not fit the security guards' image of what a Native American protester would look like) and a French newswoman were ejected for protesting. I knew that the sixtieth item, a Hopi Crow Mother mask, would far exceed pre-auction estimates of €40,000–€50,000, because of its majestic visage and its dramatic black feather Crow wings, a detail of which had been featured on the cover of the auction catalogue. When the gavel fell at €160,000, I surprised myself by standing and, in a quavering but loud voice, admonishing the participants in the transaction, in my mix of English and poor French: "Shame on you! This is not an economic transaction. This is a sacred being. *C'est dégueulasse. Dégueulasse!* [This is disgusting. Disgusting!]." I was forcibly ejected from the room and the building by a security guard the size of a sumo wrestler.[7]

Another such auction was held in December 2013, this time by Estimations et Ventes aux Enchères (EVE) auction house. The Annenberg Foundation made headlines by secretly buying twenty-one of the twenty-four Hopi items offered for sale, then holding a press conference announcing their gift to the Hopi. Tom Mashberg of the *New York Times* wrote that the contents of this auction were "held by a number of French collectors, all of whom said they had owned the items for many years and had good title to them. Several collectors said they had been impressed by prices realized at an April auction of 70 Hopi artifacts."[8] Yet another EVE auction was held in June 2014, and a fourth on December 9, 2014. After the third such auction I began to feel a mounting skepticism at the large number of Pueblo and Navajo masks suddenly available for sale. The masks from the first sale were said to have been owned by a Frenchman who had lived in the United States early in the twentieth century.[9] Was this true? And were dozens of masks in subsequent auctions really emerging from great family homes in the Parisian suburbs, stockpiled since trips to the Southwest by previous generations? Were American collectors—now cognizant of the fact that they could neither give their masks to American museums nor sell them at American auctions—sending them to Europe?[10] Donald Ellis, a well-known dealer in Native North American art, told me that he believed a dealer in Santa Fe had assembled masks from a number of American collectors and dealers to sell on consignment at the subsequent auctions, after the success of the first.[11] It seemed equally likely that the first auction had engendered a new zeal in fakers of such objects and that the other auctions were perhaps offering masks of lesser aesthetic merit that had been refurbished, repainted, and artificially aged to present the correct look valued by collectors of rare works of art. Another art dealer of my acquaintance, who preferred to remain anonymous, concurred.

Jim Enote, director of the A:shiwi A:wan Museum and Heritage Center at Zuni, was the first to raise a concern about fakes. In an opinion piece for *Indian Country Today* a month before the first auction, Enote wrote that in many museums "a substantial number of objects labeled as ceremonial are actually fakes" and cautioned: "[Zuni experts] have not authenticated items in the Paris auctions. Consequently, the auction house and the buyers can only be assured of one thing, they may be possessing and purchasing fakes."[12]

When I interviewed Enote in 2017, he told me that even just looking at the online catalogue before the April 2013 auction, it was clear to him that "some things were not right." He surmised that they "were probably made by a Zuni, but as replicas, not for ceremonial use." He told me that religious specialists within the community can easily pinpoint the mistakes: "Some objects are manufactured from the wrong materials, such as the wrong kind of feather. Or they are not painted and tied according to the correct protocol." Moreover, he believed that the ones sold in subsequent auctions (which I had suggested to him were made in Europe specifically for those auctions) were probably made in Zuni or nearby, by people, as he diplomatically put it, "responding to the market."[13] He stressed that Zuni people would characterize such a person as "damaged," for only someone damaged in some way (through mental illness, alcoholism, or witchcraft, for example) would do such a thing.

Many Native people and their allies are outraged at the public sale of such masks, for reasons having to do with politics, freedom of religion, and sovereignty. But for an even deeper understanding of the true outrage, it is crucial to understand the specific meanings of these objects to Hopi and Zuni people. Yet even discussing this is considered by some to be problematic, for many believe it is not the business of outsiders to know or talk about such things. Nonetheless, I draw on decades' worth of readily available, published ethnographic accounts to help the reader understand why these sales were considered to be such travesties. I do this knowing that surely there are inaccuracies in the accounts published by anthropologists in the nineteenth and twentieth centuries and that some readers would prefer that I not cite this literature. In my opinion, it is only by seeking to understand—no matter how imperfectly—the complexity, solemnity, and beauty of the religion of others that we can come to an empathetic regard for the positions they hold that may be at odds with Western legal and scholarly standards of openness. I add to these outsiders' accounts the words of Pueblo scholars and religious specialists.

Just as Roman Catholic belief revolves around the sacred transubstantiation of bread and wine into the living body of Christ, so too, in Zuni thought, materials of the natural world can be transformed into a living sacred being through a series of ritual steps and prayers. Shaping, feeding, and painting a Zuni mask transforms it into a person. As one step in this transformation, the head priest mixes various seeds and ceremonially feeds the mask, saying, "Now I have given you life. . . . I have made you into a person." Painting the mask is another such step.[14] For this reason, the ways that scholars customarily speak about ceremonial performances in which people don masks are inaccurate, for the words we use, "they impersonate the gods," sound like the description of an actor taking on a role. Notably, in the Zuni language it is said that when a man dons a mask that has been made in the proper ceremonial way, he is allowing the god to become a living person, or to take on a form that human beings, with our limited capacities, can apprehend.[15]

Native scholars have written about such events, too. The distinguished Tewa anthropologist Alfonso Ortiz (Ohkay Owingeh, 1939–1998), analyzing Pueblo ritual drama, memorably wrote that "kachinas remind men that if they but join their hearts periodically in these rites of mass supplication to the ancestral deities, life will continue as before in abundance and harmony."[16] Hopi linguist Emory Sekaquaptewa (Hotevilla, 1928–2007) wrote that in ceremonial performance a man who dons the katsina mask "loses his identity and actually becomes what he is representing."[17] In a document prepared for the Smithsonian in 1978, near the start of their fourteen-year process of negotiation toward the repatriation of sacred materials (discussed below), Zuni religious leaders wrote that the creative process involved in the making of *kokko* and other sacred items "bestows a spiritual life on formerly inanimate materials of which the religious objects are made."[18]

The dramatic Hopi mask featured on the cover of the auction catalogue that achieved such a high price at the April 2013 Paris auction represents Tü'mash, or Angwusnasomtaqa. Crow Mother, as this spirit being is called in English, appears in February at Powamu, a complex ceremony in which children are initiated and the promise of the new growing season is revealed. Hopi scholar and carver Alph Secakuku says that "she displays an aggressive temperament and is furiously active, ensuring that she receives attention in order to deliver to the initiates her message of the importance and significance of the katsina culture."[19] She is also the mother of the "whipper" katsinam (plural of *katsina*), those who enforce proper protocol and maintain order with their yucca whips. Some might say that Crow Mother will exact her own punishment on those who defame her visage or involve her in an economic transaction far from Hopitutskwa.[20]

PRIOR EPISODES OF REPLICATION, MISREPRESENTATION, SALE, AND FORGERY

The reproduction of Zuni objects by and for outsiders has a long and troubled history. Frank Hamilton Cushing (1857–1900), who went to Zuni in 1879 as part of a Smithsonian expedition to collect objects and information for the recently founded Bureau of American Ethnology, stayed for four years after the rest of the expedition went home. As is well known, he lived as a Zuni, was initiated into the Society of Bow Priests, and sought to understand objects in all of their material complexity by making them himself. This was considered acceptable at a time when most ethnographic museums had replicas of objects. John Wesley Powell, the first director of the bureau, described Cushing's process as "a new method of research by experimental reproduction," remarking (one hopes, somewhat archly) that "there was nothing that a Zuñi could make [that] he could not reproduce with greater skill."[21] Among the things that Cushing made were ceremonial objects, such as Ahayu:da (War God effigies).[22]

Matilda Coxe Stevenson (1849–1915), who, with her husband, was part of that 1879 expedition as well, spent six months at Zuni collecting objects and information, though, as the quotation at the beginning of this chapter indicates, she was not then able to buy masks for the Smithsonian. Indeed, about that expedition she wrote that even the "carrying away on paper" of such sacred items was met with extreme disapproval: "While the priests and other high officials favored photographing the ceremonials—in fact, seemed eager to serve the expedition in every way—the populace were so opposed to having their masks and rituals 'carried away on paper,' that it was deemed prudent to make but few ceremonial pictures with the camera, and the altars and masks were sketched in color by the writer without the knowledge of the people."[23]

It was only in the 1890s, "after her long acquaintance with the priests and their attachment to her," she claims, that the purchase of masks was possible. Yet this assertion may be somewhat disingenuous, for what she did was commission replicas (of rawhide rather than the ritually correct deer hide), and she had to provide the priests who made the replicas "a house about 50 miles away from Zuni, where the priests could feel entirely safe from intrusion."[24]

On museum collecting trips from 1902 to 1907, the curator Stewart Culin (1858–1929) sought to follow in the footsteps of Cushing, who was his hero. Zuni people sold him many things, though in Culin's reports to the Brooklyn Museum, he readily admitted that when he sought to buy masks and other sacred objects, "A cryer was sent around, who called out to the people and cautioned them against selling me any masks, and I was told that the sale of masks was punished by death."[25] Yet, as the art historian Diana Fane has documented, Culin deliberately circumvented this strict and sacred prohibition by buying several dozen masks and other objects for the museum from the missionary and trader Andrew Vanderwagen, who managed a brisk trade in the manufacture and sale of sacred materials.[26] Culin described Vanderwagen as having hired Zuni men to secretly make masks, *tihu* (katsina dolls), and other sacred items in his basement, echoing Stevenson's practice of removing the actions from the community, where it would be a grievous breach of protocol.[27] The anthropologist Ruth Bunzel, who worked at Zuni in the 1920s, affirmed the strength of these prohibitions:

> Revelation of the secrets of the katcina cult to the uninitiated is a crime against the gods and is punishable by death by decapitation. Punishment is meted out by masked impersonators of the gods, appointed by the heads of the katcina society. No such executions have taken place within the memory of living men, but they figure prominently in folklore, and the authority and readiness of the priests to so act is never questioned in Zuñi. Flogging by masked impersonators has recently been substituted for execution. During

> one of the writer's visits [i.e., her own visits] katcinas were summoned to administer punishment to a youth found guilty of selling a mask. The accused escaped so the katsinas whipped all men in the kiva for purification.[28]

While replicas may be made for sale by Native artisans, either surreptitiously or for public consumption, far more common is the making of replicas by outsiders—even those who have never visited the community of the objects' origin. For nearly a century, La Junta, Colorado, a town of about seven thousand people 175 miles southeast of Denver, has drawn an outsize share of attention because of its so-called Koshare Boy Scouts (or, more formally, Explorer Post 2230 of the Boy Scouts of America). As mentioned in chapter 2, this group is nationally known for its museum and its teenage boys who have performed Native dances to great public acclaim—and sometimes contention—since the 1930s. In 1953, it came to the attention of Zuni tribal leaders that this Explorer post had added to its repertoire a new public enactment: the famous early winter Shalako "dance" of Zuni.

Shalako is actually a cycle of performances taking place after the harvest and before the winter solstice. While it features many masked beings, the most memorable are the six ten-foot-tall beaked Shalako themselves. The performance takes place outside as well as within certain homes that have been prepared with great care to receive them. Outsiders have traditionally been welcomed at Shalako, for their witnessing of these events is thought to bring additional blessings (though in recent decades it has usually been closed to outsiders who do not have a personal invitation). As the anthropologist Barbara Tedlock has observed, "At this special time, if everyone remains serene, kind, and cheerful, then the host family, village, nation, and even the entire world can know the end of anger and the beginning of profound peace."[29]

In 1958, Val Gendron, who wrote for popular, Western, and youth audiences, published a youth novel titled *Behind the Zuni Masks* that addressed the values and culture of the Koshare Boy Scouts as well as their very public run-in with Zuni tribal leaders in 1953. This run-in was significant, for Zuni leaders promised they would close the pueblo's dances permanently to outsiders if it was not resolved to their satisfaction.[30] In the novel, the leader is called Buck Burshears, the actual nickname of the real leader, James Burshears. The Scouts, in contrast, are composite characters with fictional names.[31] One, a young boy named Charlie from Gendron's own home region of Cape Cod, Massachusetts, arrives in La Junta and is invited by Burshears to study Native customs in order to prepare for possible election into this troop, which requires craft skills, good grades, knowledge of Native lore, and dance skills. In what becomes a significant development for the troop, Burshears lends him the *Forty-Seventh Annual Report of the Bureau of American Ethnology*, a weighty tome containing Bunzel's publications on the Zuni.[32] In studying it, Charlie is fascinated both by the Koyemshi (the Zuni version of the clown-like Hopi Koshares for which the troop is named) and by the tall Shalako figures and their attendants. Charlie eventually persuades the troop to make Shalako costumes and to "put on what seemed to him the greatest of all Indian dances."[33]

In the novel, the seemingly prescient scoutmaster reminds Charlie that this dance is still ongoing among the Zuni and is sacred. Charlie replies, "But we wouldn't be making a mock of it. We would be helping to promote understanding between the two races. The Zunis are wonderful people and they are different from us. Isn't understanding between peoples one of the things the Koshares are supposed to be doing?" He even memorizes Zuni prayers to be recited as the Council of the Gods enters the performance arena.[34]

In the novel (as in real life), the new Boy Scout performance was a success, with audiences responding

> with rapt attention and respect that Charlie had not dared anticipate. The stately and beautiful Shalako created an impression of dignity and benevolence; the audiences were impressed with the gentleness and goodness of the great ten-foot images. They laughed at the antics of the Koyemshi, gasped at the sight of Sayatasha with his long turquoise horn; and the little fire god, Shulaawitsi, with his painted body of many spots always stole the show; and the Salimobiya with their feathered ruffs and cruel yucca whips made little shivers run down their backs, but the total effect of the dance was to create a feeling of wonder and reverence. They looked at a part of Indian culture for the most part unknown to them.[35]

In real life, as well as in the novel, pictures of this dramatic new performance were carried in many newspapers. The publicity reached Zuni, and Zuni leaders registered a formal protest with the Indian commissioner in Gallup. Burshears invited representatives from Zuni at his expense to witness the performance in December 1953 and to discuss the issue. In the novel, the representatives are not named, but Jack Kelly's book *Koshare* names Leo Quetawke as head councilman in charge of law and order and Oscar Sheka as keeper of the sacred masks.[36] Gendron invents far more protracted dialogue, but *Time* magazine quotes one of the Zuni leaders as saying, "This is too real, too true. What you do is not imitation. These are living gods, and we must take the Shalakos and the Mudheads to the home of the Masked Gods where they belong."[37] In the novel, Charlie understands that "good will isn't enough": "Maybe in addition to good will you need knowledge and understanding. I had some knowledge of the Zunis, I'd read all the books available, but I just lacked understanding. I never thought they'd object."[38] In real life, Burshears and a delegation of boys did return the sacred regalia to Zuni in late December 1953, receiving a formal letter of thanks from Zuni governor Conrad Lesarlley.[39]

It is it noteworthy not only that in 1953 the Zuni sought to confiscate regalia made by outsiders in imitation of their own Shalako but also that this was deemed newsworthy by both *Time* and the *New York Times*. This was an era when stories featuring Native agency and taking Native religious claims seriously were rare.[40] Kelly, a popular author, characterized this episode as "one of Scouting's finest hours"; yet Explorer Post 2230 continues to be in the news for its appropriation of Native performance.[41] Its relinquishing of Shalako regalia in 1953 was an exception to its wholesale appropriation of Native dances that has been ongoing for nearly a century.

As Gwyneira Isaac has so lucidly delineated, an essential flaw in trying to make distinctions between the "authentic," the "replica," and the "fake" at Zuni is that these terms have no meaning in Zuni epistemology. A fundamental schism divides post-Enlightenment European worldviews and those of many indigenous peoples across the world concerning notions of originality and replication, and the Zuni are no exception.

At the National Museum of Natural History of the Smithsonian Institution, the Zuni *kokko* acquired by Stevenson were on display for much of the twentieth century. In 1970, five of them were in a glass case with items of clothing, as an example of the "colorful rites" of the Zuni, according to the wall text.[42] That year, Robert Lewis, governor of Zuni, came to Washington on behalf of Zuni religious leaders and asked the museum's anthropologists to take the masks off display and return them to their rightful owners. After months of memos, meetings, disagreements, and deliberations, the masks were taken off display, but the Smithsonian declined to return the masks; some of the scientists involved felt strongly that because some were "replicas" commissioned by Stevenson, they neither were "real" nor belonged to Zuni. The Zuni politely disagreed, citing the successful conclusion to the Shalako Boy Scout incident some seventeen years earlier.[43] A decade later, as part of their campaign seeking the return of all Ahayu:da from museums, Governor Lewis sent a report to the Smithsonian titled "Request for the Return of Zuni Sacred Material and Recommendations for the Care and Curation of Objects of Zuni Religious Significance in the Collection of the Smithsonian." In the report, all material held at the Smithsonian was divided into five classes. Items in classes 1 and 2 included collectively held items such as Ahayu:da and other sacred objects. Class 3 consisted of masks, with the request that a delegation of religious specialists be allowed to come to the museum to dismantle the masks, with the component parts remaining at the Smithsonian.[44] Classes 4 and 5 were items that could remain on display, including dance kilts, rattles, and pottery. As of this writing, the masks have been neither dismantled nor returned. A coauthor of the report, Edmund Ladd (a Zuni as well as an anthropologist), in a separate statement, noted that objects made specifically for museum exhibits are considered by Zuni people to be sensitive materials and that even cardboard mask replicas made as a Works Progress Administration project at the Museum of New Mexico in the 1930s were returned to Zuni for proper disposal.[45]

Consultation with Zuni representatives in preparation for *Objects of Myth and Memory*, the 1991 exhibit at the Brooklyn Museum of the works that Culin acquired, resulted in the repatriation of Ahayu:da to Zuni. No Zuni masks were on display in that exhibit, nor do they appear as objects in the catalogue. During subsequent visits to the Brooklyn Museum in 1996 and 1997, the Pueblo of Zuni Cultural Advisory Team identified all Zuni masks in the collection as sacred and restricted. Since that visit, the Brooklyn Museum has complied with their request to keep all masks off view and restrict access to them. As of this writing, the Zuni have not asked for their repatriation.[46]

Museum exchanges were common in the twentieth century, and in 1948 the Denver Art Museum acquired two Zuni *kokko* in trade from the Brooklyn Museum. These were, of course, ones that Culin had acquired (a Koyemshi, no. 1948.235, and a Salimobiya, no. 1948.236). The Zuni ritual experts who examined these masks in Denver in 1996 and 1997 determined that the Koyemshi *kokko* appeared to have been used, for it had staining and dirt on both the exterior and the interior. The other appeared to be a replica that Culin had perhaps acquired from Vanderwagen; it was both incomplete and pristine, and certain aspects of its construction were incorrect.[47] Of the latter, the repatriation claim that the Zuni issued to the Denver Art Museum stated: "The Zuni Tribe has an interest in asserting control over religious items, and hereby requests that DAM deaccession this mask and offer it as a gift to the Zuni tribe. The Zuni tribe regards NAGPRA [the Native American Graves Protection and Repatriation Act], and possibly other laws, as having potential applicability to replicas, but needs to develop appropriate research and analysis on this point."[48]

In pointing out the inconsistency of these actions concerning Zuni masks held in museums, I am not criticizing Zuni actions. Differing directives emanating from a changing roster of busy Zuni leaders over several decades should not be surprising. As the authors William Merrill, Edmund Ladd, and T. J. Ferguson point out in their detailed discussion of the protracted process of returning Ahayu:da from the Smithsonian, religious and civil leaders step down, and others take their places, just as in government and religious organizations in the dominant culture.[49] Priorities and viewpoints change.

HOPI AND ZUNI IN THE AMERICAN CULTURAL IMAGINARY

The concept of a social or cultural imaginary has had a complicated genealogy across several disciplines since the mid-twentieth century, but suffice it to say that the cultural imaginary consists of the implicit (and usually unexamined) understandings of the world held by a particular group. Notably, such understandings can remain remarkably stable over long periods of time.[50] People participate in many overlapping social imaginaries, some related to gender, religion, nationality, or ethnicity. These allow us to occupy a specific place in society and bolster that place with images and stories that express our sense of the world. Dakota historian Philip J. Deloria has remarked that "we construct identity by finding ourselves in relation to an array of people and objects who are not ourselves," going on to examine the way that, for far too many Americans, finding themselves in relation to others has involved impersonating them.[51] For many Americans, as discussed throughout this book, selective notions about Native Americans have underpinned much of what is transmitted through popular culture: Indians look a certain way (typically in nineteenth-century Plains warrior garb); Indians partake of the past rather than of modernity; Indians are more spiritual and ecological than others and are worth emulating.

Though Zuni, Hopi, and other Pueblo peoples do not occupy the central place in the American imaginary that Plains nations have since the late nineteenth century, they do maintain a certain undeniable hold.[52] Hopi and Zuni ceremonial practices, in particular, were not only central to American anthropological literature in the late nineteenth and early twentieth centuries but were also widely reported in the press. From reports about the Snake Dance in *Harper's Weekly* in 1889 and 1896 to former president Theodore Roosevelt's travel piece on his own experience of the Snake Dance at Walpi in 1913, the American public came to have these images lodged firmly in their imagination.[53] In *Imagining Indians in the Southwest*, the cultural critic Leah Dilworth has persuasively demonstrated that the cultural primitivism focused on this region between the 1880s and the 1920s set the pattern for the way that people continue to mythologize Pueblo Indians.[54]

Of course, this was not just an American phenomenon. In the spring of 1896, the young German art historian Aby Warburg (1866–1929) traveled to Pueblo communities, ostensibly to deepen his understanding of the mystical and "primitive" strands of ancient Mediterranean art by visiting what he saw as the last vestige of a parallel way of thinking. He witnessed a Hemis katsina dance at the Hopi village of Oraibi (facilitated by Mennonite missionary H. R. Voth), took pictures and notes for slide lectures he gave in Germany the following year, and, most shockingly for us today, posed with a Hemis katsina mask atop his head, like a hat.[55] The British writer D. H. Lawrence (1885–1930) spent nearly two years in Taos, New Mexico, between 1922 and 1925 and saw and wrote about the Snake Dance and other ceremonies for the modernist literary magazine the *Dial* and other publications.[56]

All of this firmly lodged Pueblo peoples and their arts in the modern Euro-American imaginary and led to white men, from teenage Boy Scouts to adult men, appropriating Pueblo dress and dance and making Zuni masks. American artist John Sloan's famous etching *The Indian Detour* (1927), depicting tourists and their buses overrunning a Pueblo dance, portrays the hectic flavor of the times (figure C.1). And in the second decade of the twenty-first century, wealthy white buyers continued to seek a primal authenticity, paying tens of thousands of euros to buy Hopi and Zuni "masks" in Paris, carting them away in paper bags, like so much merchandise.

On Doppelgängers, Echoes, and Encores

Doppelgänger is a loan word from German—literally "double-goer"—a phrase for an inexplicable twin, a ghostly shadow of oneself.[57] Popular culture today is full of an interest in doppelgängers, who are often portrayed as evil spirits intent on preying on their human counterparts. Does that which is "not Native

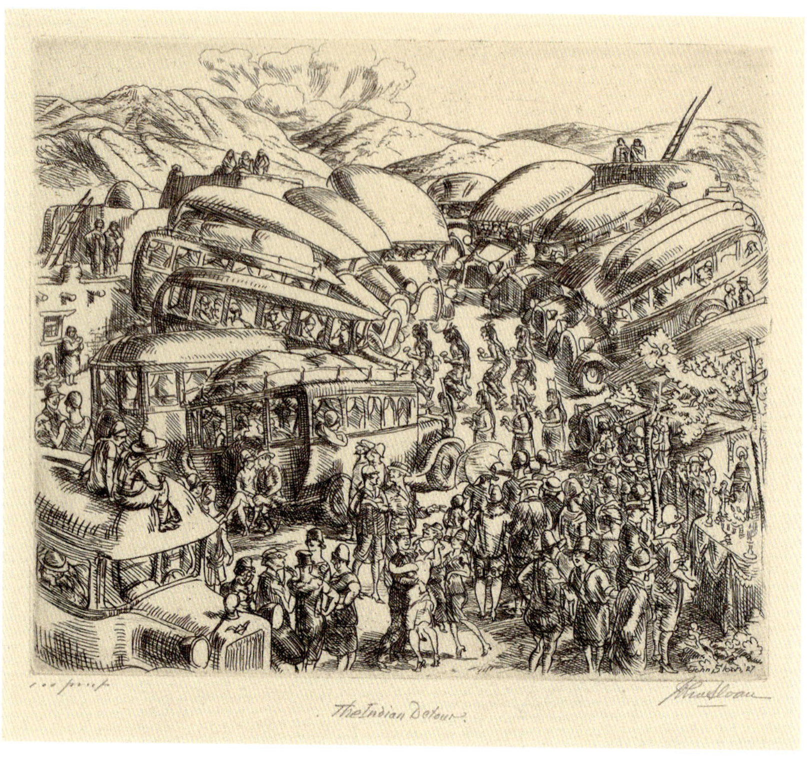

FIG. C.1 John Sloan, *The Indian Detour*, 1927. Etching. Yale University Art Gallery, no. 1969.109.2.

American art," as chronicled in this book, prey on its Native counterparts? Many people would say yes. Today, by means of the internet and face-recognition software, people arrange to meet their real-life doppelgängers and post pictures of them side by side for all to see.[58] In so doing, some of the spookiness of the encounter seems to be dissipated. Perhaps this book is a scholarly version of that—bringing the doppelgängers of Native art history into the light and examining them. Are they as malevolent as some believe?

I would like to offer a seemingly unlikely metaphor for the effect that the flood of fakes, replicas, forgeries, copies, pastiches, and surrogates has on the world of real Native art. The 2021 film *The Loneliest Whale: The Search for 52* makes the point that whale songs travel tens of thousands of miles. But the noise from shipping lanes (the dominant source of anthropogenic, or human-made, noise in the sea), which has increased dramatically since 1950, threatens to drown out their communication. It also interferes with their health in significant ways.[59] In a loosely analogous way, I suggest that the din of all that is *not* Native art threatens to drown out—or at least significantly interfere with—the eloquent communications sent out by real Native American art, both historical and contemporary. Moreover, it is not insignificant that the flood of works made by outsiders affects both the economic and emotional health of Native artists. Too much "noise" interference and the real Native artists cannot communicate with each other, and with their intended audiences, as effectively.

Dilworth points out that for white America, "the Indian, supposedly a model for authenticity, was conceived of as an oppositional other to the self, and so, paradoxically, authentic states of being were apparently only accessible through acting, impersonation, and/or acquisition." In this way, Native history is elided, "and Indians emerge as free-floating signifiers available for all kinds of signification."[60] She was speaking specifically of Pueblo Indians, though as other chapters here, and many books in the bibliography, point out, this was true to an equal or even greater extent for other parts of Native North America.

If, as I have suggested here, some of the masks sold at Paris auctions in the past decade are counterfeit, this certainly does give rise to a sense of unease, as these have been repatriated. In comparing Haida artist Don Yeomans's mask and its Indonesian doppelgänger (see figure 1.11), the malevolence of the marketplace is made apparent. As some of the examples in this book show, many artists have taken pleasure and pride in what I call the "echoes and encores" that their work embodies, including Paul and Laurel Thornburg and their "authentic" Mimbres replicas (see figure 4.12) and Cathy A. Smith and her Plains Shirtwearers (see figure 3.8). But surely such echoes and encores are even more meaningful when artists are deliberately updating works of their *own* cultural heritage and bringing them into the modern era. Many Northwest Coast artists have taken up the challenge of re-creating and reinterpreting the work of their ancestors with far more credibility than Lelooska, for example (see figure 1.14). Years ago, the anthropologists Margaret Blackman and Edwin Hall chronicled the many contemporary Northwest Coast artists of the 1970s and 1980s who were replicating and reimagining the work of their nineteenth-century forebears, pointing out how crucial the visual images in exhibition catalogues were in this regard.[61] The important exhibition *Chiefly Feasts: The Enduring Kwakiutl Potlatch* at the American Museum of Natural History in 1992, one of the first to include substantive Native consultation and collaboration, provided an occasion for the artist Calvin Hunt (Kwakwa̱ka̱'wakw, b. 1956), who is now a chief at Fort Rupert, to replicate a nineteenth-century Nulami'sta dance apparatus that he had never before seen. Notably, Hunt is the great-grandson of George Hunt, the local Native man who collected the original for the museum in 1904.[62] The original work, a theatrical prop with working movable parts made of painted wood and a collapsible painted cloth screen, was too fragile to be exhibited in a traveling show, so the curator Aldona Jonaitis commissioned Hunt to make a new version. As the art historian Judith Ostrowitz has written,

> The nineteenth-century version may itself be modeled on earlier works, and each one of them would, in all probability, have been made a little differently than the one before it. None of them would be considered less useful in ceremony because they derived from an earlier model. Similarly, we have no reason to believe that the AMNH set of screens represents a fixed form to be copied or followed slavishly for all time. Neither should Calvin Hunt's rendition of the screens be conceived as the last of its line, nor should its form be thought to dictate the correct appearance of all versions to follow.[63]

While Hunt altered a few of the details, he took careful measurements and tracings of the piece when he was at the American Museum of Natural History as part of a consulting team for the exhibit in 1990.

That same year, Hunt's nephew, Tom Hunt (Kwakwa̱ka̱'wakw, b. 1964), who worked in his uncle's studio, made yet another version, now owned by the Microsoft Corporation.[64] As Ostrowitz eloquently demonstrates in *Privileging the Past*, one of the first books to take up the issue of replication within Native art itself, such objects can move seamlessly between ceremonial use in Indigenous communities and "use" by art collectors. In the historical era, much Native regalia was confiscated (though the American Museum of Natural History, through George Hunt and the anthropologist Franz Boas, did pay for the works they collected). In contrast, today artists can command top dollar for work that both references the past and participates in a modern world of connoisseurs and collectors. Whatever their destination, such works are acts of recuperative grace and should not be seen as "merely" replicas.

In recent years, a new generation of Native museum curators and cultural critics have been grappling with the doppelgängers of Native art history as they reinvent museum practices and modes of display. Artists, too, have been confronting doppelgängers, and none more directly than Nicholas Galanin.

Coda: "The Destruction of Mimicry"—
Nicholas Galanin's Iconoclasm as Cultural Critique

In colloquial usage, the term *iconoclast* can refer to a skeptic, or someone who does not follow the rules, but art historians know that the etymology of the term *iconoclasm*—literally "image-breaking"—goes back to ancient Greek. Iconoclastic movements have occurred in many societies for a variety of reasons. Maya royal portrait sculptures of ancestral rulers were defaced by those who ruled after them in the eighth century CE; painted images of the saints were banned and destroyed in Byzantium in the same era. In the *Beeldenstorm* (image storm) of 1566, Calvinists destroyed Catholic religious images in the Netherlands. The Taliban dynamited the monumental Bamiyan Buddhas of Afganistan in 2002, and anti-racists toppled Confederate monuments in North Carolina in the summer of 2017 and elsewhere in the summer of 2020.[65]

As these examples indicate, iconoclasm is generally a collective act of destruction, sometimes for zealously political or religious reasons, other times to redress decades or centuries of racism. In the hands of the extraordinarily talented Alaskan artist Nicholas Galanin (Yéil Ya-Tseen) (Tlingit/Unangax, b. 1979), the destruction and reconstitution of fake Northwest Coast–style carvings made in Indonesia is a singular act of cultural commentary and artistic sovereignty. In chapter 1 (see figure 1.11), I discussed the faking of Northwest Coast masks and small totem poles as a cottage industry in the craft-oriented towns of Bali. Such commodities then circulate to the tourist towns of Alaska, especially those where cruise ships dock, and are sold as inexpensive alternatives to authentic Native Northwest Coast art. Galanin has purchased a number of these "curios" and out of their destruction makes new works of art. In the sculptural installation *I Think It Goes like This?* (figure C.2), the artist painted several Indonesian totem poles black and split them, as if they were destined to be firewood in a blaze that would consume their illegitimacy.[66] It is an elegant yet disturbing work, reminiscent of Louise Nevelson's mid-twentieth-century black-painted wood constructions, if they were to be chopped into pieces.[67] As the art historian Christopher Green mordantly notes, in these works that use fake Indonesian masks as the medium, Galanin "offers kitsch a path to salvation through the blade of his adze."[68]

In *Unceremonial Dance Mask, 21st Century* (2017), a performance captured in a short YouTube video, Galanin takes a Tlingit-made hand adze to a fake mask, reducing it to shavings and flinders. The resulting pile of detritus is

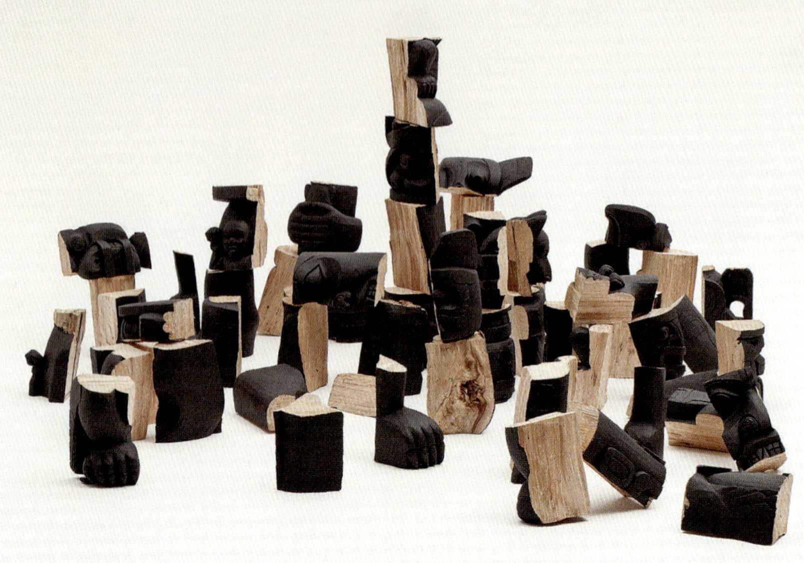

FIG. C.2 Nicholas Galanin, *I think it goes like this?*, 2012. Indonesian-carved curio totem, wood and paint, dimensions variable. Photo courtesy of the artist.

carefully shaped into the approximate form of a mask and cemented together, with long black braids attached to each side. The noise the adze makes during this act of destruction is the only soundtrack. At the end, the artist holds the fragmented and reconstituted mask—a pile of chips with no facial features—up to his face and dances in front of a fire while the echoing sound of the adze, now electronically manipulated, forms the musical accompaniment.[69] In the statement accompanying this video, the artist has written, "The action is a reclamation of cultural form through destruction and dissolution of a hollow impersonation. The mask fragments are gathered and re-formed into a mask by Tlingit hands." While the romantic collector of Indigenous art avidly seeks the ceremonial, this mask is decidedly unceremonial, as its title indicates. The artist's statement characterizes the actions that the performance and video document as the "destruction of mimicry." The artist, as he dances with the destructed/deconstructed mask, also performs a reversal of mimicry: the Native artist mimes non-Native impersonations of Native ceremony, presenting them in all their clumsy imperfection.[70]

Chapter 5 considered occasions in which Navajo sandpainters performed simulacra of their ritual work at world's fairs, art museums, and other public spaces. Native practitioners performing their artistry for others has long been a familiar trope across the continent—from Pueblo and Navajo jewelers to Navajo weavers, Haudenosaunee bead workers, and Haida totem pole carvers, among others.[71] Galanin has turned this trope on its head in the performance work *White Carver*, which he has staged multiple times in museums and galleries since 2012, sometimes behind glass, sometimes simply cordoned off in a corner of the gallery (figure C.3). The substitution of a white artist within the familiar scenario renders absurd the time-honored act of Native art-making that is so beloved by museums. Just like his Native counterparts in such circumstances, the White Carver is inexplicably dressed in what is not typically an artist's working attire: a crisp white shirt and a dark tie under his apron. The earnest performer is hard at work carving a sex toy, according to drawings presumably provided by Galanin himself.[72] He sits on a stool, or in an armchair, with a flat-top section of tree trunk as his work surface, adzes, mallets, awls, and gimlets at his feet.

In some cases, non-Native people who make Native-style art are proud to demonstrate their skills (as seen, for example, in chapter 3). But Native-style art that veers toward the fake, the ersatz, or the forgery is more typically made in anonymity behind the scenes. Here, Galanin seeks to provoke an uneasiness in his viewers as they not only watch the white man carve a wooden replica of a sex toy but also imagine something that should be soft and comfortable on the skin being made of cedar wood. The work is provocative in its suggestive association between the white fetishization of all things Native and the carving of a sexual fetish object.

In chapter 2, I cited the performance artist Guillermo Gómez-Peña's observations on what he termed in 1996 the "benign colonialism" inherent in the work of "ventriloquists, impresarios, *flaneurs*, messiahs, or cultural transvestites." He said that examining these is a necessary part of healing colonial and postcolonial wounds.[73] As is evident from government betrayals and subsequent social unrest in the United States after the federal election of 2016, and in Canada since the uncovering of hundreds of unmarked graves of Native schoolchildren in 2020, the healing of colonial and postcolonial wounds is a far larger and more complex process than some of us could ever have imagined. For those who do it, cultural cross-dressing, and the making of historical objects from a tradition not their own, can feel liberatory. For

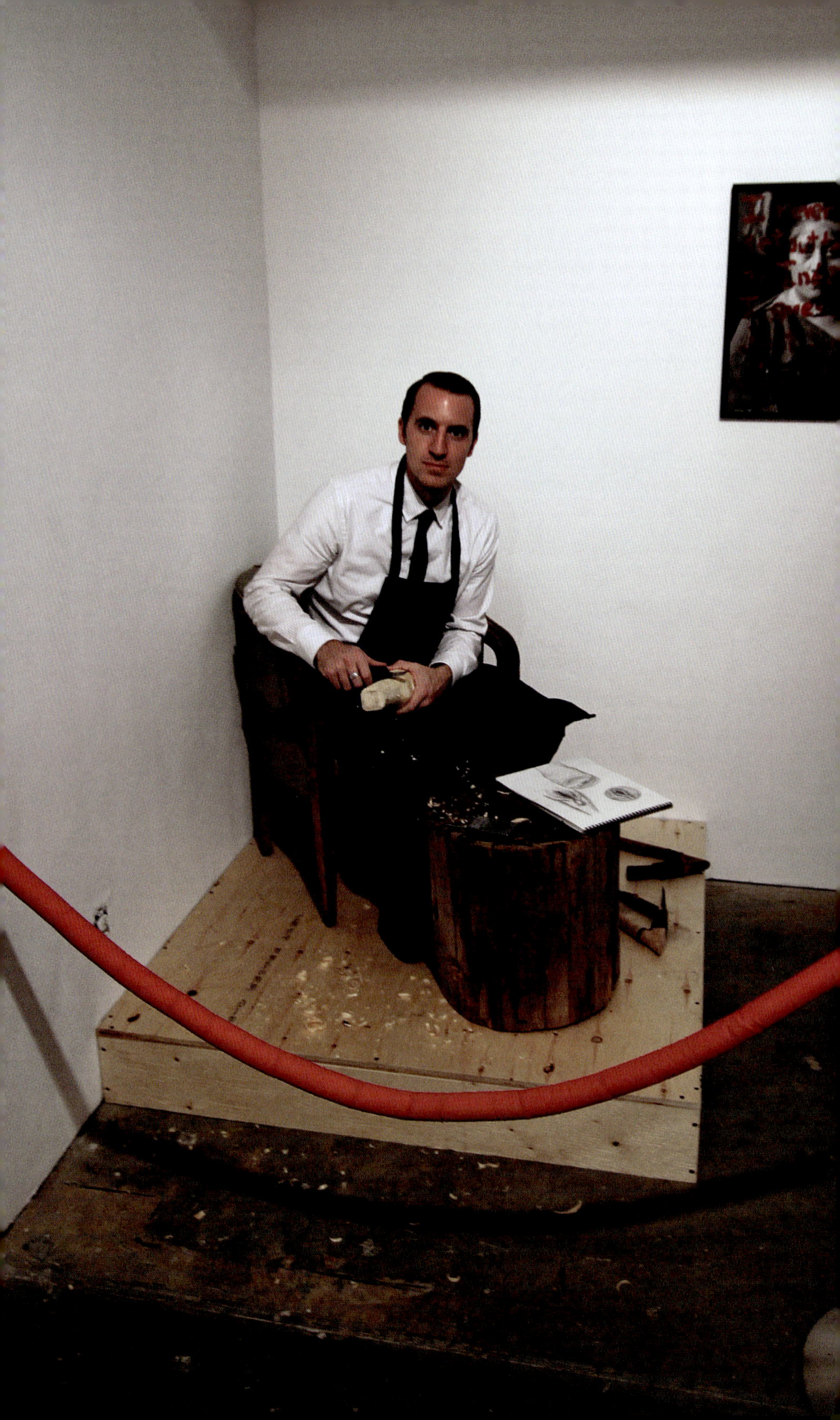

FIG. C.3 Nicholas Galanin, *White Carver*, photo of performance, 2012–present. Photo courtesy of the artist.

those who are being mimicked, mocked, appropriated, or "being paid tribute to," it is never liberatory. It lacerates. It repeatedly reopens old wounds.

As a historian, I believe that before such healing can truly take place, a deeper and fuller understanding of the past is necessary. I have offered a partial look at the making of "Native American" objects that were not Native American. Much more such analysis is needed. In a world where the making, using, and circulating of Native North American imagery by non-Natives is ubiquitous, this book sheds light on some of the countless ways that such actions can constitute real harm to Native people. Such objects and actions offer misunderstanding and misrepresentation more often than homage. Nonetheless, it is important to understand the many nuances and particular historical moments that gave rise to such practices.

Notes

Introduction

1. See C. Wilson, *The Myth of Santa Fe.*
2. US Department of Justice, US Attorney's Office, District of New Mexico, "Federal Grand Jury Indicts Five in Connection with International Scheme to Fraudulently Import and Sell Filipino-Made Jewelry as Native American-Made," press release, February 9, 2017, www.justice.gov/usao-nm/pr/federal-grand-jury-indicts-five-connection-international-scheme-fraudulently-import-and.
3. See Sheffield, *The Arbitrary Indian.*
4. United States v. Aysheh, No. 1:17-cr-00370-JCH (D.N.M. Apr. 26, 2019).
5. Steiner, *African Art in Transit.*
6. Appadurai, *The Social Life of Things.*
7. Berlo, *Teotihuacan Art Abroad*; *Plains Indian Drawings*; *Arthur Amiotte: Collages.*
8. See, for example, Appiah, *Cosmopolitanism* and *The Lies That Bind.* See also Enwezor et al., *Creolité and Creolization*; and Mercer, *Cosmopolitan Modernisms.*
9. Berlo, "Anthropologies and Histories of Art."
10. See, for example, Begay, "Crossroads and Navajo Weaving"; and Baillargeon, *North American Aboriginal Hide Tanning.*
11. Kelker and Bruhns, *Faking Ancient Mesoamerica*; Bruhns and Kelker, *Faking the Ancient Andes.*
12. Berlo and Senuk, "Caveat Emptor."
13. In 1984, the annual Plains Indian Seminar at the Buffalo Bill Historical Center (now called the Buffalo Bill Center of the West) considered the topic of "artifacts/artifakes"; the resulting publication, Horse Capture and Tyler, *Artifacts/Artifakes*, from 1992, was a much-needed first look at an important issue,

but it was limited solely to Plains material. A companion publication, written in 1993 by a lawyer, discussed the legal ramifications of "artifaking." See Edwards, *Artifacts/Artifakes*.

1 *Authenticity and Its Discontents*

1. Painter, *American Indian Artifacts*, 10.
2. Kalshoven, "Things in the Making" and *Crafting "the Indian."*
3. Kalshoven, "Things in the Making," 61.
4. Ruth B. Phillips, personal communication, September 2019.
5. Ellis, "'More Real than the Indians Themselves'"; P. Deloria, *Playing Indian*.
6. See Penney, *Art of the American Indian Frontier*, especially 299–322.
7. Catlinite, named for the artist George Catlin, who was the first to publish an account of it, is a claylike substance hardened under geological pressure. It is easily carved. The red color results from the presence of hematite in the deposit; black pipestone differs slightly in its mineralogical composition.
8. George Catlin, *Pipestone Quarry on the Coteau des Prairies*, 1836–37, Smithsonian American Art Museum, no. 1985.66.337, http://americanart.si.edu/collections/search/artwork/?id=4319, accessed July 1, 2021.
9. Catlin, *Letters and Notes*, 2:172.
10. Nydahl, "The Pipestone Quarry and the Indians."
11. Murray, *Pipestone National Monument*.
12. Holmes, "Catlinite," 219.
13. Wied-Neuwied, *Reise in das innere Nord-America*; Wied-Neuwied, *Travels in the Interior of North America*; Gallagher and Hunt, *Karl Bodmer's America*; Wied-Neuwied, *The North American Journals*.
14. Ewers, "George Catlin," 493.
15. Dippie, "Green Fields and Red Men," 32.
16. Catlin, *Letters and Notes*; Eisler, *The Red Man's Bones*, 124.
17. Catlin, *Notes of Eight Years' Travels*, 1:2. The Egyptian Hall, built in 1812 and demolished in 1905, was a large space for natural history and art exhibits.
18. Catlin, *Notes of Eight Years' Travels*, 1:90–91.
19. Catlin, *Notes of Eight Years' Travels*, 1:91–94.
20. Ronan, "Buffalo Dancer," 127.
21. Ronan, "Buffalo Dancer," 127–28.
22. Catlin, *Letters and Notes*, 1:11–12.
23. Schoolcraft, *Historical and Statistical Information*.
24. Catlin, *Letters and Notes*, 1:11–12.
25. Catlin, *Notes of Eight Years' Travels*, 1:52–59.
26. Catlin, *Letters and Notes*, 1:92, 114–17 and plate 62.

27. Catlin, *Letters and Notes*, 1:145–54 and plates 64 and 65a, b, and c.
28. Catlin, *Letters and Notes*, vol. 1, plate 64.
29. Holm, "Four Bears' Shirt," 50.
30. Holm, "Four Bears' Shirt," 47.
31. Holm, "Four Bears' Shirt," 47.
32. Eisler, *The Red Man's Bones*, 202.
33. See, for example, Warnock and Warnock, *Splendid Heritage*; Horse Capture and Horse Capture, *Beauty, Honor, and Tradition*; and Torrence, *The Plains Indians*.
34. Ewers, "George Catlin," 493.
35. Catlin, *Notes of Eight Years' Travel*, 1:96. A *tableau vivant*, or "living picture," in which people posed in costume re-creating famous paintings or historical events, was an amusement that took hold in Europe in the late eighteenth century, came to the United States in the early nineteenth century, and went out of fashion with the development of silent films. See Chapman, "'Living Pictures'"; and Holmström, *Monodrama, Attitudes, Tableaux Vivants*. On Catlin's *tableaux vivants*, see Horton, "Ojibwa *Tableaux Vivants*."
36. Halpin, introduction to Catlin, *Letters and Notes* (1973 ed.), 1:xii–xiii.
37. See Catlin, *Souvenir of the North American Indians*. The original, a suite of fifty watercolors, was made in 1849 (Gilcrease Museum, Tulsa, OK, no. 4776.5).
38. See George Catlin, *Souvenir of the N. American Indians: As They Were in the Nineteenth Century*, 1850, New York Public Library, Rare Book Division, no. b14311842, https://digitalcollections.nypl.org/collections/souvenir-of-the-n-american-indians-as-they-were-in-the-nineteenth-century?&keywords=&sort=keyDate_st+desc#/?tab=about, accessed February 1, 2020. In this portfolio, the final eleven plates depict pictorial hide robes. Plate 156 is a variant of Mató-tópe's robe in Catlin, *Letters and Notes*, vol. 1, plate 65, and plate 157 is a reprise of a Mandan robe in Catlin, *Letters and Notes*, vol. 2, plate 312. Slight differences suggest that these are not simply reused or retraced plates, but variants on a theme. The British Museum holds a bound volume of twenty-three oil paintings on cardboard titled *A Selection of Indian Pipes in Catlin's North American Indian Collection*, 1852, Department of Ethnology, no. Am2006, https://research.britishmuseum.org/research/collection_online/collection_object_details.aspx?objectId=3201893&page=1&partId=1&searchText=George+Catlin&sortBy=imageName, accessed February 21, 2020. This portfolio was published in full in Ewers, *Indian Art in Pipestone*. Plates 1–21 depict pipes. Plates 22 and 23 depict painted hides in which pipes appear. The British Museum website gives the portfolio a date of 1852, but Brownstone, "Animal Arrays" (15), suggests that it may date from 1864–66.

39. Brownstone, "Anatomy of a Fake," 56. I am grateful to Arni Brownstone for bringing these works by Catlin to my attention.
40. Ewers, *Indian Art in Pipestone*, 66.
41. Ewers, *Indian Art in Pipestone*, 66.
42. Ewers, *Indian Art in Pipestone*, 66.
43. Brownstone, "Animal Arrays," 17.
44. Lakota men had (and some continue to have) vulgar nicknames. See chapter 4, note 53.
45. See Greene and Drescher, "The Tipi with Battle Pictures"; Berlo, "Dreaming of Double Woman"; and Dauenhauer, "Tlingit *At.óow*."
46. Lowie, *The Religion of the Crow Indians*, 419.
47. The literature on such topics is vast. See Codell and Hughes, *Replication in the Long Nineteenth Century*.
48. G. Isaac, "Whose Idea Was This?," 211.
49. The essays in "Theorizing Imitation in a Global Context," a special issue of *Art History*, vol. 37, no. 4 (2014), guest edited by Paul Duro, provide a good starting point for consideration of replication and imitation.
50. A version of this section, as well as portions of the text on replica, surrogate, fake, and vexed identity in this chapter, was published in Berlo and Jonaitis, "From 'Artifakes' to 'Surrogates.'"
51. Holm, *Northwest Coast Indian Art*.
52. Holm always signed or even burned his name into his carvings so that they could not be misattributed. Kathryn Bunn-Marcuse, curator of Northwest Coast art, Burke Museum, personal communication, May 2018. While many of us repeatedly heard him use the term *artifakes* about his own work, it is hard to find in print. According to Robin K. Wright (his student and successor as professor of art history and curator of Native art at the Burke Museum), Holm seldom wrote about his own work. Robin K. Wright, personal communication, April 2018.
53. See Jonaitis, *Chiefly Feasts*, plate 4.16, 198–99.
54. The Burke Museum at the University of Washington, where Holm was professor and curator for seventeen years, holds twenty-five totem poles, masks, bracelets, and other objects made by Holm. The museum's database lists these as "replicas," and their maker is named and listed as a "Euro-American artist." See Burke Museum, Collections Databases, www.burkemuseum.org/collections-and-research/collections-databases, accessed October 3, 2022.
55. These works are fully illustrated in Herem, "A Historic Tlingit Artist."
56. S. Brown, "From Taquan to Klukwan," 158.
57. Chief Shakes IV (?–1840) is of the venerable Nanya'ayi clan of the Stikine Tlingit. On the succession of the chiefs named Shakes, see Ostrowitz,

Privileging the Past, 20–46; on dates for Chief Shakes IV, see 24 and 160n8.

58. S. Brown, "From Taquan to Klukwan," 173.
59. See Ostrowitz, *Privileging the Past*, 20–46; and Moore, *Proud Raven, Panting Wolf*.
60. Moore, *Proud Raven, Panting Wolf*, 49. Moore points out that the non-Natives in charge of New Deal initiatives routinely sought preservative replication, which fit their standards of what replication should be. Steve Brown has written, "Typically in the whole coastal area, the intent of a traditional Native 'copy' is to duplicate the crest images involved, not the object's literal appearance. Each artist is free to interpret the prescribed figures in his own individual way." S. Brown, "In the Shadow of the Wrangell Master," 78.
61. Herem, "A Historic Tlingit Artist."
62. Giovanni Morelli (1816–1891), an Italian physician and art connoisseur, asserted that such details in a painting or sculpture could provide information useful in attributing the work of art. Lee Sorensen, "Morelli, Giovanni," in *Dictionary of Art Historians*, https://web.archive.org/web/20130403033713/http://www.dictionaryofarthistorians.org/morellig.htm, accessed October 3, 2022. For the listing of such attributes, see S. Brown, "From Taquan to Klukwan," 162.
63. Herem, "A Historic Tlingit Artist," 50.
64. Often, people used to seeing an important work in its worn condition will object to the new life that a thorough cleaning or restoration bestows. For example, Michelangelo's paintings in the sixteenth-century Sistine Chapel in Rome were restored and cleaned to great acclaim and controversy in the 1980s. See Beck and Daley, *Art Restoration*; and Pietrangeli, *The Sistine Chapel*.
65. Averill, *A Man from Roundup*, 23–29. The Hamatsa, also called Cannibal Dancers for the enactments they perform as part of the winter ceremonial cycle, are men of high rank.
66. Chief Calvin Hunt, personal communication with Kathryn Bunn-Marcuse, January 19, 2019.
67. This fact is not always recognized by contemporary writers. The curator Candice Hopkins (Carcross/Tagish First Nation) completely misrepresented Holm, writing that he collapsed "the distance between himself and those who were the objects of his study, by not only taking part in their ceremonies, but by mimicking their cultural production as well. Not only did he 'turn Indian,' he also claimed that he was better at it than Native people themselves." Hopkins, "Commodification of Native Culture," 35. Of course, she was speaking from outside the culture that had validated his actions.
68. See, for example, S. Brown, *The Spirit Within*; and S. Brown, *Native Visions*.

69. Steve Brown, personal communication, April 20, 2018. See also Shibata, "Meet Steven Clay Brown."
70. Benjamin, "Mechanical Reproduction," 220.
71. The website for Arriero Zapotec Rugs, owned by the weaver Pantaleon Ruiz Martinez and located in Teotitlán del Valle, illustrates rugs for sale with the same imagery I noted some thirty-five years ago, in 1985: pre-Columbian murals from Cacaxtla, Mexico; paintings by Diego Rivera and Frida Kahlo; African rock art; Navajo textiles; and Saltillo serape designs. See Arriero Zapotec Rugs, www.arrierorugs.com, accessed January 19, 2021.
72. Moreover, modern Navajo rugs less often have cotton warps; most Zapotec rugs do, and the Zapotec weaver puts a double warp at either edge for strength. See Hedlund, "Modern Navajo Rugs"; and Mark Sublette, "How to Identify Fake Navajo Rugs," Medicine Man Gallery, video, www.medicinemangallery.com/native-american-art/navajo-rugs-navajo-blankets-for-sale, accessed January 21, 2021. Sublette notes that in recent years, Zapotec weavers have begun to weave the warp ends in, thus omitting the fringes but forming ridges that can easily be detected.
73. Berdan and Durand-Forest, *Matrícula de tributos.*
74. On cochineal, see Greenfield, *A Perfect Red.*
75. W. Wood, *Made in Mexico*, 11–22.
76. *The Weaver from the Place of the Gods*, dir. Ricardo Palavecino (Paris: Aldabra Films, 2016), https://vimeo.com/204604021.
77. W. Wood, *Made in Mexico*, 122–23, 46.
78. See Demetrio Bautista Lazo, www.teotitlan.com/index.htm, accessed January 19, 2021. In addition to dyeing and weaving, Lazo runs a bed-and-breakfast in his home, where he and his wife offer classes in weaving, dyeing, and traditional Oaxacan cuisine—the complete touristic experience.
79. See Blomberg, *Navajo Textiles.*
80. W. Wood, *Made in Mexico*, 92; see also unnumbered plates 12 and 13 after p. 114. Some of the Zapotec copies have been accessioned by the Natural History Museum of Los Angeles County (formerly the Los Angeles County Museum of History), which houses the original Hearst collection.
81. See Blomberg, *Navajo Textiles*, 233.
82. See Wheat, *Blanket Weaving in the Southwest*; Hedlund, *Gloria F. Ross and Modern Tapestry*; and Kent, *Navajo Weaving.*
83. W. Wood, "Art by Dispossession." Wood discusses examples woven in India. For internet vendors selling Navajo-style rugs from Turkey and Nepal, see, for example, the Rugman of Santa Fe's "American Classics Collections," www.therugmanofsantafe.com/rug-collection/southwest-navajo-rugs, accessed January 21, 2021. This collection of mostly recognizable Navajo designs is

available in up to a dozen stock sizes. Some are cut-pile rugs, rather than the flat weaves characteristic of the Navajo.

84. A century later, the Italian Francesco Milizia (1725–1798) wrote that pastiches "are neither originals, nor copies, but composed of different parts taken from here and there." De Piles and Milizia, quoted in Loh, "New and Improved," 498.
85. See, for example, Hoesterey, *Pastiche*.
86. See Penney, *Art of the American Indian Frontier*, 110–11.
87. Flint Institute of Arts, *The Art of the Great Lakes Indians*.
88. David Penney, email to author, April 5, 2017.
89. Feder and Chandler, "Grizzly Claw Necklaces." For more on Feder, see chapter 2.
90. Benson Lanford, "Milford G. Chandler's Pawnee-Style Grizzly Bear Claw Necklace," Skinner, online catalogue, 2013, www.skinnerinc.com/auctions/2636B/lots/78.
91. Lanford, "Pawnee-Style Grizzly Bear Claw Necklace."
92. Wied-Neuwied, *The North American Journals*, 3:74. Footnote 68 says that Maximilian had just purchased an otter skin for fifty cents and beads for one dollar and that the finished necklace may be the one in the Linden Museum in Stuttgart (no. 36110C).
93. The story of its repatriation and replication is recounted in Hollinger et al., "Tlingit-Smithsonian Collaborations."
94. Hollinger et al., "Tlingit-Smithsonian Collaborations," 204, 212. On *at.óow*, see Dauenhauer, "Tlingit *At.óow*."
95. Hollinger et al., "Tlingit-Smithsonian Collaborations," 215.
96. R. Eric Hollinger, personal communication, July 2019.
97. G. Isaac, "Perclusive Alliances," S288.
98. Hollinger et al., "Tlingit-Smithsonian Collaborations," 216.
99. The pioneering works on this topic were Graburn, *Ethnic and Tourist Arts*; and Jules-Rosette, *The Messages of Tourist Art*. Subsequently, many scholars have taken up this issue.
100. Pearlstone, "Hopi Doll Look-Alikes." See also Pearlstone, *Katsina*. On dolls made by Navajo carvers, which I am not addressing here, see B. Walsh, "The Navajo Doll."
101. Pearlstone, "Hopi Doll Look-Alikes," 587.
102. B. Walsh, "Kikmongwi as Artist." These dolls were and still are distinguished from *tihu*, educational dolls made and given to children ostensibly by the supernaturals who visit Hopi villages between February and late June. See Secakuku, "Authentic Hopi Katsina Dolls."
103. Sotheby's, "Important American Indian, African, Oceanic and Other Works

of Art from the Studio of Enrico Donati," auction, New York, May 14, 2010, www.sothebys.com/en/auctions/2010/important-american-indian-african-oceanic-and-other-works-of-art-from-the-studio-of-enrico-donati-n08685.html.

104. S. Scott, "Art of Subtle Resistance," 597.
105. Otte, *Le paléolithique supérieur ancien en Belgique*, 33.
106. See Prairie Edge, "Imitation Elk Teeth," https://prairieedge.com/all-products/imitation-elk-teeth/?gclid=Cj0KCQjw24qHBhCnARIsAPbdtlLtWs505viUjKLnS10Iz91u6jw5KqOmEIEhRG55s61Xk6y2YG2GjrMaAn8TEALw_wcB, accessed July 5, 2021; and Her Many Horses, *Identity by Design*, plates on 40, 41, 144.
107. Wong, *Van Gogh on Demand*, 1.
108. Richard and Joan Chodosh, interview with author, Santa Fe, NM, May 15, 2017, and subsequent email correspondence.
109. Halpin, "Northwest Coast Indigenous Art."
110. Lazarus owned the well-respected Red Cedar Gallery in Montreal from 1990 to 2002 and now sells privately from his home. He has represented many of the finest contemporary Northwest Coast Native artists, including Robert Davidson and Don Yeomans.
111. Stephen Lazarus, email communication and Facetime with author, late April and early May 2017. Wyatt, *Spirit Faces*, 46.
112. "Northwest Coast Indian Mask," eBay, www.ebay.com/gds/Northwest-Coast-Indian-Mask-THESE-ARENT-AUTHENTIC-/10000000008405941/g.html, accessed April 25, 2017. Lazarus, for years, has posted under the nickname "Komokwa" on eBay sites and on Antiquers.com to alert buyers to these fakes and to teach them to recognize the difference between high-quality Native-made works and Indonesian fakes. "About Komokwa," eBay, https://community.ebay.com/t5/user/viewprofilepage/user-id/5486847, accessed October 3, 2022.
113. Don Yeomans, email to author, May 1, 2017.
114. Lazarus, email communication and Facetime.
115. Trevor Isaac, telephone and email interviews with author, May 2017. I am grateful to Kathryn Bunn-Marcuse for introducing me to Isaac.
116. Esperanza, "Outsourcing Otherness," 77.
117. Lenain, *Art Forgery*, 36. See also Keats, *Forged*.
118. Nagel, "The Copy and Its Evil Twin," 102.
119. Lucic and Bernstein, "In Pursuit of the Ceremonial." This episode is complex, and Lucic and Bernstein have fully documented its many bizarre details, from the amount of money involved to the relationship between these pots and real Zuni vessels. It is perhaps the most unusual situation of forgery in Native

American art. They use the term *pseudo-ceremonial* in figure captions in Lucic and Bernstein, "In Pursuit of the Ceremonial," 52–55, and in Bernstein and Lucic, "Sacred Illusions."

120. See, for example, J. Stevenson, "Illustrated Catalogue" (1883) and "Illustrated Catalogue" (1884), 511–94; M. Stevenson, "The Zuñi Indians"; Cushing, *Zuñi*; Bunzel, "Introduction to Zuñi Ceremonialism" and "Zuñi Katcinas"; and Hodge, *The History of Hawikuh*.
121. C. G. (Charles Garrett) Wallace (1898–1993) went to Zuni in 1919 and worked for the Ilfeld Indian Trading Company, before starting C. G. Wallace Trading Company in 1927. He worked with Zuni people for more than three decades.
122. M. Stevenson, "The Zuñi Indians," 381–82.
123. As quoted in Lucic and Bernstein, "In Pursuit of the Ceremonial," 25.
124. Lucic and Bernstein, "In Pursuit of the Ceremonial," 62.
125. Lucic and Bernstein say that the drawings by William Baake of vessels excavated at Hawikuh were widely circulated in the years after the excavations. The site report itself was not published until 1966. Lucic and Bernstein, "In Pursuit of the Ceremonial," 62. See Smith, Woodbury, and Woodbury, *The Excavation of Hawikuh*. The bowl in Smith et al.'s fig. 51k is the source for the vessel illustrated here.
126. Lucic and Bernstein, "In Pursuit of the Ceremonial," 59–62.
127. Bernstein and Lucic, "Sacred Illusions," 51.
128. Bernstein and Lucic, "Sacred Illusions," 54.
129. Lucic and Bernstein, "In Pursuit of the Ceremonial," 32.
130. Lucic and Bernstein, "In Pursuit of the Ceremonial," 77.
131. Nagel, "The Copy and Its Evil Twin," 105.
132. S. Scott, "Art of Subtle Resistance," 597.
133. Hobsbawm and Ranger, *The Invention of Tradition*, 1–14.
134. See, for example, M. Stevenson, "The Zuñi Indians," 127, 165, 324, 415, 428.
135. Cushing, "Zuñi Fetiches."
136. On Zuni fetishes made for sale, see Rodee, *The Fetish Carvers of Zuni*.
137. Lucic and Bernstein, "In Pursuit of the Ceremonial," 30.
138. Bruce Bernstein notes that today it is far more likely for the vessel to be a far less costly Mexican import (personal communication, spring 2017). In the twentieth century, slip-cast Acoma vessels were probably used, rather than the more time-consuming Zuni coiled vessels, for they were lighter weight and less expensive.
139. See Adair, *Navajo and Pueblo Silversmiths*. In 1938, when Adair did his research at Zuni, he observed that "Ted Wiakwe" was one of the two most expert turquoise workers in the village (148).

140. Slaney, "Zuni Figurative Carving," 73.
141. Nusbaum, "Turquoise-Incrusted Pottery of Zuñi."
142. Nusbaum, "Turquoise-Incrusted Pottery of Zuñi," 98.
143. Kirk, "Introduction to Zuni Fetishism."
144. Kirk, "Introduction to Zuni Fetishism," 148–49.
145. Jim Enote, interview with author, Zuni Pueblo, NM, May 4, 2017. For a debunking of the sacredness of the prayer meal bowl with stepped sides, see Romancito, "Is It Art? Is It Sacred?" Noting that objects "sometimes sold better if they had a story behind them" (54), Romancito goes on to quote Zuni anthropologist Edmund Ladd that "the bowl is considered special only while it contains corn meal and while it is used during a ceremony." Ladd also concurs that pots covered with ground turquoise and what he dismissively refers to as "antler gee-gaws" are made for the tourist market (55).
146. For example, the Fred Jones Jr. Museum of Art, University of Oklahoma, contains two, nos. NA 1996.017.243 and 2008.017.094. The National Museum of the American Indian holds two that came from George Heye's Museum of the American Indian, both purchased from collectors and dealers in southern California in 1936 (no. 19/607) and 1951 (no. 17/5983), respectively.
147. For discussion of such stagecraft, see Jonaitis, *Art of the Northwest Coast*, 112–20.
148. I am grateful to Aldona Jonaitis for an explanation of the iconography of this mask and for determining that the Bob Harris mask in the National Museum of the American Indian was the model for it.
149. See Hawker, *Tales of Ghosts*, chap. 2, "The Cranmer Potlatch and Indian Agent Halliday's Display." Heye's collection at the Museum of the American Indian became the National Museum of the American Indian (Smithsonian Institution) in 1989. The other confiscated masks were sent to the Royal Ontario Museum (Toronto) and to the National Museum of Canada (Ottawa; today called the Canadian Museum of History). Those masks have since been repatriated to the U'mista Cultural Centre (Alert Bay, BC) and the Cape Mudge Museum (Quadra Island, BC), operated by the descendants of their original makers and owners. See U'mista Cultural Centre, "The History of the Potlatch Collection," www.umista.ca/pages/collection-history, accessed April 24, 2017.
150. Don Smith's mask was illustrated, along with a seven-foot totem pole also by the artist, in the Montclair Art Museum's 2007 annual report, both gifts to the museum in that year from private collectors. Montclair Art Museum, *Annual Report, 2007*, 4, 31, www.montclairartmuseum.org/docs/Annual Report2007.pdf, accessed April 17, 2017. The transformation mask was included in a 2014 reinstallation of the museum's Native American galleries,

titled *Undaunted Spirit: Native American Art*. Illustrated in Montclair Art Museum, *Undaunted Spirit: Native American Art*, Artsy, www.artsy.net/show/montclair-art-museum-undaunted-spirit-native-american-art, accessed April 10, 2017.

151. This artist was variously called Don Morse Smith, Don Lelooska Smith, Lelooska, or Chief Lelooska. The facts of Smith's life are drawn principally from Friday, *Lelooska*. This biographer makes it clear that he has close ties to the Lelooska family and that his book is "largely the story that Lelooska chose to tell" (viii).
152. Friday, *Lelooska*, 37–76.
153. Friday, *Lelooska*, 96.
154. For this period in Smith's life, see Friday, *Lelooska*, 77–120.
155. Friday, *Lelooska*, 124, and chap. 5, "A Kind of Hunger." On Feder, see Friday, *Lelooska*, 124.
156. Friday, *Lelooska*, 131. In 2000, the Indian Arts and Crafts Board transferred its art collection (formerly housed in the Bureau of Indian Affairs, Department of the Interior, Washington, DC) to the National Museum of the American Indian. Among this large collection are more than seventy works by Smith, purchased by the board's staff in 1964–66. These include jewelry, wool felt appliqué robes, and carved masks and implements. Moreover, the museum owns a Northwest Coast–style mask made by Smith circa 1980 and donated to the museum in 2002 (no. 26/1527). See National Museum of the American Indian, "Collections Search: Lelooska," https://americanindian.si.edu/collections-search/search?edan_q=Lelooska, accessed October 4, 2022. For discussion of Smith's Indian Arts and Crafts Board work, see Friday, *Lelooska*, 130–46.
157. For Smith's own evaluation of this work, see Friday, *Lelooska*, 193–96. On the college's website it says, "Chief Lelooska of the Cherokee tribe designed these figures which combine ancient Christian symbolism with the symbolism of the Northwest Coast Native American people." Lewis and Clark College, "Agnes Flanagan Chapel," www.lclark.edu/offices/spiritual_life/agnes_flanagan_chapel, accessed October 4, 2022.
158. Duff, Holm, and Reid, *Arts of the Raven*. Of an exhibit consisting of 546 objects, nos. 517–46 were by contemporary artists, including nos. 543–46 by Smith.
159. Sewid, *Guests Never Leave Hungry*. The narrative ends in 1966, so it does not cover the 1967 potlatch.
160. See Malin, "Lelooska," 4–6. See also Malin, *Masks and Totems*, 7, 195.
161. See Malin, *Masks and Totems*, plates 86, 87, 106, 107, 108 and the description of events on 199–207.

162. Glass, "Conspicuous Consumption," 839.
163. See Lelooska Foundation, www.lelooska.org, accessed October 4, 2022; and Glass, "Conspicuous Consumption," 935–37. The problematics of the public performance of Northwest Coast Native identity for more than four decades by the Lelooska family in Ariel (even after Smith's death in 1996) is a far more complex issue than can be addressed here.
164. Sheffield, *The Arbitrary Indian*, 15–16. Sheffield quotes a range of Native people who have experienced difficulty because of the problematic aspects of the law (26–28). One further complicating factor in terms of Lelooska's making of Kwakwa̱ka̱ʼwakw-style masks is that it is likely that Kwakwa̱ka̱ʼwakw people of British Columbia, Canada, would have had no standing when it came to this 1990 US statute, even if they had chosen to protest Smith's commercial activity.
165. Friday, *Lelooska*, 213.
166. Stephen Dow Beckham, professor emeritus of history, Lewis and Clark College, Portland, OR, telephone interview with author, July 21, 2021. Moreover, Beckham told me that the Lelooska family had provided some thirty masks and numerous silk-screened banners for a potlatch held after Sewid's death; the mask described and illustrated here was not a one-off commission.
167. Beckham, interview.
168. See Confederated Tribes of Grand Ronde, "Chachalu Museum and Cultural Center," www.grandronde.org/history-culture/culture/chachalu-museum-and-cultural-center, accessed October 7, 2021.
169. For critiques of blood quantum, see TallBear, "DNA, Blood, and Racializing the Tribe"; and Barker, "Indian™ U.S.A." Barker advocates that determination of tribal membership should be "grounded in an ethics of relationship and responsibility informed by genealogy" (56).
170. Samuels, *Fantasies of Identification*, 3, 9.
171. Painter, *American Indian Artifacts*, 10.
172. Hooper, "A Cross-Cultural Theory of Relics," 193–94.
173. Works that have been important to me include Foster, *Coca-Globalization*; and Roth, *Incorporating Culture*.
174. Miller and Woodward, "A Manifesto for the Study of Denim"; on aspirin, Gardiner Harris, "The Safety Gap," *New York Times*, October 31, 2008; Eric Schaal, "10 'American' Cars That Are Really Made Overseas," *MotorBiscuit*, October 13, 2017, www.motorbiscuit.com/3-american-cars-that-are-barely-made-in-america.
175. Schrader, *The Indian Arts and Crafts Board*, scrupulously documents the history of this issue and the implementation of the board's many initiatives. Schrader includes the 1935 act itself in the appendix (299–302).
176. See Inuit Art Foundation, "About the Igloo Tag," www.inuitartfoundation

.org/igloo-tag-trademark/about-igloo-tag, accessed October 4, 2022. Today the program is administered by the Inuit Art Foundation.

177. Roth, "Argillite, Faux-Argillite and Black Plastic," 302.
178. Esperanza, "Outsourcing Otherness," 92.
179. See, for example, Mukerji, *From Graven Images*, 166–209.
180. See, for example, Lowe and Smith, *James Luna*; Passalacqua, "Tanis Maria S'eiltin"; and Samuels, *Fantasies of Identification*, 141–60.
181. Tommy Orange, "How Native American Is Native American Enough?," *BuzzFeed News*, June 5, 2018, www.buzzfeednews.com/article/tommyorange/tommy-orange-there-there-native-americans-indians.
182. As the anthropologist Patricia Albers has written, the taking of captives "maintains, yet rearranges, the social nexus through which tribes were able to rework their relationships." Albers, "Symbiosis, Merger, and War," 128.
183. Hallowell, "American Indians, White and Black," 523.
184. J. Brooks, *Captives and Cousins*, 37.
185. V. Brooks, "On Creating a Usable Past," 338.
186. See, for example, Lowenthal, *The Heritage Crusade*; Hall, "Whose Heritage?"; and Harrison, *Heritage: Critical Approaches*.
187. Haney-López, "The Social Construction of Race."
188. See Berlo and Phillips, "'Our (Museum) World Turned Upside Down'"; M. Brown, *Who Owns Native Culture?*; Phillips, *Museum Pieces*; and Colwell, *Plundered Skulls and Stolen Spirits*.

2 *Cultural Cross-Dressers*

1. Letter from Joyce Herold to Reginald and Gladys Laubin, June 18, 1987, and reply from the Laubins, September 9, 1987, box 84, Reginald and Gladys Laubin Papers, Record Series no. 15/34/50, University of Illinois Urbana-Champaign Archives.
2. P. Deloria, *Playing Indian*, 12.
3. Doxtator, *Fluffs and Feathers*; R. Green, "The Tribe Called Wannabee."
4. White, *The Middle Ground*. Portions of this section are condensed from Berlo, "Men of the Middle Ground."
5. Shannon, "The World That Made William Johnson." See also O'Toole, *White Savage*, 28. Many books have been written about Johnson. I have relied on O'Toole.
6. O'Toole, *White Savage*, 47.
7. W. Johnson, *Papers*, 2:898–900.
8. Colden, *Five Indian Nations of Canada*, vol. 2, pt. 3, 164, as quoted in O'Toole, *White Savage*, 77.

9. See, for example, O'Toole, *White Savage*, 114–15, 161–62, and chap. 28.
10. For example, Kevin Muller describes Guy Johnson as wearing "Mohawk garb." Muller, "Pelts and Power, Mohawks and Myth," 47, 65.
11. See J. O'Neil, *Their Bearing Is Noble and Proud.*
12. See Benjamin West, *The Death of General Wolfe*, National Gallery of Canada, www.gallery.ca/collection/artwork/the-death-of-general-wolfe-0, accessed August 7, 2021.
13. For example, see Bostonian Ann Powell's account of "Captain David" (David Karonghyontye Hill), whom she met at Fort Erie. "Appendix: Extract from the Journal of Ann Powell," in Reinhardt, "British and Indian Identities," 299.
14. For a discussion of the widespread use of such items, see Ray, "Indians as Consumers"; and Axtell, "The First Consumer Revolution."
15. In a statistical study of eight trading posts in the Great Lakes region, for example, Dean Anderson calculated that cloth and clothing ranged from 43 percent to 75 percent of goods dispersed. Weaponry was the second-largest category, ranging from 10 percent to 25 percent. See Anderson, "European Trade Goods," especially table 4.
16. See Baggs, Jurica, and Sheils, "Stroud"; and Kidd, "The Cloth Trade."
17. West owned several pairs. See J. King, "Woodlands Artifacts," figs. 12, 14, 15, 17.
18. Phillips, "Reading and Writing between the Lines."
19. For Brandt, see George Romney's 1776 portrait, *Thayendanegea (Joseph Brandt)*, in the National Gallery of Canada, www.gallery.ca/collection/artwork/thayendanegea-joseph-brant-0, accessed August 7, 2021.
20. P. Deloria, *Playing Indian*; Huhndorf, *Going Native*; Trachtenberg, *Shades of Hiawatha.*
21. Seton was trained as an artist, but in his forties he turned his attention to youth clubs and collecting Native objects. Seton, *Trail of an Artist-Naturalist.*
22. Ellis, "'More Real than the Indians Themselves,'" 8.
23. Seton, *Two Little Savages*. It contains some five hundred pages of stories, nature lessons, and the occasional instruction on tipi making (151–56), the making of a warbonnet (327–34), and moccasin construction (429–42).
24. Yost, *A Man as Big as the West*, 129.
25. Vinson, "Sun Dancers." See also Koshare Museum, www.koshares.com, accessed October 11, 2022. Jack Kelly's *Koshare* provides an uncritical and unscholarly "appreciation" that is the only lengthy publication on this group. See also Mechling, "'Playing Indian.'" Millions of tourists and Boy Scouts from elsewhere have seen these dances, so the naturalizing of this kind of mimicry continues, despite protests by Native activists and educators. I discuss the Koshare Boy Scout appropriation of Zuni masks, and the critique of this practice, in the book's conclusion.

26. For example, Tuscarora chief Clinton Rickards (1882–1971), who founded the Indian Defense League, was often photographed wearing a Plains feathered headdress. See the cover of Graymont, *Fighting Tuscarora.*
27. Notably, the making and wearing of US military paraphernalia by outsiders is illegal and punishable by imprisonment. "18 U.S. Code § 704—Military Medals or Decorations," Legal Information Institute, Cornell Law School, www.law.cornell.edu/uscode/text/18/704, accessed May 29, 2019.
28. Hunt, "Indian Moccasins."
29. Penney, *Art of the American Indian Frontier.*
30. Pohrt, "A Collector's Life," 306 and fig. 20.
31. Ellis, *"More Indian than the Indians Themselves."*
32. Powers, "The Indian Hobbyist Movement in North America." Feder (1930–1995) was in his early twenties when he started the magazine he would publish until 1960. He was curator of American Indian art at the Denver Art Museum from 1961 to 1971, but his influence there is hard to assess, for he apparently destroyed or took with him most of his files when he left. (John Lukavic, curator, Denver Art Museum, personal communication, 2019.) On Feder's publications and influence, see Feest, *Studies in American Indian Art*, which includes a complete listing of Feder's publications.
33. Feder, "Old Time Sioux Costume."
34. Feder, *American Indian Art*; Conn, *Circles of the World* and *A Persistent Vision*. Like Feder, Conn also wrote for hobbyist publications.
35. Jennifer Dunning, "Reginald Laubin, 96, Performer of Authentic Plains Indian Dance," *New York Times*, April 11, 2000.
36. Ellis, "'More Real than the Indians Themselves.'"
37. Reginald Laubin, "How to Be an Indian," undated typescript, box 11, Laubin Papers.
38. S. Jones, *Reginald and Gladys Laubin*, 11–12.
39. Despite her Native-sounding surname, Tortoiseshell was born in New Jersey to a British father and a French Canadian mother.
40. S. Jones, *Reginald and Gladys Laubin*, 25–26. Neither in their books nor in their unpublished manuscripts do the Laubins credit Hubbard as their teacher.
41. Reginald apparently made many more objects than Gladys did.
42. Laubin Collection, undated objects nos. 1996.24.0048B and 1996.24.0052D, respectively, Spurlock Museum, University of Illinois Urbana-Champaign, www.spurlock.illinois.edu/collections/notable-collections/profiles/laubin.html, accessed May 23, 2019.
43. Zahn (1891–1966) was a mixed-blood (German/Dakota) interpreter at Standing Rock Reservation, to whom many outsiders turned for information about

Sioux history and the old ways of doing things. Curt Eriksmoen, "Standing Rock Native Navigated Different Cultures with Success," *West Fargo (ND) Pioneer*, July 30, 2017, www.westfargopioneer.com/news/4305132-standing-rock-native-navigated-different-cultures-success.

44. Campbell published under the name Stanley Vestal. See Vestal, *Sitting Bull.*
45. Letter from W. S. Campbell ("Stanley Vestal") to Reginald Laubin, April 10, 1934, box 27, Laubin Papers.
46. The Laubins refer to this event many times in their writings, without being specific about when it occurred. The biographer Starr West Jones places it in late August 1934. See S. Jones, *Reginald and Gladys Laubin*, 30–39. Reginald Laubin recounted this story in many places, but most fully in Laubin and Laubin, *Indian Dances of North America*, xxxiii–xxxviii.
47. Letter from One Bull to Reginald Laubin, February 9, 1941, One Bull file, box 75, Laubin Papers.
48. Ellis discusses Reginald Laubin's increasing aggrandizement of this story over the years. Ellis, "'More Real than the Indians Themselves,'" 17–18.
49. See, for example, Laubin and Laubin, *Indian Dances of North America*, 296–98, 337–38.
50. In one typescript, he writes that his first tipi, which he made at about age ten, was constructed according to the plans in a book by Seton. Reginald Laubin, "White Indians," 2, undated typescript, box 12, Laubin Papers; Laubin and Laubin, *The Indian Tipi*.
51. Laubin and Laubin, *Indian Dances of North America*, xxxiii, xxxvi.
52. Walter Terry, "Reginald and Gladys Laubin, the Indian's Dancing Envoys," *New York Herald Tribune*, August 3, 1947.
53. S. Jones, *Reginald and Gladys Laubin*, 22. An undated (but probably from 1935–40) flyer in the Laubin Papers lists thirty high schools where they performed, principally in the East and the Midwest. See "Reginald and Gladys Laubin, Foremost Exponents of American Indian Dancing Present Special Club and Assembly Programs," undated circular, box 48, Laubin Papers.
54. *Jacob's Pillow Dance Festival, Season 1947*, July 18–19, 1947, program, box 49, Laubin Papers.
55. *Program*, January 1948, box 26, Laubin Papers.
56. Walter Terry, "The Dance," *New York Herald Tribune*, July 19, 1947. Terry, dance critic for the *New York Herald Tribune*, and John Martin, dance critic for the *New York Times*, offered much praise for the Laubins' dancing over the years. See Terry, "The Indian's Dancing Envoys." See also by Terry, from the *New York Herald Tribune*: "Indian Dance," December 30, 1947; "The Dance," January 1, 1948; and "The Laubins," December 5, 1960. Articles by Martin, from the *New York Times*, include "The Dance: An Indian Twosome,"

December 10, 1950; and "The Laubins Star in Dance Program," December 30, 1947.

57. *Three Important Films: Plains Indian Culture*, brochure, 1955, box 26, Laubin Papers. See also Hockman, "Motion Picture Production"; figures on 4, 7, and 8 depict the Laubins and their film sets in use.
58. S. Jones, *Reginald and Gladys Laubin*, 52.
59. Letter from Reginald Laubin to Kenneth Leonard, Garrison, ND, November 16, 1964, box 73, Laubin Papers.
60. S. Jones, *Reginald and Gladys Laubin*, 69; "Jackson Hole's American Indian Dancers," *Jackson Hole Historical Society and Museum Chronicle* 35, no. 4 (Autumn 2015): 1, 4–5, https://jacksonholehistory.org/wp-content/uploads/Newsletter-Fall-2015.pdf.
61. Clyde Ellis, personal communication, May 29, 2022.
62. Laubin and Laubin, *Indian Dances of North America*, 490.
63. Lutz, "German Indianthusiasm," 169.
64. Penny, *Kindred by Choice*, 35–36. Feest, *Indians and Europe*, was the first detailed consideration of this topic; many others have followed. Among the best is Calloway, Gemünden, and Zantop, *Germans and Indians*. I am not covering British hobbyists, but they are addressed briefly by Colin Taylor, "The Indian Hobbyist Movement in Europe."
65. Penny, *Kindred by Choice*, 43, 105–26.
66. On May's novels, see Berman, "Orientalism, Imperialism, and Nationalism."
67. Penny, *Kindred by Choice*, 66.
68. Penny, *Kindred by Choice*, 60–64.
69. Penny, *Kindred by Choice*, chap. 4.
70. Penny, *Kindred by Choice*, fig. 22.
71. Penny, *Kindred by Choice*, 199–213.
72. Penny has documented that the gift was transferred from the American soldier to the German hobbyist, rather than vice versa. See Penny, "Not Playing Indian," 181.
73. Joe D. Horse Capture, personal communication, April 2017.
74. Arthur Amiotte, personal communication, August 12 and 13, 2021. All quotations from Amiotte are from this communication.
75. See, for example, Erdoes, *The Sun Dance People*; and Mails, *The Mystic Warriors of the Plains*.
76. Edward Two-Two (Lakota, 1851–1914), a resident of Pine Ridge, South Dakota, who died in Germany, was the subject of a German documentary, *Bury My Heart in Dresden*, directed by Bettina Renner (Deckert Distribution, Leipzig, 2012).
77. Penny, "Not Playing Indian," 171.

78. Penny, "Not Playing Indian."
79. G. Isaac, "Perclusive Alliances," S288.
80. Welskopf-Henrich was also an economist who had been active in the resistance during the Second World War and was a professor at Humboldt University in Berlin. See Penny, "Red Power." In the 1970s, Welskopf-Henrich traveled to Alcatraz and to the Pine Ridge Reservation, where she met with Amiotte, a young art teacher, about sending an exhibit of Lakota children's drawings to East Germany. She also raised money for Native causes. Amiotte reports that the German interest in Native rights is ongoing, telling that "when lecturing in Stuttgart in the early twenty-first century, the first question from the audience was 'What are you doing to get Leonard Peltier out of prison?'" In contrast, most American audiences under the age of seventy would not recognize this name as that of an AIM activist who is serving two life sentences in an American prison for allegedly killing two Federal Bureau of Investigation agents at Pine Ridge in 1975.
81. Lutz, "German Indianthusiasm," 169.
82. Broyles-González, "Cheyennes in the Black Forest," 71.
83. Broyles-González, "Cheyennes in the Black Forest," 82.
84. Kalshoven, "Things in the Making," 64.
85. Kalshoven, "Things in the Making," 67–68.
86. In July 1956, Belden was in Dinkelsbühl, Germany, taking photos and writing an article on another subject for *National Geographic*. It is likely that he traveled the hundred miles to Munich during this trip.
87. Clyde Ellis, personal communication, November 6, 2021.
88. *Pawnee Bill's Indian Trading Post (Oldtown), Pawnee, Oklahoma, Wholesale Catalog No. 5* (1932), 22. I am grateful to Clyde Ellis for sending me photos of pages from this catalogue and for commenting on the outfits in the Belden photo.
89. R. Green, "The Tribe Called Wannabee," 31, 50.
90. American Folklore Society, "What Is Folklore?," https://whatisfolklore.org, accessed October 10, 2022. Indeed, Penny reports that an exhibit of Native objects made by the Indian hobbyist club Manitou, in Radebeul, was held at the nearby Folk Art Museum in Dresden (Museum für Sächsische Volkskunst), date unspecified. Penny, "Not Playing Indian,"171.
91. R. Green, "The Tribe Called Wannabee," 31.
92. See Lippard and Berger, *The Transportation of Place*. Photos from this series are owned by the San Francisco Museum of Modern Art.
93. On the Civil War, see, for example, Allred, "Catharsis, Revision, and Reenactment"; and W. Davis, *The Civil War Reenactors' Encyclopedia*.

94. For a concise history, see Old Fort Niagara, "History and Collections," www.oldfortniagara.org/history, accessed July 1, 2019.
95. Old Fort Niagara, "Old Fort Niagara Reenactor Information," www.oldfortniagara.org/reenactor-information, accessed July 1, 2019.
96. Letter from George Washington to Major General John Sullivan, May 31, 1779, Founders Online, National Archives, https://founders.archives.gov/documents/Washington/03-20-02-0661, accessed August 17, 2021. The letter's original source is Washington, *Papers*, 20:716–19. See also Koehler, "Hostile Nations."
97. Some viewers are avocational photographers who post their photos on living history websites or Revolutionary War websites. For photos of reenactors engaging in battle, see, for example, Ken Bohrer, Battle of Newtown, 2010, American Revolutionary Photos, www.americanrevolutionphotos.com/p717950771, accessed August 17, 2021.
98. Reenactors Jack Andrus and Duane Saxton, interview with author, reenactment of the Battle of Newtown, Newtown Battlefield State Park, Elmira, NY, August 24, 2019.
99. Members of the center describe themselves on their website as "history buffs, nature lovers, educators, living historians, re-enactors, and just plain people." "About 30 years ago, we decided to join together with the common purpose of enjoying history, and about 20 years ago, we were given permission to hold Living History events at the Newtown Battlefield State Park." See Chemung Valley Living History Center, "Revolutionary War Weekend," https://ksa2662.wixsite.com/cvlhc, accessed October 10, 2022.
100. Paul D. Weiss, Trumansburg, NY, personal communication, August 15, 2021.
101. National Endowment for the Arts, "National Heritage Fellowships," www.arts.gov/honors/heritage, accessed August 23, 2021. Boudreaux was not the first to be so honored: in 1987, Chief Allison "Tootie" Montana (1922–2005) was awarded this fellowship. See Ya Salaam, *"He's the Prettiest."*
102. Michael P. Smith (1937–2008), who documented Mardi Gras Indians for decades, dates the first larger interest in them to the first New Orleans Jazz and Heritage Festival, held in 1970, for several "tribes" performed there. M. Smith, "New Orleans' Carnival Culture," 29.
103. See Roach, *Cities of the Dead*, 202–5. Many authors discuss Buffalo Bill's Wild West as the source. See Lipsitz, "Mardi Gras Indians," 104. Lipsitz is the only scholar to reference a participant as the source for this origin story: "One former Chief of the Golden Blades tribe suggests that both blood ties and consumer tastes played a role in the formation of an early Indian tribe, telling a reporter that, 'In 1895, Robert Sam Tillman got the idea to mask Injun by

seeing a Wild West show that came through N'Awlins. Brother Tillman came from Indians himself, and in 1897 he started the [Yellow] Pocahontas tribe'" (104).

104. M. Smith, "New Orleans' Carnival Culture," 26.
105. See R. Brown, "Don't Bow Down," fig. 1; and Becker, "New Orleans Mardi Gras Indians," figs. 2 and 4.
106. Karen Morell, *Mardi Gras Indians*, 1986, video, Africa, Trinidad, and New Orleans Multimedia Collection, University of Washington Libraries, https://digitalcollections.lib.washington.edu/digital/collection/p16786coll8/id/160, accessed October 10, 2022.
107. Joseph Pierre "Big Chief Monk" Boudreaux, interview with Josephine Reed, 2016, National Endowment for the Arts, www.arts.gov/honors/heritage/joseph-pierre-big-chief-monk-boudreaux, accessed October 10, 2022.
108. Usner, *American Indians in Early New Orleans*, 118.
109. *All on a Mardi Gras Day: Big Chief Demond of the Young Seminole Hunters*, dir. Michal Pietrzyk, 2019, 22 min., https://vimeo.com/343592050, accessed August 23, 2021.
110. Larry E. Bannock, conversations with Karen Morrell, Louisiana Folklife Festival, Baton Rouge, October 18 and 20, 1986, typescript, https://content.lib.washington.edu/morellweb/neworleans.html, accessed October 10, 2022.
111. For example, George "Big Chief Jolly" Landry (1915–1980) claimed mixed African American, Caucasian, and Choctaw heritage.
112. See Hobsbawm and Ranger, *The Invention of Tradition*. See also the section "Invented Tradition" in my chapter 1.
113. Becker, "New Orleans Mardi Gras Indians," 40.
114. See Usner, *American Indians in Early New Orleans*, chaps. 1 and 2. See also Usner, *Indians, Settlers, and Slaves*.
115. Usner, *American Indians in Early New Orleans*, 124.
116. Ya Salaam, *"He's the Prettiest."*
117. The date of carnival varies, for it occurs on Fat Tuesday (the literal translation of the French *Mardi gras*), the last day of exuberance before the austerity of the forty days of Lent beginning on Ash Wednesday. Mardi Gras can occur any Tuesday between March 17 and April 20. When Sicilians came to New Orleans in the 1880s, bringing their customs with them, many settled in the Black neighborhoods and intermarried. St. Joseph's Feast Day (March 19) became a day of Sicilian altars for the saint and public masking by African Americans as well. See James Cullen, "St. Joseph's Is an Important Day in Two Cultures: Italian and Black Masking Indians," *Very Local New Orleans*, March 18, 2019, https://nola.verylocal.com/the-sacred-and-divine-st-josephs-day-and-night/43953.

118. I am referencing Francis, *The Imaginary Indian*.
119. See, for example, Nunley and Bettelheim, *Caribbean Festival Arts*. Caribbean carnival sometimes features Native North American imagery, too. See Nunley and Bettelheim, 96–97 and fig. 74.
120. Gómez-Peña, *The New World Border*, 10.
121. A. Johnson, "Coco Fusco and Guillermo Gómez-Peña."
122. J. Alexander, "Toward a Theory of Cultural Trauma," 1. Such ideas build on the work of the influential French social theorist Maurice Halbwachs, whose book *On Collective Memory* (1992) was first published in French in 1952.
123. Sieg, "Ethnic Drag and National Identity," 297.
124. Hewitt, "Cyborgs, Drag Queens, and Goddesses," particularly 143–44.
125. Diana Taylor, *The Archive and the Repertoire*, xvi–xix.
126. Diana Taylor, *The Archive and the Repertoire*, 49.
127. Roach, *Cities of the Dead*, 188.
128. See archival video of Swimmer dancing at Jacob's Pillow, recorded August 22, 1995: American Indian Dance Theatre, "Hoop Dance," Jacob's Pillow Interactive Dance, https://danceinteractive.jacobspillow.org/american-indian-dance-theatre/hoop-dance, accessed June 20, 2019.
129. Scott McKie Brings Plenty, "Around the Rez: Eddie Swimmer Is a Great Ambassador for Tribe," *Cherokee One Feather*, January 5, 2018, https://theonefeather.com/2018/01/05/around-the-rez-eddie-swimmer-is-a-great-ambassador-for-tribe. See also American Indian Dance Theatre, "Hoop Dance."
130. Laubin and Laubin, *Indian Dances of North America*, 478.
131. Julia Carmel, "Nakotah LaRance, Acclaimed Native American Hoop Dancer Dies at 30," *New York Times*, July 19, 2020. LaRance performed in Cirque du Soleil and the Brooklyn Ballet, as well as in Native venues.

3 *Replication and Reproduction*

1. Lévi-Strauss, The Savage Mind, 23; Stewart, On Longing, 69; Phillips, Trading Identities, 102.
2. See, for example, Nottage, "Illusions and Deceptions."
3. Frederick Hoxie illustrated several in color. See Hoxie, *The Crow*, cover and 73–80.
4. See Ewers, "The Awesome Bear in Plains Indian Art," fig. 9.
5. In 2013, the Buffalo Bill Historical Center changed its name to Buffalo Bill Center of the West.
6. Museum documents show that several went to the National Museum of Anthropology in Mexico City. Others passed through collectors' hands and

today are at the Colter Bay Indian Art Museum at Grand Teton National Park. Bill Mercer, email communication, August 10, 2009. See also Nancy L. Fagin, "Any Certain Thing: The Simms Collection of Crow Shields at FMNH," unpublished manuscript, ca. 1990, Field Museum of Natural History, Chicago, in the author's possession.

7. See Penney, *Art of the American Indian Frontier*, 283, fig. caption 213.
8. Lowie, *The Religion of the Crow Indians*, 418–19.
9. Fagin, "Any Certain Thing," 39.
10. Wording on original typed card catalogue, National Museum of Natural History, Smithsonian Institution. Photocopy of original card catalogue from the museum, in the author's possession.
11. Douglas and d'Harnoncourt, *Indian Art of the United States*; in addition to the dust jacket, the shield was illustrated on 133. Feder, *American Indian Art*, fig. 28; Walker Art Center, *American Indian Art*, 23; Maurer, *Visions of the People*, fig. 23.
12. Laubin's bear shield is painted with commercial paint on commercial steer hide. No. 1996.24.2098, Spurlock Museum, University of Illinois Urbana-Champaign.
13. Prairie Edge, "Shop," www.prairieedge.com/category/22/435, accessed July 2011.
14. Prairie Edge, "Mini Bear Shield," www.prairieedge.com/mini-bear-shield, accessed July 2011.
15. Prairie Edge, "Bear Shield," https://prairieedge.com/products/bear-shield, accessed May 13, 2019.
16. Rosoff and Zeller, *Tipi*, fig. 40.
17. Prairie Edge, "Beaded Black Bear Robe," www.prairieedge.com/beaded-black-bear-robe, accessed June 29, 2011.
18. I was told by the current general manager of Prairie Edge, Dan Tribby, that the designation of "Native" and "non-Native" artist at Prairie Edge is not as simple as it appears. He asserts that Dan Chapman, who is no longer affiliated with Prairie Edge, was actually Osage, but lacked the documentation to prove it. "We follow the letter of the law," Tribby said, "but the truth is sometimes something else. Some artists are unwilling to give out their enrollment number, even when we tell them that we cannot sell their work as Native without it. Others lack documentation for any number of reasons." Dan Tribby, telephone interview with author, May 26, 2022.
19. Lynn Thomas, manager of the Native American Gallery at Prairie Edge, interview with author, June 23, 2011.
20. Further information on the history of the store, and the Hillenbrand family, is recounted in the *Rapid City (SD) Journal* and other newspapers over the

past few decades. See, for example, Jim Holland, "Prairie Edge Owner Ray Hillenbrand Dies at Age 84," *Rapid City (SD) Journal*, May 31, 2019, https://rapidcityjournal.com/news/local/prairie-edge-owner-ray-hillenbrand-dies-at-age/article_082ea524-ff69-5d33-9ee3-b718eae93a45.html. See also Prairie Edge, "Our History," www.prairieedge.com/sioux-trading-post, accessed June 6, 2019. The Hillenbrands also own the famous 26,000-acre 777 Ranch, with its herd of some fifteen hundred buffalo, used in the making of the 1990 film *Dances with Wolves*.

21. In addition to Czechoslovakia, the Murano islands in the lagoons of Venice were the source of seed beads used in Plains beadwork. When the Società Veneziana Conterie closed in 1992, Prairie Edge bought its inventory of more than seventy tons of beads (Prairie Edge brochure, 2011). *Conterie* is the Italian term for seed beads.
22. L. Thomas, interview.
23. L. Thomas, interview.
24. Tribby, interview.
25. L. Thomas, interview.
26. See Visit Rapid City, "Main Street Square," www.visitrapidcity.com/ClassLibrary/Page/Information/DataInstances/343/Files/1156/Main_Street_Square.pdf, accessed June 28, 2011; and Barbara Soderlin, "Prairie Edge Owner Buys Downtown Block Adjacent to Plaza," *Rapid City (SD) Journal*, December 22, 2010, www.rapidcityjournal.com/news/article_807e7364-0d62-11e0-93b8-001cc4c03286.html. See also Hunhoff, "The Story behind the Square."
27. See Visit Rapid City, "Main Street Square."
28. See Brasser, "In Search of Métis Art."
29. Chris Ravenshead and Neta Bald Eagle, interview with author, at their home, June 23, 2011. All quotations from Ravenshead and Bald Eagle are from this interview.
30. An influential and widely distributed video, *Lakota Quillwork: Art and Legend*, directed by H. Jane Nauman (Custer, SD: Sun Dog Films, 1990), features the work of Alice New Holy Blue Legs (1925–2003), who was a 1985 National Endowment for the Arts National Heritage Fellow.
31. Penney, *Art of the American Indian Frontier*, plate 103.
32. See Berlo, "Dreaming of Double Woman."
33. Cathy A. Smith, interviews with author, April and May 2017 and April 2018. The information in this section, unless otherwise noted, derives from these conversations as well as from Diana Vela's "Oral History Interview with Cathy A. Smith," National Cowgirl Museum and Hall of Fame, 2013, www.youtube.com/watch?v=39v2_ENbR3w.

34. From Maximilian's detailed notes, Kristine Ronan has determined that Mató-tópe visited their quarters fifty-six times from November 1833 to April 1834. Ronan, "Buffalo Dancer," 57.

35. Catlin, *Letters and Notes*, 1:145. Smith said it would be exceedingly difficult to remake this robe, for mountain sheep hides are almost impossible to come by now.

36. Mató-tópe made a wooden replica of the metal knife that he took from a Cheyenne in battle and used to kill his enemy. Catlin, *Letters and Notes*, 1:152–53.

37. Haldeman, "Spreading Out in Santa Fe." See also "R. Michael Kammerer Jr.," *Aspen (CO) Times*, May 18, 2007, www.aspentimes.com/news/r-michael-kammerer-jr.

38. Smith was inducted into the Cowgirl Hall of Fame, and *Han Skaska—the Shirtwearers: The Art of Cathy A. Smith* was displayed at the museum from October 24, 2013, to April 27, 2014.

39. *Ein Prinz unter Indianern: Die Reisen des Maximilian zu Wied*, written and directed by Philipp Greiss and Eike Schmitz, 43 min. (Berlin: Atlantis-Film, 2017), https://atlantis-film.de/en/the-journeys-of-prince-of-wied-2.

40. See Berlo, "Dreaming of Double Woman."

41. Bertha Hump (1908–1984) lived in Red Scaffold, South Dakota; her husband, John Hump, was the grandson of Hump, Crazy Horse's mentor.

42. Sotheby's, "American Indian Art," auction, New York, May 18, 2011, www.sothebys.com/en/auctions/2011/american-indian-art-n08752.html; Lot 16: "Oglala Sioux Beaded and Fringed War Shirt," pictured online at Sotheby's, *American Indian Art*, auction catalogue (New York: Sotheby's, 2011), www.sothebys.com/en/auctions/ecatalogue/2011/american-indian-art-n08752/lot.16.html.

43. Joe D. Horse Capture, interview with author, March 2017; in addition, we have had ongoing conversations as friends and colleagues for more than two decades.

44. Cathy A. Smith, personal communication, August 2019.

45. Sedikides et al., "Nostalgia," 304.

46. Hofer, "Medical Dissertation on Nostalgia."

47. The literature on nostalgia and the social movements to which it gives birth is vast. See, for example, Cumming and Kaplan, *The Arts and Crafts Movement*. In the United States, central to the Arts and Crafts movement was a valuing of Native art objects such as Pueblo pottery, Navajo weavings, and California baskets. See Hutchinson, *The Indian Craze*. For American examples, see Ulrich, *The Age of Homespun*.

48. Boym, "Nostalgia and Its Discontents," 453.

49. Stewart, *On Longing*, ix.
50. Kammen, *Mystic Chords of Memory*, 33.
51. Rosaldo, "Imperialist Nostalgia," 108.
52. Kalshoven, "Things in the Making," 61.
53. J. Horse Capture, interview.
54. Nora, *Les lieux de mémoire* (7 vols.); abridged in English as *Realms of Memory* (3 vols.). The series includes, for example, essays on topics as diverse as Lascaux, the cathedral, and French gastronomy. For a critique of the limitations of such a project, and its failure to properly incorporate French colonial history and other multidimensional approaches, see Rothberg, "Introduction: Between Memory and Memory." Rothberg suggests the term *noeuds* ("nodes" or "knots") to supplant the more simplistic *lieux* (sites).
55. See, for example, Krech, *The Ecological Indian*. Even while scholars labor to deepen and complicate our picture of US history, the version that continues to loom large in the public imagination glorifies westward expansion, and militaristic actions, both past and present. Vine Deloria Jr. and Howard Zinn were among the first to counter this jingoistic narrative. See V. Deloria, *Custer Died for Your Sins*; and Zinn, *A People's History of the United States*.
56. I am grateful to Kathryn Bunn-Marcuse, scholar of Northwest Coast Indigenous art, for offering this insight.
57. J. Alexander, *Trauma: A Social Theory*; Caruth, *Trauma: Explorations in Memory*.
58. Jan Garrison, "Native American Exhibit Opens at Crisp Center," Culver Academies, 2018, https://news.culver.org/native-american-exhibit-opens-at-crisp-center; Culver Summer Schools and Camps, "Day in the Life of a Culver Woodcrafter," April 28, 2011, video, 8:49, www.youtube.com/watch?v=KdyAJZAAIb8; Dick Zimmerman, "Culver Military Academy Woodcraft Council Fire," *Culver (IN) Citizen*, July 28, 2011, www.maxinkuckee.history.pasttracker.com/cef_cma_woodcraft/woodcraft_coucil_fire.htm.

4 *The Forgery, Fake, Fiction, and Replica*

1. See Crossley and Wagner, "Ask Mexico's Masterly Brigido Lara"; Kelker and Bruhns, *Faking Ancient Mesoamerica*, 66–71.
2. Instead, at least since the rise of processual archaeology around 1960 (the so-called New Archaeology), these practitioners seek to look at objects quantitatively, using rigorous scientific methods in order to discern larger cultural trends and forces. This approach first took hold in the archaeology of the Americas, in part in reaction to the often text-based and antiquarian pursuits

of an older generation of classical archaeologists. The founding text for the New Archaeology was Willey and Phillips, *Method and Theory in American Archaeology*. As the distinguished Mesoamerican archaeologist William T. Sanders (1926–2008) said to me dismissively at a Dumbarton Oaks conference in the 1980s, "Works of art are epiphenomenal."

3. Kopytoff, "The Cultural Biography of Things."
4. Timbrook, "Six Chumash Presentation Baskets."
5. Gamble, "Shell Beads as Adornment and Money," 86.
6. See Schumacher, "Ancient Graves and Shell-Heaps"; de Cessac, "Observations sur des fétiches."
7. A. Benson, *The Noontide Sun*, 13.
8. The numbers of graves plundered was staggering. To report only a few examples: a surveyor who conducted excavations for the Smithsonian in the 1870s routinely reported having dug hundreds of burials at a time at different places in the Channel Islands. See Schumacher, "Ancient Graves and Shell-Heaps," 341 (150 burials); Schumacher, "Etwas über Kjökken Möddinge," 219 (300–400 burials); and Schumacher, "Researches in the Kjökkenmöddings and Graves," 38 (250 burials), 54 (400 burials). In 1919, George Heye's team excavated 343 burials on San Miguel Island. See Heye, *Certain Aboriginal Artifacts*, 34. From 1939 to 1941, O. T. Littleton and Arthur Sanger, in their excavations for Heye, excavated 140 burials at Sequit Canyon and 200 burials at lower Ramera Canyon. See Burnett, "Inlaid Stone and Bone Artifacts," 16, 19.
9. During the second half of the twentieth century, an ambitious program of scientific excavations shed light on ancient Chumash society. An excellent introduction for the nonspecialist is Gamble, *First Coastal Californians*.
10. Heye, *Certain Aboriginal Artifacts*; Burnett, "Inland Stone and Bone Artifacts." Heye, who bought Native objects practically by the boxcar-load, was easy prey for forgers. See Kidwell, "Every Last Dishcloth."
11. See Carder, *A Home of the Humanities*. Elizabeth Benson, the first curator of the Pre-Columbian Collection, provides a personal view of the Blisses as collectors in "Bliss Collection of Pre-Columbian Art."
12. Stendahl began selling art in 1917 and was a major force in the art market in southern California. He famously exhibited Picasso's *Guernica* in his gallery in 1939, charging admission to raise money for those orphaned by the Spanish Civil War. See Dammann, *Exhibitionist*, 118–19. From 1935 to his death in 1966, Stendahl was one of the foremost dealers in pre-Columbian art. Subsequently, the gallery was run by his son, Alfred Stendahl, and then by his grandson, Ronald Dammann. The gallery closed in 2017. *Exhibitionist*, by Dammann's wife, April Dammann, is a thorough—if uncritical—history of Earl Stendahl's career. See also Nelson, Sherman, and Hoobler, *Hollywood Arensberg*.

13. See, for example, Keleman, *Medieval American Art.*
14. The other Chumash objects include a so-called bird figure, well known from other collections, a sailfish, and a seal (all of steatite); a crystal-topped bone blade; and another embellished bone whistle.
15. For cloud blowers and sucking tubes, see Hudson and Blackburn, *The Material Culture of the Chumash*, 4:118–29, 285–90. Far more bizarre ones than the Dumbarton Oaks cloud blower, from the Heye Collection, are pictured in Burnett, "Inlaid Stone and Bone Artifacts," plates 10 and 16–20.
16. Corbett, "Chumash Bone Whistles."
17. The species of bone of these specimens has not been identified, but most are made of deer tibia. These have been found in many excavated burials, and a particularly large cache of forty-five deer tibia whistles was discovered in Bowers Cave in northern Los Angeles County. See Elsasser and Heizer, *The Archaeology of Bowers Cave*, 17–22 and plates 6 and 7; and Hudson and Blackburn, *The Material Culture of the Chumash*, 4:354–62.
18. Asphaltum is also known as bitumen, but in the literature on Chumash archaeology, *asphaltum* is the preferred term. Heizer, "Aboriginal Use of Bitumen."
19. Gamble, "Fact or Forgery," 11–12.
20. I am grateful to Juan Antonio Murra, curator of the Pre-Columbian Collection at Dumbarton Oaks, who made the Stendahl-Bliss correspondence and the Chumash pieces available for my examination in March 2018.
21. Walter Arensberg (1878–1954), a collector of modern and pre-Columbian art, was Stendahl's friend and next-door neighbor on Hillside Avenue in Los Angeles. See Nelson, Sherman, and Hoobler, *Hollywood Arensberg.*
22. Taking inflation into account, the $3,000 that Bliss paid in 1948 for the three objects discussed here, and one minor steatite sculpture, is equivalent to more than $33,000 in 2021. DollarTimes, http://dollartimes.com, calculated on July 31, 2021.
23. This investment is not their only failure. See J. Walsh, "The Dumbarton Oaks Tlazolteotl," on a famous Aztec-style sculpture now widely accepted as a fake.
24. Koerper, "More on Arthur Sanger's Skullduggeries," 17.
25. Bryan, "San Nicolas Island," pt. 2, 216.
26. Lee, "Fake Effigies," 211.
27. Lee, "Fake Effigies," 209.
28. Lee, "Fake Effigies," 209.
29. Letter from Travis Hudson, curator of archaeology, Santa Barbara Museum of Natural History, to Elizabeth Boone, director of studies and curator of the Pre-Columbian Collection, Dumbarton Oaks, June 13, 1984. Held in the accession files of the "Chumash" objects at Dumbarton Oaks.

30. See Gamble, "Fact or Forgery," 11–12.
31. Rockefeller, a well-known businessman and philanthropist, served as governor of New York State from 1959 to 1973. He was a trustee of the Museum of Modern Art (which his mother helped found) for nearly fifty years. See R. Smith, *On His Own Terms*. Rockefeller's "Chumash" whistle was published in Museum of Primitive Art, *Art of Oceania, Africa, and the Americas*, 654. This is now Metropolitan Museum no. 1979.206.399.
32. Fairservis, *Exotic Art*, fig. 754. Carnegie Museum of Art accession no. 75.60.13. Leff bought pre-Columbian art from Stendahl; perhaps he acquired this piece as well.
33. I am grateful to Seattle Art Museum curator Barbara Brotherton for providing me with copies of these catalogue cards. Seattle Art Museum accession no. 63.80.
34. Rust, "Archaeological Frauds," 79.
35. Dammann, *Exhibitionist*, 123–43.
36. See Berlo, *Plains Indian Drawings*.
37. The auction catalogue enumerates them as "thirty-five single drawings, forty-eight additional drawings appearing as double pages, the sheets numbered 29 through 100, and then unnumbered." Sotheby's, *Important American Indian Art, June 4, 1997* (New York: Sotheby's, 1997), Sale 7002, Lot 96.
38. A sample includes Petersen, *Plains Indian Art*; Szabo, *History of Ledger Art*; Berlo, *Plains Indian Drawings*; Greene, *Silver Horn*. Gallery catalogues of works for sale include McCoy, *Kiowa Memories*; and Petersen, *American Pictographic Images*.
39. Sotheby's, *Fine American Indian Art, October 1994*, auction catalogue (New York: Sotheby's, 1994), Lot 174. Sotheby's announced this record price in a full-page ad titled "A History of Excellence," in *American Indian Art Magazine* 20, no. 4 (Autumn 1995): 19, boasting, "Sotheby's holds the majority of all world record prices in the field. This pictographic drawing, one from a group of Sioux Pictographic Drawings drawn by Black Hawk, sold for $428,750 at Sotheby's in October 1994, a World Record for an example of Plains Indian art at auction and the second highest price for an American Indian object sold at auction. Whether buying or selling, we invite you to see for yourself all that Sotheby's has to offer in the field of Fine American Indian Art."
40. Letter from author to head of Department of American Indian Art, Sotheby's New York, August 3, 1996.
41. What follows is covered in greater depth in Berlo, "Transgressing Borders."
42. See Kastner, *Miguel Covarrubias*, where many of his drawings are illustrated.
43. *Codex* (plural: *codices*) is a term used first in medieval studies to describe

illustrated Christian books made of papyrus, parchment, or vellum. Secondarily, it describes the screen-fold manuscripts of ancient Mesoamerica.

44. Covarrubias immediately began selling drawings and caricatures to leading American newspapers and magazines. See Williams, *Covarrubias*, chap. 2.

45. D'Harnoncourt (1901–1968) worked for the Indian Arts and Crafts Board in the 1930s and curated an exhibit of Native art for San Francisco's Golden Gate Exhibition in 1939 and another for the Museum of Modern Art in 1941. He was director of the Museum of Modern Art from 1949 to 1967. See Hellman, "Profiles—Imperturbably Noble."

46. Covarrubias and Rubín de la Borbolla, *El arte indígena de Norteamérica*; Covarrubias, *The Eagle, the Jaguar, and the Serpent*.

47. Pijoán, *Arte de los pueblos aborígenes*. The survey of American Indian art runs on pages 245–438. Illustrations germane to my argument are ledger drawings (figs. 396, 405, 415, 416, 430); tipi paintings of spirit visions (fig. 408); Arapaho paintings (plates 18 and 21, figs. 420–22); pictographic calendars (plate 20, fig. 431); and paintings on shields (figs. 438–39).

48. H. Alexander, *Sioux Indian Painting*. See Berlo, "The Szwedzicki Portfolios," pt. 2; and Ewers, *Plains Indian Painting*.

49. Among the many ledger drawings held by the American Museum of Natural History are Little Finger Nail's Ledger and Last Bull's Ledger (Northern Cheyenne, nos. 50.1/6618 and 50.1/6619); Cut Flesh's Ledger (Lakota, no. 50.2/3352); a large drawing of dancers by Turning Bear (Sioux, no. 50.2/6590); and 112 drawings mostly by Sioux artists collected by Rudolf Cronau (no. 50.2100). For the Cronau drawings, see Berlo, *Plains Indian Drawings*, 216–19.

50. Sotheby's, *Important American Indian Art*, Lot 96, unpaginated. The drawing book did not appear in Sotheby's fall 1996 auction; apparently the staff needed more time to find a scholar who would offer an opinion more to their liking. I subsequently discovered that Joyce Szabo and Candace Greene, scholars of Plains drawings, had been consulted and had also expressed the opinion that these were not authentic (personal email communications, January 14, 2020). I was apparently the only one who suggested that the clue to the authorship of these bizarre drawings was in their provenance—the estate of Miguel Covarrubias.

51. To my knowledge, there are no known Hidatsa ledger drawing books. The Sotheby's essay notes that on the flyleaf the ledger is inscribed "George S. Savage, Springfield, Massachusetts, 1868" and suggests, with no evidence whatsoever, that a man by this name, employed in a Massachusetts firearms factory, was possibly "sent out west during this time." In my experience of handling many inexpensive nineteenth-century ledgers for sale at flea markets and antique

shops over the past thirty years, I have observed that many record the name of the original owner, accompanied by a date; how the book is used in subsequent decades bears no relationship to this original mark of ownership. Covarrubias could easily have purchased such an item, with many blank pages, at a flea market.

52. The scholar Bill Holm later told me that Cowdrey had written the essay for Sotheby's (Bill Holm, email to author, September 7, 2007). Cowdrey is an avocational writer about Native arts of the West.
53. These names are customarily invoked only by one's male cohort, through some—including Meat Prick, Tobacco Ass, Rough Nuts, and Pretty Rump—are recorded in the Crazy Horse Surrender Ledger of 1877. See Buecker and Paul, *The Crazy Horse Surrender Ledger*, ledger pp. 65, 69, and 77.
54. Even the animals in the manuscript evince a Deco sensibility; a stylized dog compares stylistically with canids on the door grills of the 1927 Fidelity Mutual building in Philadelphia (now the Perelman Building of the Philadelphia Museum of Art). See Sotheby's, *Important American Indian Art*, ledger pp. 74–75 and 76–77. On the Fidelity Mutual doors, see Society of Architectural Historians, "Ruth and Raymond G. Perelman Building (Fidelity Mutual Life Insurance Offices)," SAH Archipedia, https://sah-archipedia.org/buildings/PA-02-PH124, accessed August 2, 2021.
55. G. Wilson, *Hidatsa Eagle Trapping*, 129–32 and fig. 6.
56. See Sotheby's, *Important American Indian Art*, Lot 96, ledger p. 59. A number of the drawing book's other odd images (unknown in authentic nineteenth-century ledger drawings) can be explained with reference to Wilson's ethnographic studies, including scenes of catfish. Compare G. Wilson, *Hidatsa Eagle Trapping*, 120–21, and Sotheby's, *Important American Indian Art*, Lot 96, ledger pp. 119–20. Boats made from buffalo skins occur in Sotheby's ledger pp. 70–71; these are pictured in another of Wilson's early works: G. Wilson, *The Horse and the Dog*, figs. 40, 84, and 85. On perusing the report on eagle trapping, it is evident why it captivated Covarrubias's imagination. Wilson, more than any other anthropologist of his era, tried to convey the flavor of Native people's own voices and stories. Much of his doctoral dissertation was in the words of Buffalo Bird Woman, his adoptive mother and principal informant. *Hidatsa Eagle Trapping* is in the words of Wolf-Chief, as translated and illustrated by Goodbird. Other works by Wilson, well known to modern scholars, were only published after Covarrubias's death: his doctoral dissertation was published as G. Wilson, *Buffalo Bird Woman's Garden*.
57. See Kastner, *Miguel Covarrubias*.
58. The angularity of bodily forms is also an Art Deco feature. While the drawings in Codex Covarrubias are not modeled and shaded like his numerous

well-known drawings of Balinese dancers, some have a similar angularity and articulation of limbs. See, for example, Covarrubias, *Island of Bali*, double-page foldout after p. 226. His well-known drawing of the dancer José Limón is similar in its style and articulation of limbs. See Kastner, *Miguel Covarrubias*, plate 15. For horses on tiptoe in Codex Covarrubias, see Sotheby's, *Important American Indian Art*, ledger pp. 47, 49, 78–79, and 134, among others.

59. Bill Holm, email correspondence with author, September 7, 2007–January 23, 2008.
60. I have chronicled in detail Covarrubias's eight-year-long struggle to honor his contract and to send a completed manuscript to Knopf while laboring on a dozen other projects. Berlo, "Transgressing Borders," 81–83.
61. See, for example, a cartoon about archaeology drawn for Covarrubias by his colleague d'Harnoncourt, illustrated in Villela, "Miguel Covarrubias," fig. 3.3.
62. For a small example of such perspectives, see Wilton and Barringer, *American Sublime*; Lévy, *A Transatlantic Avant-Garde*; A. Miller et al., *American Encounters*; and Neff, *American Adversaries*.
63. For an excellent introduction to Mimbres culture, see Nelson and Hegmon, *Mimbres Lives and Landscapes*.
64. For an explanation of this practice, on the basis of historic Pueblo beliefs, see Moulard, *Within the Underworld Sky*, xviii–xix.
65. See Fewkes, *Archaeology of the Lower Mimbres Valley*; *Designs on Prehistoric Pottery from the Mimbres Valley*; and *Additional Designs on Prehistoric Mimbres Pottery*. These were reprinted as Fewkes, *The Mimbres*.
66. The Cosgroves' research has been ably documented by C. Davis, *Treasured Earth*. See also Cosgrove and Cosgrove, *The Swarts Ruin*.
67. "America's Finest Pre-historic Pottery: 'Incredible' Mimbres Art," *Illustrated London News*, March 30, 1929; Bryan, "Excavation of the Galaz Ruin"; Jenks, "Geometric Designs on Mimbres Bowls"; Watson, "The Laughing Artists of the Mimbres Valley."
68. Sloan and La Farge, *Introduction to American Indian Art*, 129. The exposition billed itself, on the title page of the catalogue, as "the first exhibition of American Indian art selected entirely with consideration of esthetic value."
69. See Berlo and Phillips, *Native North American Art*, fig. 2.8.
70. The problem was particularly acute in the Gila National Forest, as one report stated: "Looting is so severe in this area, that all traces of the Mimbres culture will probably be destroyed within the next few years." United States General Accounting Office, *Cultural Resources*, 103. See also Edelman, "Pot-Hunting."
71. Brody, *Mimbres Painted Pottery* (1977), 5. For earlier attention, see Covarrubias, *The Eagle, the Jaguar, and the Serpent*, 214–17. Covarrubias calls Mimbres pottery "without doubt the outstanding artistic achievement of

Southwestern ceramic art" (214). Dunn, *American Indian Painting*, devotes five pages and one illustration to Mimbres painting (60–64).

72. Carlebach, a well-known dealer in so-called primitive art, had a store in New York City in the 1940s and 1950s.
73. Brody, *Mimbres Painted Pottery* (1977), 5.
74. The late Julie Jones was Rockefeller's curator at the Museum of Primitive Art and then curator in charge of the Department of the Arts of Africa, Oceania, and the Americans at the Metropolitan Museum. Julie Jones, personal email communication, May 3, 2011.
75. See Brody, Scott, and LeBlanc, *Mimbres Pottery*. During the 1980s and 1990s, Mimbres bowls were regularly on offer in the catalogues of Sotheby's New York auctions of fine American Indian art, with prices reaching over $60,000 for the finest figurative vessels.
76. Brody, Scott, and LeBlanc, *Mimbres Pottery*. The itinerary of this tour was the Heard Museum, Phoenix (winter 1984); Nelson-Atkins Museum of Art, Kansas City, Missouri (spring 1984); Museum of New Mexico, Santa Fe (summer 1984); University Art Museum of the University of Minnesota, Minneapolis (winter 1985); Colorado Historical Society, Denver (spring 1985); Southwest Museum, Los Angeles (summer 1985); Metropolitan Museum of Art, New York (autumn 1985). This information was provided by Michaelyn Mitchell, former publications director of the American Federation of Arts, in email correspondence with author, August 5, 2011.
77. Kronkright was trained in conservation at the Peabody Museum at Harvard and taught in the highly regarded art conservation graduate program at the State University of New York at Buffalo, as well as the Getty Conservation Institute. He is a member of the American Institute for Conservation and coauthor of Florian, Kronkright, and Norton, *The Conservation of Artifacts*.
78. Dale Kronkright, interview with author, May 24, 2017. All quotations from Kronkright are from this interview.
79. Anonymous A, interview with author, June 5-6, 2011; Anonymous B, interview with author, May 2017. All quotations from the two men are from these interviews.
80. In 2005, for example, the Art Institute of Chicago mounted a remarkable exhibition titled *Casas Grandes and the Ceramic Art of the Ancient Southwest*. While most of the pottery in this exhibit was made almost a millennium ago, the pieces on display were in superb condition. The exhibit's curator chose not to display fragmentary works of the sort that are common to anthropology and natural history museums or that routinely are published in books on pottery of the ancient Southwest. Almost all of the vessels were from private

collections, and some were "repaired" by one of the individuals whose work I discuss in this section. See Townsend, *Casas Grandes.*

81. For scientific studies of Mimbres vessels and what has been done to them, see Lee and Khandekar, "Embellishments on Classic Mimbres Vessels."
82. The American Institute for Conservation Code of Ethics, sec. 2.E,.notes that conservators must be guided by the "principle of reversibility" in their treatments and should avoid the use of materials of which future removal could endanger the object and should avoid techniques that cannot be undone. See Appelbaum, "Criteria for Treatment," 73n1.
83. See Getty Conservation Institute, "Cultural Heritage Policy Documents: The Venice Charter," www.getty.edu/conservation/publications_resources/research_resources/charters/charter12.html, accessed October 11, 2022. For an update to the charter, see Hardy, *The Venice Charter Revisited.*
84. For a study of such objects in the corpus of ancient Maya painted pottery, see Dicey Taylor, "Classic Maya Vases."
85. Thompson and Elliott, "The Mimbres Journey," 119.
86. The "restored" bowl is pictured in a color plate in Moulard, *Re-creating the World*, plate 132.
87. See Brody, *Mimbres Painted Pottery* (1977), dust jacket and color plate 16.
88. See tDAR (the Digital Archaeological Record), Mimbres Pottery Images Digital Database, https://core.tdar.org/collection/22070/mimbres-pottery-images-digital-database-with-search, accessed May 25, 2017. It is not always possible to determine the current whereabouts of a bowl photographed in a private collection years ago.
89. See Kabotie, *Designs from the Ancient Mimbreños*, no. 39.
90. Anonymous A, interview with author, June 5–6, 2011. He explains that Duco, a nitrocellulose, is an excellent all-purpose cement that lasts about fifty years and is easily removed with acetone. Professional conservators formerly used it as well. See Barov, "The Reconstruction of a Greek Vase."
91. Lowenthal, *The Heritage Crusade*, 120–21.
92. Laurel and Paul Thornburg, interview with author, Thornburgs' studio, June 7, 2011; this interview was clarified in follow-up correspondence during the summer of 2011. All quotations from the Thornburgs are from this interview and correspondence.
93. The originals of these bowls are published in, respectively, Brody, *Mimbres Painted Pottery* (1977), figs. 119–20 and color plate 38; and Moulard, *Within the Underworld Sky*, plate 39.
94. DeWald, "Art of the Ancients—Revived," 28. Elsewhere, a feature on the Thornburgs was a sidebar to an article on looting: Howard LaFranchi, "Indian

Digs Raise Question, 'Who Owns the Past?,'" *Christian Science Monitor*, November 29, 1988.

95. See Nelson and Hegmon, "Mimbres Lives and Landscapes." 7.
96. Ramona Sakiestewa, interview with author, Sakiestewa's studio, Santa Fe, NM, April 2017.
97. The Thornburgs give Jelks credit in DeWald, "Art of the Ancients—Revived," 28. Scheelite ($CaWO_4$) is found in many parts of the world, including southern Arizona.
98. Martin Kim, personal communication, June 7, 2011. In a visit I made to the shop in 2019, none of the Thornburgs' bowls were in evidence.
99. See Pillers, "Visiting Potters in Nicaragua."
100. Reese Guth, owner of Mayta Clay, based in Maryland, telephone interview with author, July 12, 2011. All otherwise unattributed quotations from Guth came from this interview. His domain name, MaytaClay.com, is no longer active.
101. Giammattei and Reichert, *Art of a Vanished Race*.
102. All of these bowls were available for purchase in 2011 at the Mayta Clay website, under "Native American Designs." The website carefully noted, "These pieces are not intended to be sold as or represented as the artwork of Native Americans from the Southwestern United States." Mayta Clay, www.maytaclay.com, accessed July 14, 2011. This domain name is no longer active.
103. See Wade, "Straddling the Cultural Fence," where he explains the uniquely Pueblo way of avoiding the strife caused by the clamor for the pots by Maria Poveka Martinez, which brought far higher prices than those of others: Martinez sometimes signed works made or painted by others, thus allowing them to achieve higher prices. This was an effective Pueblo solution to an intractable problem, in which everyone achieved what they desired: the buyers who sought a Martinez pot were happy, the potters whose own work did not earn them such a high price were better paid, and Martinez kept peace in the community.
104. Guth and Van den Berghe, "The Potters of San Juan de Oriente."
105. Mayta Clay, "About Mayta Clay," www.maytaclay.com, accessed June 10, 2011.
106. Mayta Clay, "Native American Pottery," www.maytaclay.com, accessed June 10, 2011.
107. Mayta Clay, "A Brief History of San Juan de Oriente," www.maytaclay.com, accessed June 10, 2011. On the far better-known project of pottery making in Mata Ortiz, Mexico, where Mimbres imagery also graces many vessels, see G. Johnson, *From Paquimé to Mata Ortiz*; and Lowell et al., *The Many Faces of Mata Ortiz*.
108. Ginsburg, "Vetoes and Compatibilities," 536.

109. See, for example, D. Miller, *Materiality*; and Bennett and Joyce, *Material Powers*. Such studies explore how material things shape social relations as they move through different networks.
110. Kopytoff, "The Cultural Biography of Things," 68, 78.

5 *Cross-Cultural Replication and Native Revitalization*

1. Urry, The Tourist Gaze.
2. This section is a greatly abbreviated version of Berlo, "Navajo Sandpainting in the Age of Cross-Cultural Replication." It appears here with the permission of the journal *Art History*.
3. See Witherspoon, *Language and Art in the Navajo Universe*, 151–78.
4. Zolbrod, foreword to Matthews, *The Mountain Chant*, xiii.
5. Matthews, *The Mountain Chant*, 46.
6. Matthews, *The Mountain Chant*, 22; Parezo, "Discovery of Navajo Drypaintings," 60.
7. Matthews, "Mythic Dry-Paintings of the Navajos," 931, reprinted in Halpern and McGreevy, *Washington Matthews*, 221.
8. Matthews, *The Mountain Chant*, 28.
9. Kubler, *The Shape of Time*, 39; for discussion of prime objects and the replica-mass, see 39–40.
10. See Parezo, *Navajo Sandpainting*.
11. Franciscan Fathers, *An Ethnologic Dictionary of the Navaho Language*, 393.
12. Newcomb, *Hosteen Klah*.
13. Epple, "Navajo *Nádleehí*"; Thomas, "Navajo Cultural Constructions of Gender and Sexuality."
14. Newcomb, *Hosteen Klah*, 116.
15. Franc Johnson Newcomb, "Autobiography and Life Data," handwritten manuscript, 3–4, unpublished and undated materials, box 1, Archives of the Wheelwright Museum of the American Indian, Santa Fe, NM.
16. Newcomb, *Hosteen Klah*, 124–26.
17. Newcomb, *Hosteen Klah*, 126.
18. Newcomb, *Hosteen Klah*, 126; Newcomb, "Autobiography and Life Data," 4. In the unpublished drafts she wrote: "And when Klah offered to help me record these transient paintings with paints and cardboard, I decided to make this a special endeavor. In thirty years I succeeded in recording nearly 600 Navajo sandpaintings." These were not all with Klah, for Newcomb worked with other *hataałii* as well.
19. Newcomb observed, "It was not long before I gained the name of *Atsay Ahson*, or Medicine Woman, and to this day when I visit the Navajo country, I hear

'*Atsay Ahson*' whispered behind my back." Newcomb, "Autobiography and Life Data," 4.

20. Lange, "Franc Johnson Newcomb."
21. McGreevy, *Woven Holy People.*
22. For example, see Newcomb and Reichard, *Sandpaintings of the Navajo Shooting Chant.*
23. Friess, "Professor Bush and His Collection."
24. These items exist today in the archives of the Wheelwright Museum in Santa Fe, in both handwritten and typescript drafts.
25. Franc Johnson Newcomb, "Restoring the Mountain Chant, Chuska Mountains," chap. 5 in "In Quest of Navajo Chanters," unpublished and undated manuscript, box CB09, Archives of the Wheelwright Museum.
26. See P. Deloria, *Playing Indian*; Nicks and Phillips, "'From Wigwam to White Lights'"; Phillips, "Performing the Native Woman"; Myers, *Painting Culture*; Gladstone and Berlo, "The Body in the (White) Box"; and Graham and Penny, *Performing Indigeneity.*
27. Newcomb, *Hosteen Klah*, 113, 191–97; McLerran, *A New Deal for Navajo Weaving.*
28. Newcomb, *Hosteen Klah*, 193. Notably, a book of Newcomb's miniature sandpainting replicas, complete with photos and short biographies of several *hataałii*, was also exhibited there. Franc Johnson Newcomb, "Navajo Sand-Paintings: From a Personal Collection of over 250 Sand-Painting Sketches by Franc Johnson Newcomb," unpublished hand-lettered and hand-painted buckskin-bound volume, circa 1930, Archives of the Wheelwright Museum.
29. Armstrong, *Mary Wheelwright*, 127–29.
30. Armstrong, *Mary Wheelwright*, 136.
31. Leatrice Armstrong, assistant director, Wheelwright Museum, personal communication to the author, July 26, 2012.
32. Museum of Modern Art, "Navaho Medicine Men Make Sacred Sand Paintings at Museum of Modern Art," press release, March 1941, www.moma.org/momaorg/shared/pdfs/docs/press_archives/683/releases/MOMA_1941_0022_1941-03-25_41325-21.pdf.
33. Horton, "Rebalancing the Cold War," 86. See also Horton, *Earth Diplomacy.*
34. Navajo *hataałii*, personal communication, 2013; see also Bryant, *The Wheel of Time Sand Mandala.*
35. Benjamin, "Mechanical Reproduction," 220.
36. Benjamin, "Technological Reproducibility," 22. For decades, the shorter and widely reproduced essay was translated as "The Work of Art in the Age of Mechanical Reproduction," though the 2008 version and translation, "The Work of Art in the Age of Its Technological Reproducibility," is now more widely

favored. I use the former title in this section because of its resonance in the modern intellectual imagination.

37. Benjamin, "Technological Reproducibility," 24, 21. He extended the notion of ritual to secular ritual, such as the cult of beauty, or art for art's sake.
38. Maybury-Lewis, *Millennium*.
39. Begay, "*Shi' sha' hane'* (My Story)," 22–23.
40. Franc Johnson Newcomb, "Trip into the Reservation on the Arizona Side to Obtain Material for the Smithsonian," July 5, 1938–July 12, 1938, box B, Si–Y, Franc Newcomb Papers, Archives of the Wheelwright Museum. The quotation is from the entry for July 6, 1938.
41. I lack the detailed knowledge—or even the right to know—how the Wheelwright Museum serves as a resource for Navajo ceremonial practitioners. The decision that archival materials, especially recordings of songs, should be open only to ritual specialists was made in collaboration with officials at the Navajo Nation Museum and Cultural Center. Neither the large collection of sandpainting textiles nor the painted replicas of sandpaintings have been on display since the early 1990s, but scholars are allowed to use them. Some of the chants first recorded in pictures by Newcomb and others—and later published by the Museum of Navajo Ceremonial Art in 1956—were reprinted in 1988 through a publishing venture with Navajo Community College in Tsaile, Arizona (now Diné College, established in 1968 as the first tribally controlled community college in the United States). See Wheelwright, *The Myth and Prayers*.
42. Jennifer McLerran, email communication, January 2022.
43. Parezo, "Discovery of Navajo Drypainting," 61, 59.
44. Parezo, "Discovery of Navajo Drypainting," 60–61. For similar doubts and prohibitions about Navajo stories, see Toelken, "The Yellowman Tapes."
45. For discussions of such issues, see M. Brown, *Who Owns Native Culture?*
46. At the archives of the Museum of Northern Arizona in Flagstaff, a repository of many anthropologists' field notes and photographs, I was told in the summer of 2006 that their Navajo cultural consultants had flagged many images and field notes of prominent anthropologists as off-limits to non-Navajo. I pointed out that one flagged image was the photo of the sandpainting performance at the Museum of Modern Art—a photo taken in a public context and published repeatedly since 1941.
47. See Zolbrod, foreword to Matthews, *The Mountain Chant*, xviii; and Rickard, "Visualizing Sovereignty."
48. Benjamin, "Technological Reproducibility," 21.
49. Reichard calls the paintings done by Newcomb and others "authentic copies." See Reichard, *Navajo Medicine Man*, 2. I thank Jennifer McLerran for

information on recruitment of Walmart customers to Diné College (personal communication, 2006).

50. I was unable to learn anything more than that the sandpainting replicas had been taken down "a couple of years ago," when the ceiling was repainted. Presumably, they were returned to Diné College.
51. See McLerran, "Woven Chantways."
52. On the inalienability of knowledge and "strategic acts of silence" among Navajo weavers today, see Yohe, "Weaving Knowledge in Contemporary Navajo Life."
53. The people who spoke to me in the late spring of 2013 knew that I was writing about such issues, and I shared with them my publications that focused on textiles with sandpainting imagery: Berlo, "Navajo Cosmoscapes"; and Berlo, "Alberta Thomas, Navajo Pictorial Arts." Yet they chose not to be quoted by name, for reasons of privacy, or fear of being criticized by others, or offending those whose beliefs and actions are different from their own. Notably, both men whom I am quoting are college-educated professionals who have chosen the ethical stance of returning and working within the Navajo Nation to rebuild traditional values among the younger generation.
54. The anthropologist Gary Witherspoon estimated that there were more than three hundred thousand conjugations of the verb *to go* in Navajo and that if one were to add to this the conjugations of the verb *to move*, "the number of conjugations would be well into the millions." Witherspoon, *Language and Art in the Navajo Universe*, 49.
55. Kabotie, *Designs from the Ancient Mimbreños.*
56. Mimbres pottery was not the only ancestral image system that animated Pueblo potters. Nampeyo (Hopi-Tewa, ca. 1856–1942) and her husband, Lesou (Hopi, ca. 1850–1932), who often painted her pots, used ancestral Hopi pots from nearby Sikyatki as a design source even in the late nineteenth century, sparking what came to be called the Sikyatki Revival. Lesou worked on the Hemenway Expedition, which excavated hundreds of Sikyatki wares. See McCoy, "Nampeyo"; and Elmore, *In Search of Nampeyo*. According to the author Charles S. King, their great-granddaughter Dextra Quotskuyva recalled of Lesou: "[He] used to go out there where they were digging at Sikyatki. He painted the designs with charcoal on cardboard. He would save those." C. King, *Spoken through Clay*, 81.
57. Julian Martinez worked with Edgar Lee Hewett at Bandelier starting in 1907. By 1908, he and Maria Poveka Martinez were making pottery that drew inspiration from the potsherds collected there. See Spivey, *The Legacy of Maria Poveka Martinez*, 11.
58. Richard L. Spivey calls it "practically an exact copy from the prehistoric

Mimbres." Spivey, *The Legacy of Maria Poveka Martinez*, caption to plate 20. Plate 34 on 39 of Spivey depicts the identical design in black-on-black ware, also from the 1920s.

59. See Fewkes, *Additional Designs on Prehistoric Mimbres Pottery*, 30, fig. 12.
60. Bernstein, "Potters and Patrons," 77.
61. LeBlanc, *Painted by a Distant Hand*, 47.
62. For images of Lewis's Mimbres-influenced vessels, see Peterson, *Lucy M. Lewis*, figs. 324, 325, 338, and 339, and see 43–44. For Berlant, see LeBlanc, *Painted by a Distant Hand*, 105n28.
63. Dillingham, *Fourteen Families in Pueblo Pottery*, 100–101. See also Fred Jones Jr. Museum of Art and Philbrook Museum of Art, *The Eugene B. Adkins Collection*, 236–37; and Coe, *Lost and Found Traditions*, fig. 276.
64. Charmae Shields Natseway, interview with author, Santa Fe, NM, August 2011. Unless otherwise noted, all quotations are from this interview with the artist.
65. Schultz (1923–2019) was on the board of the Wheelwright Museum, was active in Native arts across New Mexico, and with her husband, Sid, was a collector and supporter of contemporary Native artists, encouraging them to follow their singular visions, rather than worrying about the market. Jonathan Batkin, former director of the Wheelwright Museum, personal communication, September 29, 2021.
66. See, for example, Brody, *Mimbres Painted Pottery* (2004), fig. 30.
67. Tonawanda is the home of the Tonawanda Seneca Nation in western New York; most of it is in Genesee County. Other Seneca reservations include the Allegany Reservation in Cattaraugus County, New York, and the Cattaraugus Reservation in Chautauqua County, New York. The Seneca are one of the Six Nations of the Haudenosaunee (Iroquois) Confederacy.
68. An exact count of objects made during the project is not possible; some were exchanged with other museums, and some were burned in two fires at Tonawanda in 1937 and 1941.
69. Hauptman, "The Iroquois School of Art," provides the best general history of the program; McLerran, *A New Deal for Native Art*, places it in the context of other initiatives benefiting Native Americans. See also Hauptman, *The Iroquois and the New Deal*. The Seneca Arts Project is sometimes called the Indian Arts Project, but, following Hauptman, "The Iroquois School of Art," I use the more specific name here, except when citing the archives at the RMSC, where the files call it the Indian Arts Project (hereafter cited as RMSC, IAP).
70. See Cornplanter, *Legends of the Longhouse*. The masks were widely displayed and published in the fifty years after the program. In recent decades, the Haudenosaunee have deemed them to be culturally sensitive; they were

repatriated to the Seneca in 2011. Smith's paintings of ceremonies are no longer exhibited or published. On the subject of the repatriation of masks, principally in Canada, see Phillips, "Disappearing Acts."

71. For an expanded version of this section, see Berlo, "Women of the Seneca Arts Project."
72. Morgan, as quoted in Tooker, *Morgan on Iroquois Material Culture*, 20.
73. Tooker, *Morgan on Iroquois Material Culture*, 170.
74. See Porter, *To Be Indian*. While Arthur Parker spent his first eleven years on the Cattaraugus Reservation of the Seneca Nation in western New York, his father was mixed-race and his mother was white, so in this matrilineal society he was not eligible to be enrolled as Seneca, though he was accepted by, and later formally adopted into, the Seneca Nation.
75. Hirsch, "New York State Indians," 1.
76. Letter from Temporary Emergency Relief Administration of the State of New York to Frederick Daniels, April 24, 1934, RMSC, IAP, TERA File.
77. Letter from Arthur C. Parker to John C. Brennan, January 11, 1935, Arthur Caswell Parker Papers, Rush Rhees Library, Department of Rare Books, Special Collections, and Preservation, University of Rochester, Rochester, NY.
78. People at Cattaraugus participated in only the first two years; after that, the project focused on Tonawanda.
79. Parker, "Museum Motives," 12.
80. Issues of contact and change in Haudenosaunee arts are addressed in Phillips, *Trading Identities*; and Kasprycki, *On the Trails of the Iroquois*.
81. Parker, "Museum Motives," 12.
82. On this phenomenon, see Ewers, "Symbol of the North American Indian." For Haudenosaunee examples, see Kasprycki, *On the Trails of the Iroquois*, figs. 417–32 and fig. 452.
83. The many plates in Parker, "Certain Iroquois Tree Myths and Symbols," certainly were used as models by SAP bead workers.
84. Hill and Fenton, "Reviving Indian Arts among the Senecas," 13. While this article is coauthored with William Fenton, the young anthropologist working for the Indian Service at Tonawanda who would later become the most prolific scholar of Iroquoian studies of the twentieth century, it is written in the voice of Cephas Hill.
85. See, for example, Kasprycki, *On the Trails of the Iroquois*, 207, fig. 361; and Holler, "Fashion, Nationhood, and Identity," fig. 9.
86. Today we think of broadcloth as being a cotton fabric, but, historically, "broadcloth" referred to wool cloth woven on a wide loom (therefore "broad") and then shrunk by means of heat, water, and agitation, causing the fibers to interlock. Because of this process, broadcloth did not easily unravel

when cut; it was warm, sturdy, and water-repellent. Broadcloth was much favored in the Indian trade in the eighteenth and nineteenth centuries and was used across the Northeast for intercultural garments. See Montgomery, *Textiles in America*, 177. It is still available at companies that provide materials for reenactors. See, for example, Crazy Crow, "Wool Trade Cloth," www.crazycrow.com/wool-trade-cloth, accessed August 30, 2021. In museum records and exhibit catalogue descriptions, the ribbon used in SAP clothing is described as silk, but the leftover spools of ribbon in storage at the museum are labeled "satin taffeta ribbon, rayon and silk, made in U.S.A."

87. Walco, a large concern that sold beads across North America during much of the twentieth century, was later subsumed into the Halcraft Collection. See Halcraft Collection, "About Us," www.halcraftcollection.com/pages/about-us, accessed February 1, 2021.

88. Twenty-six women at Cattaraugus worked from 1935 to 1936. Because of the far smaller output of beadwork artists, I am not considering them here. With a few exceptions, Cattaraugus women seemed to perform occasional labor, perhaps only when sorely in need of cash. Most women there made fewer than a dozen items, some only three or four.

89. The photo, taken by William G. Frank of the Rochester Museum of Arts and Sciences, is undated, but Martha Skye took part in the SAP only until 1938. Moreover, 1936 was the only year that Melinda Skye made hats, and she is pictured with a hat on her lap. Therefore, I have established 1936 as the date of this photo. RMSC, IAP, chronological list of participants in the Indian Arts Project and their works.

90. These assessments were determined from my own counting of objects made by individuals as recorded in the chronological files and individual workers' files. RMSC, IAP.

91. RMSC no. 6461, made in thirty-five and a half hours.

92. See Holler, "The Remarkable Caroline G. Parker Mountpleasant," 12. The normal school (a nineteenth-century term for a school devoted to the education of teachers) was established in Albany in 1844 and is now the State University of New York at Albany. State University of New York at Albany, "About UAlbany," www.albany.edu/about, accessed October 7, 2022.

93. The federal minimum wage rose to thirty cents per hour in 1939. See United States Department of Labor, "Federal Minimum Wage Chart," www.dol.gov/whd/minwage/chart.htm, accessed July 20, 2019. The Native supervisors earned slightly more than fifty cents per hour.

94. "WPA-sponsored Federal Project #1 (Art, Music, Theatre, and Writing)," contract, December 16, 1935, RMSC, IAP, Legal File.

95. "Indian Arts and Crafts Forwarded to World's Fair," undated typed list of

objects, RMSC, IAP. The world's fair ran from late April to late October in both 1939 and 1940. Memo of December 14, 1939, RMSC, IAP, Alphabetical Correspondence Files. On Indian art at the Golden Gate International Exposition, see Schrader, *The Indian Arts and Crafts Board*, chaps. 8 and 9.

96. RMSC, IAP, Alphabetical Correspondence Files: Loans.
97. "Iroquois Art, Crafts on Way to Israel," *Democrat and Chronicle* (Rochester, NY), June 13, 1962, RMSC, IAP, Clipping File.
98. On Douglas and his Indian Fashion Shows, see Parezo and Blomberg, "Indian Chic"; and Parezo, "The Indian Fashion Show." Figure 7 in Parezo shows a model wearing the skirt, overdress, and leggings that were acquired by the Denver Art Museum in 1936.
99. Curated by Betty Prisch of the RMSC staff, the exhibit ran from July 6 to August 13, 1989. Exhibition files for *A Seneca Renaissance*, RMSC.
100. Wall label, *Bridging the Gap* exhibition at the RMSC, 2018. The Melissa Smith quotation in this paragraph derives from the text for wall labels. The exhibit was organized by museum staff member Jamie Jacobs and marked the two hundredth anniversary of the birth of Lewis Henry Morgan, upon whom the Seneca had bestowed the name Tayadaowuhkuh, or One Bridging the Gap.
101. Jacques, "Discipline of a Good Mind," unpaginated; Jacques, "Good Minds."
102. "*Bridging the Gap: Seneca Art across Generations*: Curated Panels from the Exhibit," RMSC, https://rbscp.digitalscholar.rochester.edu/wp/Morgan200/exhibits/bridging-the-gap-seneca-art-across-generations/rmsc-exhibit-panels, accessed July 15, 2019.
103. Michael Galban, interview with author, Ganondagan State Historic Site, Victor, NY, August 1, 2019.
104. Parker, "The Indian Arts Project," 9.
105. Parker, "Art Reproductions of the Seneca Indians," 33.
106. Ulrich, *The Age of Homespun*, 39.
107. See McLerran, "The History and Progress of the Navajo People"; and Moore, *Proud Raven, Panting Wolf*.
108. See Peers, *Playing Ourselves*, for a fine ethnography of Native reenactors/educators who do this as a profession.
109. Michael Galban, "Playing Indian [. . .]," *Edge of the Woods* (blog), January 30, 2013, htttp://edgeotw.blogspot.com/2013/01/playing-indian-as-child-growing-up-in.html.
110. Much of this section, unless otherwise noted, is based on the interview I had with Galban at Ganondagan on August 1, 2019, and subsequent email conversations.
111. Ganondagan, "About Us," https://ganondagan.org/about-us, accessed February 9, 2021.

112. Morgan, "Fabrics, Inventions, Implements," 85.
113. Parker, "Art Reproductions of the Seneca Indians," discusses the revival of finger weaving of basswood fiber bags and tumplines. The article illustrates Tom Two Arrows doing finger weaving. See also Hauptman, "The Iroquois School of Art," 297, which references the film *Making the Basswood Burden Strap* (1936), featuring Everett Parker doing all stages of the process, from stripping the basswood tree in the spring to making fine cording and completing the weaving.
114. Kasprycki, *On the Trails of the Iroquois*, plates 258 and 259; Galban, "The Oldest Surviving Quilled Bag." Galban's blog is titled *Edge of the Woods*, http://edgeotw.blogspot.com.
115. Galban, *The Historical Art of Robert Griffing*, vol. 3.
116. Michael Galban, "Paddles, Perspectives, and Pickers," *Edge of the Woods* (blog), February 2, 2013, http://edgeotw.blogspot.com/2013/02/paddles-perspectives-and-pickers-ok-i.html.
117. Jamie Jacobs, conversations with author, RMSC, July 15 and 22, 2019. This section is based principally on these conversations. The Iroquois Museum in Howe's Cave, New York, sponsored his virtual lecture on quillwork in July 2020; some details come from there. "Quill Worker Jamie Jacobs," Facebook, www.facebook.com/watch/?v=288749742550612, accessed February 10, 2021.
118. Kasprycki, "Quilled Drawstring Pouches," fig. 15. The one Jacobs modeled his after is in the Folkens Museum-Etnografiska in Stockholm.
119. For the catalogue, see Ganondagan, *2020 Hodinöhsö:ni' Virtual Art Show Winners*, https://ganondagan.org/files/documents/28dfff4e-f4ae-4ca5-a38b-680fada4d8f1.pdf, accessed October 7, 2022.
120. G. Isaac, "Whose Idea Was This?," 211.
121. Urry, *The Tourist Gaze*.
122. Trimble, *Talking with the Clay*, 80.
123. Kabotie, *Designs from the Ancient Mimbreños*.
124. King and Spivey, *The Life and Art of Tony Da*; J. Scott, *Changing Woman*, 112.
125. Ramona Sakiestewa, interview with author, Sakiestewa's studio, Santa Fe, NM, April 2017. See also Ramona Sakiestewa, "Scalamandré Ancient Blanket Series," https://ramonasakiestewa.com/collaborations/scalamandre-ancient-blanket-series, accessed October 7, 2022.
126. The gambling image has been repeatedly published; it is in the collection of the School for Advanced Research in Santa Fe. See Brody, *Mimbres Painted Pottery* (2004), fig. 36.
127. On Romero, see Clark, *Free Spirit*; and Coe, *The Responsive Eye*, 270.
128. Romero, "Diego Romero: Cochiti."

Conclusion

1. Hopi today prefer the term *katsina* (plural: *katsinam*), though in the twentieth-century literature, the term *kachina* was more often used. The Zuni term is variously spelled *ko-ko* or *kokko*.
2. M. Stevenson, "The Zuñi Indians," 381–82.
3. Néret-Minet, Tessier et Sarrou, *Masques katsinam des indiens Hopis de l'Arizona, indiens Acoma du Nouveau-Mexique, indiens Jemez, indiens Zuñi, vendredi 12 avril 2013* (Paris: Néret-Minet, Tessier et Sarrou, 2013). The eighty-eight-page full-color catalogue was long available for download online but, since 2018, has been removed. Masks by Hopi, Zuni, Navajo, and other Southwestern peoples were for sale.
4. Comité de Solidarité members handed out flyers on the sidewalk. On the front, the headline urged: "Respect du peuple Hopi et des droits des peuples autochtones. Ce vendredi 12 avril, pas de vente d'objets sacrés Hopi à l'Hôtel Drouot!" (Respect for the Hopi people and the rights of indigenous peoples. This Friday, April 12, no sale of sacred Hopi objects at the Hotel Drouot!). The text stressed that the United Nations Declaration on the Rights of Indigenous Peoples (2007), to which France was a signatory, declared that indigenous people have the right to use and control their ceremonial objects. On the back of the flyer, a long letter from LeRoy N. Shingoitewa, president of the Hopi Tribe, to Gilles Néret-Minet, dated April 4, 2013, insisted that this sale was not an homage to Hopi culture (as Néret-Minet had publicly opined) but a profaning of their religion and that the masks were Hopi cultural patrimony. By using these words, Shingoitewa was using the precise legal language in the 1992 Native American Graves Protection and Repatriation Act. (Flyer in the author's possession.)
5. For discussion of the French civil code and the disposition of this issue, see Cornu, "About Sacred Cultural Property"; and Nicolazzi, Chechi, and Renold, "Case Hopi Masks."
6. Tom Mashberg, "Hopis Try to Stop Paris Sale of Artifacts," *New York Times*, April 14, 2013. By the same author, see also "Embassy Discourages Sale of Hopi Ritual Items," *New York Times*, April 9, 2013; and "Auction of Hopi Masks Proceeds after Judge's Ruling," *New York Times*, April 12, 2013.
7. My actions were reported, without naming me, and with several inaccuracies, in Mashberg, "Auction of Hopi Masks Proceeds"; and Tom Mashberg, "Protested Sale of Hopi Works Brings $1.2 Million," *New York Times*, April 13, 2013.
8. Tom Mashberg, "Secret Bids Guide Hopi Indians' Spirits Home," *New York Times*, December 16, 2013. The Annenberg Foundation was established in 1989 by well-known American philanthropists Walter and Lenore Annenberg,

whose fortune came from magazine publishing and television broadcasting. Best known for support of the visual arts and university programs in communication and journalism, their website notes that in recent years the foundation's mandate has expanded to include "environmental stewardship, social justice, and animal welfare." In its timeline of "milestones and moments," the foundation's website lists as a 2013 milestone its actions on behalf of the Hopi Nation. See Annenberg Foundation, "Who We Are," www.annenberg.org /who-we-are, accessed June 2, 2020.

9. Some American art dealers and museum curators apparently know the identity of the owner of the objects in the first sale, identified on the title page of the catalogue only as "L.S." and described on page 3 by the catalogue's author, Daniel DuBois (characterized as a "spécialiste des Indiens d'Amérique"), as someone who assembled the collection "durant les 30 ans de son séjour aux U.S.A." (i.e., during his thirty years' stay in the United States). A photo of Hopi chief Wilson Tawaquaptewa and his *tihu* (painted katsina carvings) taken by Paul Coze at the village of Oraibi in 1935 graces page 2 of the auction catalogue. Some scholars believe that some of these masks had belonged to Coze (1903–1974), a French writer and artist who traveled in the American Southwest in the early twentieth century, eventually settling in Phoenix. He wrote about American Indians for French audiences and curated two exhibits at Musée d'Ethnographie du Trocadéro in the 1930s. During his years in the Southwest, Coze wrote for American audiences as well. See Coze, "Kachinas," which opens with a full-page color plate of a Crow Mother masked figure and recounts the author's experiences at Pueblo and Navajo ceremonials; see also Coze, "Twenty-Four Hours of Magic." See also Horton, "Performing Paint, Claiming Space."

10. In 1991, Sotheby's proceeded with the sale of one Navajo and two Hopi masks in its New York auction of May 21, despite written protests from the Navajo and Hopi cultural centers asking that these not be auctioned. See Rita Reif, "Three Indian Masks to Stay in Auction," *New York Times*, May 21, 1991. After several such incidents were widely covered in the press, Sotheby's New York stopped selling such masks, presumably because of the bad publicity.

11. Donald Ellis, personal email communication, March 11, 2020.

12. Enote, "Buyer Beware." In 2017, Enote told me that the Zuni deliberately chose not to engage with the French auction houses or with the Annenberg Foundation. Jim Enote, interview with author, A:shiwi A:wan Museum, Zuni Pueblo, May 4, 2017.

13. Enote, interview.

14. Bunzel, "Zuñi Katcinas," 851.

15. Bunzel, "Zuñi Katcinas," 848.

16. Ortiz, "Ritual Drama and the Pueblo World View," 160.
17. Sekaquaptewa, "Hopi Indian Ceremonies," 39.
18. "Statement of Religious Leaders of the Pueblo of Zuni concerning Sacred Zuni Religious Items/Artifacts," September 20, 1978, as quoted in Merrill, Ladd, and Ferguson, "The Return of the *Ahayu:da*," 532.
19. Secakuku, *Following the Sun and Moon,* 17. See also Stephen, *Hopi Journal*, fig. 156.
20. Hopitutskwa is the Hopi name for their ancestral land. See the Hopi Tribe's official website, www.hopi-nsn.gov, accessed July 2, 2020.
21. J. Green, introduction to Cushing, *Zuñi*, 17, 10.
22. See G. Isaac, "Whose Idea Was This?" In part, this essay deals with an Ahayu:da that Cushing made and sent to the Pitt Rivers Museum at Oxford as a gift and the Zuni attempt to repatriate this object. Cushing also made one for the Ethnological Museum of Berlin. See Tedlock, "Aesthetics and Politics," 157–64.
23. M. Stevenson, "The Zuñi Indians," 17.
24. M. Stevenson, "The Zuñi Indians," 243, note a.
25. As quoted in Fane, Jacknis, and Breen, *Objects of Myth and Memory*, 60.
26. Andrew and Effa Vanderwagen (or Vander Wagen), who arrived in Zuni in 1897, were missionaries for the Dutch Christian Reformed Church.
27. Fane, Jacknis, and Breen, *Objects of Myth and Memory*, 62. Figure 15 in Fane et al. depicts about eighteen of the masks on display at the Brooklyn Museum circa 1910; the *tihu* are illustrated in figures 68–83.
28. Bunzel, "Introduction to Zuñi Ceremonialism," 479.
29. Tedlock, *The Beautiful and the Dangerous*, 252. The first and most thorough description of Shalako was written by Stevenson, who witnessed the ceremonial cycle in 1876, 1891, and 1896. See "Annual Festival of the Sha'lako," in M. Stevenson, "The Zuñi Indians," 227–83.
30. "Boys Drop Zuni Rites," *Gallup (NM) Independent*, December 30, 1953. I am grateful to my friend and colleague Clyde Ellis for giving me a copy of this article.
31. Gendron, *Behind the Zuni Masks*, acknowledgments, 213.
32. Along with papers on non-Zuni topics, the *Forty-Seventh Annual Report of the Bureau of American Ethnology, 1929–1930* contains Bunzel's "Introduction to Zuñi Ceremonialism," "Zuñi Origin Myths," "Zuñi Ritual Poetry," and "Zuñi Katcinas."
33. Gendron, *Behind the Zuni Masks*, 131.
34. Gendron, *Behind the Zuni Masks*, 148. The prayers (160–62) are adapted directly from Bunzel, "Zuñi Ritual Poetry," 690–92.
35. Gendron, *Behind the Zuni Masks*, 167.

36. Kelly, *Koshare*, 45.

37. "The Return of the Gods," *Time*, January 11, 1954, 60, 62. This story was picked up by newspapers across the nation, as evidenced by its appearance in one in the small town of Mexico, Missouri, about one hundred miles west of St. Louis: "When the Koshares Made a Treaty with Zuni Indians," *Mexico (MO) Evening Ledger*, June 25, 1954. I am grateful to my colleague Clyde Ellis for giving me copies of these newspaper clippings concerning the Boy Scout Shalako incident. For the fictionalized account, see Gendron, *Behind the Zuni Masks*, 188–91, 195–99.

38. Gendron, *Behind the Zuni Masks*, 201.

39. Kelly, *Koshare*; the entire letter is published on 52.

40. Gregory Hawkins, "Guarding a Ritual: Indians Stop Imitations of a Sacred Dance," *New York Times*, February 21, 1954. This was not, strictly speaking, "repatriation," for it was not a return to the place where these objects were made, but a confiscation by people who insisted that outsiders had no right to copy such things. While we think of requests for repatriation as beginning in the 1980s, in the decade leading up to the passage of the Native American Graves Protection and Repatriation Act of 1990, in fact, Haudenosaunee (Iroquois) people first requested the return of their wampum belts from public institutions beginning in the 1890s. See Fenton, "Return of Eleven Wampum Belts"; the effort to recover wampum belts in the 1890s is mentioned on 403–4.

41. Kelly, *Koshare*, 49. See, for example, DesJarlait, "Appropriation of Native American Dance." DesJarlait (Red Lake Anishinaabe) writes: "The stereotypes that mark the Koshare dancers are not any different than professional models in headdresses, logos and mascots of professional sports teams like the Washington [Redskins] team or Disney's Peter Pan Indians. . . . It represents the dark side of colonialism that, by its nature, subjugates the things that culturally diverse people value, and turns them into a commodity that they can profit from." See also Houska, "Boy Scout Koshare Dancers." Houska (Couchiching First Nation of Canada) writes, "Sentimental racism is still racism."

42. Merrill, Ladd, and Ferguson, "The Return of the *Ahayu:da*," 528 and 529, fig. 4. The sequence of events of the next few months is discussed in detail (528–30). It involved directives that came from the highest levels of the Smithsonian, afraid of setting a precedent that could be used by fundamentalist Christians, creationists, and others who disagreed with the free dissemination of scientific and cultural knowledge.

43. The Zuni acknowledged that these masks had been made "voluntarily," with materials supplied primarily by the Smithsonian, yet still found their

display deeply problematic. Merrill, Ladd, and Ferguson, "The Return of the *Ahayu:da*," 540.

44. Merrill, Ladd, and Ferguson, "The Return of the *Ahayu:da*," 539.
45. Ladd, statement following Merrill, Ladd, and Ferguson, "The Return of the *Ahayu:da*," 547.
46. Nancy Rosoff, senior curator, Arts of the Americas, Brooklyn Museum, personal communication, June 10, 2020.
47. See appendix A, "Repatriation Claim of the Zuni Tribe at the Denver Art Museum," in Echo-Hawk, *Keepers of Culture*, 183–88. (No author is given, but it is described as a "joint project between the Zuni Heritage and Historic Preservation Office and the Native Arts Department at the Denver Art Museum, included here[in] as an example of a model claim under NAGPRA, April 2001" [77].)
48. Echo-Hawk, *Keepers of Culture*, 188.
49. Merrill, Ladd, and Ferguson, "The Return of the *Ahayu:da*."
50. See Castoriadis, *The Imaginary Institution of Society*; and Charles Taylor, *Modern Social Imaginaries*. In French cultural studies, "the imaginary" has more of a psychoanalytic dimension. Works in Native studies that implicitly critique the place of Native people in the American imaginary, without necessarily using the term, include P. Deloria, *Playing Indian*, and Krech, *The Ecological Indian*.
51. P. Deloria, *Playing Indian*, 21.
52. See McFeely, *Zuni and the American Imagination*. McFeely notes that "Stevenson, Cushing, and Culin were inventing their methods as they were inventing an anthropological version of Zuni, and so their stories are simultaneously those of Zuni, of anthropology, of three idiosyncratic Americans, and of America itself" (42). In her first chapter, McFeely chronicles the way in which "a grand teleological narrative" began when Esteban, the Black survivor of a Spanish shipwreck, came upon the "Seven Cities of Cibola" in 1539, when he beheld Zuni Pueblo (3–23).
53. Edwardy, "Snake Dance of the Moqui Indians"; Garland, "Among the Moki Indians"; Roosevelt, "The Hopi Snake Dance."
54. Dilworth, *Imagining Indians in the Southwest*, fully analyzes the place of the Hopi Snake Dance—as ethnography and spectacle—in the American cultural imaginary. Also relevant is the work of the writer Frank Waters (1902–1995). His *Masked Gods* (1970; a reprint of the 1950 original, republished for the counterculture generation) and *Book of the Hopi* (1969) both catered to a romantic ahistorical audience during the second half of the twentieth century. Both remain available today. For a critique from a rigorous anthropological and religious studies perspective, see Geertz, "Book of the Hopi."

55. For some reason, Warburg's brief touristic jaunt has fascinated modern scholars concerned with what Christopher Wood has so aptly characterized as art history's "ancestor cult." Indeed, Warburg is one of the most vexing of art history's patriarchal ancestors. See C. Wood, "Aby Warburg, *Homo victor*"; and Warburg, *Images from the Region of the Pueblo Indians*. Warburg's book illustrates and discusses what he calls the "Humiskachina" (Hemis katsina) dances that he witnessed at Oraibi in May 1896 (figs. 14–19, 22 and pp. 21–33). See also Freedberg, "Warburg's Mask." Freedberg's figure 2 illustrates the infamous picture of the thirty-year-old German art historian wearing the Hemis katsina mask.
56. See Meyers, "D. H. Lawrence and the American Indians"; Lawrence, "Indians and an Englishman" and "Taos"; and Bachrach, *D. H. Lawrence in New Mexico*.
57. The term has been around in German literature since the late eighteenth century. According to the Merriam-Webster dictionary, it was coined by German romantic novelist Jean Paul Richter in 1796. *Merriam-Webster*, s.v. "doppelgänger (*n.*)," www.merriam-webster.com/dictionary/doppelgänger, accessed July 5, 2021.
58. See Twin Strangers, https://twinstrangers.net, accessed July 5, 2021; and YouTube's official Twin Strangers channel: www.youtube.com/channel/UCeiNMDTRFR_QTiVHLYlufEw, accessed July 5, 2021.
59. *The Loneliest Whale: The Search for 52*, dir. Joshua Zeman (New York: Bleecker Street Films, 2021). The doubling of ship traffic from 1950 to 2000 has been accompanied by a doubling of anthropogenic noise every decade. See Frisk, "Noiseonomics"; and N. Jones, "Ocean Uproar."
60. Dilworth, *Imagining Indians in the Southwest*, 209.
61. Blackman and Hall, "The Afterimage and Image After"; Blackman, "Facing the Future, Envisioning the Past."
62. George Hunt (1854–1933) was the son of a British father and a Tlingit mother but grew up in the Kwakwa̱ka̱'wakw community of Fort Rupert, was fluent in the language, and married two local women. See Jacknis, "George Hunt."
63. Ostrowitz, *Privileging the Past*, 119. See also Jonaitis, *Chiefly Feasts*, 62–64.
64. S. Brown, *Native Visions*, fig. 7.20.
65. M. O'Neil, "Marked Faces, Displaced Bodies"; Karlin-Hayter, "Iconoclasm"; Arnade, *Beggars, Iconoclasts, and Civic Patriots*; Flood, "Between Cult and Culture"; Maggie Astor, "Protesters in Durham Topple a Confederate Monument," *New York Times*, August 14, 2017; Anna Dubenko, "Right and Left on Removal of Confederate Statues," *New York Times*, August 18, 2017.
66. Like a number of Galanin's works, *I think it goes like this?* exists in multiple forms. The Anchorage Museum has a white painted version (no.

2016.008.001). Anchorage Museum, "Artists: Nicholas Galanin," www.online collections.anchoragemuseum.org/#/artist/3561, accessed June 4, 2020.

67. See, for example, Rapaport, *The Sculpture of Louise Nevelson*.
68. C. Green, "Break Open This Container."
69. Nicholas Galanin, *Unceremonial Dance Mask, 21st Century*, July 29, 2017, video, 2:33, www.youtube.com/watch?v=CfD4l2o6y5U.
70. The art critic Tania Willard (Secwépemc First Nation, British Columbia) discusses other examples of Galanin's use of or reference to fake masks. See Willard, "Nicholas Galanin."
71. See, for example, Batkin, *The Native American Curio Trade*; Phillips, *Trading Identities*; Jonaitis and Glass. *The Totem Pole*; and Weigle, "Exposition and Mediation."
72. Colloquially called a "pocket pussy," and manufactured by the Fleshlight company, this object is a sheath the size of a large flashlight, with realistically molded vaginal lips. Fleshlight, "The Original Pocket Pussy," www.fleshlight .com/collections/pocket-pussy?utm_source=google&utm_medium=cpc &source=&gclid=Cj0KCQjww_f2BRCARIsAP3zarFQzpcnpE0QCNj5 YM6hnkBBuyUwPJ7GB8pxZOswxjdYmx60SJqlU6IaAnvFEALw_wcB, accessed June 8, 2020. For one made of yellow cedar, see *I Looooove Your Culture! Fine Woodworking*, in Willard, "Nicholas Galanin," 68.
73. Gómez-Peña, *The New World Border*, 10.

Bibliography

Abbott, Larry. *A Time of Visions: Interviews by Larry Abbott*. Ca. 1994–96. http://dev.cushing.org/abbott/main.htm.

Adair, John. *Navajo and Pueblo Silversmiths*. Norman: University of Oklahoma Press, 1944.

Albers, Patricia. "Symbiosis, Merger, and War: Contrasting Forms of Intertribal Relationships among Historic Plains Indians." In *The Political Economy of North American Indians*, edited by John H. Moore, 94–132. Norman: University of Oklahoma Press, 1993.

Alexander, Hartley Burr. *Sioux Indian Painting*. 2 vols. Nice, France: l'Edition d'Art C. Szwedzicki, 1938.

Alexander, Jeffrey C. "Toward a Theory of Cultural Trauma." In *Cultural Trauma and Collective Identity*, by Jeffrey C. Alexander, Ron Eyerman, Bernhard Giesen, Neil J. Smelser, and Piotr Sztompka, 1–30. Berkeley: University of California Press, 2004.

———. *Trauma: A Social Theory*. Cambridge, UK: Polity, 2012.

Alexander, Jeffrey C., Ron Eyerman, Bernhard Giesen, Neil J. Smelser, and Piotr Sztompka. *Cultural Trauma and Collective Identity*. Berkeley: University of California Press, 2004.

Allred, Randal. "Catharsis, Revision, and Re-enactment: Negotiating the Meaning of the American Civil War." *Journal of American Culture* 19, no. 4 (1996): 1–13.

American Institute for Conservation. "Code of Ethics and Guidelines for Practice." www.culturalheritage.org/about-conservation/code-of-ethics. Accessed March 21, 2022.

Anderson, Dean. "The Flow of European Trade Goods into the Western Great Lakes Region, 1715–1760." In *The Fur Trade Revisited: Selected Papers of the Sixth North American Fur Trade Conference*, edited by Jennifer Brown, W. J. Eccles,

and Donald Heldman, 93–115. East Lansing: Michigan State University Press, 1994.
Appadurai, Arjun, ed. *The Social Life of Things: Commodities in Cultural Perspective*. Cambridge: Cambridge University Press, 1986.
Appelbaum, Barbara. "Criteria for Treatment: Reversibility." *Journal of the American Institute for Conservation* 25, no. 2 (1987): 65–73.
Appiah, Kwame Anthony. *Cosmopolitanism: Ethics in a World of Strangers*. New York: W. W. Norton, 2006.
———. *The Lies That Bind: Rethinking Identity*. New York: W. W. Norton, 2018.
Armstrong, Leatrice. *Mary Wheelwright: Her Book*. Santa Fe, NM: Wheelwright Museum of the American Indian, 2016.
Arnade, Peter. *Beggars, Iconoclasts, and Civic Patriots: The Political Culture of the Dutch Revolt*. Ithaca, NY: Cornell University Press, 2008.
Averill, Lloyd. *A Man from Roundup: The Life and Times of Bill Holm*. Seattle: Burke Museum of Natural History and Culture, University of Washington, 2003. www.burkemuseum.org/sites/default/files/2019-10/Holm_Averill_ManFromRoundup.pdf.
Axtell, James. "The First Consumer Revolution." In *Beyond 1492: Encounters in Colonial North America*, 126–51. New York: Oxford University Press, 1992.
Bachrach, Arthur. *D. H. Lawrence in New Mexico*. Albuquerque: University of New Mexico Press, 2006.
Baggs, A. P., A. R. J. Jurica, and W. J. Sheils. "Stroud: Economic History." In *A History of the County of Gloucester*, vol. 11, *Bisley and Longtree Hundreds*, edited by N. M. Herbert and R. B. Pugh, 119–32. London: Victoria County History, 1976. British History Online, www.british-history.ac.uk/vch/glos/vol11/pp119-132.
Baillargeon, Morgan. *North American Aboriginal Hide Tanning: The Act of Transformation and Revival*. Ottawa: University of Ottawa Press, 2010.
Barker, Joanne. "Indian™ U.S.A." *Wicazo Sa Review* 18, no. 1 (2003): 25–79.
Barov, Zdravko. "The Reconstruction of a Greek Vase: The Kyknos Krater." *Studies in Conservation* 33, no. 4 (1988): 165–77.
Batkin, Jonathan. *The Native American Curio Trade in New Mexico*. Santa Fe, NM: Wheelwright Museum of the American Indian, 2008.
Beck, James, and Michael Daley. *Art Restoration: The Culture, the Business, and the Scandal*. London: John Murray, 1993.
Becker, Cynthia. "New Orleans Mardi Gras Indians: Mediating Racial Politics from the Backstreets to Main Street." *African Arts* 46, no. 2 (2013): 36–49.
Begay, D. Y. "Crossroads and Navajo Weaving: A Weaver's Narrative." In *Navajo Textiles: The Crane Collection at the Denver Museum of Nature and Science*, by Laurie Webster, Louise Stiver, D. Y. Begay, and Lynda Teller Pete, 78–86.

Denver: Denver Museum of Nature and Science; Boulder: University Press of Colorado, 2017.

———. "*Shi' sha' hane'* (My Story)." In *Woven by the Grandmothers: Nineteenth-Century Navajo Textiles from the National Museum of the American Indian*, edited by Eulalie H. Bonar, 13–27. Washington, DC: Smithsonian Institution Press in association with the National Museum of the American Indian, Smithsonian Institution, 1996.

Benjamin, Walter. "The Work of Art in the Age of Mechanical Reproduction." 1935. In *Illuminations: Essays and Reflections*, edited by Hannah Arendt, translated by Harry Zohn, 217–52. New York: Schocken Books, 1968.

———. "The Work of Art in the Age of Its Technological Reproducibility: Second Version." In *The Work of Art in the Age of Its Technological Reproducibility, and Other Writings on Media*, edited by Michael Jennings, Brigid Doherty, and Thomas Y. Levin, translated by Edmund Jephcott, Rodney Livingstone, Howard Eiland, et al., 19–55. Cambridge, MA: Belknap Press of Harvard University Press, 2008.

Bennett, Tony, and Patrick Joyce, eds. *Material Powers: Cultural Studies, History and the Material Turn*. London: Routledge, 2010.

Benson, Arlene. *The Noontide Sun: The Field Journals of the Reverend Stephen Bowers, Pioneer California Archaeologist*. Menlo Park, CA: Ballena Press, 1997.

Benson, Elizabeth. "The Robert Woods Bliss Collection of Pre-Columbian Art: A Memoir." In *Collecting the Pre-Columbian Past*, edited by Elizabeth Hill Boone, 15–34. Washington, DC: Dumbarton Oaks Research Library and Collection, 1993.

Berdan, Frances, and Jacqueline de Durand-Forest. *Matrícula de tributos (Códice de Moctezuma)*. Graz, Austria: Akademische Druck- und Verlagsanstalt, 1980.

Berlo, Janet Catherine. "Alberta Thomas, Navajo Pictorial Arts, and Ecocrisis in Dinétah." In *A Keener Perception: Ecocritical Studies in American Art History*, edited by Alan C. Braddock and Christoph Irmscher, 237–53. Tuscaloosa: University of Alabama Press, 2009.

———. "Anthropologies and Histories of Art: A View from the Terrain of Native North American Art History." In *Anthropologies of Art*, edited by Mariët Westermann, 178–92. Williamstown, MA: Clark Art Institute, 2005.

———. *Arthur Amiotte: Collages 1988–2006*. Santa Fe, NM: Wheelwright Museum of the American Indian, 2006.

———. "Dreaming of Double Woman: The Ambivalent Role of the Female Artist in North American Indian Mythology." *American Indian Quarterly* 17, no. 1 (1993): 31–43.

———. "Men of the Middle Ground: The Visual Culture of Native-White

Diplomacy in Eighteenth-Century North America." In *American Adversaries: West and Copley in a Transatlantic World*, edited by Emily Ballew Neff, 104–15. Houston: Museum of Fine Arts, 2013.

———. "Navajo Cosmoscapes—Up, Down, Within." *American Art* 25, no. 1 (2011): 10–13.

———. "Navajo Sandpainting in the Age of Cross-Cultural Replication." *Art History* 37, no. 4 (2014): 688–707.

———, ed. *Plains Indian Drawings, 1865–1935: Pages from a Visual History*. New York: Harry N. Abrams, 1996.

———. *Spirit Beings and Sun Dancers: Black Hawk's Vision of the Lakota World*. New York: George Braziller, in association with the New York State Historical Association, 2000.

———. "The Szwedzicki Portfolios of American Indian Art, 1929–1952." Pt. 2. *American Indian Art Magazine* 34, no. 3 (2009): 58–67.

———. *Teotihuacan Art Abroad: A Study of Metropolitan Style and Provincial Transformation in Incensario Workshops*. Oxford: British Archaeological Reports, 1984.

———. "Transgressing Borders: Miguel Covarrubias and the Development of Native American Art History." In *Miguel Covarrubias: Drawing a Cosmopolitan Line / Georgia O'Keeffe Museum*, edited by Carolyn Kastner, 76–99. Austin: University of Texas Press, 2014.

———. "Women of the Seneca Arts Project, 1935–1941: Beading across the Generations." Unpublished longer manuscript on Seneca beadwork, possession of the author, 2021.

Berlo, Janet Catherine, and Aldona Jonaitis. "From 'Artifakes' to 'Surrogates': The Replication of Northwest Coast Carving by Non-Natives." In *Unsettling Native Art Histories on the Northwest Coast*, edited by Kathryn Bunn-Marcuse and Aldona Jonaitis, 76–91. Seattle: University of Washington Press, 2020.

Berlo, Janet Catherine, and Ruth B. Phillips. *Native North American Art*. Oxford: Oxford University Press, 1998.

———. "'Our (Museum) World Turned Upside Down': Re-presenting Native American Arts." *Art Bulletin* 77, no. 1 (March 1995): 6–10.

Berlo, Janet Catherine, and Raymond Senuk. "Caveat Emptor: The Misrepresentation of Historic Maya Textiles." *Archaeology* 38, no. 2 (1985): 84.

Berman, Nina. "Orientalism, Imperialism, and Nationalism: Karl May's *Orientsyklus*." In *The Imperialist Imagination: German Colonialism and Its Legacy*, edited by Sara Friedrichsmeyer, Sara Lennox, and Susanne Zantop, 51–67. Ann Arbor: University of Michigan Press, 1998.

Bernstein, Bruce. "Potters and Patrons: The Creation of Pueblo Art Pottery." *American Indian Art Magazine* 20, no. 1 (1994): 70–79.

Bernstein, Bruce, and Karen Lucic. "Sacred Illusions: A Unique Collection of Zuni Pots Comes to Light." *American Indian Art Magazine* 27, no. 3 (2002): 50–57.

Blackman, Margaret. "Facing the Future, Envisioning the Past: Visual Literature and Contemporary Northwest Coast Masks." *Arctic Anthropology* 27, no. 2 (1990): 27–39.

Blackman, Margaret, and Edwin Hall Jr. "The Afterimage and Image After: Visual Documents and the Renaissance in Northwest Coast Art." *American Indian Art Magazine* 7, no. 2 (1982): 1–39.

Blomberg, Nancy. *Navajo Textiles: The William Randolph Hearst Collection*. Tucson: University of Arizona Press, 1988.

Boym, Svetlana. "Nostalgia and Its Discontents." In *The Collective Memory Reader*, edited by Jeffrey K. Olick, Vered Vinitzky-Seroussi, and Daniel Levy, 452–57. Oxford: Oxford University Press, 2011.

Brasser, Ted. "In Search of Métis Art." In *The New Peoples: Being and Becoming Métis in North America*, edited by Jacqueline Peterson and Jennifer Brown, 221–29. Winnipeg: University of Manitoba, 1985.

Breunlin, Rachel. "Bridge Work: Repatriating Mardi Gras Indian Photography with the House of Dance and Feathers." *African Arts* 46, no. 2 (2013): 50–61.

Brody, J. J. *Mimbres Painted Pottery*. Santa Fe, NM: School of American Research Press, 1977.

———. *Mimbres Painted Pottery*. Rev. ed. Santa Fe, NM: School of American Research Press, 2004.

Brody, J. J., Catherine Scott, and Steven A. LeBlanc. *Mimbres Pottery: Ancient Art of the American Southwest*. With an introduction by Tony Berlant. New York: Hudson Hills Press in association with the American Federation of Arts, 1983.

Brody, J. J., and Rina Swentzell. *To Touch the Past: The Painted Pottery of the Mimbres People*. New York: Hudson Hills Press, 1996.

Brooks, James F. *Captives and Cousins: Slavery, Kinship, and Community in the Southwest Borderlands*. Chapel Hill: University of North Carolina Press, 2002.

Brooks, Van Wyck. "On Creating a Usable Past." *Dial* 64, no. 4 (April 1918): 337–41.

Brown, Michael F. *Who Owns Native Culture?* Cambridge, MA: Harvard University Press, 2004.

Brown, Robert N. "Don't Bow Down on That Dirty Ground: A Photographic Essay of the Mardi Gras Indians of New Orleans." *Focus on Geography* 57, no. 3 (November 2014): 103–13.

Brown, Steve. "From Taquan to Klukwan: Tracing the Work of an Early Tlingit Master Artist." In *Faces, Voices and Dreams*, edited by Peter Corey, 157–75. Juneau: Alaska State Museum, 1987.

———. "In the Shadow of the Wrangell Master." *American Indian Art Magazine* 19, no. 4 (1994): 74–85.

———. *Native Visions: Evolution in Northwest Coast Art from the Eighteenth through the Twentieth Century*. Seattle: Seattle Art Museum in association with University of Washington Press, 1998.

———, ed. *The Spirit Within: Northwest Coast Native Art from the John H. Hauberg Collection*. New York: Rizzoli; Seattle: Seattle Art Museum, 1995.

Brownstone, Arni. "Anatomy of a Fake." *European Review of Native American Studies* 16, no. 2 (2002): 55–56.

———. "Animal Arrays and Geometric Pictorials: Commercial Aspects of Plains Paintings." *European Review of Native American Studies* 18, no. 1 (2004): 9–19.

Broyles-González, Yolanda. "Cheyennes in the Black Forest: A Social Drama." In *The Americanization of the Global Village: Essays in Comparative Popular Culture*, edited by Roger Rollin, 70–86. Bowling Green, OH: Bowling Green State University Popular Press, 1989.

Bruhns, Karen Olsen, and Nancy Kelker. *Faking the Ancient Andes*. Walnut Creek, CA: Left Coast Press, 2010.

Bryan, Bruce. "Excavation of the Galaz Ruin, Mimbres Valley, New Mexico." *Art and Archaeology* 32, no. 1–2 (July 1931): 35–42.

———. "San Nicolas Island, Treasure House of the Ancients." Pt. 1. *Art and Archaeology* 29, no. 4 (April 1930): 147–56.

———. "San Nicolas Island, Treasure House of the Ancients." Pt. 2. *Art and Archaeology* 29, no. 5 (May 1930): 215–23.

Bryant, Barry. *The Wheel of Time Sand Mandala: The Visual Scripture of Tibetan Buddhism*. 2nd ed. Ithaca, NY: Snow Lion Publications, 2003.

Buecker, Thomas, and R. Eli Paul, eds. *The Crazy Horse Surrender Ledger*. Lincoln: Nebraska State Historical Society, 1994.

Bunzel, Ruth. "Introduction to Zuñi Ceremonialism." In *Forty-Seventh Annual Report of the Bureau of American Ethnology, 1929–1930*, 465–545. Washington, DC: Government Printing Office, 1932.

———. "Zuñi Katcinas." In *Forty-Seventh Annual Report of the Bureau of American Ethnology, 1929–1930*, 837–1108. Washington, DC: Government Printing Office, 1932.

———. "Zuñi Origin Myths." In *Forty-Seventh Annual Report of the Bureau of American Ethnology, 1929–1930*, 545–609. Washington, DC: Government Printing Office, 1932.

———. "Zuñi Ritual Poetry." In *Forty-Seventh Annual Report of the Bureau of American Ethnology, 1929–1930*, 611–835. Washington, DC: Government Printing Office, 1932.

Bureau of American Ethnology. *Forty-Seventh Annual Report of the Bureau of American Ethnology, 1929–1930*. Washington, DC: Government Printing Office, 1932.

Burnett, E. K. *Inlaid Stone and Bone Artifacts from Southern California*. Contributions from the Museum of the American Indian, Heye Foundation, vol. 13. New York: Museum of the American Indian, Heye Foundation, 1944.

Calloway, Colin, Gerd Gemünden, and Susanne Zantop, eds. *Germans and Indians: Fantasies, Encounters, Projections*. Lincoln: University of Nebraska Press, 2002.

Carder, James, ed. *A Home of the Humanities: The Collecting and Patronage of Mildred and Robert Woods Bliss*. Washington, DC: Dumbarton Oaks Research Library and Collection, 2010.

Caruth, Cathy, ed. *Trauma : Explorations in Memory*. Baltimore: Johns Hopkins University Press, 1995.

Castoriadis, Cornelius. *The Imaginary Institution of Society*. Translated by Kathleen Blamey. Cambridge, MA: MIT Press, 1987.

Catlin, George. *Catlin's Notes of Eight Years' Travels and Residence in Europe, with His North American Indian Collection*. 2 vols. New York: Burgess, Stringer, 1848.

———. *George Catlin's Souvenir of the North American Indians: A Facsimile of the Original Album*. With an introductory essay and chronology by William Truettner. Tulsa, OK: Gilcrease Museum, 2003.

———. *Letters and Notes on the Manners, Customs, and Condition of the North American Indians*. 2 vols. London: privately printed, 1841.

Cessac, Leon de. "Observations sur des fétiches de pierre sculptés en forme d'animaux, découverts à l'île de San Nicolas (Californie)." *Revue d'ethnographie* 1 (1882): 30–40.

Chapman, Mary. "'Living Pictures': Women and *Tableaux Vivants* in Nineteenth-Century American Fiction and Culture." *Wide Angle* 18, no. 3 (July 1996): 22–52.

Clark, Garth. *Free Spirit: The New Native American Potter*. 's-Hertogenbosch, Netherlands: Stedelijk Museum 's-Hertogenbosch, 2006.

Codell, Julie, and Linda Hughes, eds. *Replication in the Long Nineteenth Century: Re-makings and Reproductions*. Edinburgh: Edinburgh University Press, 2018.

Coe, Ralph T. *Lost and Found Traditions: Native American Art 1965–1985*. Seattle: University of Washington Press, 1986.

———. *The Responsive Eye: Ralph T. Coe and the Collecting of American Indian Art*. With contributions by J. C. H. King and Judith Ostrowitz. New York: Metropolitan Museum of Art, 2003.

Colden, Cadwallader. *History of the Five Indian Nations of Canada* [. . .]. 2 vols.

London: printed for T. Osborne, 1747. Reprint, New York: New Amsterdam Book Company, 1902.

Colwell, Chip. *Plundered Skulls and Stolen Spirits: Inside the Fight to Reclaim Native America's Culture*. Chicago: University of Chicago Press, 2017.

Conn, Richard. *Circles of the World: Traditional Art of the Plains Indians*. Denver: Denver Art Museum, 1982.

———. *A Persistent Vision: Art of the Reservation Days*. Denver: Denver Art Museum, 1986.

Corbett, Ray. "Chumash Bone Whistles." In *The Foundations of Chumash Complexity*, edited by Jeanne Arnold, 65–73. Los Angeles: Cotsen Institute for Archaeology, University of California, Los Angeles, 2004.

Cornplanter, Jesse. *Legends of the Longhouse*. Philadelphia: J. B. Lippincott, 1938.

Cornu, Marie. "About Sacred Cultural Property: The Hopi Masks Case." *International Journal of Cultural Property* 20, no. 4 (2013): 451–66.

Cosgrove, Harriet, and Cornelius B. Cosgrove. *The Swarts Ruin: A Typical Mimbres Site in Southwestern New Mexico*. Papers of the Peabody Museum of American Archaeology and Ethnology, Harvard University, vol. 15, no. 1. Cambridge, MA: Peabody Museum, 1932.

Covarrubias, Miguel. *The Eagle, the Jaguar, and the Serpent: Indian Art of the Americas; North America: Alaska, Canada, and the United States*. New York: Alfred A. Knopf, 1954.

———. *Island of Bali*. New York: Alfred A. Knopf, 1938.

Covarrubias, Miguel, and Daniel F. Rubín de la Borbolla, eds. *El arte indígena de Norteamérica*. Mexico City: Fondo de Cultura Económica, 1945.

Coze, Paul. "Kachinas: Masked Dancers of the Southwest." *National Geographic* 112 (August 2, 1957): 218–36.

———. "Twenty-Four Hours of Magic . . . the Zuñi Shalako." *Arizona Highways*, 30, no. 11 (November 1954): 10–27, 34–35.

Crossley, Mimi, and E. Logan Wagner. "Ask Mexico's Masterly Brigido Lara: Is It a Fake?" *Connoisseur* 217, no. 905 (1987): 98–103.

Cumming, Elizabeth, and Wendy Kaplan. *The Arts and Crafts Movement*. New York: Thames and Hudson, 1991.

Cushing, Frank Hamilton. *Zuñi: Selected Writings of Frank Hamilton Cushing*. Edited by Jesse Green. Lincoln: University of Nebraska Press, 1979

———. "Zuñi Fetiches." In *Second Annual Report of the Bureau of American Ethnology, 1880–1881*, 9–44. Washington, DC: Government Printing Office, 1883.

Dammann, April. *Exhibitionist: Earl Stendahl, Art Dealer as Impresario*. Los Angeles: Angel City Press, 2011.

Dauenhauer, Nora Marks. "Tlingit *At.óow*: Traditions and Concepts." In *The Spirit*

Within: Northwest Coast Native Art from the John H. Hauberg Collection, edited by Steve Brown, 20–29. New York: Rizzoli; Seattle: Seattle Art Museum, 1995.

Davis, Carolyn O'Bagy. *Treasured Earth: Hattie Cosgrove's Mimbres Archaeology in the American Southwest*. Tucson, AZ: Sanpete Publications and Old Pueblo Archaeology Center, 1995.

Davis, William. *The Civil War Reenactors' Encyclopedia*. Guilford, CT: Lyons Press, 2002.

Deloria, Philip J. *Playing Indian*. New Haven, CT: Yale University Press, 1998.

Deloria, Vine, Jr. *Custer Died for Your Sins: An Indian Manifesto*. New York: Macmillan, 1969.

DesJarlait, Robert. "The Koshares and the Appropriation of Native American Dance." *Intercontinental Cry / IC*, December 15, 2015. https://intercontinentalcry.org/koshares-appropriation-native-american-dance.

DeWald, Louise. "Art of the Ancients—Revived." *Arizona Highways* 65, no. 8 (August 1989): 14–28.

Dillingham, Rick. *Fourteen Families in Pueblo Pottery*. Albuquerque: University of New Mexico Press, 2002.

Dilworth, Leah. *Imagining Indians in the Southwest: Persistent Visions of a Primitive Past*. Washington, DC: Smithsonian Institution Press, 1996.

Dippie, Brian. "Green Fields and Red Men." In *George Catlin and His Indian Gallery*, edited by George Gurney and Therese Heyman, 26–61. New York: W. W. Norton, 2002.

Douglas, Frederic, and René d'Harnoncourt. *Indian Art of the United States*. New York: Museum of Modern Art, 1941.

Doxtator, Deborah. *Fluffs and Feathers: An Exhibit on the Symbols of Indianness*. Brantford, ON: Woodland Cultural Center, 1988.

Duff, Wilson, Bill Holm, and Bill Reid. *Arts of the Raven: Masterworks by the Northwest Coast Indian*. Vancouver, BC: Vancouver Art Gallery, 1967.

Dunn, Dorothy. *American Indian Painting of the Southwest and Plains Areas*. Albuquerque: University of New Mexico Press, 1968.

Duro, Paul, ed. "Theorizing Imitation in a Global Context." Special issue, *Art History* 37, no. 4 (September 2014).

Echo-Hawk, Roger. *Keepers of Culture: Repatriating Cultural Items under the Native American Graves Protection and Repatriation Act*. Denver: Denver Art Museum, 2002.

Edelman, Bernard. "Pot-Hunting: The Looting of History." *Police Magazine* 4 (January 1, 1981): 23–26.

Edwards, Richard W., Jr. *Artifacts/Artifakes: Plains Indian Art Reproductions: The Law*. Cody, WY: Buffalo Bill Historical Center, 1993.

Edwardy, W. M. "Snake Dance of the Moqui Indians." *Harper's Weekly*, November 2, 1889.

Eisler, Benita. *The Red Man's Bones: George Catlin, Artist and Showman*. New York: W. W. Norton, 2013.

Ellis, Clyde. *A Dancing People: Powwow Culture on the Southern Plains*. Lawrence: University Press of Kansas, 2003.

———. *"More Indian than the Indians Themselves": A History of the Indian Lore Movement in the US, 1900–2020*. Norman: University of Oklahoma Press, forthcoming.

———. "'More Real than the Indians Themselves': The Early Years of the Indian Lore Movement in the United States." *Montana: The Magazine of Western History* 58, no. 3 (2008): 3–22, 92–94.

Elmore, Steve. *In Search of Nampeyo: The Early Years, 1875–1892*. Santa Fe, NM: Spirit Bird Press, 2015.

Elsasser, Albert, and Robert Heizer. *The Archaeology of Bowers Cave, Los Angeles County, California*. Reports of the University of California Archaeological Survey, no. 59. Berkeley: University of California Archaeological Survey, 1963.

Enote, Jim. "Buyer Beware." *Indian Country Today*, March 13, 2013.

Enwezor, Okwui, Carlos Basualdo, Ute Meta Bauer, Susanne Ghez, Sarat Maharaj, Mark Nash, and Octavio Zaya, eds. *Creolité and Creolization: Documenta_Platform 3*. Ostfildern-Ruit: Hatje Cantz Publishers, 2003.

Epple, Carolyn. "Coming to Terms with Navajo *Nádleehí*: A Critique of *Berdache*, 'Gay,' 'Alternate Gender,' and 'Two-Spirit.'" *American Ethnologist* 25, no. 2 (May 1998): 267–90.

Erdoes, Richard. *The Sun Dance People*. New York: Random House, 1972.

Esperanza, Jennifer. "Outsourcing Otherness: Crafting and Marketing Culture in the Global Handicrafts Market." In *Hidden Hands in the Market: Ethnographies of Fair Trade, Ethical Consumption, and Corporate Social Responsibility*, edited by Geert De Neve, Peter Luetchford, Jeffrey Pratt, and Donald C. Wood, 71–95. Bingley, UK: Emerald Publishing, 2008.

Ewers, John. "The Awesome Bear in Plains Indian Art." *American Indian Art Magazine* 7, no. 3 (1982): 36–45.

———. "The Emergence of the Plains Indian as the Symbol of the North American Indian." In *Annual Report of the Board of Regents of the Smithsonian Institution*, 1964, 531–44. Washington, DC: Government Printing Office, 1965.

———. "George Catlin, Painter of Indians and the West." In *Annual Report of the Board of Regents of the Smithsonian Institution*, 1955, 483–528. Washington, DC: Government Printing Office, 1956.

———. *Indian Art in Pipestone: George Catlin's Portfolio in the British Museum*. London: British Museum, 1979.

———. *Plains Indian Painting: A Description of an Aboriginal Art*. Palo Alto, CA: Stanford University Press, 1939.

Fairservis, Walter A., Jr. *Exotic Art, from Ancient and Primitive Civilizations: Collection of Jay C. Leff*. Pittsburgh: Carnegie Institute, 1959.

Fane, Diana, Ira Jacknis, and Lise Breen. *Objects of Myth and Memory: American Indian Art at the Brooklyn Museum*. Brooklyn, NY: Brooklyn Museum in association with University of Washington Press, 1991.

Feder, Norman. *American Indian Art*. New York: Harry N. Abrams, 1971.

———. "Old Time Sioux Costume." *American Indian Hobbyist* 4, no. 3–4 (December 1957): 23–30.

Feder, Norman, and Milford Chandler. "Grizzly Claw Necklaces." *American Indian Tradition* 8, no. 1 (1961): 7–16.

Feest, Christian F. *Frederick Weygold: Artist and Ethnographer of North American Indians*. Altenstadt, Germany: ZKF Publishers, 2017.

———, ed. *Indians and Europe: An Interdisciplinary Collection of Essays*. Aachen, West Germany: Rader Verlag, 1987.

———, ed. *Studies in American Indian Art: A Memorial Tribute to Norman Feder*. Altenstadt, Germany: European Review of Native American Studies, 2001.

Fenton, William. "Return of Eleven Wampum Belts to the Six Nations Iroquois Confederacy on Grand River, Canada." *Ethnohistory* 36, no. 4 (1989): 392–410.

Fewkes, Jesse Walter. *Additional Designs on Prehistoric Mimbres Pottery*. Smithsonian Miscellaneous Collections, vol. 76. Washington, DC: Smithsonian Institution, 1924.

———. "Animal Figures in Prehistoric Pottery from the Mimbres Valley, New Mexico." *American Anthropologist* 18, no. 4 (1916): 535–45.

———. *Archaeology of the Lower Mimbres Valley, New Mexico*. Smithsonian Miscellaneous Collections, vol. 63. Washington, DC: Smithsonian Institution, 1914.

———. *Designs on Prehistoric Pottery from the Mimbres Valley, New Mexico*. Smithsonian Miscellaneous Collections, vol. 74. Washington, DC: Smithsonian Institution, 1923.

———. *The Mimbres: Art and Archaeology*. Albuquerque, NM: Avanyu Publishing, 1989.

Flint Institute of Arts. *The Art of the Great Lakes Indians*. Flint, MI: Flint Institute of Arts, 1973.

Flood, Finbarr Barry. "Between Cult and Culture: Bamiyan, Islamic Iconoclasm, and the Museum." *Art Bulletin* 84, no. 4 (2002): 641–59.

Florian, Mary-Lou, Dale Kronkright, and Ruth Norton. *The Conservation of Artifacts Made from Plant Materials*. Los Angeles: Getty Conservation Institute, 1990.

Foster, Robert. *Coca-Globalization: Following Soft Drinks from New York to New Guinea*. New York: Palgrave Macmillan, 2008.

Francis, Daniel. *The Imaginary Indian: The Image of the Indian in Canadian Culture*. Vancouver, BC: Arsenal Pulp Press, 1992.

Franciscan Fathers. *An Ethnologic Dictionary of the Navaho Language*. St. Michaels, AZ: Franciscan Fathers, 1910.

Fred Jones Jr. Museum of Art and Philbrook Museum of Art. *The Eugene B. Adkins Collection: Selected Works*. Norman: University of Oklahoma Press, 2011.

Freedberg, David. "Warburg's Mask: A Study in Idolatry." In *Anthropologies of Art*, edited by Mariët Westermann, 3–25. Williamstown, MA: Clark Art Institute, 2005.

Friday, Chris. *Lelooska: The Life of a Northwest Coast Artist*. Seattle: University of Washington Press, 2003.

Friess, Horace. "Professor Bush and His Collection of Religion and Culture." *Columbia University Quarterly*, April 1941, 159–64.

Frisk, George V. "Noiseonomics: The Relationship between Ambient Noise Levels in the Sea and Global Economic Trends." *Scientific Reports* 2, no. 437 (June 2012): 1–4. https://doi.org/10.1038/srep00437.

Galban, Michael. *The Historical Art of Robert Griffing*. Vol. 3, *An Amazing Journey*. Panama, NY: Paramount Press, 2018.

———. "The Oldest Surviving Quilled Bag in America." *Iroquoia*, no. 4 (2018): 77–104.

Gallagher, Marsha, and David Hunt. *Karl Bodmer's America*. Lincoln: University of Nebraska Press, 1984.

Gamble, Lynn. "Fact or Forgery: Dilemmas in Museum Collections." *Museum Anthropology* 25, no. 2 (2002): 3–20.

———, ed. *First Coastal Californians*. Santa Fe, NM: School for Advanced Research Press, 2015.

———. "Shell Beads as Adornment and Money." Chap. 12 in *First Coastal Californians*, edited by Lynn Gamble. Santa Fe, NM: School for Advanced Research Press, 2015.

Garland, Hamlin. "Among the Moki Indians." *Harper's Weekly*, August 15, 1896.

Geertz, Armin. "Book of the Hopi: The Hopi's Book?" *Anthropos* 78, no. 3–4 (1983): 547–56.

Gendron, Val. *Behind the Zuni Masks*. New York: Longmans, Green, 1958.

Giammattei, Victor, and Nanci Greer Reichert. *Art of a Vanished Race: The Mimbres Classic Black-on-White*. Woodland, CA: Dillon-Tyler, 1975.

Ginsburg, Carlo. "Vetoes and Compatibilities." *Art Bulletin* 77, no. 4 (1995): 534–36.

Gladstone, Mara, and Janet Catherine Berlo. "The Body in the (White) Box:

Corporeal Ethics and Museum Representation." In *Routledge Companion to Museum Ethics: Redefining Ethics for the Twenty-First-Century Museum*, edited by Janet Marstine, 353–78. New York: Routledge, 2011.

Glass, Aaron. "Conspicuous Consumption: An Intercultural History of the Kwakwa̱ka̱'wakw Hamat'sa." PhD diss., New York University, 2006.

Gómez-Peña, Guillermo. *The New World Border: Prophecies, Poems, and Loqueras for the End of the Century*. San Francisco: City Lights Books, 1996.

Graburn, Nelson, ed. *Ethnic and Tourist Arts: Cultural Expressions from the Fourth World*. Berkeley: University of California Press, 1976.

Graham, Laura R., and H. Glenn Penny, eds. *Performing Indigeneity: Global Histories and Contemporary Experiences*. Lincoln: University of Nebraska Press, 2014.

Graymont, Barbara, ed. *Fighting Tuscarora: The Autobiography of Chief Clinton Rickard*. Syracuse, NY: Syracuse University Press, 1973.

Green, Christopher. "Break Open This Container." *Art in America*, January 1, 2018. www.artnews.com/art-in-america/features/break-open-this-container-63317.

Green, Jesse, ed. Introduction to *Zuñi: Selected Writings of Frank Hamilton Cushing*, 3–34. Lincoln: University of Nebraska Press, 1979.

Green, Rayna. "The Tribe Called Wannabee: Playing Indian in America and Europe." *Folklore* 99, no. 1 (1988): 30–55.

Greene, Candace. *Silver Horn: Master Illustrator of the Kiowas*. Norman: University of Oklahoma Press, 2001.

Greene, Candace, and Thomas Drescher. "The Tipi with Battle Pictures: The Kiowa Tradition of Intangible Property Rights." *Trademark Reporter* 84, no. 4 (July 1994): 418–33.

Greenfield, Amy Butler. *A Perfect Red: Empire, Espionage, and the Quest for the Color of Desire*. New York: Harper Perennial, 2005.

Guth, Reese, and Eric van den Berghe. "The Potters of San Juan de Oriente: Portraits and Stories." Unpublished manuscript, 2007. In author's possession, obtained from Reese Guth, July 13, 2011.

Halbwachs, Maurice. *On Collective Memory*. Edited and translated by Lewis Coser. Chicago: University of Chicago Press, 1992.

Haldeman, Peter. "Spreading Out in Santa Fe." *Architectural Digest*, June 2008.

Hall, Stuart. "Whose Heritage? Un-settling 'The Heritage,' Re-imagining the Post-Nation." *Third Text* 13, no. 49 (1999): 3–13.

Hallowell, A. Irving. "American Indians, White and Black: The Phenomenon of Transculturalization." *Current Anthropology* 4, no. 5 (1963): 519–31.

Halpern, Katherine S., and Susan Brown McGreevy, eds. *Washington Matthews: Studies of Navajo Culture, 1880–1894*. Albuquerque: University of New Mexico Press, 1997.

Halpin, Marjorie. Introduction to *Letters and Notes on the Manners, Customs, and*

Conditions of the North American Indians, by George Catlin, 1:vii–xiv. Reprint, New York: Dover, 1973.

———. "Northwest Coast Indigenous Art." In *The Canadian Encyclopedia*, Historica Canada, February 7, 2006. www.canadianencyclopedia.com/en/article/northwest-coast-aboriginal-art.

Handler, Richard, and William Saxton. "Dyssimulation: Reflexivity, Narrative, and the Quest for Authenticity in 'Living History.'" *Cultural Anthropology* 3, no. 3 (August 1988): 242–60.

Haney-López, Ian. "The Social Construction of Race." In *Critical Race Theory: The Cutting Edge*, edited by Richard Delgado and Jean Stefancic, 163–75. 2nd ed. Philadelphia: Temple University Press, 2000.

Hanson, James. *Firearms of the Fur Trade*. Vol. 1 of *The Encyclopedia of Trade Goods*. Chadron, NE: Museum of the Fur Trade, 2011.

Hardy, Matthew, ed. *The Venice Charter Revisited: Modernism, Conservation, and Tradition in the 21st Century*. Newcastle upon Tyne, UK: Cambridge Scholars, 2008.

Harrison, Rodney. *Heritage: Critical Approaches*. New York: Routledge, 2013.

Hauptman, Laurence. *Coming Full Circle: The Seneca Nation of Indians, 1848–1934*. Norman: University of Oklahoma Press, 2019.

———. *In the Shadow of Kinzua: The Seneca Nation of Indians since World War II*. Syracuse, NY: Syracuse University Press, 2014.

———. *The Iroquois and the New Deal*. Syracuse, NY: Syracuse University Press, 1988.

———. "The Iroquois School of Art: Arthur C. Parker and the Seneca Arts Project, 1935–1941." *New York History*, July 1979, 282–312.

Hawker, Ron. *Tales of Ghosts: First Nations Art in British Columbia, 1922–1961*. Vancouver: University of British Columbia Press, 2003.

Hedlund, Ann Lane. "Commercial Materials in Modern Navajo Rugs." *Textile Museum Journal* 25 (1986): 83–94.

———. *Gloria F. Ross and Modern Tapestry*. New Haven, CT: Yale University Press, 2010.

Heizer, Robert. "Aboriginal Use of Bitumen by the California Indians." *California Division of Mines Bulletin* 118 (April 1943): 74.

Hellman, Geoffrey. "Profiles—Imperturbable Noble: René d'Harnoncourt." *New Yorker*, May 7, 1960, 49–112.

Her Many Horses, Emil, ed. *Identity by Design: Tradition, Change, and Celebration in Native Women's Dresses*. Washington, DC: National Museum of the American Indian, Smithsonian Institution, 2007.

Herem, Barry. "A Historic Tlingit Artist: The Trail of His Work and Its Modern Re-creation." *American Indian Art Magazine* 15, no. 3 (1990): 48–55.

Hewitt, Marsha. "Cyborgs, Drag Queens, and Goddesses: Emancipatory Regressive Paths in Feminist Theory." *Method and Theory in the Study of Religion* 5, no. 2 (1993): 135–54.
Heye, George. *Certain Aboriginal Artifacts from San Miguel Island, California*. Indian Notes and Monographs, vol. 7, no. 4. New York: Museum of the American Indian, Heye Foundation, 1921.
Hill, Cephas, and William Fenton. "Reviving Indian Arts among the Senecas." *Indians at Work*, June 15, 1935, 13–15.
Hirsch, Harry. "New York State Indians." *Social Welfare Bulletin* (New York State Department of Social Welfare) 7, no. 1–2 (January 1936): 1.
Hobsbawm, Eric, and Terence Ranger, eds. *The Invention of Tradition*. Cambridge: Cambridge University Press, 1984.
Hockman, Ned. "Motion Picture Production at the University of Oklahoma." *Journal of the University Film Producers Association* 6, no. 2 (1953): 3–9.
Hodge, Frederick Webb. *The History of Hawikuh, New Mexico*. Los Angeles: Southwest Museum, 1927.
Hoesterey, Ingeborg. *Pastiche: Cultural Memory in Film, Art, Literature*. Bloomington: Indiana University Press, 2001.
Hofer, Johannes. "Medical Dissertation on Nostalgia [1688]." Translated by Carolyn Kiser Anspach. *Bulletin of the Institute of the History of Medicine* 2, no. 6 (1934): 376–91.
Holler, Deborah R. "Fashion, Nationhood, and Identity: The Textile Artistry of Caroline G. Parker." *American Indian Art Magazine* 37, no. 4 (2012): 58–65.
———. "The Remarkable Caroline G. Parker Mountpleasant, Seneca Wolf Clan." *Western New York Heritage* 14 (2011): 9–18.
Holley, Linda. *Tipis, Tepees, Teepees: History and Design of the Cloth Tipi*. Layton, UT: Gibbs Smith, 2007.
Hollinger, R. Eric, Edwell John Jr., Harold Jacobs, Lora Moran-Collins, Carolyn Thome, Jonathan Zastrow, Adam Metallo, Günter Waibel, and Vince Rossi. "Tlingit-Smithsonian Collaborations with 3D Digitization of Cultural Objects." *Museum Anthropology Review* 7, no. 1–2 (2013): 201–53.
Holm, Bill. "Four Bears' Shirt: Some Problems with the Smithsonian Catlin Collection." In *Artifacts/Artifakes: The Proceedings of the 1984 Plains Indian Seminar*, edited by George P. Horse Capture Sr. and Suzanne G. Tyler, 43–59. Cody, WY: Buffalo Bill Historical Center, 1992.
———. *Northwest Coast Indian Art: An Analysis of Form*. Seattle: University of Washington Press, 1965.
Holmes, William Henry. "Catlinite." In *Handbook of American Indians North of Mexico*, edited by Frederick Webb Hodge, 217–19. Washington, DC: Government Printing Office, 1907.

Holmström, Kirsten. *Monodrama, Attitudes, Tableaux Vivants: Studies on Some Trends of Theatrical Fashion, 1770–1815*. Stockholm: Almqvist och Wiksell, 1967.

Hooper, Steven. "A Cross-Cultural Theory of Relics: On Understanding Religion, Bodies, Artefacts, Images and Art." *World Art* 4, no. 2 (July 2014): 175–207.

Hopkins, Candice. "On the Commodification of Native Culture." In *Without Boundaries: Visual Conversations*, edited by Sonya Kelliher-Combs, 32-40. Anchorage, AK: Anchorage Museum, 2016.

Horse Capture, George P., Sr., and Suzanne G. Tyler, eds. *Artifacts/Artifakes: The Proceedings of the 1984 Plains Indian Seminar*. Cody, WY: Buffalo Bill Historical Center, 1992.

Horse Capture, Joe D., and George P. Horse Capture Sr. *Beauty, Honor, and Tradition: The Legacy of Plains Indian Shirts*. Washington, DC: National Museum of the American Indian, Smithsonian Institution, 2001.

Horton, Jessica. *Earth Diplomacy: Indigenous American Art and Reciprocity, 1953–1973*. Durham, NC: Duke University Press, forthcoming, 2024.

———. "Ojibwa *Tableaux Vivants*: George Catlin, Robert Houle, and Transcultural Materialism." *Art History* 39, no. 1 (February 2016): 124–51.

———. "Performing Paint, Claiming Space: The Santa Fe Indian School Posters on Paul Coze's Stage in Paris 1935." *Transatlantica—Revue d'études américaines / American Studies Journal* 32, no. 2 (2017). https://journals.openedition.org/transatlantica/11220#article-11220.

———. "Rebalancing the Cold War: Diné Sandpainting and Earth Diplomacy." *Art Bulletin* 104, no. 3 (2022): 84–116.

Horton, Jessica, and Janet Catherine Berlo. "Pueblo Painting in 1932: Folding Narratives of Native Art into American Art History." In *A Companion to American Art*, edited by John Davis, Jennifer Greenhill, and Jason LaFountain, 264–80. Chichester, West Sussex, UK: Wiley, Blackwell, 2015.

Houska, Tara. "Boy Scout Koshare Dancers Need to Stop Stealing from Natives." *Indian Country Today*, February 12, 2016. https://indiancountrytoday.com/archive/houska-boy-scout-koshare-dancers-need-to-stop-stealing-from-natives.

Hoxie, Frederick. *The Crow*. New York: Chelsea House Publishers, 1989.

Hudson, Travis, and Thomas Blackburn. *The Material Culture of the Chumash Interaction Sphere*. Vol. 4, *Ceremonial Paraphernalia, Games, and Amusements*. Menlo Park, CA: Ballena Press, 1986.

Huhndorf, Shari. *Going Native: Indians in the American Cultural Imagination*. Ithaca, NY: Cornell University Press, 2001.

Hunhoff, Bernie. "The Story behind the Square." *South Dakota Magazine*, April 2013. www.southdakotamagazine.com/main-street-square.

Hunt, Ben. "Indian Moccasins." *Boys' Life*, November 1947, 10–11.

Hutchinson, Elizabeth. *The Indian Craze: Primitivism, Modernism, and Transculturation in American Art, 1890–1915*. Durham, NC: Duke University Press, 2009.

Isaac, Gwyneira. "Perclusive Alliances: Digital 3-D, Museums, and the Reconciling of Culturally Diverse Knowledges." *Current Anthropology* 56, no. S12 (December 2015): S286–96.

———. "Whose Idea Was This? Museums, Replicas, and the Reproduction of Knowledge." *Current Anthropology* 52, no. 2 (April 2011): 211–33.

Jacknis, Ira. "George Hunt, Collector of Indian Specimens." In *Chiefly Feasts: The Enduring Kwakiutl Potlatch*, edited by Aldona Jonaitis, 177–224. Seattle: University of Washington Press, 1991.

Jacques, Freida. "Discipline of a Good Mind." In *Neighbor to Neighbor, Nation to Nation: Readings about the Relationship of the Onondaga Nation with Central New York, USA*, edited by Neighbors of the Onondaga Nation. Syracuse, NY: Neighbors of the Onondaga Nation, 2014.

———. "Good Minds." Friends of Ganondagan, 2020. https://ganondagan.org/learn/good-mind.

Jenks, Albert. "Geometric Designs on Mimbres Bowls." *Art and Archaeology* 33, no. 3 (May 1932): 137–39.

Johnson, Anna. "Coco Fusco and Guillermo Gómez-Peña." *Bomb Magazine*, January 1, 1993. https://bombmagazine.org/articles/coco-fusco-and-guillermo-gómez-peña.

Johnson, Grace, ed. *From Paquimé to Mata Ortiz: The Legacy of the Ancient Casas Grandes*. San Diego, CA: San Diego Museum of Man, 2001.

Johnson, William. *The Papers of Sir William Johnson*. Vol. 2. Prepared for publication by James Sullivan. Albany: University of the State of New York, 1922.

Jonaitis, Aldona. *Art of the Northwest Coast*. Seattle: University of Washington Press, 2006.

———, ed. *Chiefly Feasts: The Enduring Kwakiutl Potlatch*. Seattle: University of Washington Press, 1991.

Jonaitis, Aldona, and Aaron Glass. *The Totem Pole: An Intercultural History*. Seattle: University of Washington Press, 2010.

Jones, Nicola. "Ocean Uproar: Saving Marine Life from a Barrage of Noise." *Nature* 568 (April 10, 2019): 158–61.

Jones, Starr West. *Reginald and Gladys Laubin, American Indian Dancers*. Urbana: University of Illinois Press, 2000.

Jules-Rosette, Bennetta. *The Messages of Tourist Art*. New York: Plenum, 1984.

Kabotie, Fred. *Designs from the Ancient Mimbreños with a Hopi Interpretation*. Flagstaff, AZ: Northland Press, 1982. First published 1949 by Grabhorn Press (San Francisco).

Kahng, Eik, ed. *The Repeating Image: Multiples in French Painting from David to Matisse*. Baltimore: Walters Art Museum, 2007.

Kalm, Peter. *Travels into North America* [. . .]. Translated by John Reinhold Forster. 2 vols. London: T. Lowndes, 1773. Online facsimile of the second edition at www.americanjourneys.org/aj-117a/summary/index.asp.

Kalshoven, Petra. *Crafting "the Indian": Knowledge, Desire, and Play in Indianist Reenactment*. New York: Berghahn Books, 2012.

———. "Things in the Making: Playing with Imitation." *Etnofoor* 22, no. 1 (2010): 59–74.

Kammen, Michael. *Mystic Chords of Memory: The Transformation of Tradition in American Culture*. New York: Alfred A. Knopf, 1991.

Karlin-Hayter, Patricia. "Iconoclasm." In *The Oxford History of Byzantium*, edited by Cyril Mango, 153–62. New York: Oxford University Press, 2002.

Kasprycki, Sylvia, ed. *On the Trails of the Iroquois*. Berlin: Nicolai, 2013.

———. "Quilled Drawstring Pouches of the Northeastern Woodlands." *American Indian Art Magazine* 23, no. 3 (1997): 64–75.

Kastner, Carolyn, ed. *Miguel Covarrubias: Drawing a Cosmopolitan Line / Georgia O'Keeffe Museum*. Austin: University of Texas Press, 2014.

Keats, Jonathon. *Forged: Why Fakes Are the Great Art of Our Age*. Oxford: Oxford University Press, 2013.

Keleman, Pal. *Medieval American Art*. 2 vols. New York: Macmillan, 1943–44.

Kelker, Nancy, and Karen Olsen Bruhns. *Faking Ancient Mesoamerica*. Walnut Creek, CA: Left Coast Press, 2010.

Kelly, Jack. *Koshare*. Boulder, CO: Pruett Publishing, 1975.

Kent, Kate Peck. *Navajo Weaving: Three Centuries of Change*. Santa Fe, NM: School of American Research Press, 1985.

Kidd, Kenneth E. "The Cloth Trade and the Indians of the Northeast during the Seventeenth and Eighteenth Centuries." *Annual*, Art and Archaeology Division, Royal Ontario Museum, Toronto, 1961, 48–56.

Kidwell, Clara Sue. "Every Last Dishcloth: The Prodigious Collecting of George Heye." In *Collecting Native America, 1870–1960*, edited by Shepard Krech and Barbara Hail, 232–58. Washington, DC: Smithsonian Institution Press, 1999.

King, Charles S. *Spoken through Clay: Native Pottery of the Southwest*. Santa Fe: Museum of New Mexico Press, 2017.

King, Charles S., and Richard L. Spivey. *The Life and Art of Tony Da*. Tucson, AZ: Rio Nuevo Publishers, 2011.

King, J. C. H. "Woodlands Artifacts from the Studio of Benjamin West." *American Indian Art Magazine* 17, no. 1 (1991): 34–47.

Kirk, Ruth F. "Introduction to Zuni Fetishism." 5 pts. *El Palacio: The Magazine of the Museum of New Mexico* 50, no. 6 (June 1943): 117–29; no. 7 (July 1943):

146–59; no. 8 (August 1943): 183–98; no. 9 (September 1943): 206–19; no. 10 (October 1943): 235–45.

Koehler, Rhiannon. "Hostile Nations: Quantifying the Destruction of the Sullivan-Clinton Genocide of 1779." *American Indian Quarterly* 42, no. 4 (2018): 427–53.

Koerper, Henry. "More on Arthur Sanger's Skullduggeries." *Pacific Coast Archaeological Society Quarterly* 52, no. 2 (2016): 17–42.

Kopytoff, Igor. "The Cultural Biography of Things: Commoditization as Social Process." In *The Social Life of Things: Commodities in Cultural Perspective*, edited by Arjun Appadurai, 64–91. Cambridge: Cambridge University Press, 1986.

Krech, Shepard. *The Ecological Indian: Myth and History*. New York: W. W. Norton, 2000.

Kubler, George. *The Shape of Time: Remarks on the History of Things*. New Haven, CT: Yale University Press, 1962.

Lange, Patricia Fogelman. "The Spiritual World of Franc Johnson Newcomb." *New Mexico Historical Review* 73, no. 3 (July 1998): 253–74.

Laubin, Reginald, and Gladys Laubin. *Indian Dances of North America*. Norman: University of Oklahoma Press, 1977.

———. *The Indian Tipi: Its History, Construction, and Use*. Norman: University of Oklahoma Press, 1957.

Lawrence, D. H. "Indians and an Englishman." *Dial* 74 (1923): 144–52.

———. "Taos." *Dial* 74 (1923): 251–54.

LeBlanc, Steven A. *Painted by a Distant Hand: Mimbres Pottery from the American Southwest*. Cambridge, MA: Peabody Museum Press, Harvard University, 2004.

Lee, Georgia. "Fake Effigies from the Southern California Coast? Robert Heizer and the Effigy Controversy." *Journal of California and Great Basin Anthropology* 15, no. 2 (1993): 195–215.

Lee, Lynn, and Narayan Khandekar. "An Analytical Approach to Detect Non-original Embellishments on Classic Mimbres Vessels." *Studies in Conservation* 57, no. 4 (2012): 218–26.

Lenain, Thierry. *Art Forgery: The History of a Modern Obsession*. London: Reaktion Books, 2011.

Lévi-Strauss, Claude. *The Savage Mind*. Chicago: University of Chicago Press, 1970.

Lévy, Sophie. *A Transatlantic Avant-Garde: American Artists in Paris, 1918–1939*. Giverny, France: Musée d'Art Américain Giverny in association with University of California Press, 2003.

Lippard, Lucy, and Maurice Berger. *The Transportation of Place*. New York: Aperture Press, 2006.

Lipsitz, George. "Mardi Gras Indians: Carnival and Counter-Narrative in Black New Orleans." *Cultural Critique*, no. 10 (1988): 99–121.

Loh, Maria H. "New and Improved: Repetition and Originality in Italian Baroque Practice and Theory." *Art Bulletin* 86, no. 3 (September 2004): 477–504.

Lowe, Truman T., and Paul Chaat Smith, eds. *James Luna: Emendatio*. Washington, DC: National Museum of the American Indian, Smithsonian Institution, 2005.

Lowell, Susan, Jim Hills, Jorge Quintana Rodriguez, Walter Parks, and Michael Wisner. *The Many Faces of Mata Ortiz*. Tucson, AZ: Rio Nuevo Publishers, 1999.

Lowenthal, David. *The Heritage Crusade and the Spoils of History*. Cambridge: Cambridge University Press, 1998.

Lowie, Robert. *The Religion of the Crow Indians*. Anthropological Papers of the American Museum of Natural History, vol. 25, pt. 2. New York: American Museum of Natural History, 1922.

Lucic, Karen, and Bruce Bernstein. "In Pursuit of the Ceremonial: The Laboratory of Anthropology's 'Master Collection' of Zuni Pottery." *Journal of the Southwest* 50, no. 1 (2008): 1–102.

Lutz, Hartmut. "German Indianthusiasm: A Socially Constructed German National(ist) Myth." In *Germans and Indians: Fantasies, Encounters, Projections*, edited by Colin Calloway, Gerd Gemünden, and Susanne Zantop, 167–84. Lincoln: University of Nebraska Press, 2002.

Mails, Thomas E. *The Mystic Warriors of the Plains*. New York: Doubleday, 1972.

Malin, Edward. "Lelooska." *Smoke Signals* 49 (1966): 3–17.

———. *Masks and Totems: A Northwest Coast Odyssey*. Privately printed, 2012.

Matthews, Washington. "The Mountain Chant: A Navajo Ceremony." In *Fifth Annual Report of the Bureau of Ethnology, 1883–84*, edited by J. W. Powell, xliv–xlvii. Washington, DC: Smithsonian Institution, 1887.

———. *The Mountain Chant: A Navajo Ceremony*. Reprint, Salt Lake City: University of Utah Press, 1997.

———. "Mythic Dry-Paintings of the Navajos." *American Naturalist* 19, no. 10 (October 1885): 931–39. Reprinted in *Washington Matthews: Studies of Navajo Culture, 1880–1894*, edited by Katherine S. Halpern and Susan Brown McGreevy, 221–28. Albuquerque: University of New Mexico Press, 1997.

Maurer, Evan. *Visions of the People: A Pictorial History of Plains Indian Life*. Minneapolis: Minneapolis Institute of Art, 1992.

Maybury-Lewis, David. *Millennium: Tribal Wisdom and the Modern World*. New York: Viking Press, 1992.

McCoy, Ronald. *Kiowa Memories: Images from Indian Territory, 1880*. Santa Fe, NM: Morning Star Gallery, 1987.

———. "Nampeyo: Giving the Indian Artist a Name." In *Indian Lives: Essays on*

Nineteenth- and Twentieth-Century Native American Leaders, edited by L. G. Moses and Raymond Wilson, 43–57. Albuquerque: University of New Mexico Press, 1985.

McFeely, Eliza. *Zuni and the American Imagination*. New York: Hill and Wang, 2001.

McGreevy, Susan Brown. *Woven Holy People: Navajo Sandpainting Textiles from the Permanent Collection*. Santa Fe, NM: Wheelwright Museum of the American Indian, 1982.

McLaughlin, Castle. *Arts of Diplomacy: Lewis and Clark's Indian Collection*. Cambridge, MA: Peabody Museum of Archaeology and Ethnology, Harvard University; Seattle: University of Washington Press, 2003.

McLerran, Jennifer. "D. Y. Begay: Traditional Environmental Knowledge in Form and Practice." In *The Weavings of D. Y. Begay*, edited by Victoria Passalacqua, 10–16. Davis: C. N. Gorman Museum, University of California, Davis, 2013.

———. "The History and Progress of the Navajo People: Dual Signification in Gerald Nailor's Navajo Nation Council Chamber Murals." *American Indian Art Magazine* 38, no. 1 (2012): 40–49.

———. *A New Deal for Native Art: Indian Arts and Federal Policy, 1933–1943*. Tucson: University of Arizona Press, 2009.

———. *A New Deal for Navajo Weaving: Reform and Revival of Diné Textiles*. Tucson: University of Arizona Press, 2022.

———. "Woven Chantways: The Red Rock Revival." *American Indian Art Magazine* 28, no. 1 (2002): 64–73.

Mechling, Jay. "'Playing Indian' and the Search for Authenticity in Modern White America." *Prospects* 5 (1980): 17–33.

Mercer, Kobena, ed. *Cosmopolitan Modernisms*. Cambridge, MA: MIT Press, 2005.

Merrill, William, Edmund Ladd, and T. J. Ferguson. "The Return of the *Ahayu:da*: Lessons for Repatriation from Zuni Pueblo and the Smithsonian Institution." *Current Anthropology* 34, no. 5 (1993): 523–67.

Meyers, Jeffrey. "D. H. Lawrence and the American Indians." *Michigan Quarterly Review* 56, no. 2 (2017). http://hdl.handle.net/2027/spo.act2080.0056.221.

Miller, Angela, Janet Catherine Berlo, Bryan Wolf, and Jennifer Roberts. *American Encounters: Art, History, and Cultural Identity*. Upper Saddle River, NJ: Pearson / Prentice Hall, 2007.

Miller, Daniel. *Materiality*. Durham, NC: Duke University Press, 2005.

Miller, Daniel, and Sophie Woodward. "A Manifesto for the Study of Denim." www.ucl.ac.uk/anthropology/people/academic-and-teaching-staff/daniel-miller/manifesto-study-denim. Accessed February 4, 2012.

Miller, T. Michael. *Artisans and Merchants of Alexandria, Virginia, 1780–1820*. 2 vols. Bowie, MD: Heritage Books, 2009.

Montgomery, Florence. *Textiles in America, 1650–1870*. New York: W. W. Norton, 1984.

Moore, Emily L. *Proud Raven, Panting Wolf: Carving Alaska's New Deal Totem Parks*. Seattle: University of Washington Press, 2018.

Morgan, Lewis Henry. "Report on the Fabrics, Inventions, Implements, and Utensils of the Iroquois." In *Fifth Annual Report of the Regents of the University, on the Condition of the State Cabinet of Natural History, and the Historical and Antiquarian Collection Annexed Thereto*, 67–117. Albany, NY: Charles van Benthuysen, 1852.

Moulard, Barbara. *Re-creating the World: Painted Ceramics of the Prehistoric Southwest*. Santa Fe, NM: Schenk Southwest Publishing, 2002.

———. *Within the Underworld Sky: Mimbres Ceramic Art in Context*. Pasadena, CA: Twelvetrees Press, 1984.

Mukerji, Chandra. *From Graven Images: Patterns of Modern Materialism*. New York: Columbia University Press, 1983.

Muller, Kevin. "Pelts and Power, Mohawks and Myth." *Winterthur Portfolio* 40, no. 1 (2005): 47–75.

Murray, Robert A. *A History of Pipestone National Monument Minnesota*. Pipestone, MN: Pipestone Indian Shrine Association, 1965. www.nps.gov/park history/online_books/pipe2/index.htm.

Museum of Primitive Art. *Art of Oceania, Africa, and the Americas from the Museum of Primitive Art*. New York: Museum of Primitive Art, 1969.

Myers, Fred R. *Painting Culture: The Making of an Aboriginal High Art*. Durham, NC: Duke University Press, 2002.

Nagel, Alexander. "The Copy and Its Evil Twin: Thirteen Notes on Forgery." *Cabinet*, no. 14 (2004): 102–5.

Neff, Emily Ballew, ed. *American Adversaries: West and Copley in a Transatlantic World*. Houston: Museum of Fine Arts, 2013.

Nelson, Margaret C., and Michelle Hegmon. "Mimbres Lives and Landscapes." In *Mimbres Lives and Landscapes*, edited by Margaret C. Nelson and Michelle Hegmon, 1–7. Santa Fe, NM: School for Advanced Research Press, 2010.

Nelson, Mark, William Sherman, and Ellen Hoobler. *Hollywood Arensberg: Avant-Garde Collecting in Midcentury L.A.* Los Angeles: Getty Research Institute, 2020.

Newcomb, Franc Johnson. *Hosteen Klah, Navaho Medicine Man and Sand Painter*. Norman: University of Oklahoma Press, 1964.

Newcomb, Franc Johnson, and Gladys A. Reichard. *Sandpaintings of the Navajo Shooting Chant*. New York: J. J. Augustin, 1937.

Nicks, Trudy, and Ruth B. Phillips. "'From Wigwam to White Lights': Princess White Deer's Indian Acts." In *Three Centuries of Woodlands Indian Art: A*

Collection of Essays, edited by J. C. H. King and Christian F. Feest, 144–60. Altenstadt, Germany: ZKF Publications, 2007.
Nicolazzi, Laetitia, Alessandro Chechi, and Marc-André Renold. "Case Hopi Masks—Hopi Tribe v. Néret-Minet and Estimations & Ventes aux Enchères." Platform ArThemis (Art-Law Centre, University of Geneva), 2015. http://unige.ch/art-adr.
Nora, Pierre, ed. *Les lieux de mémoire*. 7 vols. Paris: Gallimard, 1984–92. Abridged in English as *Realms of Memory*, 3 vols., translated by Arthur Goldhammer. New York: Columbia University Press, 1996–98.
Nottage, James. "Illusions and Deceptions: The Indian in Popular Culture." In *Powerful Images: Portrayals of Native America*, edited by Sarah Boehme, 75–111. Seattle: University of Washington Press, 1998.
Nunley, John, and Judith Bettelheim. *Caribbean Festival Arts: Each and Every Bit of Difference*. St. Louis, MO: St. Louis Art Museum in association with University of Washington Press, 1988.
Nusbaum, Aileen. "Turquoise-Incrusted Pottery of Zuñi." *Masterkey* 12, no. 3 (May 1938): 97–99.
Nydahl, Theodore. "The Pipestone Quarry and the Indians." *Minnesota History* 31 (December 4, 1950): 193–208.
O'Neil, James F., II. *Their Bearing Is Noble and Proud: A Collection of Narratives regarding the Appearance of Native Americans from 1740–1815*. Dayton, OH: J.T.G.S. Publishing, 1995.
O'Neil, Megan. "Marked Faces, Displaced Bodies: Monument Breakage and Reuse among the Classic-Period Maya." In *Striking Images, Iconoclasms Past and Present*, edited by Stacy Boldrick, Leslie Brubaker, and Richard Clay, 47–64. Farnham, Surry, UK: Ashgate, 2013.
Ortiz, Alfonso. "Ritual Drama and the Pueblo World View." In *New Perspectives on the Pueblos*, edited by Alfonso Ortiz, 135–61. Albuquerque: University of New Mexico Press, 1972.
Ostrowitz, Judith. *Privileging the Past: Reconstructing History in Northwest Coast Art*. Seattle: University of Washington Press; Vancouver: University of British Columbia Press, 1999.
O'Toole, Fintan. *White Savage: William Johnson and the Invention of America*. New York: Farrar, Strauss and Giroux, 2005.
Otte, Marcel. *Le paléolithique supérieur ancien en Belgique*. Brussels: Musées Royaux d'Art et d'Histoire, 1979.
Painter, John. *American Indian Artifacts: The John Painter Collection*. Cincinnati: George Tassian Organization, 1991.
Parezo, Nancy. "The Indian Fashion Show: Fighting Cultural Stereotypes with Gender." *Journal of Anthropological Research* 69, no. 3 (2013): 317–46.

———. "Matthews and the Discovery of Navajo Drypaintings." In *Washington Matthews: Studies of Navajo Culture, 1880–1894*, edited by Katherine S. Halpern and Susan Brown McGreevy, 53–73. Albuquerque: University of New Mexico Press, 1997.

———. *Navajo Sandpainting: From Religious Act to Commercial Art*. Albuquerque: University of New Mexico Press, 1991.

Parezo, Nancy, and Nancy Blomberg. "Indian Chic: The Denver Art Museum's Indian Style Show." *American Indian Art Magazine* 23, no. 1 (1997): 44–55.

Parker, Arthur C. "Art Reproductions of the Seneca Indians." *Museum Service: Bulletin of the Rochester Museum of Arts and Sciences* 14, no. 9 (1941): 31–33.

———. "Certain Iroquois Tree Myths and Symbols." *American Anthropologist* 14, no. 4 (December 1912): 608–20.

———. "The Indian Arts Project." *Museum Service: Bulletin of the Rochester Museum of Arts and Sciences* 9, no. 1 (January 15, 1936): 9.

———. "Museum Motives behind the New York Arts Project." *Indians at Work*, June 15, 1935, 11–12.

Passalacqua, Veronica. "Tanis Maria S'eiltin: Coming Full Circle." In *Into the Fray: The Eiteljorg Fellowship for Native American Fine Art, 2005*, edited by James Nottage, 97–109. Indianapolis: Eiteljorg Museum of American Indians and Western Art in association with University of Washington Press, 2005.

Pearlstone, Zena. "Hopi Doll Look-Alikes: An Extended Definition of Inauthenticity." *American Indian Quarterly* 35, no. 4 (2011): 579–608.

———, ed. *Katsina: Commodified and Appropriated Images of Hopi Supernaturals*. Los Angeles: Fowler Museum of Cultural History, University of California, Los Angeles, 2001.

Peers, Laura. *Playing Ourselves: Interpreting Native Histories at Historic Reconstructions*. Lanham, MD: AltaMira Press, 2007.

Penney, David. *Art of the American Indian Frontier: The Chandler-Pohrt Collection*. Detroit: Detroit Institute of Arts in association with University of Washington Press, 1992.

Penny, H. Glenn. *Kindred by Choice: Germans and American Indians since 1800*. Chapel Hill: University of North Carolina Press, 2013.

———. "Not Playing Indian: Surrogate Indigeneity and the German Hobbyist Scene." In *Performing Indigeneity: Global Histories and Contemporary Experiences*, edited by Laura R. Graham and H. Glenn Penny, 169–205. Lincoln: University of Nebraska Press, 2014.

———. "Red Power: Liselotte Welskopf-Henrich and Indian Activist Networks in East and West Germany." *Central European History* 41, no. 3 (September 2008): 447–76.

Petersen, Karen Daniels. *American Pictographic Images: Historical Works on Paper by the Plains Indians*. Santa Fe, NM: Morning Star Gallery, 1988.

———. *Plains Indian Art from Fort Marion*. Norman: University of Oklahoma Press, 1971.

Petersen, Karen Daniels, and Jean Afton. *The Edwards Ledger Drawings: Folk Art by Arapaho Warriors*. New York: David A. Schorsch, 1990.

Peterson, Susan. *Lucy M. Lewis: American Indian Potter*. New York: Kodansha International, 1984.

Phillips, Ruth B. "Disappearing Acts: Traditions of Exposure, Traditions of Enclosure, and the Sacrality of Onkwehonwe Medicine Masks." In *Museum Pieces: Toward the Indigenization of Canadian Museums*, 111–31. Montreal: McGill-Queen's University Press, 2011.

———. *Museum Pieces: Toward the Indigenization of Canadian Museums*. Montreal: McGill-Queen's University Press, 2011.

———. "Performing the Native Woman: Primitivism and Mimicry in Early Twentieth-Century Visual Culture.'" In *Antimodernism and Artistic Experience: Policing the Boundaries of Modernity*, edited by Lynda Jessup, 26–49. Toronto: University of Toronto Press, 2001.

———. "Reading and Writing between the Lines: Soldiers, Curiosities, and Indigenous Art Histories." *Winterthur Portfolio* 45, no. 2/3 (Summer/Autumn 2011): 107–24.

———. *Trading Identities: The Souvenir in Native North American Art from the Northeast, 1700–1900*. Seattle: University of Washington Press; Montreal: McGill-Queen's University Press, 1998.

Pietrangeli, Carlo, ed. *The Sistine Chapel: A Glorious Restoration*. New York: Harry N. Abrams, 1994.

Pijoán, José. *Arte de los pueblos aborígenes*. Summa artis: Historia general del arte, vol. 1. Madrid: Espasa-Calpe, 1931.

Pillers, Beverly. "Visiting Potters in Nicaragua." *Ceramics Monthly* 46, no. 6 (1998): 16–18.

Pohrt, Richard A. "A Collector's Life." In *Art of the American Indian Frontier: The Chandler-Pohrt Collection*, by David Penney, 299–322. Detroit: Detroit Institute of Arts in association with University of Washington Press, 1992.

Popper, Deborah, and Frank Popper. "The Great Plains: From Dust to Dust." *Planning* 53, no. 2 (1987): 12–18.

Porter, Joy. *To Be Indian: The Life of Iroquois-Seneca Arthur Caswell Parker*. Norman: University of Oklahoma Press, 2001.

Powers, William K. "The Indian Hobbyist Movement in North America." In *Handbook of North American Indians*, vol. 4, *History of Indian-White Relations*, edited by Wilcomb Washburn, 557–61. Washington, DC: Smithsonian Institution, 1988.

Rapaport, Brooke, ed. *The Sculpture of Louise Nevelson: Constructing a Legend*. New York: Jewish Museum, 2007.

Ray, Arthur. "Indians as Consumers in the Eighteenth Century." In *Old Trails and New Directions: Papers of the Third North American Fur Trade Conference*, edited by Arthur Ray and Carol Judd, 255–71. Toronto: University of Toronto Press, 1980.

Reichard, Gladys A. *Navajo Medicine Man: Sandpaintings*. New York: Dover, 1977.

Reinhardt, Leslie. "British and Indian Identities in a Picture by Benjamin West." *Eighteenth-Century Studies* 31, no. 3 (1998): 283–305.

Rickard, Jolene. "Visualizing Sovereignty in the Time of Biometric Sensors." *South Atlantic Quarterly* 110, no. 2 (2011): 465–86.

Roach, Joseph. *Cities of the Dead: Circum-Atlantic Performance*. New York: Columbia University Press, 1996.

Rodee, Marian. *The Fetish Carvers of Zuni*. Albuquerque: Maxwell Museum of Anthropology, University of New Mexico, 1995.

Romancito, Rick. "Is It Art? Is It Sacred?" *Indian Trader*, 1992, 54–55.

Romero, Diego. "Diego Romero: Cochiti." Interview with Larry Abbott. In *A Time of Visions: Interviews by Larry Abbott*, ca. 1994–96. http://dev.cushing.org/abbott/dromero.htm.

Ronan, Kristine. "Buffalo Dancer: The Biography of an Image." PhD diss., University of Michigan, 2016.

Roosevelt, Theodore. "The Hopi Snake Dance." *Outlook* 105 (October 18, 1913): 365–73.

Rosaldo, Renato. "Imperialist Nostalgia." *Representations*, no. 26 (1989): 107–22.

Rosoff, Nancy, and Susan Kennedy Zeller, eds. *Tipi: Heritage of the Great Plains*. Brooklyn, NY: Brooklyn Museum in association with University of Washington Press, 2011.

Roth, Solen. "Argillite, Faux-Argillite and Black Plastic: The Political Economy of Simulating a Quintessential Haida Substance." *Journal of Material Culture* 20, no. 3 (2015): 299–312.

———. *Incorporating Culture: How Indigenous People Are Reshaping the Northwest Coast Art Industry*. Vancouver: University of British Columbia Press, 2018.

Rothberg, Michael. "Introduction: Between Memory and Memory: From *Lieux de mémoire* to *Noeuds de mémoire*." *Yale French Studies*, no. 118/119 (2010): 3–12.

Rust, Horatio Nelson. "Archaeological Frauds." *American Archaeologist* 2, no. 3 (March 1898): 79.

Samuels, Ellen. *Fantasies of Identification: Disability, Gender, Race*. New York: New York University Press, 2014.

Schoolcraft, Henry. *Historical and Statistical Information respecting the History, Condition, and Prospects of the Indian Tribes of the United States*. 6 vols. Philadelphia: J. B. Lippincott, 1851–57.

Schrader, Robert Fay. *The Indian Arts and Crafts Board: An Aspect of New Deal Indian Policy*. Albuquerque: University of New Mexico Press, 1983.

Schumacher, Paul. "Ancient Graves and Shell-Heaps of California." In *Annual Report of the Board of Regents of the Smithsonian Institution*, 1874, 335–50. Washington, DC: Government Printing Office, 1875.

———. "Etwas über Kjökken Möddinge und die Funde in alten Gräbern in Südcalifornien." *Archiv für Anthropologie* 8 (1875): 217–21.

———. "Researches in the Kjökkenmöddings and Graves of a Former Population of the Santa Barbara Islands and the Adjacent Mainland." *Bulletin of the United States Geological and Geographical Survey of the Territories* 3, no. 1 (1877): 37–56.

Scolieri, Paul. *Ted Shawn: His Life, Writings, and Dances*. New York: Oxford University Press, 2019.

Scott, Jay. *Changing Woman: The Life and Art of Helen Hardin*. Flagstaff, AZ: Northland Publishing, 1989.

Scott, Sascha. "Awa Tsireh and the Art of Subtle Resistance." *Art Bulletin* 95, no. 4 (2013): 597–622.

Secakuku, Alph. "Authentic Hopi Katsina Dolls." In *Katsina: Commodified and Appropriated Images of Hopi Supernaturals*, edited by Zena Pearlstone, 162–65. Los Angeles: Fowler Museum of Cultural History, University of California, Los Angeles, 2001.

———. *Following the Sun and Moon: Hopi Kachina Tradition*. Flagstaff, AZ: Northland Publishing in cooperation with the Heard Museum, 1995.

Sedikides, Constantine, Tim Wildschut, Jamie Arndt, and Clay Routledge. "Nostalgia: Past, Present, and Future." *Current Directions in Psychological Science* 17, no. 5 (2008): 304–7.

Sekaquaptewa, Emory. "Hopi Indian Ceremonies." In *Seeing with a Native Eye: Essays on Native American Religion*, edited by Walter H. Capps, 35–43. New York: Harper and Row, 1976.

Seton, Ernest Thompson. *Trail of an Artist-Naturalist: The Autobiography of Ernest Thompson Seton*. New York: C. Scribner's Sons, 1940.

———. *Two Little Savages, Being the Adventures of Two Boys Who Lived as Indians and What They Learned*. New York: Doubleday, Page, 1903.

Sewid, James. *Guests Never Leave Hungry: The Autobiography of James Sewid, a Kwakiutl Indian*. Edited by James Spradley. New Haven, CT: Yale University Press, 1969.

Shannon, Timothy. "The World That Made William Johnson." *New York History* 89, no. 2 (2008): 111–25.

Sheffield, Gail. *The Arbitrary Indian: The Indian Arts and Crafts Act of 1990*. Norman: University of Oklahoma Press, 1997.

Shibata, Stephanie. "Meet Steven Clay Brown." *Sea Magazine*, June 2016. https://issuu.com/dmcinc/docs/2016-06-sea-combo-srgb.

Sieg, Katrin. *Ethnic Drag: Performing Race, Nation, Sexuality in West Germany*. Ann Arbor: University of Michigan Press, 2002.

———. "Ethnic Drag and National Identity: Multicultural Crises, Crossings, and Interventions." In *The Imperialist Imagination: German Colonialism and Its Legacy*, edited by Sara Friedrichsmeyer, Sara Lennox, and Susanne Zantop, 295–319. Ann Arbor: University of Michigan Press, 1998.

Slaney, Deborah. "Zuni Figurative Carving from the C. G. Wallace Collection." *American Indian Art Magazine* 19, no. 1 (1993): 68–75.

Sloan, John, and Oliver La Farge. *Introduction to American Indian Art*. New York: Exposition of Indian Tribal Arts, 1931.

Smith, Michael P. "New Orleans' Carnival Culture from the Underside." *Plantation Society in the Americas* 3, no. 1 (1990): 11–32.

Smith, Richard N. *On His Own Terms: A Life of Nelson Rockefeller*. New York: Random House, 2014.

Smith, Watson, Richard Woodbury, and Nathalie Woodbury. *The Excavation of Hawikuh by Frederick Webb Lodge: Report of the Hendricks-Hodge Expedition, 1917–1923*. Contributions from the Museum of the American Indian, Heye Foundation, vol. 20. New York: Museum of the American Indian, Heye Foundation, 1966.

Spivey, Richard L. *The Legacy of Maria Poveka Martinez*. Santa Fe: Museum of New Mexico Press, 2003.

Steiner, Christopher. *African Art in Transit*. Cambridge: Cambridge University Press, 1994.

Stephen, Alexander M. *Hopi Journal of Alexander M. Stephen*. Edited by Elsie Clews Parsons. New York: Columbia University Press, 1936.

Stevenson, James. "Illustrated Catalogue of the Collections Obtained from the Pueblos of New Mexico and Arizona in 1880." In *Second Annual Report of the Bureau of Ethnology, 1880–81*, 429–66. Washington, DC: Government Printing Office, 1883.

———. "Illustrated Catalogue of the Collections Obtained from the Pueblos of New Mexico and Arizona in 1881." In *Third Annual Report of the Bureau of Ethnology, 1881–82*, 511–94. Washington, DC: Government Printing Office, 1884.

Stevenson, Matilda Coxe. "The Zuñi Indians: Their Mythology, Esoteric Fraternities, and Ceremonies." In *Twenty-Third Annual Report of the Bureau of American Ethnology, 1901–1902*, 3–608. Washington, DC: Government Printing Office, 1904.

Stewart, Susan. *On Longing: Narratives of the Miniature, the Gigantic, the Souvenir, the Collection*. Baltimore: Johns Hopkins University Press, 1984.

Szabo, Joyce. *Howling Wolf and the History of Ledger Art*. Albuquerque: University of New Mexico Press, 1994.

TallBear, Kimberly. "DNA, Blood, and Racializing the Tribe." *Wicazo Sa Review* 18, no. 1 (2003): 81–107.

Taylor, Charles. *Modern Social Imaginaries*. Durham, NC: Duke University Press, 2003.

Taylor, Colin. "The Indian Hobbyist Movement in Europe." In *Handbook of North American Indians*, vol. 4, *History of Indian-White Relations*, edited by Wilcomb Washburn, 562–69. Washington, DC: Smithsonian Institution, 1988.

Taylor, Diana. *The Archive and the Repertoire: Performing Cultural Memory in the Americas*. Durham, NC: Duke University Press, 2003.

Taylor, Dicey. "Problems in the Study of Narrative Scenes on Classic Maya Vases." In *Falsifications and Misreconstructions of Pre-Columbian Art*, edited by Elizabeth Hill Boone, 107–24. Washington, DC: Dumbarton Oaks, Trustees for Harvard University, 1982.

Tedlock, Barbara. "Aesthetics and Politics: Zuni War God Repatriation and Kachina Representation." In *Looking High and Low: Art and Cultural Identity*, edited by Brenda Jo Bright and Liza Bakewell, 151–72. Tucson: University of Arizona Press, 1995.

———. *The Beautiful and the Dangerous: Encounters with the Zuni Indians*. New York: Viking Penguin, 1992.

Thomas, Wesley. "Navajo Cultural Constructions of Gender and Sexuality." In *Two-Spirit People: Native American Gender Identity, Sexuality, and Spirituality*, edited by Sue-Ellen Jacobs, Wesley Thomas, and Sabine Lang, 156–73. Urbana: University of Illinois Press, 1997.

Thompson, Mina, and Angela Elliott. "The Mimbres Journey: How Shifting Contexts Necessitate a Multi-disciplinary Conservation Approach." In *The Object in Context: Crossing Conservation Boundaries*, edited by David Saunders, Joyce Townsend, and Sally Woodcock, 116–22. London: International Institute for Conservation of Historic and Artistic Works, 2006.

Timbrook, Jan. "Six Chumash Presentation Baskets." *American Indian Art Magazine* 39, no. 3 (2014): 50–57.

Toelken, Barre. "The Yellowman Tapes, 1966–1997." *Journal of American Folklore* 111, no. 442 (1998): 381–91.

Tooker, Elisabeth. *Lewis H. Morgan on Iroquois Material Culture*. Tucson: University of Arizona Press, 1994.

Torrence, Gaylord, ed. *The Plains Indians: Artists of Earth and Sky*. New York: Skira/Rizzoli, 2014.

Townsend, Richard, ed. *Casas Grandes and the Ceramic Art of the Ancient Southwest.* Chicago: Art Institute of Chicago in association with Yale University Press, 2005.

Trachtenberg, Alan. *Shades of Hiawatha: Staging Indians, Making Americans, 1880–1930.* New York: Hill and Wang, 2004.

Trimble, Stephen. *Talking with the Clay: The Art of Pueblo Pottery.* Santa Fe, NM: School of American Research Press, 1987.

Ulrich, Laurel Thatcher. *The Age of Homespun: Objects and Stories in the Creation of an American Myth.* New York: Alfred A. Knopf, 2001.

United States General Accounting Office. *Cultural Resources: Problems Protecting and Preserving Federal Archeological Resources; Report to Congressional Requesters.* Washington, DC: General Accounting Office, 1987. www.gao.gov/assets/rced-88-3.pdf.

Urry, John. "How Societies Remember the Past." *Sociological Review* 43, no. S1 (May 1995): S45–65.

———. *The Tourist Gaze.* 2nd ed. London: Sage, 2002.

Usner, Daniel. *American Indians in Early New Orleans.* Baton Rouge: Louisiana State University Press, 2018.

———. *Indians, Settlers, and Slaves in a Frontier Exchange Economy: The Lower Mississippi Valley before 1783.* Chapel Hill: University of North Carolina Press, 1992.

Vestal, Stanley. *Sitting Bull, Champion of the Sioux: A Biography.* Boston: Houghton Mifflin, 1932.

Villela, Khristaan. "Miguel Covarrubias and Twenty Centuries of Pre-Columbian Latin American Art, from the Olmec to the Inka." In *Miguel Covarrubias: Drawing a Cosmopolitan Line / Georgia O'Keeffe Museum,* edited by Carolyn Kastner, 49–75. Austin: University of Texas Press, 2014.

Vinson, Charles. "Sun Dancers." *Boys' Life,* May 1947, 8–9, 33–35.

Wade, Edwin. "Straddling the Cultural Fence: The Conflict for Ethnic Artists within Pueblo Societies." In *The Arts of the North American Indian: Native Traditions in Evolution,* edited by Edwin Wade, 243–54. New York: Hudson Hills Press, 1986.

Walker Art Center. *American Indian Art: Form and Tradition.* Minneapolis: Walker Art Center and E. P. Dutton, 1972.

Walsh, Barry. "Kikmongwi as Artist: The Katsina Dolls of Wilson Tawaquaptewa." *American Indian Art Magazine* 23, no. 1 (1998): 52–59.

———. "The Navajo Doll and the Dispute with the Hopi." *Indian Trader,* March 1994, 5–9.

Walsh, Jane MacLaren. "The Dumbarton Oaks Tlazolteotl: Looking beneath the Surface." *Journal de la Société des américanistes* 94, no. 1 (2008): 7–43.

Warburg, Aby. *Images from the Region of the Pueblo Indians of North America.* Translated by Michael P. Steinberg. Ithaca, NY: Cornell University Press, 1995.

Warnock, John, and Martha Warnock. *Splendid Heritage: Perspectives on American Indian Art.* Salt Lake City: University of Utah Press, 2009.

Washington, George. *The Papers of George Washington: Revolutionary War Series.* Vol. 20, *8 April–31 May 1779*, edited by Edward G. Lengel. Charlottesville: University of Virginia Press, 2010.

Waters, Frank. *Book of the Hopi.* New York: Ballantine Books, 1969. First published 1963 by Swallow Press.

———. *Masked Gods: Navaho and Pueblo Ceremonialism.* New York: Ballantine Books, 1970. First published 1950 by Swallow Press.

Watson, Editha L. "The Laughing Artists of the Mimbres Valley." *Art and Archaeology* 33, no. 4 (July 1932): 188–93.

Weigle, Marta. "Exposition and Mediation: Mary Colter, Erna Fergusson, and the Santa Fe / Harvey Popularization of the Native Southwest, 1902–1940." *Frontiers: A Journal of Women Studies* 12, no. 3 (1992): 116–50.

Wheat, Joe Ben. *Blanket Weaving in the Southwest.* Edited by Ann Lane Hedlund. Tucson: University of Arizona Press, 2003.

Wheelwright, Mary Cabot. *The Myth and Prayers of the Great Star Chant and the Myth of the Coyote Chant.* Edited by David McAllester. Tsaile, AZ: Navajo Community College Press, 1988.

White, Richard. *The Middle Ground: Indians, Empires, and Republics in the Great Lakes Region, 1650–1815.* Cambridge: Cambridge University Press, 1991.

Wied-Neuwied, Maximilian, Prince of. *The North American Journals of Prince Maximilian of Wied.* Edited by Stephen Witte and Marsha Gallagher. Translated by William J. Orr, Paul Schach, and Dieter Karch. 3 vols. Norman: University of Oklahoma Press, 2009–11.

———. *Reise in das innere Nord-America in den Jahren 1832 bis 1834.* 2 vols. Koblenz, Germany: J. Hoelscher, 1839–41.

———. *Travels in the Interior of North America.* Translated by H. Evans Lloyd. London: Ackermann, 1843.

Willard, Tania. "Nicholas Galanin: Translate Transpose Transmit—Shifting Indigenous Aesthetics." In *RED: Eiteljorg Contemporary Art Fellowship, 2013*, edited by Jennifer Complo McNutt and Ashley Holland, 65–79. Indianapolis: Eiteljorg Museum of American Indians and Western Art, 2013.

Willey, Gordon, and Philip Phillips. *Method and Theory in American Archaeology.* Chicago: University of Chicago Press, 1958.

Williams, Adriana. *Covarrubias.* Edited by Doris Ober. Austin: University of Texas Press, 1994.

Wilson, Chris. *The Myth of Santa Fe: Creating a Modern Regional Tradition*. Albuquerque: University of New Mexico Press, 1997.

Wilson, Gilbert L. *Buffalo Bird Woman's Garden*. St. Paul: Minnesota Historical Society Press, 1987.

———. *Hidatsa Eagle Trapping*. Anthropological Papers of the American Museum of Natural History, vol. 30, pt. 4. New York: American Museum of Natural History, 1928.

———. *The Horse and the Dog in Hidatsa Culture*. Anthropological Papers of the American Museum of Natural History, vol. 15, pt. 2. New York: American Museum of Natural History, 1924.

Wilton, Andrew, and Tim Barringer. *American Sublime: Landscape Painting in the United States, 1820–1880*. Princeton, NJ: Princeton University Press, 2002.

Witherspoon, Gary. *Language and Art in the Navajo Universe*. Ann Arbor: University of Michigan Press, 1977.

Wong, Winnie Won Yin. *Van Gogh on Demand: China and the Readymade*. Chicago: University of Chicago Press, 2013.

Wood, Christopher. "Aby Warburg, *Homo victor*." *Journal of Art Historiography* 11 (December 2014): 1–24.

Wood, W. Warner. "Art by Dispossession at El Paso Saddleblanket Company: Commodification and Graduated Sovereignty in Global Capitalism." In *Art and Sovereignty in Global Politics*, edited by Douglas Howland, Elizabeth Lillehoj, and Maximilian Mayer, 169–95. New York: Palgrave Macmillan, 2017.

———. *Made in Mexico: Zapotec Weavers and the Global Ethnic Art Market*. Bloomington: Indiana University Press, 2008.

Wyatt, Gary. *Spirit Faces: Contemporary Masks of the Northwest Coast*. Seattle: University of Washington Press, 1994.

Wyman, Leland. "Navajo Ceremonial System." In *Handbook of North American Indians*, vol. 10, *Southwest*, edited by Alfonso Ortiz, 536–57. Washington, DC Smithsonian Institution, 1983.

Ya Salaam, Kalamu. *"He's the Prettiest": A Tribute to Allison "Tootie" Montana's 50 Years of Mardi Gras Indian Suiting*. New Orleans: New Orleans Museum of Art, 1997. www.louisianafolklife.org/LT/Virtual_Books/Hes_Prettiest/hes_the_prettiest_tootie_montana.html.

Yohe, Jill Ahlberg. "The Circulation and Silence of Weaving Knowledge in Contemporary Navajo Life." *American Indian Culture and Research Journal* 36, no. 4 (2012): 107–26.

Yohe, Jill Ahlberg, and Teri Greeves, eds. *Hearts of Our People: Native Women Artists*. Minneapolis: Minneapolis Institute of Art, 2019.

Yost, Nellie Snyder. *A Man as Big as the West*. Boulder, CO: Pruett Publishing, 1979.

Zinn, Howard. *A People's History of the United States*. New York: Harper and Row, 1980.

Zolbrod, Paul. Foreword to *The Mountain Chant: A Navajo Ceremony*, by Washington Matthews, vii–xxiii. Reprint, Salt Lake City: University of Utah Press, 1997.

Index

Page numbers in *italics* refer to illustrations.